Queering and Querying the Paradise of Paradox

Queering and Querying the Paradise of Paradox

LGBT Language, New Media, and Visual Cultures in Modern-Day Brazil

Steven F. Butterman

ROWMAN & LITTLEFIELD
Lanham • Boulder • New York • London

Credits and acknowledgments for material borrowed from other sources, and reproduced with permission, appear on the appropriate page within the text.

Published by Rowman & Littlefield
An imprint of The Rowman & Littlefield Publishing Group, Inc.
4501 Forbes Boulevard, Suite 200, Lanham, Maryland 20706
www.rowman.com

British Library Cataloguing in Publication Information Available

Library of Congress Cataloging-in-Publication Data
Names: Butterman, Steven F. (Steven Fred), author.
Title: Queering and querying the paradise of paradox : LGBT language, new media, and visual cultures in modern-day Brazil / Steven F. Butterman.
Description: Lanham, Maryland : Rowman & Littlefield, an imprint of The Rowman & Littlefield Publishing Group, Inc., [2021] | Includes bibliographical references and index. | Summary: "This book provides readers with a study of the characteristics that make life unique for sexual minorities in Brazil while also viewing Brazil in relation to global LGBT sociopolitical movements, as well as providing the first comprehensive discourse analysis of the dynamics and features of the largest LGBT Pride parade in the world"— Provided by publisher.
Identifiers: LCCN 2021009834 (print) | LCCN 2021009835 (ebook) | ISBN 9781538150887 (cloth) | ISBN 9781538150900 (pbk) | ISBN 9781538150894 (epub)
Subjects: LCSH: Sexual minorities—Brazil—Social conditions. | Gay pride parades—Brazil.
Classification: LCC HQ73.3.B6 B88 2021 (print) | LCC HQ73.3.B6 (ebook) | DDC 306.76—dc23
LC record available at https://lccn.loc.gov/2021009834
LC ebook record available at https://lccn.loc.gov/2021009835

I dedicate this book to the memory of the lives and loves of the thousands of lesbian, gay, bisexual, transgender, and *travesti* Brazilian citizens who have been brutally murdered, both in spirit and in body.

Though this is part and parcel of my life's work, I began to research and compose this manuscript ten years ago, in 2011. COVID-19 is the most recent calamity to remind us that statistics can record but never reconstitute the human lives they represent, lives that transcend the tragic deaths they can only quantify. Nevertheless, these numbers also concretize truths that must be spoken.

Hence, this contribution is not merely my own, for it is informed by and stands in solidarity with our queer family, in proud tribute to their lives, which meant so much more than their atrocious deaths.

I humbly offer these pages to the **266** lives lost in 2011, the **388** victims in 2012, the **312** murdered in 2013, the **326** brutally assassinated in 2014, the **318** members of the LGBT+ community executed in 2015, the **343** who perished in 2016 at the hateful hands of others, and the **445** individuals massacred in 2017. This book is for the lives and the loves of the **420** documented assassinations in 2018 and the **329** homicides in 2019.

This long list of lives lost represents **3,147** Brazilian citizens killed for being L, G, B, and/or T in the period of one decade, the time it took for me to research, write, and publish this book. These numbers do not include those citizens whose internalized homolesbotransphobia resulted in their choice to die.

As I finish this book chronicling life in LGBTI+ Brazil and its cultural representations within and beyond its borders, setting my pen down halfway through 2020 and in the midst of a deadly invisible pandemic. Soaring in Brazil as it has in the United States, this devastating new reality has had little impact in a climate where one LGBTI Brazilian is either murdered or takes their own life every twenty-six hours.

This book is also for the countless others who are thriving or merely surviving and whose invisibility, in itself tragic, may be the reason they are still alive today.

I dedicate this book to the readers it will likely never have, to the perpetrators of these atrocious crimes that have transfigured human lives into mortality statistics, for it is they who suffer from the most insidious disease of all, one that is diminished, negated, or minimized, one that is called many different names but which I posit here for full visibility: homolesbotransphobia.

Finally, this book is for the vast majority who continue to be denied the justice they deserve, the right to be punished for hateful crimes against would-be versions of their **selves** they so bitterly and brutally repress.

Contents

Contents

Figures and Illustrations

INTRODUCTION

CHAPTER 3

CHAPTER 6

CHAPTER 7

CHAPTER 8

ABOUT THE AUTHOR

Acknowledgments

For my dad, Dr. Norman Butterman (in memoriam), and all other victims of the coronavirus and all the families who grieve the loss of their loved ones from afar. So many of us now know the acute anguish of loss compounded by the suffering of not being able to say goodbye.

For my mom, Marilyn Silver Butterman, whose recovery from COVID-19 is a blessing and an inspiration to move forward in dire times. Living valiantly and vibrantly with dementia, my mother occupies a magical parallel universe. Thank you, Mom, for nurturing within me the love of language and the gift of creativity.

To Susan Rose, my loving sister tirelessly fighting the good fight, and to all the members of my family who support and love me unconditionally.

To those who did not live to see this work come to fruition but were very influential in its trajectory. For my beloved grandmother, Etta Silver, who showed the world by example how to live and to love for nearly a century. For my brother Bruce (in memoriam), who, despite official records, died also from internalized homophobia. For my brilliant activist nephew Jordan (in memoriam), who suffered the consequences of continued stigmatization around mental illness in addition to the complexity of leukemia.

For all the families who grieve loved ones in so much pain that death was their only relief.

For the members of my chosen family who have supported my efforts to persevere through this project and so many others. For my partners and best friends who patiently stood by me as I grappled with my own limitations (perceived and real), through thick and thin, proving that water can be just as thick as blood despite what conventional chemistry may tell us. For Nelson Villafane, for Alan Otto Parshley, my guardian angel bears and my cheerleaders in far too many ways to even begin to record here.

To Lidiana de Moraes, my *alma gêmea platônica* (platonic soulmate) with the wisdom of an owl, for her creativity in preparing pedagogical slides to go with this project and her tireless moral support throughout the process.

For my extended queer family throughout the Americas and omnipresent in all corners of my heart: Maureen Seaton, Samuel Ace, Sonny Nordmarken, Lidiana de Moraes and Marcia Fanti Negri (in the United States), Meta Loei, Eliéser Pedroso de Oliveira, Volnei Righi, Laura Guerim, Tatiana Vargas Maia, and Fabrício Pontin (in Brazil).

This book would not exist without the light and *lampião* (lamp) of the LGBT movement in Brazil and the folks who bravely paved the way for a much brighter future despite the grim past and present. For all the LGBT activists "on the ground" in Brazil since the 1970s or earlier, especially to those (s)heroes who have touched my life in such profound ways. For João Silvério Trevisan, Leila Míccolis, Urhacy Faustino, Glauco Mattoso, Akira Nishimura, Jean Wyllys (in exile), and Marielle Franco (in memoriam).

A deep debt of gratitude goes to all my colleagues and friends at the University of Miami, far too numerous to list here, but especially to professor and professional photographer Sean Black, whose invaluable insights and nurturing support significantly enriched the chapter on photography. To Thomas Heinke for sharing creative insights on the images in chapter 8.

My sincere thanks to my chairperson Yolanda Martínez-San Miguel, whose mentoring and endless support inspired me to persevere despite profound professional and personal challenges.

Heartfelt appreciation and love to my dear friends Gema Pérez-Sánchez and Pamela S. Hammons, whose enduring partnership inspires my admiration and trust. Together, you have literally saved my life, both physically and emotionally.

Utmost esteem and appreciation for Tracy Devine Guzmán, my partner in social justice and generous colleague in the Portuguese program at the University of Miami, which she has so capably directed during times when I have been on research leave or sabbatical.

I also wish to thank the following colleagues who, through their distinguished work and service, have modeled for me how to reach my own scholarly potential, inside and outside the classroom: Maureen Seaton, Lillian Manzor, Merike Blofield, Belkys Torres, Claire Oueslati-Porter, George Yúdice, Ralph Heyndels, David Ellison, and Viviana Díaz-Balsera. Special mention goes to Beth Giulianelli, my high school Spanish teacher who encouraged me on my linguistic adventures. And to the team of wonderful professors that made me fall in love with Portuguese, from the early days of Lusorapture inspired by Prof. Isolde Jordan at CU-Boulder, to the Fulbright-Hayes scholarship program in Belo Horizonte led by Lúcia Helena Costigan at the Ohio State University. I would not have attained my doctoral degree were it not for the conscientious support of Severino João Albuquerque (my PhD mentor), Ellen W. Sapega, and Mary Lou Daniel at the University of Wisconsin-Madison. Thank you for believing in me!

Teaching is the greatest passion in my life. This book is also dedicated to the hundreds of students who have touched my life, have worked in leaning communities to recognize intersectionality in real and not simply discursive terms. You are our future activists, artivists, and academics.

For the countless ways in which my graduate students have invested confidence in me as their mentor. You have afforded me the chance to witness invaluable pedagogical and scholarly projects under development and carried to fruition. For Mary Bartsh, Nathan Watson, Carlos de Oro, Marcia Fanti Negri, Emily Powell, Bella Campbell, Akua Akyeamponmaa Banful, Jordan Brasher, Mackenzie Teek, Ronke Sokunbi, Emily Vallillo, Yaliza Núñez-Gutiérrez, Lidiana de Moraes, María Gracia Pardo, Myriam Mompoint, Volnei José Righi, Josefina Raquel Cicconetti, Guilherme Miorando Smee, Fernando Rodrigues da Motta Bertoncello, Diego Moreira, Arthur Tang, Joanne Pol, Monica Faust, Melyssa Haffaf, Zayer Baazaoui, Manuel Rilo, Dora Romero, Guillermo Rivera, Samuel Johnson, Pablo Vespasiano, Rafael Torralvo da Silva, Jessica Osborn, Julie Carter Pierabella, Katherine C. Davis, Kai Kenttamaa Squires, Jordan Strickler, Ricardo Zulueta, Gabriela Zaviezo, Ariana Magdaleno, Anna Wilking, Bryn Hafemeister, and Ken Peyser, whose brilliant theses and dissertations I am honored to have directed or helped to advise. Your work continues to inspire my own.

My gratitude goes to the hundreds of University of Miami undergraduate and graduate students I have had the pleasure to teach during two decades as a faculty member there, with kudos to those brave souls who survived and thrived despite rigorous curricula and a demanding professor in "Brazilian Portugays: LGBT Language and Culture in Contemporary Brazil" (Portuguese 322/691). For the several iterations—now generations—of "Queer Studies" (Gender and Sexuality Studies 305) students doing their part to promote social, racial, and sexual justice in the 305 and well beyond the borders of South Florida, where I have made my home for twenty years.

I would also like to thank my colleagues at the Roger Thayer Stone Center for Latin American Studies (SCLAS) at Tulane University who accommodated me with such hospitality when I was named the Richard E. Greenleaf distinguished scholar and visiting professor in Latin American Studies in spring 2016. This opportunity allowed me to make significant advances on this manuscript at the Latin American Library while allowing me to develop an interdisciplinary graduate seminar in gender and sexuality studies. Special thanks to faculty members Christopher J. Dunn, Rebecca Atencio, Idelber Avelar, Edie Wolfe, and Mauro Porto. My gratitude to Thomas F. Reese, executive director of the SCLAS and James D. Hick, Jr., assistant director of the SCLAS, for making me feel so welcome in beautiful NOLA (New Orleans), perhaps the closest site in heart and soul (if not geography) to Brazil.

Finally, thank you to my colleagues and students in the Portuguese School at Middlebury College, where I have had the pleasure to teach an intensive course for seven consecutive years, creating an invaluable laboratory for my research to dovetail with pedagogy and second language acquisition. Special thanks to Luci Moreira, director, and Regina Santos, assistant director, and the dozens of exceptional students who have enriched my cultural studies courses on *Brasil: o pa(ra)ís(o) do paradoxo?* and *(Contra)cultura e (Con)tradição brasileira* through the years.

My appreciation goes to the following colleagues who so graciously provided extended interviews and access to materials during this project: Barry Michael Wolfe, Fred Libi, João Silvério Trevisan, and Glauco Mattoso.

Alain-Philippe Durand and two confidential reviewers read and critiqued the earlier versions of parts of this manuscript, improving the quality of this work.

Intramural funding and support for this project and my larger body of research have been provided by University of Miami Provost's Awards, University of Miami Office of Research Administration, University of Miami College of Arts and Sciences International Travel Fund, The Andrew W. Mellon Foundation CREATE Grants Program, and University of Miami Libraries.

External funding and support for this project and others were awarded by the Richard E. Greenleaf Distinguished Scholar in Residence at the Stone Center for Latin American Studies at Tulane University, the National Endowment for the Humanities in the United States, and the Fundação do Amparo à Pesquisa do Estado de São Paulo and Conselho Nacional de Desenvolvimento Científico e Tecnológico in Brazil.

I remain extremely grateful to the following colleagues and institutions who invited me for on-campus visits and opportunities to present earlier versions of this work in progress:

University of New Mexico (Leila Lehnen and Jeremy Lehnen):
Department of Spanish and Portuguese; Latin American Studies

Smith College (Marguerite Itamar Harrison and Malcolm McNee):
Lecture Committee; Department of Spanish & Portuguese; Resource Center for Gender and Sexuality; Lewis Global Studies Center; Africana Studies; Study of Women and Gender; Latin American and Latino/a Studies; Comparative Literature.

University of Utah's Global Sexualities Series (Christopher Lewis and Elena Shtromberg):
Department of World Languages and Cultures
Center for Latin American Studies

Ohio State University's Cultures of Sexual Diversity in Contemporary Latin America (Ignacio Corona and Lúcia Costigan):

Department of Spanish and Portuguese
Center for Latin American Studies
Sexuality Studies Program

Pontifícia Universidade Católica-Rio Grande do Sul (Nythamar de Oliveira, Fabrício Pontin, and Laura Guerim):
Department of Philosophy

Unilsasalle-Canoas (Rio Grande do Sul) (Lucas Graeff, Cleusa Maria Gomes Graebin, Tatiana Vargas Maia, and Laura Guerim)
Programa de Pós-Graduação (PPG) em Memória Social e Bens Culturais (2017–2018)

Unilsasalle-Canoas (Rio Grande do Sul):
PPG em Direito e Sociedade (Winter School 2019) (Raffaella Pallamolla and Daniel Achutti)

Universidade de São Paulo (Valéria Barbosa de Magalhães and José Renato de Campos Araujo):
Grupo de Estudo e Pesquisa em História Oral e Memória (GEPHOM) da Escola de Artes, Ciências e Humanidades (EACH)

Universidade Federal de Alagoas (Susana Souto Silva):
Faculdade de Letras

Universidade Federal de Santa Catarina (Joca Wolff and Diego Moreira):
Faculdade de Letras
Programa de Pós-Graduação em Literatura

University of Arizona "Translating Transgender" Conference (Susan Stryker, Samuel Ace, and David J. Gramling):
College of Humanities
The Institute for LGBT Studies
Transgender Studies Quarterly

Last but certainly not least, I would like to emphatically thank the entire editorial and production staff at Rowman & Littlefield in London, especially Dhara Snowden and Rebecca Anastasi, who have patiently helped me steer this manuscript through various stages of development despite the uncertainties of an ongoing international pandemic. They have shown remarkable allyship in times of anguish while reinforcing respect for the creative process and furnishing resources for their authors.

Jasti Bhavya, for carefully reading and annotating the entire manuscript during the copy-editing process.

Christine Ritchlin for designing the cover of the book with an expert's eye to showcase and bring to the center the relatively unknown new artworks that I analyze in these pages.

Lisa Rivero, for her expert indexing, encouragement, careful reading and consultation.

HAUS OF X

A Haus of X é uma drag family e coletivo de artistas transformistas, fundado em 2016 em Maringá (PR/BR). Entre as múltiplas frentes que atuamos, estão: performances, dublagens, produção de eventos próprios e temáticos, participação em eventos regionais específicos da linguagem drag, eventos acadêmicos, nas produções de textos, de material midiático e nas experimentações metodológicas de cursos, oficinas e palestras. Criando, desse modo, um movimento de vislumbrar, disseminar e dignificar o transformismo enquanto uma linguagem própria e autônoma.

SOBRE O #HAUSOFXCHALLENGE

Durante o período de quarentena nos desafiamos a piratear as drags de nossas irmãs. A proposta era sortear uma de nós, a cada dois ou três dias, para as integrantes do coletivo piratearem suas ideias, conceitos, estéticas. . . . Incluindo a própria sorteada, pois montar-se de si pode ser tão desafiador quanto montar-se das outras. Os resultados desses pirateamentos foram postados no Instagram, ao longo do desafio.

A imagem presente na Queerentena, exposição promovida pelo Museu de Diversidade Sexual, apresenta o resultado desses pirateamentos. A ideia era criar um mapa dessas experimentações devido a praticidade de cruzar dados: quem é quem, quem se montou de quem. Organizamos a imagem de modo que horizontalmente temos as montações feitas por cada artista, e verticalmente, os pirateamentos feitos a partir dessa mesma artista. Uma vez que nem todas se montaram de todas, ou de si mesmas, obrigatoriamente surgem lacunas. A estética dialoga com a ideia de amizade enquanto um devir outro do mesmo, pois é pela amizade que compartilhamos os processos de subjetivação que nos atravessam. Para além, a organização das imagens tem o intuito de projetar uma estrutura de confinamento individual—cada drag em sua linha e/ou coluna, conversando com a ordem de isolamento, mas inevitavelmente abaladas pelo caos, pelo incerto, pelas lacunas ocasionadas pela pandemia.

BACK COVER

As artistas presentes na arte por linha:
1ª linha: Lua Lamberti
2ª linha: Gustavo Barrionuevo
3ª linha: Ludmila Castanheira
4ª linha: Uriel Canille
5ª linha: Serena Vieira
6ª linha: Anyelle Cordeiro
7ª linha: Gaby Belline
8ª linha: Oliva Dentello

FRONT MATTER

English Translation by Steven F. Butterman

MISSION STATEMENT: HAUS OF X

The Haus of X is a drag family and collective of trans artists, founded in 2016 in Maringá, Paraná, Brazil. Our interventions include various facets and aspects such as performances, voiceovers, productions of our own original thematic events, participation in regional activities specific to "drag language," academic conferences, development of texts, multimedia materials and experimental methodologies for courses, workshops, and lectures. Our objective is to foster a movement intended to discern, disseminate, and dignify non-binary gender performances as its own autonomous language.

ARTISTS' STATEMENT: ABOUT THE #HAUSOFXCHALLENGE

In the middle of the pandemic, we challenged each other to hack into our drag queen sisters. We drew names from the drag house every two or three days to determine which queen would be the one whose ideas, concepts, aesthetics we would "pirate." This lottery would include the winner of the raffle because performing one's own identity can be just as challenging as performing the identity of other queens. The results of these first piracies were posted on Instagram throughout the duration of the challenge.

The image presented in the *Queerentena*, an art exhibit promoted by the Museum of Sexual Diversity, presents the result of these piracies. The idea is to map out these experimental trials using the practicality of cross-referencing: who is who, who is performing whom. We organized the artwork in such a way that we horizontally showcase all the works of each artist. Vertically, however, we are displaying the "hacks" of each individual artist. Since not every artist performs one another or even themselves, gaps or omissions obligatorily occur. These aesthetics dialogue with the concept of friendship in which one becomes the other of the same because it is through friendship that we share the processes of subjectivity passing through ourselves and one another. The organizational apparatus of the images also bears the intention to reflect a structure of individual confinement—each drag queen within her own line and/or column, interacting with (dis)order of isolation (lockdown), but inevitably shattered by the chaos, the uncertainty, the blank spaces that the pandemic has created.

Introduction: Pondering the Paradise of Paradox: LGBTI+ Culture in Brazil Today

> Cultural analysis is (or should be) guessing at meanings, assessing the guesses, and drawing explanatory conclusions from the better guesses, not discovering the Continent of Meaning and mapping out its bodiless landscape. . . . I have never gotten anywhere near to the bottom of anything I have ever written about. . . . Cultural analysis is intrinsically incomplete. And, worse than that, the more deeply it goes the less complete it is.
> —Clifford Geertz, *The Interpretation of Cultures*, 20, 29

World-renowned cultural anthropologist Clifford Geertz published these words nearly half a century ago, in a different century, a different millennium, a different time, place, and space, suggesting a strong dose of humility (and humanity) for any intellectual cross-cultural journey. The role of the cultural studies critic today has changed in a myriad of ways, but one tenet that seems to remain stable is the liberty to blend theoretical questions with political concerns and, even more importantly, the permission to leave questions unanswered, though in a tense state of constant interrogation. Dissolution of ambiguities or resolution of contradictions is not necessarily a goal of a cultural studies project, and certainly not of this one, which promises to not confine itself to monolithic definitions or conceptions, thereby allowing exploration of the richness of cultural complexities and paradoxes. This study subscribes to Stuart Hall's (1991) famous contention that "both in the British and the American context, cultural studies has drawn the attention itself . . . because it holds theoretical and political questions in an ever irresolvable but permanent tension. It constantly allows the one to irritate, bother, and disturb the other, without insisting on some final theoretical closure" (284).

And so our cultural analysis begins, but it is hardly a bodiless one as Geertz mentions. Nor are we any "worse" off for embracing contradictions

1

as the ambiguity increases with each step we take deeper into this study of cultural representations of contemporary LGBT life in Brazil. The cultural studies methodology I choose to employ in this book is one that is inherently interdisciplinary in nature and not in rhetoric. The constructiveness of anti-disciplinarity resides in the fact that such an approach liberates any study of culture from prefabricated discourses locked into each of the social sciences, each with its own language, terminology, and jargon. The permission to borrow from discourses of sociology, anthropology, and political science, and to combine approaches from literary criticism, textual, and discourse analysis, and the study of visual cultures is one of the fundamental principles, as well as one of the most contested sites, in the vast body of theoretical scholarship around contemporary cultural studies. It is my belief that an eclectic and trans disciplinary interrogation of cultural representation affords us the chance to view cultural processes that are often themselves eclectic, dynamic, and para-doxical in nature. To suggest that this is a project at the same time interdisci-plinary, multidisciplinary, and antidisciplinary does by no means undermine the methodological foundations of this work. The act of resisting intellectual classifications is a queer gesture that challenges the imagined boundaries of intellectual fields while cultivating more complex reconsiderations of mul-tiple languages, words, and concepts that speak simultaneously to dismantle institutional limitations that constrict us from opening new constructions, conversations that through their very conflicted viewpoints have the potential to bridge the humanities and the social sciences. At the very least the rejection of disciplinary paradigms also frees us from having (the discipline) to make a Solomonic decision, the sophism of Sophie's choice in academic scholar-ship, to relegate one set of interdisciplines to a more "scientific" or more "humanistic" existence than the other. We can be bi and "do" both at the same time without dichotomously subscribing to hierarchies that placate or para-lyze their dynamism and cross-contamination. The rejection of intellectual binary structure reflects the spirit of this book, welcoming readers to question the multiplicities and the ambiguities of its very foundations, knowledges conventionally conceived as "theoretical" *or* "empirical," as "academic" *or* "activist." Resistance to these artificial categories is at the heart of a project like this one, echoing recent queer methodologies that, as Heather Love put it in 2019, "can exemplify the intimacy, uncertainty, erotics, boundary-crossing, and activist energies that gave rise to it, while engaging critically and productively with the resources of traditional disciplinary knowledge" (35). I would add to Love's list "interdependencies" and "internal(ized) contradictions." To state that this piece of scholarship is invested in queer studies requires a kind of "thick description" that takes root but goes beyond Clifford Geertz's revolutionary understanding of the complexities of (writing about) culture. As Love affirms, "When scholars attend to complexity, refuse to equate behavior with identity, address stigmatized activities without judgment, or 'hustle' between disciplines and academic and vernacular frames of reference, they bear witness to core queer values (and furthermore suggest the extent to which queer studies has developed recognizable methods)" (35).

A well-researched interdisciplinary study in contemporary culture is a daunting task, for we must balance the fine line in being theoretically sophisticated to appeal to scholars while highly readable and accessible to students of a wide variety of fields. As such, my hope is that this book will be of interest to students and scholars of Latin American studies, Brazilian studies, queer studies, gender studies, urban studies, history, sociology, psychology, visual studies and new media, cultural studies, and linguistics. The thread that holds the eclectic incorporation of these disciplines together, as we call on them individually and collectively to inform the pages of this work, is a singular one with multiple avenues: language. Cultural representations of LGBT life in the Brazil of the late twentieth and early twenty-first century are complex, resisting reductive analysis. It is my belief that language, or rather, languages are the most effective tools to dig deeper into how we construct meaning and how we interpret "reality." As such, this book integrates and reflects on five different "types" of languages that express cultural phenomena. Chapters 1, 2, and 3 focus on a language Brazilians sometimes call *jornalês*, the language of the daily newspaper, as it recounts, recreates, and reconstructs meaning in its representation of the LGBT Pride Parade in São Paulo. Chapter 4 takes language to its most referential and identifiable level, examining the discourse of the dictionary not only in its hegemonic and powerful position to "define" meaning of the words we speak, think, write, and otherwise articulate but also in its ability to subvert heteronormative linguistic codes and reinvest them with more expansive (and often highly ambiguous) conceptualizations of gender and sexuality. This chapter also studies the language of the image, the drawings, and captions that accompany a book self-defining as a reference source. The language constituting chapter 5 is a well-intentioned effort to conjoin academic text with political activism, interrogating the limits of both to do their hard work to promote social justice in the context of sexual and gender identity minorities, fused at the hip and at the *bunda* (buttocks) of the body of the Brazilian *travesti*. Chapter 6 looks at the language of photography, examining the complex relationship between subject and object, the role of the camera in creating meaning, and the ethical imperatives and limitations involved in recording visual representations of bodies not to exploit them but rather to humanize them. In chapter 7, I examine cinematic production that revolves around representations of LGBT+ Brazilians both in Brazil and as members of its international diasporic communities. Finally, chapter 8 turns our lens to the language of museology, studying both artistic representations of queerness and the political, ideological, and religious conflicts that arise from such a display. In this final chapter, we come to terms with the dangers of (con)testing the curatorial as dictatorial in a relatively young democracy where community-building activities like crowd-sourcing enter into conflict with state censorship. Ultimately, I take up what constitutes queer criteria for inclusion in Brazil's one and only *Queermuseu* (Queer Museum) (2018–2019) and the cultural institutions that claim the power to make such evaluations.

The specific objectives of this study are five-fold: (1) to conduct the first comprehensive discourse analysis of the dynamics and features of the largest LGBT Pride Parade in the world; (2) to relate and critically evaluate an untold story that involves the very recent developments for the LGBT movement in Brazil; (3) to study characteristics that make life unique for sexual minorities in Brazil, while also viewing Brazil in relation to global LGBT sociopolitical movements; (4) to critically assess the complex relationship(s) between the visual arts and political activism, carefully analyzing artistic representations of LGBT identities through discourses of journalism, photography, cinema, museology, and new social media platforms; and (5) to argue for the usefulness and the challenges of Brazil as a case study for understanding the cultivation of ambiguity in contemporary (re)constructions of queer life. My hope and desire is that the present contribution to an ever-widening field may help gauge a theoretical scholarly framework promoting linkages and subsequent dialogues between political activism and academic scholarship. Language is at the core of such a dialogue, of course, whether to create or comprehend political structures or to critique them in academic discourse. As such, this study attempts to analyze the relationship between burgeoning critical sociopolitical movements while problematizing the "language" used to (re)configure and (re)conceptualize them. To accomplish these objectives, we must carefully examine the intricacies of terminology Brazilian sexual minorities themselves adopt and adapt in a variety of cultural circuits, thus illustrating the development of LGBT+ identities through performative language use and not solely the institutions that claim to speak for or on behalf of these individuals and communities.

Throughout these chapters, I explore how an interdisciplinary project such as this one may productively and simultaneously utilize tools from the social sciences while maintaining a humanities-based cultural studies methodological framework to theorize the imaginary of Brazil as an idyllically "queer space." To that end, I view Brazil's historical development and its present reality as inherently ambiguous in nature. While attempting to avoid exoticizing "difference," the theoretical foundations of this book consider *Brasilidade*[1] as a concept that is permanently in flux, resisting attempts to locate, much less placate, a "national character" or define a "profile" of the country or its collective core values. Through an eclectic process of "becoming" and by occupying a "space in-between," much in the spirit of Silviano Santiago's analysis of Latin American cultures,[2] I contend that it becomes virtually unnecessary "to queer" the Brazilian imaginary since the cultural landscape of this space is inherently and quintessentially queer. In addition to reflecting on the usefulness of a book on queer Brazil, I aim to assess both the existence and the irreconcilability of the internal contradictions, which seem to typify the trope of *Brazil* and simultaneously characterize its queer positionality as an entity fascinated with the messiness of the creative process and ultimately less interested in attaining "final results." A concrete example of this tendency is the fact that while São Paulo boasts, and various sources confirm, that it is the megalopolis which hosts the largest Pride Parade in the world, we must balance this with the sobering reality of a nation identified in various media sources (internally and internationally) as the current world leader in the perpetration of homicidal transphobic and homophobic hate crimes.

How does ambiguity co-exist with the positivistic formation of the Brazilian Republic, where "order and progress" would seem to negate the very fabric of creative energy that might lead to a continual self-reflexive process in which chaos is a welcome ingredient to help sustain contradiction?[3] I would like to posit that São Paulo constitutes the ideal "laboratory" for this study for a number of reasons. Perhaps the most important is the fact that, according to the July 2019 census conducted by Brazil's renowned *Instituto Brasileiro de Geografia e Estatística (IGBE)* (Brazilian Institute of Geography and Statistics), the megalopolis is home to some 12.25 million inhabitants or 22 million in the metropolitan area (45.9 million Brazilians reside in the state of São Paulo), making it the largest city in Brazil and the fifth largest in the world. Many *paulistanos* (inhabitants or residents of São Paulo) migrated to the financial center of Brazil from all over the country and throughout Latin America in search of a better quality of life. This is especially true in the case of LGBT-identified individuals and communities, who have traditionally faced and continue to experience severe discrimination based on sexual and/or gender orientation. Much like London or Toronto, São Paulo is one of the most ethnically and racially diverse cities in the world and certainly the most diverse in Brazil.[4] Such cultural, linguistic, racial, ethnic, and sexual diversity provides a richly textured geographical space for the analysis of questions and issues surrounding the megalopolis, both in mainstream heteronormative cultures and in LGBT cultures.

The intricacies of terminology used to refer to Brazilian sexual minorities necessitates special attention to the development and the employment of the following terms in a specifically Brazilian context: *Queer, Gay* versus *Guei* (1970s and 1980s), *GLS (Gays, Lésbicas, e Simpatizantes)* (Gays, Lesbians, and Allies), *GLBT (Gays, Lésbicas, Bissexuais, e Transgêneros)* (Gays, Lesbians, Bisexuals, and Transgender) (until 2008), *LGBT* (after 2008), *Homocultura* (Homoculture), *Homoerotismo* (Homoeroticism) (Garcia 2004, 37), *Homoarte* (Homoart) (Garcia 2004, 37), and *Homoafetividade* (Homoaffectivity). These are all terms that I will use throughout the book, though hardly interchangeably and often in productive and controversial dialogue with one another. An integral part of this study is invested in the inclusion of the "T" in the rainbow of difference, which, in a Brazilian context, is particularly challenging conceptually. I critically evaluate the specific terminology adopted within the trans communities as well as the official discourse used to classify trans-identified individuals, with special emphasis on the polysemantic term *travesti*, an in-depth examination of which reveals a high degree of mistranslatability in a North American context, *transgênero* (transgender), *transexual* (transexual), and *transformista* (*drag*) (transvestite or drag artist).[5]

It is important to acknowledge the vast contributions and analyses of a variety of both Brazilian and non-Brazilian scholars and cultural activists (most notably, James N. Green, Edward MacRae, Leila Míccolis, Luiz Mott, and João Silvério Trevisan, among others; see bibliography), but I argue it is also productive to engage in a critical discussion of the "official" history of the gay civil rights movement in Brazil, which I conduct with particular emphasis on São Paulo, especially the activist group *Somos*, the journal *Lampião da Esquina*, and the *Grupo Arco-Íris de Cidadania LGBT* (Rainbow Group of LGBT Citizenship) (founded on May 21, 1993) so as to arrive at a more informed discussion of the state of homophobia and transphobia in Brazil today. With such reflection comes another contradiction, one of a geographical nature: north–south. The LGBT-identified citizen of the Brazilian northeast, especially the state of Pernambuco, runs an 84% greater risk of being murdered than his/her counterpart residing in the south or southeastern regions of Brazil.[6]

SITUATING LGBT ACTIVISM IN BRAZIL FROM 1960 TO 1996

At the same time as I wish to acknowledge the significant contributions of the scholars and activists (and scholar-activists) I have mentioned earlier, I do not feel it is necessary to repeat or to reiterate their work here. Rather, my intentions are to trace the cultural representations of LGBT life in Brazil, embarking on an interdisciplinary, cultural studies-based journey to examine, in particular, the largest LGBT Pride Parade in the world, the use of photography and art to bring transgender Brazilians into the picture and combat their erasure from mainstream homonormative culture, and the use of language to deconstruct hegemonic and heteronormative discourses in order to forge new alternatives and richer possibilities of expression that pertain to sexual and gender identity minorities in a Brazilian context.

In this introductory chapter, I briefly trace the origins of the contemporary "LGBT movement" in Brazilian society.[7] Much like in the United States, 1950s and 1960s Brazil was characterized by police persecution of the then-called *entendidos* (literally, understood), used to refer to gay and lesbian Brazilians. Most notoriously, a movement to "clean up" downtown Rio de Janeiro, led by police officer Raimundo Padilha, would become one moment of *limpeza* (cleansing) on a long list of state and police intervention to rid urban spaces of "undesirable" Brazilian citizens (often not even considered citizens), including *travestis*, street children (*meninos de rua*), and, most recently, the murder of the homeless in the streets of São Paulo and the forced *remoções* (removal) of communities in the name of progress, as Brazil prepared for the World Cup in 2014 and the Summer Olympics in 2016. Parallel to these decades of overt persecution and severe repression, a variety of ways to represent homosexuality emerged in Brazilian popular culture, from the development of bodybuilding, quasi-pornographic magazines, to the inclusion of LGBT identities in the Carnival Clubs, the transgender "Miss Brazil" contest, and the rise of a variety of queer-identified performers, most notably singers, such as Dalva de Oliveira, Carmen Miranda, Emilinha Borba, Dolores Durán, and many others from the "Golden Age" of Brazilian radio.[8]

The year 1960 saw the opening of a bar called *Ferro* (literally translated as Iron) in São Paulo's *Bixiga* (predominantly Italian-influenced) neighborhood, mostly frequented by lesbians, who would attend readings given by Cassandra Rios, a "cult" openly lesbian Brazilian novelist. Meanwhile, in Rio de Janeiro, one would find a number of bars or clubs downtown in the Copacabana neighborhood, where a traditional white middle-class clientele used to socialize. In 1963, *Snob*, the first homosexual-themed journal, was launched, also in Rio. All the male editors of this in-house publication referred to themselves as *camp*, *effeminate*, and *entendidos* (the understood). It was not until 1967 that the use of the term *entendido* officially became equivalent to "gay." As far as language is concerned, there was a clear distinction made between *bichas* and *bofes* (roughly, "faggots" and "machos"), terms which I shall problematize in chapter 4 with a comprehensive look at the Brazilian variety of "gayspeak" emerging in contemporary linguistic codes. As James N. Green points out, these terms were not necessarily intended to portray "faggots" as submissive to "machos." On the contrary, as we shall see, the intention was to define "faggots" as those who would use their "femininity" as a powerful tool of seduction of the "machos."

While Brazil experienced a military dictatorship from 1964 to 1985, the Stonewall Riots in New York City in June 1969 and the creation of LGBT groups such as the Mattachine Society in the United States and *Arcadie* in France did not go unnoticed in Brazil,[9] even though that year and the three to follow would become the most repressive phase of the military dictatorship. The years preceding the development of an organized gay rights movement in Brazil were characterized by very rich counter-cultural manifestations, which carried into the 1970s with Rio's *Carnaval* (Carnival) opening spaces for job opportunities, parties, balls, and fashion shows that would include

LGBT citizens. In 1972, celebrated singer-poet-performer-activist Caetano Veloso returned from political exile in London, perhaps without *lenços e documentos* (handkerchiefs and documents), alludes to a famous Caetano Veloso song,[10] but with a good supply of lipstick that he would use to perform Carmen Miranda style, arguing that androgyny and ambiguity were the most effective forms of political protest against a dictatorship which suspended human rights on all levels, including the sexual. This fundamental year also saw the creation of the group *Dzi Croquettes* (Zee Croquettes), an important countercultural dance troupe, recently memorialized in an award-winning documentary film of the same name.[11] The "alternative" music scene continued to blossom in 1973, thanks in large part to the efforts of genderqueer performer Ney Matogrosso, the son of a military general and former cadet, who uses androgyny in voice, body, and dancing to subvert heteronormative models of rigid identitarian politics, helping to carve out a creative space for alternative forms of self-expression in the face of a deeply patriarchal and *machista* society. Matogrosso's band, *Secos & Molhados* (Dry and Wet Ones), a new brand of rock 'n' roll, mixed Brazilian and Portuguese folk songs and dance, to protest the military dictatorship.

Two celebrated Brazilian singers, Maria Bethânia and Gal Costa, famously exchanged a kiss on the lips after performing a duet of *"Menininha do Cantois"* (Little Gril from Cantois) (1972), a song by Dorival Caymmi evoking a *candomblé* (Afro-Brazilian syncretic religion) blessing. At the same time, disco culture arrived in Brazil, influencing the establishment of gay nightclubs in both Rio and São Paulo. Issues around gender began to be debated in universities as part of the platform of the 1975 celebration for International Women's Day, resulting in the emergence of the first feminist journal, *Nós, mulheres* (*We, Women*), in 1976. A historical meeting of gay artists, intellectuals, and journalists took place the following year, in the painter Darcy Penteado's apartment, leading to the founding of a gay press in Brazil, inspired by the work of Winston Leyland, editor of San Francisco's "Gay Sunshine Press." In 1978, the group launched the famous journal, *Lampião da Esquina* (*Streetlamp*), which marked the "official" beginning of the gay rights movement in Brazil. The same pivotal year would see the founding of the activist group *Somos* in São Paulo, whose organization was inspired by feminist groups and studied extensively by the historians and critics named earlier. *Somos* would later spark similar organizations to emerge in many urban regions throughout Brazil, including Brasília, João Pessoa, Recife, Niterói, Salvador, and, of course, Rio de Janeiro. In 1979, a division in *Somos* sparked the creation of the group *Lésbico-Feminista* (Lesbian Feminist), which in turn created the press called *Chanacomchana* (loosely translated as "Pussy with Pussy"), illustrating the beginning of a rift between gay male and lesbian activists, a situation I will examine in much greater detail in the pages to come.

There was increasing freedom in Brazil in the 1980s, as democracy slowly began to return. With less repression and more LGBT activism came the First Meeting of Organized Homosexual Groups (*I Encontro de Grupos Homossexuais Organizados*) held in São Paulo in April 1980,[12] which restricted attendance exclusively to homosexual activist groups and their guests. The event brought almost 200 people together, including members from *Somos* and the editorial board of *Lampião da Esquina*, together with many other associations. The results of this meeting led to seven specific decisions that would form the platform of the organization and many others to come: (1) to fight for the modification of the DSM regarding the classification of homosexuality as a "sexual disorder"; (2) to argue for the inclusion of "sexual option" in the text of the Brazilian Constitution; (3) to gain judicial legalization of the groups who comprised membership at the meeting; (4) to use journals and newsletters to enhance communication between and among these groups; (5) to promote a debate about homosexuality during the annual convention of the Brazilian Society for the Progress of Science; (6) to denounce discrimination against homosexuals by employers; and (7) to track investigations on police harassment against homosexuals. The *Grupo Gay da Bahia* (Gay Group of Bahia) was founded the same year by Luiz Mott, who is still quite active today and from whose organization we receive most of our statistics on LGBT assaults and assassinations on an annual basis. June 13, 1980 marked the First Demonstration of Homosexual Groups, allied with both the feminist and the black movements, held in São Paulo to protest against the then-named (and unfortunately still pertinent) "Cleaning Operation" led by the civil police, at the hands of Sheriff José Wilson Richetti, culminating in the presence of approximately 1,000 protesters.

Activism around AIDS would change the panorama of the gay rights movement in Brazil from 1982 onward. The first diagnoses of AIDS among homo/bisexual male patients in Brazil led to the problematic (and today highly controversial term) *aidético* (literally, "aidsetic") as an adjective to refer to a person with AIDS. Interestingly, the term *AIDS*, unlike in Brazil's Latin American counterparts, was never translated to *SIDA* in Brazil, despite the fact that Portuguese would render the acronym in identical ways to Spanish. Whether it is a result of North American (English-language) linguistic imperialism or a popular belief that the Spanish acronym of *SIDA* is too close to the common Portuguese nickname *Cida* (derived from the popular first name *Aparecida*), together with its implicit religious connotations as *Nossa Senhora da Aparecida* (Our Lady of the Conception Appeared), Brazil is unique among its Latin American neighbors in its abbreviated nomenclature of the disease. In 1983, São Paulo created a state program called "PE-DST/AIDS" to educate its citizens on safe-sex practices to avoid sexually transmitted diseases. An emergent movement to combat AIDS had begun in 1985, gaining significant strength by 1989 leading to major political impact in the 1990s, earning the Brazilian government a prominent place as one of the most progressive policies in the world on AIDS-related legislation. For instance, the reader may remember the bold decision by President José Inácio ("Lula") da Silva to break patents so that the Brazilian government could (and still does) provide medication free to its citizens living with HIV or AIDS, under a progressive policy of universal access to health care. This pivotal year saw the creation of the first NGO to fight AIDS, the *Grupo de Apoio e Prevenção à AIDS* (Support Group for the Prevention of AIDS), in São Paulo. The Ministry of Health financed a dozen projects developed by LGBT groups to prevent AIDS within the homosexual population. Also that year, which included Brazil's definitive final move from military dictatorship to *Abertura* (democratic elections), the Federal Board of Medicine of Brazil removed Article 302.0 from the DSM, which considered homosexuality a disease, "downgrading" it, one might say, to "other psychosocial circumstances," recoded to 206.9. Administrative rule 236 created a National Program of STD/AIDS Education and Prevention, though it became active only in 1988. The *Abertura* process is generally considered to have begun with pronouncements by President Ernesto Geisel in 1974 about *distensão* (liberalization) and is manifested by the Amnesty Law of 1979, among other measures. Hence, it is important to note that while the year 1985 technically marks the end of the military dictatorship, it actually represents the final steps of a work in progress for nearly a decade.

The group *Triângulo Rosa* (Pink Triangle) was also founded in 1985 in Rio by activist Eduardo Mascarenhas,[13] who would combine forces with the *Grupo Gay da Bahia* to change the Brazilian Constitution to prohibit discrimination against "sexual orientation" as opposed to "sexual option," a hard-fought battle which unfortunately has not proven successful to this day. Nevertheless, the 1990s witnessed significant consolidation of both LGBT identity and community in Brazil. In 1991, the acronym of PWA (people living with AIDS) was adopted, although *aidético* (literally, AIDS-carrier) is still used in some popular circles today, and not necessarily with pejorative connotations. The final decade of the last millennium in Brazil began to see increased involvement and participation of transgender citizens, such as the *Primeiro Encontro Nacional de Travestis que Trabalham na Prevenção da AIDS* (First National Meeting of *Travestis* Working for the Prevention of AIDS). By the tenth meeting, transsexuals would be included in this group. As we shall see in great detail in chapters 4 and 5, the place and the definition of the "T" in the LGBT sandwich is a hotly contested issue in Brazil, one that continues to be controversial today. In fact, it was not until 2005, during the Twelfth Meeting of the Brazilian Gay, Lesbian, and Transgender Collective, that bisexuals were publicly included in the movement, a congress which also called for the expansion of the category of "T" to represent transvestites, transsexuals, *travestis*, and transgender people.

In 1993, during the Seventh Annual Meeting of the *Encontro Nacional de Homossexuais* (National Meeting of Homosexuals), the term *lésbicas* was added to the designation. Further opening up the movement to nonheteronormative groups and individuals, in 1994, André Fischer coined the important acronym *GLS* (*Gays, Lésbicas, e Simpatizantes*—Gays, Lesbians, and Allies) when he produced the *MIX Brasil de Diversidade Sexual* film series. This is a designation still in use by many today, for its *simpatizantes* (the "S") roughly equates to what we might call gay-friendly or "straight but not narrow" in the United States. In 1995, the first edition of a gay rights magazine, *Sui Generis*, was published. Also noteworthy in 1995 was the occurrence of the first LGBT Parade in Brazil. Immediately following the Seventeenth Meeting of the International Lesbian and Gay Association (ILGA) in Rio de Janeiro, approximately 2,000 people marched in solidarity. In 1996, Federal Judge Raupp Rios, from Porto Alegre, was the first to rule in favor of the registration of a same-sex partner as a dependent in a health insurance plan. This victory would lead to a much more significant one, when in 2002, the Third Court of Justice of Rio Grande do Sul would force the National Health System to grant same-sex partners the right to receive retirement benefits in case of death or imprisonment of a registered partner.

The year 1997 would celebrate the first LGBT Pride Parade in São Paulo, modeled closely on the 1995 Parade in Rio. The São Paulo LGBT Pride Parade is the sociopolitical phenomenon I analyze extensively in the next two chapters to provide a window to understanding the cultural representations of the lives of LGBT Brazilians in the past decade or so. Pride parades for the LGBT community (also known as pride marches, gay pride parades, LGBT pride parades, pride events, and pride festivals) are events celebrating the lesbian, gay, bisexual, and transgender culture. The events also at times serve as demonstrations for legal rights such as domestic partnerships, same-sex marriage, and adoption rights. Most pride events occur annually, with many taking place around June to commemorate the Stonewall Riots, a pivotal moment in the modern LGBT rights movement.[14]

Politician and psychoanalyst Marta Suplicy, whose activities and speeches are discussed at length in chapters 1 and 2, presented legislation around registered partnerships of same-sex unions to the National Congress, a variation of which would finally be approved on May 5, 2011, when the Federal Supreme Court voted unanimously in favor of allowing same-sex couples all 112 legal rights given to married couples. Within a two-year period, approximately one-half of Brazil's twenty-seven jurisdictions began to allow same-sex marriage, and, on May 14, 2013, Brazil's National Council of Justice ruled 14 to 1 in favor that same-sex couples should not be denied marriage licenses, converting existing civil unions into full marriage equality and ordering all Brazilian civil registers nationwide to perform same-sex marriages, the law coming into effect two days later. This victory for civil rights, however, has occurred on very shaky ground. Since same-sex marriage was instituted federally, the conservative Social Christian Party appealed the decision of the Council of Justice to the Brazilian Supreme Court, creating the opportunity for the Brazilian legislature to intervene on the issue if it so desires. As a result, there is still significant uncertainty on whether same-sex marriage will be upheld or overturned in Brazil (much like the government itself) in the months and years to come.

Unfortunately, this pivotal civil rights success would be mitigated and counter-balanced by a far more significant recent setback. In December 2013, after twelve years of stunts on the part of Evangelical politicians to stall a vote on *PLC 122*, a bill to criminalize hate crimes by making it illegal to discriminate and incite violence on the basis of sexual orientation and gender identity, the proposed legislation was voted down by a significant majority of senators (29 against, 12 in favor, and 2 abstentions) in the Brazilian Congress.

What began as a book project to represent LGBTQ culture in Brazil in the first two decades of the new millennium literally found itself in flux after Bolsonaro's ascension to the presidency on January 1, 2019. The pun in the former title of this manuscript, *Brazilian Portugays: LGBT Language and Culture in Brazil Today*, is no longer funny. Nor was it ever meant to evoke laughter. But though I coined the expression to encompass an interdisciplinary marking, or rather rema(r)king, of a conventional heteropatriarchal Romance language like Brazilian Portuguese, much like the sociolects of Polari or "gayspeak" in the United Kingdom or the United States, I believe that the use of the term is no longer sustainable or responsible given the current administration in Brazil (or frankly, in the United States) at the time I write this manuscript. In the United States, for example, New York's prominent Leslie-Lohman Museum of Gay and Lesbian Art dropped its "gay and lesbian" identities, at least from its name. Disturbingly, no argument was made to replace this with "queer," LGBT, LGBTQI+, or any other variation thereof. The terms "gay and lesbian" were simply erased. To be fair, the title adopted a new tagline reading "The Future Is Queer" with the hope and the executive director's intention that everyone feel welcome to go to the museum. However, what are the costs involved in not naming the sexual minorities for whom this museum was intended and on whom it was based? What are the social and political consequences of referring to a queer future as if to acknowledge that the present time is not "queer" and the marker of queerness could occur only in a future yet to come or forever utopian? In an era when political agendas and activism have converged with and through the "Black Lives Matter" movement, the familiar counterargument that "All Lives Matter" rings painfully present, perpetuating a similar erasure and consequent inequality as the condescending (at best) or racist discourse of "All are welcome" or "All are equal under the law" ignores a global sociopolitical climate where neither is the case or the current reality.

THE RISE OF BOLSONARO: BRAZIL'S
BIGGEST BIGOTED BULLY

When Jair Bolsonaro was elected on October 7, 2018 to become Brazil's current president, a host of homotransphobic discourses led to the legitimization of a series of concerns that Brazil's already delicate dystopia for its LGBT citizens would become ever more untenable. Bolsonaro achieved many of the goals of his openly misogynist, anti-gay platform literally within the first few days of his inauguration on January 1, 2019. This section aims to briefly bring readers "up to date" on the actual policies he implemented and their effects on increasingly fragile Brazilian democratic institutions. Included among these concerns is, in no specific order of importance or consequence, the well-grounded fear that federal legalization of same-sex marriage would be reversed. Concerns about the defunding of LGBT crisis centers and community service organizations met with reality literally days after the inauguration, as did attempts to reverse public health care for trans Brazilians, plans to exclude LGBT Brazilian citizens from military service, banning LGBT people from service in public sector jobs, de facto legalization of conversion therapy for the so-called *cura gay* (the gay cure) in 2017, and legitimization of the use of hate speech toward LGBT Brazilians and other minorities, resulting in measurable increases in sometimes fatal attacks in public spaces such as the streets, nightclubs, and the urban subway stations. But Bolsonaro's dangerous agenda, damaging to LGBT individuals and communities throughout the country, did not stop there. His blatant abuses of human rights led to the "Family Statute" Proposal to legally define a family as a man, a woman, and their offspring (also marginalizing single-parent families), a proposal to add ten far-right conservative judges to the current eleven in the Supreme Court, and attempts to end sexual and gender education in public schools. The *Escola sem partido* (party-free school) equates gender and sexuality education to an "ideology of gender" seen to be imposed on children, arguing that teaching children about gender and sexuality imposes "LGBTQ values," which in turn "hyper-sexualizes" their behavior to encourage "aberrant" sexuality and pedophilia. It is no secret that Bolsonaro has vilified the LGBT community throughout his political career, having made notoriously infamous statements like "parents should beat their children if they come out as gay, he would rather have a dead son than a gay son," accusing the LGBT community as evidence of eroding family values in Brazil, and even criticizing anti-bullying programs in schools since 2011 for inventing "gay kits" ultimately designed to "convert" pupils into homosexual students. This strategy became Bolsonaro's own favorite brand of "fake news," using supposed "gender ideology" arguments to incite fear and hatred of supposed LGBT "agendas" to recruit new members for their own future sexual gratification, as he claimed in his *Gaycation* interview with Ellen Page in 2016. During his visit to the United

States in March 2019, Trump and Bolsonaro made joint statements meant
to discuss their mutual goal to undermine and even relegate LGBT citizens
to invisibility. Infamously but unsurprisingly, Bolsonaro stated as his final
remarks: "In conclusion, may I say that Brazil and the United States stand
side by side in their efforts to share liberties and respect to traditional and
family lifestyles, respect to God, our creator, against the gender ideology of
the politically correct attitudes, and fake news."

The assassination of Rio city councilor Marielle Franco and her driver
Anderson Gomes on March 14, 2018 became an emblematic consequence of
the intersectional threads of hatred that extended to anti-black racism/white
superiority, misogyny, and homophobia in post-Bolsonaro Brazil. Marielle
Franco's death also became a wake-up call for LGBT Brazilians and like-
minded allies to take real and symbolic actions to resist hate and speak out on
an increasingly grim Brazilian track record that added assassination of social
and political activists, especially those concerned with environmental and
indigenous rights, to a growing list of LGBT Brazilian citizens murdered for
no other reason than their passionate resolve for justice. At the time of this
writing, signs of resistance are visible throughout Brazil just as Bolsonaro's
approval ratings during the pandemic paradoxically increase. Filmmaker Juliana Ruhfus postulates not only on who killed Marielle but also on what the
investigation into her still unsolved and unavenged murder tells us about the
Brazil of 2019, writing, "Marielle's effective activism, courage and clarity
had made her a rising star in Brazil's increasingly divided political world. As
an Afro-Brazilian, gay, single mother from one of the city's poorest neigh-
bourhoods, she used her role as a city councilor to empower these very constituencies. Her success in doing so made her a hero to some and a threat to
others." After highlighting and then discrediting several political, economic,
and social motives that may have instigated Marielle's assassination, Ruhfus
arrives at the conclusion that there are "uncannily close ties Bolsonaro and
his family have with corrupt policemen and the militia," some of whom were
arrested as part of the investigation into the execution-style murders of Marielle and her driver. And though there are still many unanswered questions
that the arrest of the two killers does not resolve, such as who ordered the
assassination, *Al Jazeera* notes that "the outrage over Marielle's death gave
momentum to the election of three more black female legislators into Rio's
legislative assembly," showing us that in the midst of such brutal injustice,
though certainly little consolation for its occurrence, efforts at resistance create hard-won victories.

On August 21, 2019, Bolsonaro ordered that *ANCINE* (*Agência Nacional
do Cinema Brasileiro*; National Agency for Brazilian Cinema), Brazil's most
important funding mechanism for the production and proliferation of the
national film industry, would be prohibited from financially supporting *filmes*

com temática LGBT (films with LGBT content), as well as cinematic works that address racism and intersectionalities between homotransphobia and anti-black racism.[15] Minister Osmar Terra's solution to Bolsonaro's request was to suspend the entire competition (*edital*) contest with seventy initiatives in twelve different categories, including LGBT-themed productions. Just a few short weeks later, at the beginning of October, Federal Judge Laura Bastos Carvalho saw through and overturned Terra's denial of funding for the competition as being motivated by discrimination of films with LGBT content, requiring that the competition be restored with R$70 million divided between eighty projects, each with a budget capped at R$1.5 million.

Bolsonaro did not wait to legislate his hate for the LGBT community and their interests. On the first day of his tenure, he signed a decree numbered 870/19 into law, excluding LGBT populations from the list of groups that form human rights coalitions in Brazil. The modified platform, led by former Evangelical Protestant pastor Damares Alves, famous for blaming LGBT rights as a threat to Brazilian families, would take on a new name and an LGBT-less direction: *Ministério da Mulher, da Família e dos Direitos Humanos* (Ministry of Women, Family and Huam Rights). In its former structure, LGBT rights were included in several categories but now systematically excluded from each one with the new target populations attending to the rights of women, children, and adolescents; senior citizens; persons with disabilities; and Black, indigenous, and other communities designated as "ethnic and social minorities" (*minorias étnicas e sociais*), with *índio*, a politically incorrect and sometimes derogatory term for indigenous communities, placed literally at the end of the list.

Another transphobic act of legislation occurred on the second day of his presidency, January 2, 2019, when Bolsonaro demanded taking down the informational bulletin for trans men published on the government's Health Ministry website so that improvements (*melhorias*) could allegedly be made to it. The website included information on how to prevent STIs (sexually transmitted infections). One of the arguments for its removal was the inclusion of a graphic representation of female sexual organs and a "pump" used to enlarge the clitoris. In addition to being removed from the Internet, there would be no further distribution of the 23,000 physical copies already circulated to health care agencies on best practices for treating trans men.

There are as many examples of Bolsonaro's (un)veiled homotransphobic statements and policy-making as there are acts of resistance to oppose these attacks. The last two *Carnaval* celebrations, in 2019 and 2020, were considered to have been the most overtly "political" and "social" manifestations of revolt and disapproval since the end of the military dictatorship in 1985. In fact, the comparison does not stop there since themes of pro-democracy and anti-dictatorship were the engine to ignite consciousness "*De norte ao sul, escolas de samba e blocos de rua levantaram bandeira*," as the headline of an article reads in *Brasil de Fato* (*Brazil de Facto*) on February 23, 2020: "From North to South, Samba Schools and Street Blocks to Raise the Banner [of Protest]." In São Paulo, the most common floats were those that, before Bolsonaro's ascent to the presidency, would have been the least visible: tributes to famous black Brazilians that helped to construct Brazilian intellectual history, proclaiming in one particularly poignant homage to the late Marielle Franco that "*as minorias são a maioria*" ("the minorities are the majority"). Another float celebrated women's empowerment and paid tribute to female *orixás Obá, Oyá, Yabá*, and *Oxum*. The statement about the periphery becoming the new center was not only an idea or a metaphor in 2020 *blocos do carnaval* (carnival blocks or street clubs), with São Paulo alone registering a 62% increase in participating in *blocos* (blocks or clubs), marking an unprecedented regional presence, from 490 in 2019 to 796 in 2020. There was also an increased interest in decrying Bolsonaro's actions to damage the environment, deforestation, and displacement of indigenous communities in particular, and a historically large LGBT+ against Bolsonaro contingency. In Recife, the *Bloco da Diversidade* (Diversity Group) celebrated its tenth anniversary, focusing its gratitude on the five women who founded it, celebrating the slogan "*Minha Cama, Minha Vida*" ("My Bed, My Life"), a play on words of "*Minha Casa, Minha Vida*" ("My House, My Life"), a program of subsidized living that the *Partido dos Trabalhadores* (Workers' Party), under Lula's presidency, launched in Brazil in 2009 to support the acquisition or rental of homes or apartments for low-income families.

In Rio de Janeiro, the award-winning *Escola de samba Estação Primeira de Mangueira* marked its twentieth win as it took the award for the 2019 *carnaval* with the composition "*História para ninar gente grande*" ("Lullaby for Big Kids" in loose translation) with the now famous chorus, "*Brasil, chegou a vez de ouvir as Marias, Mahins, Marielles, malês*," urging Brazilians that it is time to listen to the black women who have been marginalized by official historical record despite their ever-important voices, including Marielle's. Luiza Mahin, for example, was an ex-slave who played a major role in the black revolts that occurred in Bahia in the nineteenth century, most notably the *Revolta dos Malês* (Revolt of the Malleable) in 1835. The term *malê* denotes malleability, elasticity, or adaptability. *Maria* is an allusion to Maria Felipa, also from Bahia, known as the "Black Heroine of Independence" for her participation in the 1822 war for independence, in which she led forty women to create a booby trap to lure Portuguese soldiers to their demise. In this remarkable *samba de protesto* (protest music), which deserves a much more in-depth study than I am able to provide here, the song "*A Verdade vos fará Livre*" ("The Truth Shall Set You Free") alludes to John 8:32 in the New Testament while also recalling a phrase Bolsonaro was particularly fond of using during his presidential campaign in 2018, a popularized version of the Biblical "*E *conhecereis a verdade, e a verdade vos libertará* (And you shall know the truth, and the truth shall free you)," which the samba school subverted to bring to consciousness a new conceptualization of Jesus Christ: A *"Jesus da gente, de rosto negro, sangue índio, corpo de mulher, filho de pai carpinteiro desempregado e de mãe Maria das Dores Brasil,"* loosely translated as "A Jesus of the common people, with a black face, indigenous blood, and the body of a woman, son of an unemployed carpenter and the martyr Mary of Brazil."

Despite the severe criticisms of a blatantly homolesbophobic, misogynist, racist leader like Bolsonaro, we must remind ourselves that he was democratically elected in a country that bred his ascendancy into power. In a well-written article on the "Messiah Complex: How Brazil Made Bolsonaro," Brian Winter, former correspondent based in Brazil from 2010 to 2015, highlights sociopolitical and economic conditions in Brazil that allowed the rise to power of such an authoritarian bully. Winter rehashes global factors such as resurgent nationalism and frustration over increasing economic inequality in an increasingly class-conscious global milieu. However, as he argues, "Local factors have played as large a role: in Brazil's case, the growth of evangelical Christianity and a legacy of military rule that has never been fully overcome." Winter contends that "Despite comparisons to Trump, Bolsonaro is a Brazilian invention" in a country where "hunger is rising, the middle class is shrinking, and some fear democracy itself is in danger," drawing on historical patterns leading the author to ultimately and disturbingly argue that "In the sweep of Brazilian history, Bolsonaro is not an aberration but a return to normalcy" and that "the Brazil of 2020 is more like its president than many would care to admit." Winter views the past thirty years as an exceptional period when respect for civil authority, tolerance for diversity, and lessening socioeconomic inequalities were temporarily in fashion. Despite the president's horrendous mishandling of the pandemic emergency that would earn Brazil a number two spot on the list of coronavirus-related fatalities, behind the United States but steadily catching up, polls taken as recently as February 2020 show that 61% of Brazilians support Bolsonaro's idea to open new military schools, 60% are in favor of mandatory religious instruction in schools, and there is still a majority of the population that opposes same-sex marriage and a woman's right to have an abortion.

Complicating our understanding and appreciation of the paradoxes of modern-day Brazil, there are many pro-LGBT developments that have occurred in the years preceding the Bolsonaro presidency, accomplishments that are worth mentioning even if we do not have the space to go into detail about them at this juncture. Summarizing the positive gains, I include the progressive health care policies in the access to treatment for HIV/AIDS, strengthened in 1996 and then broadened in 2013. Brazil's civil unions bill went into effect in 2011, and its Supreme Court legalized same-sex marriage in 2013. Same-sex parents have been allowed to adopt children in Brazil since

2015, and the Brazilian Supreme Court voted to prohibit psychologists from conducting gay conversion therapy, known in Portuguese as *reversão sexual* or in Brazilian slang as *a cura gay* on April 9, 2019, flying in the face of one of Bolsonaro's aspirations during his tenure as president. Significantly, on June 13, 2019, the Brazilian Supreme Court voted to criminalize homophobia and transphobia, equating acts of discrimination on the basis of sexual orientation or gender identity to hate crimes based on racism. And on May 6, 2020, after nearly four years in court, Brazil's Supreme Court overturned rules that limit gay and bisexual men from donating blood.

The years 2017 and 2018 were key years in the battle for trans rights. The Ministry of Education recognized the use of social names to replace birth names on classroom rosters for trans-identified students. One year later, on March 22, 2018, the TSE (*Tribunal Superior Eleitoral*; Superior Electoral Court) allowed the use of social names in registrations and ballots for elections, and the alteration of birth certificates were allowed to occur in notary publics without involving attorneys or judges to weigh in on these personal decisions. On March 1, 2018, Brazilian trans-identified citizens won a nine-year battle for recognition of the right to stake out a social name free from their birth names without the need for sex reassignment or gender confirming surgery, therefore legitimizing and legalizing noncisgender identities. Also in 2018, the Brazilian pre-college *ENEM* (*Exame Nacional do Ensino Médio*) College preparedness exams. The Brazilian equivalent of the S.A.T. in North America included for the first time in its history a question related to *Pajubá*, the coded language used by Brazilian *travestis* and later appropriated by gay male communities (a key topic in chapter 4 of this book). In September 2019, the Brazilian Supreme Court voted unanimously to not exclude same-sex relationships from the concept of the family unit, guaranteeing access of such couples to benefits awarded to their heterosexual counterparts.

Also noteworthy are the following local accomplishments of great cultural significance: In 2012, São Paulo's Office of Culture and Creative Economy (*Secretaria de Cultura e Economia Criativa*) inaugurated Brazil's first Sexual Diversity Museum (*Museu da Diversidade Sexual*), an entity to which we shall return in the next section. On June 19, 2019, despite pressure from Bolsonaro to close its doors, the *Centro de Referência da Diversidade em SP* (Referral Center for Diversity in São Paulo), in existence since 2008, providing services for at least 1,000 LGBT *paulistanos* in situations of vulnerability, resists these orders and remains open. Also in São Paulo, in 2019, the NGO *Eternamente SOU* (I Am Eternally Me in literal translation) launched the first Cultural Resource Center for LGBT+ Senior Citizens (*Centro de Convivência e Referência para a população LGBT+ idosa ou em processo de envelhecimento*). On July 13, 2020, a pastor of the *Igreja de São Miguel Arcanjo* (The Church of St. Michael the Archangel) in São Paulo asked for forgiveness from the LGBT community, declaring during a video he produced on Instagram that "nobody should think that homophobia comes from God. LGBT-phobia is a crime. To those pastors or religious officials who humiliate LGBT people, take note that this is a crime."[16] Meanwhile, Rio de Janeiro celebrated the inauguration of its first library named after a formidable trans history professor, Laura de Vison, on July 22, 2020. And a collective effort by the law firm *Baptista Luz Advogados*, the NGO *Casa Um* ("One House"/"First House"), and *ANTRA* (*Associação Nacional de Travestis e Transexuais*; National Association of Travestis and Transsexuals) developed and launched on the Internet in August 2019 a twenty-eight-page *Guia de retificação de prenome e gênero de pessoas não-cisgêneras* ("Guide for the Correction of Pronouns and Gender of Non-Cisgender People").

BRAZIL *COVIDIANO*: CORONAVIRUS, WHATSAPP, AND "SO WHAT?"

According to *The Lancet*, the first case of COVID-19 recorded in Brazil was on February 25, 2020. At the time of this writing, Brazil has the most cases and deaths in Latin America, and a May 9, 2020 study by Imperial College in the United Kingdom revealed that Brazil is the country with the highest rate of transmission. The article laments Bolsonaro's apathetic reaction to the spread of the virus in Brazil, critiquing in no uncertain terms that "perhaps the biggest threat to Brazil's COVID-19 response is its president." While current U.S. practices to collectively bang pots at home at 7:00 p.m. are meant to show support and appreciation for the essential workers risking their lives to provide health care and potentially life-saving supplies to Americans, pot-banging in Brazil often occurs as a protest during presidential announcements. The effects of a careless leader on the well-being of his citizens are certainly not unique to Brazil, but the marginalization of Brazil's most vulnerable minorities also continues well into the pandemic. Throwing caution to the wind, Bolsonaro was repeatedly seen greeting visitors with handshakes and shunning mask use. Put another way, simply because well over 100,000 citizens have perished from a highly contagious virus is no reason to gather antipathy on top of apathy for those Brazilians who are trying in earnest to protect themselves, their families, and the larger community. Several reports and articles on Bolsonaro mocking and taunting staffers wearing masks have been compounded by the president's unambiguous statements he articulated in public that masks are *coisa de viado* (for faggots or fairies), sending a dangerous signal to Brazilian society that would condone homophobia, and perhaps even encourage it, during a pandemic.

Indifference and antagonism are devastating in a time that requires emergency measures, but this is especially the case when such judgments are transformed into perilous action. In June and July 2020, two critical months witnessing the skyrocketing spread of the virus in Brazil, Bolsonaro weakened laws mandating the use of masks in public spaces in order to slow the coronavirus, vetoing several articles requiring employers to supply face masks for their staff. Bolsonaro rejected a decree that would require public authorities to provide face coverings for "economically vulnerable" civilians, even vetoing bills that would require the use of masks in prisons. He also trashed a law that would have obliged businesses to disseminate information for their employees to properly place and wear masks. Shortly after testing positive for the virus himself, Bolsonaro infamously attended a luncheon in honor of U.S. Independence Day without a face mask, prompting widespread international media criticism by numerous sources from the *Folha de S. Paulo*, to *France 24*, to *LGBTQ Nation* in the United States, with a headline of "Brazilian president told staff 'wearing masks' is a 'faggot thing' right before he caught coronavirus" on July 9, 2020. Bolsonaro tested positive two more times, the most recent of which was July 22, 2020.

As Brazilians continue to contract the virus at dangerous rates, studies and polls are under way to determine not only who is at high risk for developing serious, life-threatening disease but also those communities who suffer the most detrimental impacts to their mental and emotional health. A two-year national study piloted by the organization *#VoteLGBT* found social isolation to have particularly serious effects on LGBT communities. Initiated on April 28, 2019, the questionnaire confirmed that of the 10,065 LGBT respondents, 28% received a diagnosis of depressive disorder, a pre-pandemic percentage that is four times higher than the national average for the general Brazilian population. These numbers, as well as other statistics, have only compounded during and as a result of the pandemic. In 2019, according to the study, 20.7% polled possessed no income, 21.5% were unemployed, and 97% did not approve of Bolsonaro's performance, giving him the worst possible evaluation of *péssima* (horrible). It is worth noting at this juncture that these results do not correspond to more recent popular opinion polls and surveys of Brazil's general population. *Datafolha* confirmed its findings from polls on August 11–12, 2020, noting that in its sample of 2,065 participants, 47% believed that the president cannot be blamed for the coronavirus-related fatalities in Brazil, while 52% believed that he shared some responsibility. Of that slight majority, only 11% felt that the president is the primary person responsible for these deaths, while 41% agreed that the president is only one among other responsible parties. Paradoxically, the research found that the president had won the highest approval rating since beginning his tenure in office. Bolsonaro's overall approval rate climbed from 32% to 37% during the pandemic, from the end of June to the beginning of August, while his overall rejection rate fell by 10%, presumably in response to continued emergency stimulus payments of R$600 per month and less head-butting with Brazilian Congress and the Supreme Court. An August 14, 2020 article, "*Aprovação de Bolsonaro bate* *recorde no auge da pandemia* (In the Middle of the Pandemic, Bolsonaro's Approval Rate Hits a New High Record)," laments this, the latest apparent contradiction from the paradise of paradox: "Paradoxically, the significant change in the way that part of the population perceives Bolsonaro's leadership occurs at the very moment that the country enters a grave economic and health crisis."[17] This curious statistic contrasts sharply with the fact that by December 2019, the end of his first year in the presidency, Bolsonaro had earned the worst public approval rate of all Brazilian presidents elected since 1994.

Brazil's LGBT population is clearly not the only minority group at high risk during the pandemic. As we shall see in much greater detail in chapters 5 and 6, trans sex workers are the most vulnerable of all, and since COVID-19, their lives and their livelihoods are in existential danger. In a June 21, 2020 interview with *The Guardian*, Stefany Gonçalves, a trans sex worker from Espírito Santo living in Rio since 2000, put it better than any statistics or academic analysis thereof can possibly perform: "It's really difficult, because there's almost nobody on the street. . . . I work as a prostitute, so what happens? It's terrible. I still go out, I still have sex, because if I don't, I'll die of hunger." In this same piece, Indianare Siqueira, founder of the NGO *Casa Nem*, a shelter for LGBT+ people in Rio's Copacabana neighborhood that has recently devoted its attention to producing face masks that trans women work at home to make, states: "This social isolation that society is going through is what LGBT people and especially transvestites and transsexuals have always lived with. I hope people learn from this." Needless to say, regardless of sexual orientation or gender identity, Brazil's sex workers suffer not only stigmatization but exponentially increased difficulties as they attempt to survive during a pandemic. In her article, "*'Nós somos invisíveis': trabalhadoras sexuais são afetadas pela pandemia* ('We are Invisible': Sex Workers Affected by the Pandemic)," Marie Declercq interviews several sex workers about their experiences of working in and through coronavirus. Santuzza de Souza, a *mineira* (from Minas Gerais) who is a member of the *Central Única de Trabalhadoras Sexuais* (*CUTS*) (Central Union of Sex Workers), states: "We are already seen as a vector of diseases, and now they perceive us as responsible for the spread of coronavirus."[18] Irene Santos, a representative of *CUTS* in Sergipe, puts the dilemma as a hypothetical rhetorical question she would never ask her colleagues: "How do I tell the girls to maintain one meter of distance from their clients?"[19] Is virtual sex work an option? Hardly, it seems, when the streets of Brazil's urban centers still exist as (solitary?) sites of solidarity for women—cisgender, transgender, or *travestis*—to claim their space and their livelihood.

After its suspension on March 16, 2020, international tourism, whether sexual, cultural, commercial, political, or all of these, returned to Brazil on July 29, 2020, just as the nation reflected the second highest concentration of COVID-19-related deaths in the world. Brazil's decision to reopen its boundaries to international flights came with only one caveat, surprisingly not evidence of a negative coronavirus test result: proof of health insurance for the duration of the trip to Brazil, a requirement since removed on October 2, 2020. A study from the University of Oxford partnering with the Brazilian research organization *FAPESP* (*Fundação de Amparo a Pesquisa do Estado de São Paulo*; São Paulo Foundation for Research Support) shows that between late February and early March there were at least 102 international introductions of the virus into Brazil, from 18 virus strains. But only three of them—all from Europe—created a chain of transmission. Two strains of the virus prevalent in São Paulo and Rio de Janeiro were later found in the Amazonian region of northern Brazil, becoming the epicenter of the pandemic in June and doubling the overall fatality rate in the country as a whole. It is tempting but troubling to view this transmission as an invisible neocolonialist invasion that comes, once again, from European soil, devastating any individuals in its path but especially indigenous communities who, as history repeats itself, have again become victims of "First World" spreading from north (Europe) to south (Brazil) and then north (Amazon) again, mirroring patterns of European immigration to and claiming of the lands and the lives of First Nations. It is especially ironic to remember that while Brazilian borders have reopened, reciprocity is not the case. Brazilian citizens have been banned from entering the United States since May 27, 2020 and forbidden to set foot in the countries of the European Union beginning July 1, 2020.

QUEER FUTURE? CONTAMINATION
OF *QUEERENTENA* IN ISOLATION

> The real Brazil never corresponded to the clichéd image of a gentle giant, projected for export. But not even the most pessimistic Brazilian could have predicted that in 17 months Bolsonaro would hijack all the country's joy and creative power. A rising number now think it is easier to survive the virus than the president. . . . Brazil today is masked in hatred. But there are other Brazils, and they resist.
>
> —Eliane Brum, "Jair Bolsonaro Has Trashed Brazil's Image But He Hasn't Broken Its Soul: The President Has Fomented Hate, Underplayed Coronavirus and Unleashed a Financial Crash. But There Is Rising Resistance." *The Guardian*, June 3, 2020

Given the tendency of both academic and activist communities in Brazil to continue to discourage or critique the applicability of the term "queer" to a Brazilian context, how did it come to be that the use of the pun *queerentena* would take root in Brazil just as it has in multiple global contexts throughout the world? Does this one-time use of the word in virtual formats indicate that Brazil has now incorporated the word into its popular sociopolitical lexicon? Or was this particular pun simply too difficult to resist? Here I mean to deliberately use *resistance* as the operative word. To some, this may be merely a question of semantics; nevertheless, it is no coincidence that the world's largest LGBT Pride Parade has not and still does not use the "Q," whether to denote "queer" or "questioning" in its otherwise inclusive rainbow. As we shall see in chapters 1–3 to come, a host of initials from GLS, to GLBT, to the inverted LGBT, to LGBTI, to LGBTI+ and LGBT+, respectively, in the last two iterations of the Pride Parade, represents more than a shift in initials. The designation indicates which identities are included, those that are to remain invisible, and others that need not (why?) be named other than eclipsed into *in addition to* (hence, the use of the "+" sign) in 2020. What are the political circumstances that led to the recognition of "intersex" (I) in 2019 but becoming invisible again one year later, collapsed or coopted into a "+" sign that maintains its unspoken invisibility. And what shall we make of the absence of either one of the "A"s, whether designating ally or asexual, in the Brazilian sandwich of diversity? I argue, in the pages to come, that these silences are not accidental omissions but instead represent cultural differences that challenge the uniformity of definitions of allyship, an assumption that all human beings possess a sexuality (with no asexuality among them), and a continued refusal and resistance to embrace "queer" in a country that occupies, arguably, the most quintessentially "queer" imaginary, including tolerance for ambiguity and a penchant for paradox, in the world.

What follows is a selective sampling, excerpted from the sixty works from the *Museu da Diversidade Sexual*'s (Museum of Sexual Diversity) first digital exhibition, launched publically on May 25, 2020. But first let us briefly address the objective of this compelling coronavirus cultural (by)product and the parameters of the selection process for the artists who contributed to this project, part of the *Secretaria de Cultura e Economia Criativa de São Paulo*'s (São Paulo Secretariat of Culture and Creative Economy) streaming and video on demand platform, *#CulturaEmCasa*, inaugurated on April 20, 2020. This event is a testament to democratization, at least to some extent, making access to artistic and cultural works completely free and available, that is to those who own televisions, computers, tablets, and cell phones. Nevertheless, the evaluation criteria to decide which of the artists would have their works featured in the event were perhaps not as democratic as one would like. In addition to following norms regulating technological content, digital support, and other technical factors, mixed media artistic works were allowed and even encouraged, welcoming a diversity of artworks from photography, to digital design and collage, to watercolor, to sculpture, to video performance, to dance, to recorded art, and to works combining these venues. Potential candidates were required to self-identify as LGBTI+ (meaning, in reality, that no space was ceded to those who may self-define as queer, asexual, or even allies of the community, despite the international outreach of the call for contributors). The artwork is required to have been produced during the actual pandemic and have established a connection with it, demonstrating the pertinence of specific lockdown-driven parameters. Finally, contributors would not be remunerated in any way for their works, even those ultimately selected for exhibition. This last criterion seems particularly disheartening given that the competition was sponsored by a well-funded government initiative, the *Secretaria de Cultura e Economia Criativa* sponsored by the state of São Paulo, indisputably the wealthiest state in the country. As we know, artists have demonstrated particular needs for financial assistance during times of quarantine when even those with means are unable or unwilling to go out and purchase works of art. The *Museu da Diversidade Sexual* reported 358 submissions from all of Brazil, Portugal, and Germany and selected the works of thirty-one artists and one collective for participation in the virtual exposition, totaling sixty works of art. Given that virtual "space" does not require geographic feet of space that work of art would ordinarily need to conform to in a physical setting (e.g., a museum), it is worth questioning the lack of democratic ideals in upholding a selective process that eliminates nearly 90% (89.4%, to be precise) of the entries that were submitted for consideration. Of the works selected, only eight Brazilian states were represented, the vast majority of those being artists from predominantly major urban centers: São Paulo, Curitiba, Londrina, Rio de Janeiro, Brasília, Recife, Belo Horizonte, and Belém. This result bespeaks another marginalization, one that is based on regionalism and places precedence on production in city centers over artists residing in the rural areas of the country.

The final section of this introduction unlocks the rest of the book, written in isolation just as many of us now spend the majority of our days during the global pandemic. To represent the lack of mutuality in new platforms that no longer "hear" the receiver, for we find ourselves deprived of the opportunity to fully express instantaneous reactions to the material that presents itself, I invite the reader to carve out the time and space to reflect on these works produced in a virtual vacuum, artistic testimonials which speak (volumes) for themselves in solitary confinement. To respect the silences that lockdowns have imposed on human interactions, whether by choice or coercion, I limit my own interpretations here to the role of translator of only the most basic linguistic elements and allusions to Brazilian cultural references with which the reader may be unfamiliar. I encourage the reader to silently process and to feel the unspeakable effects of isolation in an age of contamination that rather ironically connects us to one another globally. The first three images, by artist

Clara de Cápua, invite us into a solitary world (view) that we had no choice to face. They tell a story that begins with the shock of realizing that we have entered a new world in which we are stuck with ourselves, finding creative and safe yet fleeting means of reconnection with others, ultimately (em)bracing our own skin, as we adapt to a world where the exchange of human touch is rare if at all possible. Ultimately, we are born and we die alone. Many of us suffer from the trauma of not being able to say goodbye in person to our loved ones, whether victims of coronavirus, homotransphobic violence, or any consequence of our own mortality. We are left to find our (inner) selves despite and precisely because of forced isolation from others. The desire to build a sense of community while we are all in our own rooms in the house called humanity recalls musician Tom Zé's now haunting neologism *unimultiplicidade* (unimultiplicity), a pre-pandemic political and philosophical utopia to which we shall return at the end of this introduction and the beginning of this new era.

Queerentena: Arte LGBT+ na quarentena (Queerentine: LGBT + Art during the Quarentine)

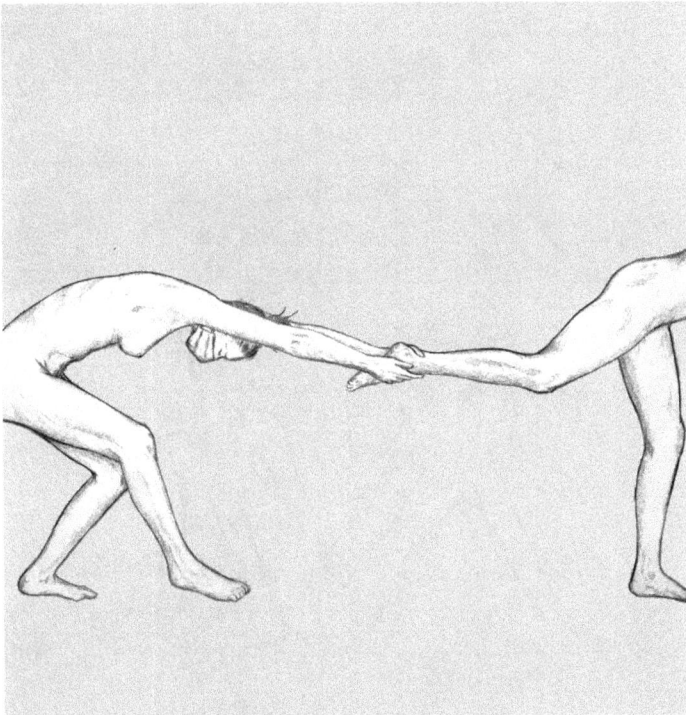

Figures I.1–I.4. *Queerentena: Primeira Exposição Digital do Museu da Diversidade Sexual* (Queerentine: The First Digital Exhibit of the Museum of Sexual Diversity) (2020). Artist: Clara de Cápua (São Paulo).

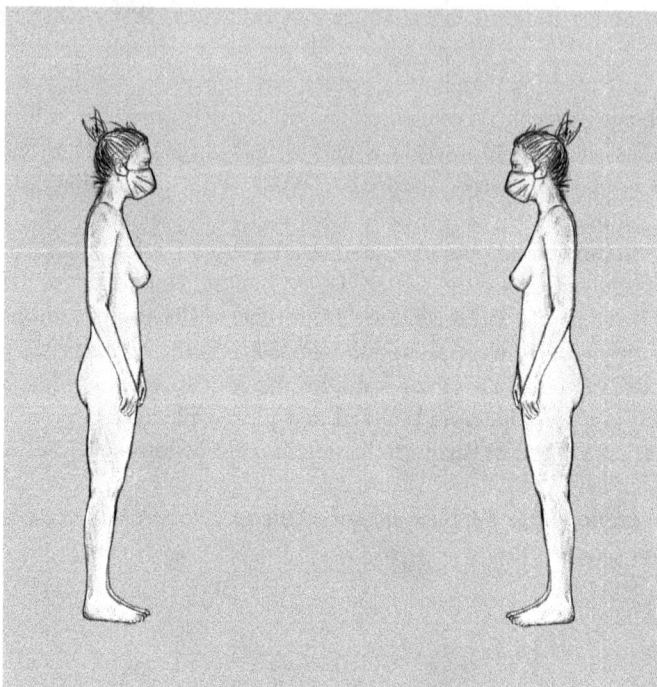

Figures I.1–I.4. (Continued)

Figures I.1–I.4. **(Continued)**

In the Brazilian indigenous language of Tupi-Guarani, *Abaporu* literally means "a man (*aba*) who eats (*ú*) people (*pora*)." This piece appropriates and reinvents Tarsila do Amaral's oil painting in which she gave birth to a mythical figure that became a hallmark of the modernist movement in arts and literature founded in São Paulo during the *Semana de Arte Moderna* (Modern Art Week) in 1922. An icon of Brazilian modernism in the 1920s, *Abaporu* represents anthropophagy (literary cannibalism), in which foreign or external influences imposed upon a Brazilian cultural context are eaten, swallowed, digested, and adapted into a specifically Brazilian context. This 2020 rendition of Abaporu reflects life in the pandemic for city dwellers who are alone despite being surrounded by vast urban landscapes, more melancholic than dynamic, not quite ready to get out of bed. The carpet reminds the viewer that Abaporu is home to stay and to dream of the future, where a basic light bulb replaces the sun in a barren new life, the desert(ing) of outdoor life that the cactus now comes to represent.

Akira Umeda's digital work, "Isolations," cleverly and compellingly draws a historical trajectory between the establishment of safe sex practices in response to HIV/AIDS, emphasized by the blue condom duly in place,

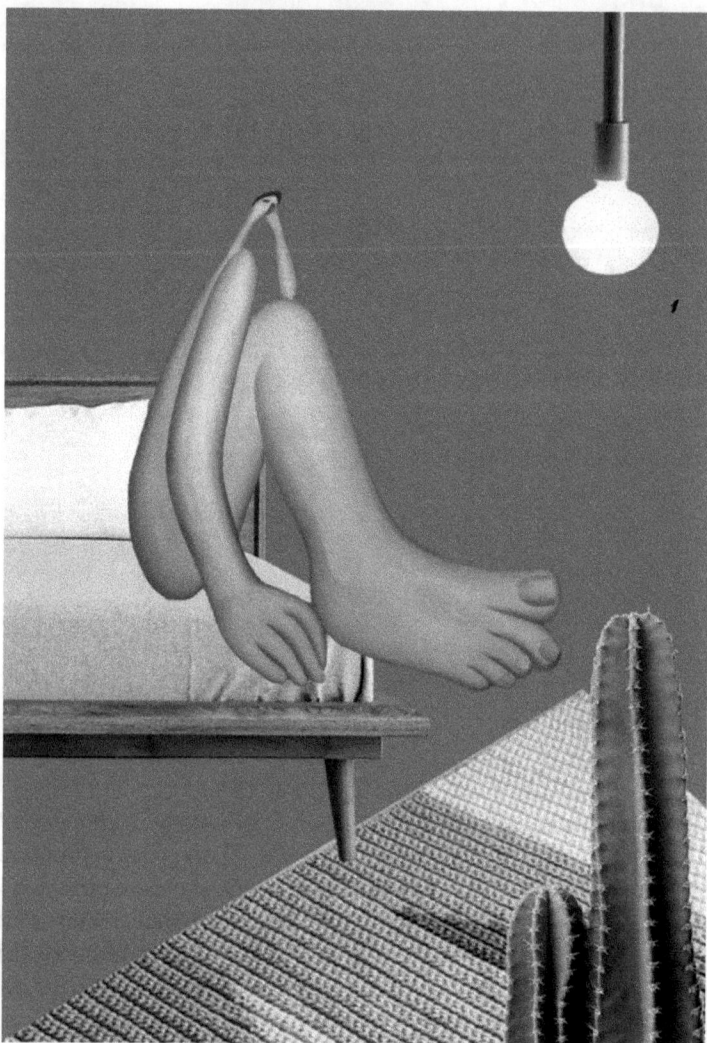

Figure I.5. *Abaporu na quarentena* (Abaporu [literally, "aba" + "pora" + "u" = Man who eats people or anthropophagist] during Quarantine) (2020). Artist: Vinicius Monção (Rio de Janeiro).

reflecting a moment in history when the medical community taught us how to handle the disease and the precautions necessary to be taken in order to save lives, one that is still relevant today not only to reducing transmission of the virus but also other sexually transmitted infections. In the current age of a highly contagious airborne virus transmitted by something as essential and involuntary as breathing, in order to safely connect to another human being, one must extend that condom to cover the entire physical landscape of the human body, thus building a barrier between the self and everyone external to that self. We cannot touch even the works that are on digital display, even as they profoundly touch us without any hope or possibility of reciprocity. Each person is an island, and not only in metaphorical terms, in a world where physical isolation encompasses our existence.

This final piece represents a contribution by the "Haus of X," a drag family and community of trans-identified artists that includes drag queens, drag kings, drag queers, and "tranimals," transcending the limitations of our own viral humanity and not simply the gender binary. The work emphasizes unity in difference and togetherness despite separation in a project to create artistic representations of the members of the "chosen family" that unifies individuals

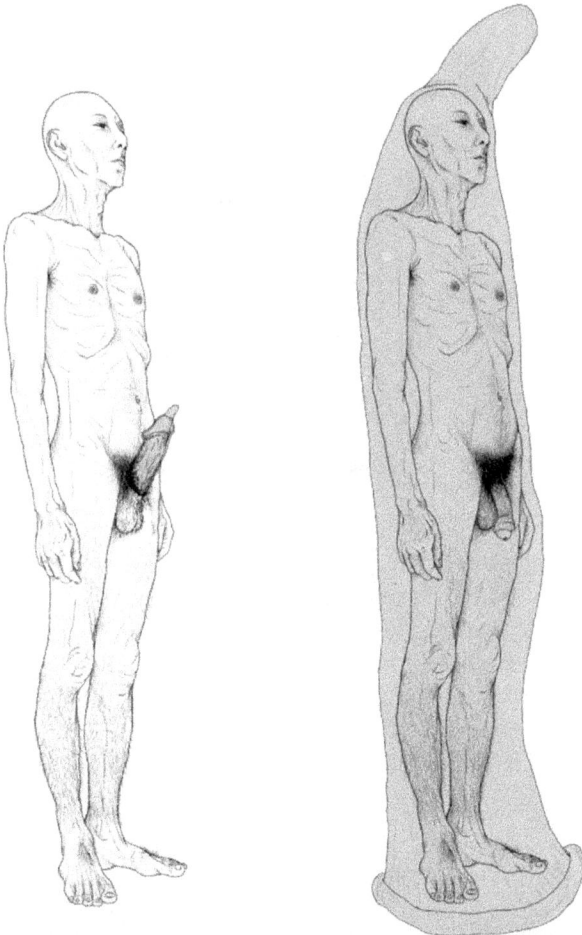

Figure I.6. *Isolamentos* (Isolations) (2020). Artist: Akira Umeda (São Paulo).

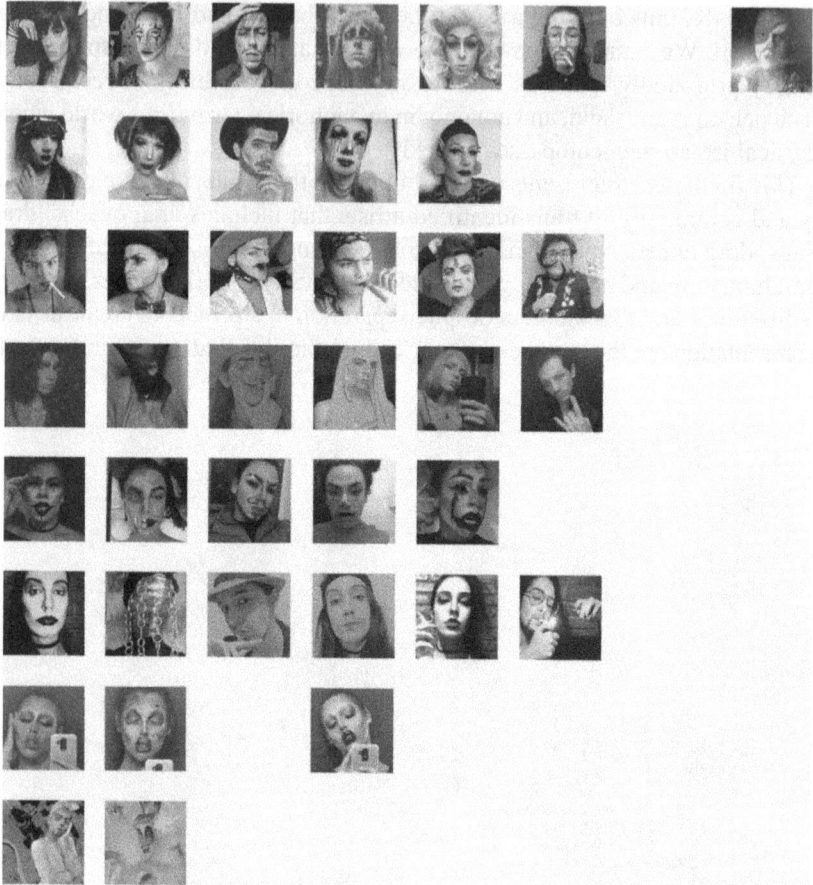

Figure I.7. *HausofXChallenge* **(Drag House of X Challenge) (2020). Artist: Coletivo HausofX (Maringá, Paraná).**

into a community of belonging. The expression of that community is virtual, as if the images crafted to represent the members existed, participating on a Zoom call. The uneven blank squares of whiteness may serve to remind the viewer that there are community members who no longer occupy those spaces through absence or through death. On the other hand, the empty spaces could very well reflect that there is always room for the family to grow and for others to join in the call to be themselves together.

OVERVIEW OF CHAPTERS

Chapter 1 discusses the first decade of the LGBT Pride Parade in São Paulo; chapter 2 takes us to 2011, and chapter 3 highlights and examines very closely the most recent stagings (2012–2020) of the event. It bears noting that I have given significant thought to the value of selecting daily newspapers that are not "mainstream" or as popular in nature in addition to choosing to concentrate on the venues that have the widest available circulation in São Paulo, and therefore are the most likely to influence public opinion on a larger scale due to widespread accessibility and affordability; hence, my methodological reasoning for eliminating alternative venues that are not as widely circulated and tend to be more sympathetic to LGBT rights and issues. For example, publications or articles that focus on LGBT issues are quite often, though not always, written from within and for distribution among the LGBT community. While such a comparison is a worthwhile project, particularly if the researcher conducts a careful discursive analysis of representations offered by these contrasting venues, I have opted to eliminate them in this discussion. I am interested in interrogating patterns of cultural representations for general, large-scale public consumption. Therefore, I have chosen to focus my critical intention here on mainstream, hegemonic sources circulating in daily Brazilian media circuits (and, for the purposes of this book in particular, in popular print media).

While examining each edition of the Pride Parades of two decades or so (1997–2020), I devote careful attention to the politics and the internal bureaucracy of the *Associação da Parada do Orgulho LGBT de São Paulo* (Association of LGBT Pride Parade of São Paulo), which plans and performs the largest Pride Parade in the world. The Pride Parade of 2007, for example, drew an estimated 3.5 million participants and spectators and in 2009 an estimated 3.1 million, according to the Military Police (this number is markedly higher if the numbers from the Parade Commission are used). In the section "The Pride in the Press," I conduct a critical study of the themes throughout the first fifteen years of the existence of this cultural phenomenon in São Paulo. To what extent has the motto of the Thirteenth Parade (2009), "*Sem Homofobia, Mais Cidadania—Pela Isonomia dos Direitos*" ("More Citizenship without Homophobia—For Equality of Rights"), evolved from earlier incarnations of the event? I continue into chapter 3 the discussion on whether the slogans are of a repetitive, cyclical, rhetorical, or chronological nature, and how this pattern may reflect the views of the Parade Commission itself in accordance with or in opposition to the actual participants in the Parade, the majority of whom do not identify as queer or LGBT themselves. The chapter also considers the now notorious and rather ironic (given the focused push toward criminalization of homophobia that year) incident of homophobic violence that erupted at the *Largo do Arouche* (the area of downtown São Paulo, which hosts the highest concentration of LGBT clubs and bars) in the 2009 Pride Parade, showing that acceptance of sexual minorities, even in a day marked internationally for celebration of difference, is still a challenge in urban Brazilian reality.

Careful analysis of each performance of the Pride Parade unique to São Paulo furnishes the researcher with valuable insights, such as contemplating whether such events are truly political mega-manifestations, as they purport themselves to be, or merely a feverish *festa* (party), which serves a secondary purpose to function as the most lucrative city-sponsored event on the official calendar. According to the Brazilian Tourism Board, the June 23, 2019 edition of the Parade yielded R$403 million in revenue (approximately US$105.5 million, at that day's exchange rate of BRL to USD of 0.2617) for the city of São Paulo. I examine the repercussions of the tension between the philosophical and ethical goals of the event, oscillating between celebration (including depoliticization) and sociopolitical protest which prompted the Association, in 2008, to mandate the removal of the floats sponsored by and advertising bars and night clubs.

The heart of chapter 2 is preoccupied with a particularly heated issue: The space conflict. In recent years, there has been a geographical (and, I argue, economic as well as symbolically ideological) battle over the *Avenida Paulista* (Paulista Avenue), the center (and centerpiece) of Brazilian financial institutions. Using the logic that the Parade had significantly outgrown its space limitations and was rapidly becoming a threat to personal and collective security, the Mayor's Office ordered that the Parade be moved to a larger space (namely, in the *Vale de Anhangabaú*) An important park in downtown São Paulo. This is particularly interesting since the March of the Evangelical Christians has also staked out the Avenue. After much negotiation, the Pride Parade Association announced that the "sacred" space of the *Paulista* was designated and dedicated for the use of the Parade until 2020, as we would come to see, the year in which the Pride Parade would cease to exist on the streets altogether and be transported online due to the coronavirus. This chapter is also informed by recent studies of Gay Pride manifestations in other countries in Latin America[15] and draws on theory on the ideological use of geographical spaces in urban settings.

Chapter 3 brings us up to date and into the digital age. While 2012 was a banner year for attracting the largest attendance in the history of Pride Parades throughout the world, this chapter will focus special attention on more recent versions of the event, taking into account the past three years, 2018–2020, when the *Primeira Parada Virtual do Orgulho LGBT de São Paulo* aired on June 14, 2020, and the COVID-delayed live event was twice scheduled and twice canceled due to the ongoing pandemic.

Chapter 4 changes the venue to the written word, focusing on colorful colloquial language that documents censure and simultaneously condemnation of sexual diversity and gender non-normativity in Brazil. I perform a detailed analysis of three recent controversial publications in Brazil and their public reception, all "passing" as reference books or even as instruction manuals that pertain to sexuality and to theorizing about sex in a Brazilian context.

Unfortunately, however, due to gross generalizations, we often encounter moments when the employed language borders—intentionally or not—on misogyny and even homophobia. The danger of these entertaining and liberating pieces, therefore, resides in their own grammar. Upon closer examination, we see that such texts, rather than *subverting* heteronormative linguistic and more specifically, semantic patterns, often serve to *reinforce* a hegemonic and monolithic view of homosexuality inscribed with racist, classist, and, at times, even misogynist undertones. Of course, there are countless texts like these which have emerged inside and outside Brazil, often bound by the dictates of homonormative models (let alone heteronormativity) which further marginalize women and queers of color by speaking for them rather than representing minority groups in an inclusive manner. In this book, one that focuses specifically on LGBT language in Brazil, it is particularly relevant to interrogate how far "gayspeak" (or, in a Brazilian context, *pajubá*) even as it has attempted to create new modes of communication and semantic codes to speak from within minority communities, is nonetheless still inscribed and even constructed by recourse to patriarchal thought and white privilege.

Chapters 5 and 6 are invested in giving some much-needed attention to the lives and the work of *travestis*, making every attempt possible to avoid exoticizing or romanticizing existences but inevitably and necessarily failing in this regard insofar as it is virtually impossible to peel off multiple layers of marginalization and misconceptions operating on complex levels to objectify one of the world's most stigmatized (if not the most despised) class of individuals. Simply by virtue of studying trans lives and attempting to represent trans voices become an objectification of lived lives, no matter how well intentioned or carefully presented. I fear this is true in any scholarly study, the present one included, which positions transgender lives at the forefront of analysis, whether the discipline is anthropology/ethnography, sociology, psychoanalysis, or historical in nature. Nevertheless, what I hope to convey in this chapter is both the merits and the dangers of the universalization of "trans" Brazilians as a category of political identity and as a metaphorical space for ambiguity and fluidity in the multiple and queerly contradictory constructions of gender identity. Clearly, conjoining "trans" identities into one monolithic category has political advantages and disadvantages. For one, the all-encompassing "trans" makes various transgender, transsexual, MTF (male to female), FTM (female to male), and *travesti* communities subject to manipulation and erasure on the basis of the important inherent differences between such identifications. On the other hand, some scholars have argued that, for the sake of collective organization, uniting forces under the same umbrella is a political necessity to attain visibility (Benedetti 2005, 17, 111–4). As Viviane Namaste also points out, trans individuals and communities, regardless of their differences, often share in common similar, if not identical, experiences of discrimination. However, as Namaste urges, "I suggest that social scientists recognize that there is not one large 'trans-gendered community,' but rather several small networks of transsexual and transgendered people, as well as many TS/TG people unaffiliated with other individuals like them. (This insight thus cautions against the simplistic use of the word 'transgendered,' since this umbrella term may erase the specificity of different transgendered, and especially transsexual, individuals.)" (267).

When writing about variation in trans communities, in any cultural context, the academic and the activist alike inevitably encounter serious ethical issues very difficult (if not impossible) to overcome. The issue of universalizing so as to build strength in numbers and a multitude of identities within those who would classify themselves as gender variant may also lead to invisibility (intentional or inadvertent) of difference among trans-identified individuals under the T-shaped umbrella. Similarly, staking out multitudinous identities runs the risk of diminishing the numbers of trans-identified individuals and manipulative erasure by both heteronormative and homonormative hegemonies who might (and often do) reject gender identity as a valid category of existence. At the least, the "T" in the rainbow of colors, when not despised, is often overlooked or neglected as a constituent worth fighting for. As such, even progressive-minded gays and lesbians sometimes feel threatened by the "T" in equation, arguing (and to some very narrow extent, correctly) that the fight for social and political equality for sexual minorities is a separate battle than the struggle for equality between and among gender variant identities.

Western tendencies to classify or categorize poses a great challenge, if not an enticing opportunity, to the scholar or activist who attempts to write about the levels of marginalization in the daily lives of trans-identified individuals. Indeed, one must confront the most obvious rift between academic research (intellectual thought) and political activism (concrete, "real" action). Can these two roles be connected without sacrificing the principles of one or the other? Is it possible for the "academic," immersed in the study of our "subject," to refrain from objectification of difference, even as he or she tries to point out the importance of not conflating nor segregating such differences? More specifically, within academic circles, is it possible to write about trans issues and trans people without the obligation to stake out an ethnographic approach, a psychoanalytic model, or a sociological platform? Can the all-encompassing "spirit" of the ambiguity of "trans" be articulated in human language without unwittingly falling victim to exoticization, victimization, over-politicization, idealization, or worst of all, dehumanization (and by this, I mean whether declaring "trans" as sub-human or sub-political or romanticizing difference to attain a sacred, godlike quality that would lift onto a pedestal otherwise ordinary human beings struggling daily to live their lives in a violently transphobic world)? As we examine the complex nature of the topics I am working to problematize throughout the book, I would like to note that my intention is not to romanticize but rather to enrich our intellectual appreciation of those complexities at play.

As part of this intellectual project, one that is deeply invested in a close examination of language and linguistic codes to create or, as is often the case, to repress meaning, there are inevitably many moments in which I criticize terminology used by other scholars and political viewpoints expressed by LGBT activists in Brazil and elsewhere. This is meant to engage in a critical and constructive dialogue, not with the purpose of finding fault with other scholars' analyses or activists' political viewpoints and not even with the pretense to offer a clear, "correct," or less simplistic, less troubling, or less problematic alternative. For example, I feel quite strongly that no academic or activist representation of *travesti* culture is capable of representing life "on the ground," as it were, and therefore is doomed to failure if a critic believes that such representation is capable of substituting for human voices. It is important to acknowledge the limits of academic studies to represent minority cultures and resist the voyeuristic tendency to unwittingly mischaracterize these communities or worse, to speak for them, for the notion that there is a "clear and correct" way to talk about *travesti* culture in Brazil, and by extension LGBT life in Brazil, is inaccurate at best and unethical at worst. I believe we have the right to intellectually challenge and interrogate the work of our colleagues without necessarily feeling compelled to propose "the solution" or the magical recipe for "the right" way to examine richly textured sociocultural phenomena which can be more profoundly understood only by problematizing its very ambiguity and complexity. These are some of the issues this chapter takes up as we transverse conceptualizations of the "trans" in a specifically Brazilian context by academics and activists alike, neither of whom is qualified to speak for individuals who live their daily lives as gender variant in a patriarchal, *machista* society such as contemporary Brazil, known internationally for its abundance of *travestis* in its borders and in diaspora. For Brazil consistently registers, year after year, the world's most common perpetrator in assassination of trans people.

Carefully examining a selection of LGBT-themed feature-length films and shorts produced in Brazil from 2001 to 2020, chapter 7 offers readings of cinematic representations of queer diasporas, with a focus on cultural representations of Brazilians moving through, between, and toward various forms of deliberate self-displacement, geographical, existential, and identitarian in nature. Emphasizing the motif of fleeing "home" in order to reinscribe and reconstruct what I call "quome," this chapter is inspired and nourished by Gloria Anzaldúa's *Borderlands/La Frontera: The New Mestiza* (1986), charting a journey that has as its objective a gradual transition to "queer home(s)" of their own invention. As such, I analyze the creation of queer utopias, alternative families and communities, and the depathologization and "normalization" of transgender, *travesti*, and transsexual character development, diverting the attention of the spectator to other societal taboos or "problems" that result from patriarchal impositions. Specifically, I will critically assess the creation of the *utopia do cu* (the utopia of the asshole) in the film *Tatuagem* (Tattoo) (Hilton Lacerda, 2013), contrasting cinematic creations of fictitious lands with the spectacularization in the fantasy worlds of *Madame Satã* (Madame Satan) (Karim Aïnouz, 2002), turning to the construction of a performative identity in queer flux as a response to and a protest of discrimination based on racism and homo/transphobia. Chapter 7 contrasts the more concrete "grounded" displacement in *Dois perdidos numa noite suja* (Two Lost in the Filthy Night) (José Joffily, 2002) and *Praia do Futuro* (Future Beach) (Karim Aïnouz, 2014), effectively "queering" the utopian North American/European dream of *trans-brasilidade* (trans-Brazilianness) abroad.

Chapter 8 brings us to the August 2018 re-re-inauguration of the "*Queermuseu: Cartografias da diferença na arte brasileira*" (Queermuseum: Cartographies of Difference in Brazilian Art) in Rio de Janeiro. After two highly controversial and successful attempts at censorship, it brought to the forefront a multiplicity of intersectional issues that echo, dramatize, and metaphorize (even metastasize) Brazil's sociopolitical divisions, despite the, as exhibit curator Gaudêncio Fidelis called it on numerous occasions, "villainy" of fascist state involvement, religious fundamentalism, and pernicious support for censorship of cultural initiatives designed to destigmatize creative production by and/or about Brazilian gender and sexual minorities. This intervention questions the paradoxically productive and destructive role of stigma when subscribing to queer theory's insistence on antinormativity. The brief but volatile history of the museum's opening, its subsequent censorship in Porto Alegre, the use of social media to resuscitate and resituate itself in Rio with the largest "crowdfunding" campaign in Brazil's history reveals larger debates on freedom of speech, citizenship as activism, art as a site of cultural resistance, and the limits of reception and spectatorship on the basis of sexuality, gender, race, and even age. For example, a judge ordered on the eve of its opening that children fourteen and under not be permitted to visit the exhibit. While the order was suspended days later by another judge, these (re)actions stage current debates in Brazil on "ideology of gender" arguments that continue to suppress gender studies and LGBT/queer studies at all levels of the curriculum, from the *kit de anti-homofobia* (anti-homphobia educational kit) at the secondary level to the repression and commission of aggression against Judith Butler's (physical and scholarly) body of knowledge.

Continuing to problematize simultaneously conflictual and consensual relationships between aesthetics (artwork), this chapter discusses the ethical imperative of the museum as a cultural institution invested in creating space for and representing the cultural artifacts of marginalized citizens, the rules of censorship, and the roles of freedom of speech in a "democracy" increasingly positioning itself in an ambivalent "queer space and time" (Halberstam) consistently questioning the fragile foundations upon which it is employed—and revoked—in today's Brazil, while calling for the democratization of contemporary curatorship, transitioning into a new collaborative model of *cuiratorship*.

The prefix *trans* remains, in fact, at the heart of this book, and in the broadest sense possible. Each of the following chapters is invested in a "crossing over" of sorts, aiming to bridge translinguistic features to transmit information and knowledge to transcend not only disciplinarity of academic discourse but also to foment a productive project of transdisciplinarity, one invested in the language that constitutes, fuels, and ruptures social movements. More to the point, I attempt to show how these very movements become transformed when orthodox or monolithic notions of gender and sexuality are themselves transgressed in a universe where multiple discourses speak simultaneously. One way in which customary and conventional notions of language may be pluralized and problematized is to argue that the discourses around human rights evolves and revolves around a multiplicity of languages, from the bodily, to the journalistic, to the satiric and humorous, and countless others. Each of these linguistic phenomena "speak to" complex performative narratives I examine in the pages to come, stories that are necessarily and most productively subject to diverse readings. I contend that what has become known as "gayspeak" in the United States since the early 1980s, a topic I examine much more thoroughly in chapter 4, this linguistic codification has transcended its own boundaries, though certainly not just within Brazil. In an era where access to new social media has transformed the very foundations of how oral and written communication are conceived, I am interested in examining cultural "texts" where words may or may not be at the crux of their construction. How does an online newspaper article incite political activism differently than, for example, printed matter or even a photograph? How does a televised scene, such as the immensely popular Brazilian soap opera, influence public opinion on homosexuality differently than an alternative dictionary offering a plethora of words and phrases "queered" and deployed in unique circumstances, designed to assert agency in a homophobic and/or transphobic environment? How do feature-length films represent LGBT+-identified Brazilians in the country and in diaspora? How does the (hetero)normativity of museum studies and artistic manifestations co-exist with queer notions of curatorship? How are these performative "texts" articulated, by whom, and in which circuits do they travel? Who are the originators of such discourses, and does their language speak to or for the marginalized populations they (cl)aim to represent? How do these respective languages—the journalistic text, the photographic image, the humorous narrative, the ethnographic study, the cinematic spectacle, the art "work" in a museum—dialogue with one another and reference themselves in connection to a larger motif of an amorphous, ambiguous imaginary known (or at least named) as LGBT Brazil? It is precisely for this reason, to enrich our understanding of translinguistic discourses, that I choose for examination disparate media sources which bear in common thematically related articulations of language. I would like to posit that studying the multiple meanings these texts denote and connote has the ability to widen our lens on Brazilian culture, provided they are allowed to speak for themselves, dialogue with each other, whether affirming or contradicting their respective discourses. Given our embracement of this Bakhtinian "heteroglossia" of voices from a variety of social registers and cultural articulations, my hope is to reinscribe an already contradictory *Brasil brasileiro* as a queer performative space where sexuality and gender remain in a constant state of flux. In utilizing and analyzing these multiple discourses, I do not make any claim that their conjunction will make it more possible or even desirable to "name" or define a space that is unique to Brazilian cultural tropes or imaginaries. Instead, I argue that the apparent contradictions that emerge from this work in constructing a collage of such languages (one that is not necessarily typified by competing confrontations but rather more invested in collaboration between and among them) is at the heart of this journey into understanding the *Portugays* that speaks for itself. The message(s) of this language are, of course, as multiple and varied as the interpretations thereof. For this scholar, though, one thing seems certain: Within the multiple deployments of these disparate discourses resides a call for liberation from both heteronormative and homonormative institutional and sociopolitical structures to transform a patriarchal past into a pluralistic present, where each text has the right and the responsibility to speak its own language, even if that language leads us to a blank page, an empty stare in a photograph, a silenced or hushed word, an interviewee's self-censored omission, and a question mark in reaction to a work of art. Is liberation from homophobia and transphobia possible to flourish in a patriarchal, rigidly gendered society like Brazil? This author believes it is conceivable insofar as Brazilian politicians and citizens alike subscribe to well-known Brazilian Popular Music composer-performers Tom Zé and Ana Carolina's "*Unimultiplicidade*" (combining or integrating unity within multiplicity, or in an alternative conceptualization, working together and through multiple sources to attain a singular finality). The neologism was coined in the 2005 song "*Brasil Corrupção*," part of an album which won Triple Platinum certification, having sold more than 300,000 copies solely in Brazil. With the trope of unity in multiplicity to ultimately transcend their separateness and become one, Tom Zé and Ana Carolina's provocative vision may lead Brazil to transform the euphemistic and *ufanista* (nationalistic propaganda and boastful pride) dream into concrete and measurable realities, combatting much more than the political corruption the lyrics of the song were designed to protest.[20]

In the final section of the book, I argue that queer life in Brazil is a pendulum—and will perhaps perpetually continue to oscillate between a politics of coming-out activism while simultaneously advocating a strategy of invisibility. My analysis takes up theoretical and ethical questions surrounding self-marginalization, North American imperialism, and the development of queer subjectivities, resulting in an in-depth discussion of assertions made by what scholars and political activists alike consider to be among the two most highly respected gay-identified thinkers in Brazil today: Denilson Lopes and Silviano Santiago. In his 2004 article *"O Homossexual Astucioso"* ("The Astute Homosexual"), novelist, literary scholar, and Professor Emeritus Silviano Santiago writes: "Does not subversion through the courageous anonymity of subjectivities in play, a slower process of consciousness-raising, add more effectively to the future dialogue between heterosexuals and homosexuals, when compared to the open declarations on the part of a group that marginalizes itself, the process perceived by North American culture as faster and more efficient?"

As informative as such a study would be, I do not make any pretense or claim that the present book is by any means an authoritative book on transnational LGBT cultures. While I recognize the significance and abundant usefulness of the work of comparatists, invested in fleshing out the similarities and differences between and among a variety of nations and cultures, I am interested here in qualitatively examining cultural representations specific to Brazilian LGBT culture. Such an analysis will occasionally and inevitably touch on Brazil in a transnational context, though I ask the reader to forgive my avoidance of cross-cultural comparisons.[21] Though they are fascinating and no doubt important, my goal is to keep the reader geographically focused and centered on Brazil, not with the intention of being exclusivist but rather with the acknowledgment of the geographical limitations of this particular project. A book of this nature, one that contemplates the use of the Portuguese language in a Brazilian context and more specifically an LGBT "revisioning" of that language, is best suited to discuss the connections and interactions, even the internal dialogues, which occur between terms that originate in English and are "Brazilianized" in completely different ways (such as the term *bicurious*, for example, which I examine in depth in chapter 4).[22] It is my belief that a side-by-side translation within the main body of the book, though my original intention, may become a distraction to the reader. For this reason, I have included all of the original Portuguese quotations from newspapers and other sources in the endnotes section for cross-referencing purposes. The reader should note that all translations performed into English are my own, and I assume full responsibility for any errors or inaccuracies within the translations themselves, and of course, the entirety of the text.

It goes without saying that all references I consider are cited in the bibliography section at the end of the book. The general bibliography of works cited precedes the more specific list of references used to document the entire collection of the newspaper and periodical sources that have informed my research on the LGBT Pride Parade of São Paulo in the three chapters to follow. The final list of references is a working filmography containing all the Brazilian films, feature-length and shorts as well as documentaries that I would like to have included but could not due to space constraints, worthy of another book. Though not exhaustive, my hope is that the reader will use this list as a guide for viewing, studying, or teaching LGBT-themed films from and about Brazil.

Chapter 1

A Decade of Decadence: The Emergence of the Largest Gay Pride Parade on the Planet (1997–2006)

Even for those who discredit the Pride Parades as a mere *Carnaval* in the wrong season, the question endures: How did we arrive at a collective consciousness that has brought throngs of people to this celebratory party, carrying flags and wearing the colors of the rainbow? It is certain that the rise to leadership of a new social group was born on the streets. And this has unfolded socially until contaminating the means of communication, awakening them to come to understand a new phenomenon.

—João Silvério Trevisan, writer and activist

Back cover of *(In)Visibilidade Vigilante: representações midiáticas da maior parada gay do planeta* (Vigilant (In)Visibility: Journalistic Representations of the Largest Gay Pride Parade on the Planet)

This chapter examines the first ten years (1997–2006) of São Paulo's *Parada do Orgulho LGBT* (LGBT Pride Parade), indisputably the largest LGBT Pride Parade in the world. For organizational purposes, I divide the history of the Parade into four specific chronological phases, as follows: Phase one (from 1997 to 1999) encompasses the birth of the event and the foundations for the development of the *Associação da Parada do Orgulho LGBT de São Paulo* (*APOGLBT*; The LGBT Pride Association of São Paulo). The *APOGLBT* characterizes itself as a not-for-profit organization with no political or religious affiliations. It was initially founded in 1999, thanks to the collaboration of a number of partners, including *InterPride* (*Associação Internacional de Organizadores de Eventos do Orgulho de Gays, Lésbicas, Bissexuais e Transgêneros*; the International Association of LGBT Pride Event Organizers) and *ABGLT* (*Associação Brasileira de Gays, Lésbicas, Bissexuais, Travestis, Transexuais e Intersexos*; Brazilian Association of Lesbians, Gays, Bisexuals, Transvestites,

Transsexuals, and Intersexes). *ABGLT*, founded in January 1995 in Curitiba at the end of a National *Encontro* (National Meeting), was the confluence of thirty-one groups and organizations, among them the *Fórum Paulista LGTTB* (São Paulo Lesbian Gay Transexual, Travesti and Bisexual Forum), The São Paulo Lesbian, Gay, *Travesti*, and Transsexual Forum, and *ANTRA* (*Articulação Nacional de Travestis, Transexuais e Transgêneros*—National Coordination of Travestis, Transsexuals and Transgenders). I designate the first phase as one of rapid construction that would, in retrospect, provide the necessary prerequisite to allow the Parade to blossom in later years. The first three years were also dedicated to the objective of achieving visibility. The discourse exploited to attain presence correlates quite well to the disciplinary academic discourse of gay and lesbian studies in the United States in the 1970s and 1980s, a political platform asserting not only that mainstream society must acknowledge that gays and lesbians exist in Brazil but also that they are productive tax-paying citizens who contribute to every sector of society. Clearly, the goal of visibility was successfully reached, for the number of participants expanded from 2,000 to 35,000 in the course of just three years (a mere three editions) of the Parade.

The second phase extended an additional three years, from 2000 to 2002, representing the consolidation of the Pride Parade into an annual festivity on the calendars of rapidly increasing numbers of *paulistanos*, and a major discursive shift from the trope of *liberation*, to one articulating the goal to concretize and conquer specific *rights* for homosexual *citizens*. The phrase of "respect for diversity" was repeatedly invoked during this period of intense growth, as Brazilians witnessed the numbers of participants increase five-fold from 100,000 to 500,000 in just three years.

Phase three encompasses the manifestations from 2003 to 2006, and is particularly concerned with the fight for human rights, specifically for all gay, lesbian, bisexual, transgender, transvestite, and *travesti* citizens. Thus, the movement clearly extends beyond the platform of sexual orientation, entering more firmly into the realm of gender identity. During this half-decade or so, São Paulo witnessed, yet again, a dramatic increase in the number of participants, from approximately 1 million (in 2003) to 3.5 million (in 2007).

The fourth phase, beginning in 2006 and continuing through 2011, focuses specifically on an *anti-homophobia* campaign, most clearly evidenced by the repetitive usage of the term as part of distinct slogans for each of the six successive years. Usage of the term throughout the six editions of the Pride Parade during this phase is noteworthy, which is as follows:[1][2] 2006: "Homophobia Is a Crime"; 2007: "For a World without Homophobia"; 2008: "Homophobia Kills"; 2009: "More Citizenship without Homophobia"; 2010: "Vote against Homophobia"; 2011: "Thou Shalt Love One Another: Put an End to Homophobia!" Simultaneously, though, the Parade has amplified its discourse of human rights to consciously cast a wider net to include other sociopolitical movements and causes, such as protection of the environment, the continued battle against racism, and even the promotion of certain religious groups and labor unions, which I will discuss later in this chapter.[3]

As we shall see through the course of this chronological study, there are four specific tropes which emerge as both part of the political rhetoric and the extensive marketing campaign of these gargantuan, arguably carnivalesque celebrations, all of which are invoked repeatedly and cyclically in each incarnation of the event but develop in distinct ways: The discourse of *family*, the trope of *citizenship*, the paradigm of *rights*, and the goal to embrace *diversity*, all emerging as a call to solidifying and reaffirming democratic processes in post-dictatorial Brazil. It is worth interrogating why these four tropes emerge in each of the multiple discourses analyzed here, whether as part of the speeches of the parade organizers or the platforms of the politicians, the slogans of the LGBT-identified participants or discourses of the *simpatizantes* (straight allies), or interpretations and representations by the popular press.

In the pages to follow, I will examine the deployment of each of these multiple discourses and look not only at how they intersect but also how they (in)form social attitudes and political positions of the Parade organizers; the participants, whether LGBT-identified or not; and mainstream popular press in São Paulo.

VIGILANT (IN)VISIBILITY

The foundation of São Paulo's Pride Parade, like much of contemporary Brazilian cultural dynamics, rests upon and often parallels an ambivalent connection to the LGBT civil rights movement in the United States. The first manifestation of the event was held on June 28, 1997 to commemorate the Stonewall Riots, which occurred in New York City on the same date in 1969.[4] It is important to point out, though, that in subsequent years, the Parade would be changed to coincide with the Corpus Christi holiday, privileging the convenience of an expanded Catholic holiday weekend over commemoration of a North American iconic moment in the history of civil rights. While this move may very well have been dictated by the practicalities of accommodating more citizens because of the official Brazilian holidays, I believe it suggests a tension that exists in much Brazilian cultural thought today. As we shall see with our examination of the journalistic representations of various editions of the São Paulo Pride Parade, I note that, in characteristic anthropophagic fashion, much of this sociocultural phenomenon derives from its North American counterparts. Nevertheless, in this (both literal and figurative) carnivalization of the political militancy of Pride Parades in the United States, we may observe a tendency for the Parade organizers to promote a deliberate *abrasileiramento* (Brazilianization) of these borrowed (yet transformed) legacies.

The first edition of São Paulo's Pride Parade, which occurred without direction from the *APOGLBT*, not yet in existence, was entitled the *Parada do Orgulho GLT* (Gays, Lesbians, and Travestis Pride Parade) (gays, lesbians, and *travestis*), which drew approximately 2,000 attendees. Perhaps more interesting than the decision to include the three categories of identities—gays, lesbians, and *travestis*—is to consider the possible rationale for the exclusion of the others (notably, bisexuals and transgendered persons), which would enter into the rainbow of visible diversity only two years later, in conjunction with the foundation of the *APOGLBT*. The motto of the first edition of the Parade, "*Somos muitos, estamos em todas as profissões*" ("We are many, we are in every occupation"), clearly concerned with visibility, runs the risk of erasing gender identity issues by ignoring the existence of openly transgender Brazilians whose gender expression may not "pass" within the parameters of the gender assigned to them at birth. Furthermore, at that time and arguably to this day, the category of *travesti*, discussed extensively in chapter 5, has been viewed as an assumed profession—sex work—not necessarily constitutive of one's personal identity. Further, the existence of bisexuals, or those who may be considered sexually oriented toward both men and women, or pansexual/polyamorous in nature, was not acknowledged, let alone celebrated. As such, the markers of identity, even though of a minority nature, were mainstreamed into visible categories based on substantial (and rigid) differentiation from any form of ambiguity, both in terms of sexual orientation and gender identity. The co-organizers and coordinators of the first parade constituted an eclectic bunch, having drawn its personnel from seven different organizations, ranging from political parties, to academia, to sexual health organizations, to anarchists. The groups involved were as follows: *CORSA* (*Cidadania, Orgulho, Respeito, Solidariedade, Amor*—Citizenship, Pride, Respect, Solidarity, Love), which would later form the basis for much of the discourse fueling the future editions of the Parade; *Núcleo de Gays e Lésbicas do PT de São Paulo* (League of Gays and Lesbians of the Workers' Party), demonstrating that the *PT*, Brazil's democratic socialist political party founded in 1980 and one of the most prominent if embroiled left-wing movements in Latin America, has been affiliated since the very beginning; the *Núcleo GLTT do PTSU* (League of Gays, Lesbians, *Travestis* and Transgendered of the United Socialist Workers' Party); the *CAHEUSP* (*Centro Acadêmico de Estudos Homoeróticos da Universidade de São Paulo*; University of São Paulo Academic Center for Studies of Homoeroticism), which would serve as a precursor to the *Associação Brasileira de Estudos da Homocultura* (*ABEH*), *Etc. e Tal* (Brazilian Association of Homocultural Studies; et cetera and such (and so on and so forth)), a gay political activist group headquartered in São Paulo; *APTA* (*Associação para Prevenção e Tratamento da AIDS*; Association for AIDS Prevention and Treatment); and the *AnarcoPunks* (Anarchopunks), which publishes its group rules as follows, mirroring in the process the obliteration of all proper rules of punctuation and capitalization: "Freedom and equality, no such thing as rules or laws, nothing will be imposed on any of you, simply think along the lines of RESPECT IN ORDER TO BE RESPECTED."[5]

The second edition of São Paulo's Pride Parade, occurring on June 28, 1998, continued to pay homage to the Stonewall Riots, increased the numbers of participants more than 300% to 7,000 attendees, but also continued to omit the existence of bisexual, transgender, and transsexual individuals. This exclusion, whether intentional or not, is highlighted quite clearly with the slogan that was selected for that year: "*Os direitos de gays, lésbicas e travestis são direitos humanos*" ("The rights of gays, lesbians, and *travestis* are human rights").

The third edition followed in the footsteps of the late June celebration, held on June 27, 1999, but witnessed a dramatic increase of 500% to 35,000 attendees and the birth of the new, more inclusive acronym of *Parada do Orgulho GLBT*. The end of the millennium also entailed the birth of *APOGLBT São Paulo*, which still directs the Pride Parade today. The slogan selected for the event was timely, "*Orgulho Gay no Brasil, rumo ao ano 2000*" ("Gay Pride in Brazil heading into the year 2000"), and the demonstration proved to be of grand proportions, for it represented the single largest public protest in the gay civil rights movement in Brazilian history. As mentioned earlier, this edition of the Parade signified the social and political visibility for the first time for Brazilian bisexual citizens, transsexuals, and transgender Brazilians in addition to *travestis*. A couple of important initiatives were also introduced that year. For the first time, night clubs and bars were admitted and included among the *trios elétricos* (carnival music floats). For many, and for better or worse, this would signal a major shift in the direction of the Parade from a militant (though ludic) political denunciation to an irrepressible and explosive celebration of gay pride, festive enough to dignify an unseasonal *Carnaval* in the peak of a cool Southern Brazil winter. This new practice would later trigger a contentious debate among the organizers, one which plays itself out in fascinating ways in subsequent editions of the mega party/celebration/manifestation. Also worth mentioning is the fact that the celebration included the presence of caravans from over fifty Brazilian cities. As such, São Paulo very quickly assumed prominence for being the gay-friendly center of Brazil, while at the same time dispelling a very common national stereotype that generally holds Latin America's financial center to be uptight, stressed out, prone to workaholism, and too serious for its own good.

The first Pride Parade of the new millennium, held on June 25, 2000, attracted a record-breaking 120,000 participants who joyfully engaged in the objective of "*Celebrando o orgulho de viver a diversidade*" ("Celebrating the pride of living diversity"). The commemoration was retrospectively assessed in a statement from the board of directors of the *APOGLBT SP*, conveyed as follows: "In order to facilitate society's understanding, which until then, had not demonstrated familiarity with the acronym of GLBT (used in Brazil until July 2008, later substituted by LGBT, as we shall see), and was also

unfamiliar with the dissemination of the theme of the Parade, it was decided
to combine all of the groups represented by the movement within the denomi-
nation of the 'Gay' rubric."[6] Certainly, we may read the trope of "diversity"
in an ironic light, considering that the umbrella term "gay" falls seriously
short of explicitly including gender identity in addition to diverse categories
of sexual orientation. This intentional omission, in my view, represents a
serious setback in the evolution of civil rights in Brazil, but the decision to
exclude more polemical, and thus more profoundly abused, sexual minorities,
including *travestis*, was likely motivated by factors other than perpetuating
the ignorance of the masses by creating a monolithic category to encompass
all sexual minorities. The first year of the new millennium brought the inauguration of the prestigious *Prêmio Cidadania em Respeito à Diversidade
Sexual* ("The Citizens' Award for Respect for Sexual Diversity"). The year
2000 was also the first time that the Parade received state support, both from
the Ministry of Health and the Mayor's Office. One cannot help but wonder
if this first but giant step in moving from the protest typical of political activism to a commercially staged celebration was not also tinged with a careful
shift of terminology to *branquear*, "to whiten" the event, in classic classist
fashion. *Branqueamento* (or "whitening"), as it conflates race and class, has
been developed and elaborated in the seminal work of Brazilianist scholars
such as Skidmore, Brookshaw, and Dzidzienyo.[7]

The fifth edition of São Paulo's Pride Parade, held on June 17, 2001,
attracted a quarter of a million participants commemorating and "*abraçando a
diversidade*" ("embracing diversity"), which became the predictable and then
especially ironic slogan of the event, now for the second year configured as
the *Parada do Orgulho Gay*. As this cultural phenomenon continued to gain
prominence and prestige, more and more *trios elétricos* paid steep fees to enter
the publicity stunt and embrace, if not diversity, the opportunity to target a
large population of like-minded individuals with spending power. Also telling
is the fact that the 2001 Parade was the first to receive private sponsorship,
which came from the Internet company IG (whereas the state aided the venture,
as mentioned before, in the previous year). Further evidence of substantive
commercialization of the Pride Parade party is the development of numerous
other parallel events which very quickly made their way to the city's calendar
of officially recognized annual events: "Gay Day" in an amusement park (Hopi
Hari), likely inspired by Gay Days at Disney World, occurring around the first
week of June in Orlando, Florida; and *Feira Cultural* (Cultural Fair) in *Largo
do Arouche*, similar to the U.S. tradition of Pride Fairs (today often referred
to as *vendor marts* to both recognize and criticize the economic interests that
take part in marketing the Parade to reap financial benefits). This was the year
when the date of the event was changed from paying homage to the internationally famous Stonewall Riots to accompany the Corpus Christi (Catholic)

holiday in Brazil, with the intention of making it possible for more Brazilians from other states to participate in the event. The question raised in the first pages of this chapter, whether the adoption of new dates may best be read as a practical adaptation or an intentional act of *abrasileiramento* (Brazilianization), not to mention the secularization of a religious holiday, will be considered in subsequent pages examining media portrayals and representations of this cultural event. The year 2001 would also introduce significant disputes over the quantitative aspects of measuring the magnitude of the Parade. For example, the Military Police related that there were twelve floats parading throughout the day, while the president of the *APOGLBT* maintained that there were eighteen. This discrepancy would foreshadow much grander ones in the years to come, as the Military Police and the *APOGLBT* constantly argued over the final numbers of spectators and participants attending the annual event.

DIVERTING DIVERSITY

The *Parada do Orgulho Gay* of June 2, 2002 continues the irony of promoting the "buzz word" of diversity while committing the ironic error of eliminating the bulk of sexual minorities that would collectively contribute to a full panorama of diversity. Even more problematic, in my view, is the didactic tone explicit in a slogan that would encourage Brazilian citizens to tolerate and, quite literally, adapt to diversity, perhaps against their own wishes: "*Educando para a diversidade*" ("Educating for diversity"). It is this particular edition of the Parade, with 500,000 attendees, that begins to garner significant media attention, as the sheer numbers of participants, including the presence of twenty-five *trios elétricos*, make the event increasingly newsworthy (or at least virtually impossible to ignore) and well on its way to rapidly becoming among the largest in the world. Our analysis, at this point, becomes richer and thicker, as we devote much more attention now to the vast array of media portrayals of the event. The remainder of this chapter, therefore, considers journalistic representations of the Pride Parade, studying how the most important newspapers of the journalism industry in São Paulo depict the manifestation. As stated in the introduction, I have chosen venues based solely on their distribution and large-scale readership and not with any particular political "bent" in mind. Rather, it is my goal to analyze the print and online media sources that are considered iconic and "mainstream" venues due to the singular criterion of possessing the largest circulation of any of the local daily publications in São Paulo. While it would be worthwhile to study and trace shifts in media representations from among various sources published within the LGBT community and/or those that are well-known to be *simpatizantes* (i.e., sympathetic to LGBT issues or allies of the gay movement for civil rights), my goal is to analyze representation in those sources that have attained the largest possible general readership so as to better measure their pervasive influence on the opinions and judgments of their readers. My intention here is to trace how both the subtext and the semantics of the language of these portrayals mirror a fairly rapid change in progressive thought from earlier events (of 2002), to a historical manifestation nearly a decade later (2011), and finally to the present day.[8]

THE PARADE IN THE PRESS

With coverage appearing on the first page for the first time in the popular press was an article written by reporter Denise Marson and published in the *Diário de São Paulo* (São Paulo Daily) on June 3, 2002, the day after the event: "Gay Pride exceeds expectations and gathers 400,000 people in the city."[9] The headline was accompanied by the rather unusual inclusion of two separate subtitles: (1) "With colorful clothes and costumes, irreverent participants left [Avenida] Paulista and marched to the [Praça da] República";[10] and (2) "According to the organizers, 700,000 people attended the Parade, considered the largest in Latin America."[11] A careful reader cannot help but notice a number of interesting, if rather problematic, features of the headlines before beginning to delve into the content of the actual article. With the reference to the colorful attire and costumes, we see that the event is already being portrayed to possess both the characteristics and the proportions of a Brazilian *Carnaval*. The performative and spectacularization of this association cast the Parade onto a stage of fantasy and utopian unreality, transforming it into a massive party, the dimensions (and, arguably, the stakes too) of the event from the sociopolitical manifestation and protest against abuses of human rights perpetuated by a system that is both homophobic and transphobic in nature and in law. Nevertheless, the subversive parody of a traditionally solemn protest met with ludic and sometimes lewd celebratory gestures is, in my view, an intentional one. Indeed, the issue of the carnivalization of the event, which occurs not only within the media but under the supervision of the Pride Parade Commission itself, is quite complex, especially when we consider that scholars tend to view the term *Parada* as merely the copying of the foreign "Parade" rather than a subversion of the military parade, which I posit here. For the purposes of this historical discussion, I think it is important to register the "birth" of this portrayal in popular mainstream media.

The use of the term *irreverentes* (the irreverent ones) to refer to the participants of the event is a troubling word choice. At the same time as the term casts the Pride Parade as a subversive or transgressive event, one may also argue that the term connotes a deliberate anti-religious gesture and that the irreverence is a product not only of transgression of legal norms but of religious codes as well. This is a perspective that would clearly be endorsed by staunch Catholics and Evangelical Christians. A third reading, if one were to exploit the term for its potentially ironic meanings, might reflect a process whereby the protest (and the protesters) is mocked or belittled into a simple gesture of irreverence, in the way that a young teenager might rebel against societal norms to *épater le bourgeois* (to shock the middle-class), to shock the middle class. However the term is dissected, bisected, or intersected, it is both fortunate and significant to mention that the problematic word choice implicit in this article would not reappear in any subsequent mainstream sources to date.

The staged "performance" is portrayed as one in which the people united together are making a "scene," a sort of theatrical spectacle not well directed, but nonetheless still spectacular, out of the ordinary, an event that will soon be forgotten, an activity that inserts itself at a particular moment of staging and solely within the context of the Pride Parade. This manifestation is reminiscent of Brazilian *Carnaval*, in which the rules are temporarily subverted, or merely suspended, before an inevitable sense of "normality" reasserts itself. Semantically, the word *parade* in a specifically Brazilian context, where authoritarianism is a part of recent history, is somewhat paradoxical; notably, the term has migrated from military vocabulary, reappropriated as an "irreverent" event that occurs against the would-be limitations imposed by any repressive force.

A similar semantic segregation of the participants of the Parade from the observers on the sidelines of the event occurs within the text of the article, which clearly "others" the *irreverentes* parading in the event as the exotic performers while characterizing spectators as *pessoas* (people) to perhaps differentiate gay attendance (read: irreverent performers) from non-gay attendance (read: normative). For the first time, the discourse of family appears in the press, but unlike future versions of the event which would configure sexual minorities *as* family members, the article does not make any effort to characterize the family of LGBT citizens but rather to accentuate the presence of heteronormative families, fulfilling their role as passive spectators or mere (read: innocent) onlookers of the event: "The Gay Pride Parade has become a family event. In addition to attracting groups of homosexual couples and gay-friendly people, a large number of people came to Paulista Avenue to attend the event simply to check out the vibrant scene and the **colorful and exotic costumes of the drag queens**" (emphasis mine).[12] The language of this piece clearly serves to exoticize difference while segregating the straight-identified spectators from the gay drag queens performing for their voyeuristic pleasure. As such, the initial media coverage of the event paints a picture where heteronormative families attend the extravagant queer spectacle from the sidelines, taking care not to mix with the gay performers while experiencing entertainment provided by the flamboyant drag queens who are offering a free (but likely perceived as bizarre) show. The language of the article also reinforces the existence of an invisible boundary, a border between observer and participant, a false dualistic construction that reinforces the binary of "us" on the outside and "them" on the inside. In reality, of course, it would be just as impossible to discern the LGBT observers on the sidelines from the LGBT participants parading as it would be to separate the gay-friendly supporters of the event marching in solidarity from the heterosexual citizens (and their families) enjoying what media sources portray as a circus-like off-season *Carnaval*. Furthermore, the use of the adverb *simplesmente* in the sentence from the article quoted before, to denote the meaning of "simply to check out" reinforces the notion of spectacle, present in the idea of performance in general and in *Carnaval* specifically. The use of the adverb, a word that has the power to modify the verb "to check out, to confirm," the adjective, or the adverb itself, alters the participation of a significant part of those who are present in the Parade, demonstrating that these onlookers are truly (and symbolically) offstage, performing a voyeuristic function. At the same time, however, and quite paradoxically, it is fair to state that drag queens who spend hours making costumes and dressing up are consciously performing the "exotic." In other words, while media may portray drag queens as "exotic," the performers themselves are actually calling attention to their "exotic" character. In fact, one of the conflicts that took place in an early parade was the fact that drag queens insisted on standing in front of the initial parade banner so as to be photographed for the press. This action, of course, resulted in the content of the banner being blocked. Much to the dismay of the organizers, the drag queens would not move because such compliance with the organizers might risk not being covered in the press.

As one of the foundational articles to describe the magnitude of the Pride Parade, it is also important to note the beginning of a more quantitative discourse, which can actually be substantiated by numbers (but even more significantly by the gaps in the variation between the numbers). This article, as is the case of many others to follow, reports on enormous discrepancies between the numbers of participants the Parade Commission calculates to have been present at the event and the "official" numbers as determined by the Military Police. In this particular Parade, the organizers claimed that 700,000 people attended the event while the Military Police stated that number was 400,000. In an event where visibility is still a key factor in determining both degree of outreach and overall impact, a margin of error of some 300,000 people, or 43%, is significant. But the enormous gap in numbers is not unique to the spectators or onlookers of the event. In fact, there is an even larger discrepancy in the article's recording of the number of floats passing through the Parade: "Taking over all of the [Avenue] Paulista, the mass of gays, lesbians, gay-friendly and curious onlookers reveled with the musical score blasting from the **seven musical floats** present in the Parade."[13] While the verb *tomar* is used by police to express general suspicion of or opposition to mass demonstrations, I cannot help but wonder if there might not be a subtle homophobic connotation in the exaggerated descriptive and figurative language used to describe the masses depicted as literally "taking" or conquering the financial center of Latin America. Obviously, the difference between seven floats and twenty-five (representing a discrepancy of 72%) is a marked one, prompting the critical observer to speculate whether this huge margin is indeed an error at all. Since it is impossible to determine the "correct" statistic that would clarify the numbers of participants and spectators, and since there is such a vast discrepancy between those numbers, we must ask the following question: What investment—social, political, financial, or otherwise—do the Military Police, the local print media, and/or the Pride Parade Commission have in distorting (i.e., dramatically reducing or inflating) the numbers of attendees? Equally telling is the obsession with quantifying the magnitude of the event, often to the detriment of ignoring or downplaying more significant qualitative factors, such as the adherence to or demonstration of the slogan or theme of the event in a particular year, or the political progress (or lack thereof) in attaining civil rights through measures like the criminalization of homophobia, which (l)anguished in the Brazilian Congress for twelve years before it was ultimately voted down in December 2013 before resurrecting itself much more recently. I will return to these questions later in this chapter, while tracing the increasing micromanagement, involvement (and consequent tension) between the Military Police, present in these events for security to the tune of 800 officers in this particular parade of 2002, and the ever-changing directorship and organization of the Pride Parade Commission. For now, I find it quite revealing that the president of the *APOGLBT* in São Paulo, when asked to theorize as to why the crowds had grown so dramatically in just one year, pointed to the increased number of floats, allegedly from eighteen in 2001 to twenty-five in 2002.[14]

A notable characteristic of the 2002 Parade is its international character, transcending national boundaries and becoming a global event. As the same article (Marson) in the *Diário de São Paulo* reports, "According to the organization, there were foreign groups present from as far away as the U.S. and South Africa."[15] Paradoxically, even though the nomenclature of the Parade continued as *Orgulho Gay*, the year 2002 maintained a solid focus on women, lending a particularly feminist character to the event. As Marson's article relates, "This year's theme was to widen the focus on matters related to homosexual women."[16] The reluctance to employ the word "lesbian" in this context is quite perplexing and, to my mind, reflects an implicit or even unconscious invisibility that the semanticization of the Pride Parade as "Gay" may, perhaps inadvertently, perpetuate. In any case, the Parade invites, for the first time, a woman-centered demonstration; its internationalization continues to reflect (or perhaps even mimic) "First World" Pride Parades, with an opening clearly inspired by the "Dykes on Bikes" tradition, in which "the first group, with about ten lesbian bikers, opened the parade."[17] Nevertheless, the 2002 edition of the Parade was distinctly and indisputably Brazilian in nature, with endless allusions to popular mass media, in a national context, to help endorse human rights. For example, the press accentuated the awarding of the guardianship of Chicão, son of the late, legendary singer Cássia Eller, to her life partner, Maria Eugênia, as a victory squarely in support of lesbian rights: "One of the main actions of support for lesbian rights was the petition arguing for Cássia Eller's son to be adopted by her partner, Maria Eugênia."[18]

While it is true that there was a notable female presence in the 2002 Parade, indicating the potential for progressive change in a patriarchal country like Brazil, we cannot overlook the exoticization of women that took place in this edition of the Parade. The personal family drama of a deceased legendary rock star seems to have been validated and valued much more highly than the everyday battles of ordinary citizens prohibited from holding their families together when a partner falls ill or dies. This ideology of success is omnipresent in the contemporary world, in which media sources pay homage to (or trash) celebrities, perpetuating the invisibility of others. The objectification of lesbian bodies, even by other lesbians, was an additional feature of the Parade that year.[19] The "rival" article published on June 3, 2002 in São Paulo's leading daily newspaper, the *Folha de São Paulo*, to which I alluded earlier, "Gay Pride: Parade Brings 400,000 People to the Streets of São Paulo, Breaking a Previous Record," co-authored by Paloma Cotes, Fabiane Leite, and Sérgio Duran, emphasizes the widespread lesbian presence as well as the spectacle of female nudity: "This year's edition of the Parade paid homage to lesbians, who were the center of attention of the party. The singer Laura Finochiaro invited the lesbian participants to 'show your breasts' and removed her T-shirt while singing the gay anthem 'Mysterious Peacock' by the composer Ednardo. Many women accepted the invitation."[20] In a moment reminiscent, perhaps, of the movement for sexual freedom in the United States in the 1960s, this gesture was particularly transgressive in the context of a traditionally hypermasculinist country like Brazil. The collective voice of protest which resulted in hundreds of women exposing their breasts, perhaps also to question why female nudity in itself is considered offensive, is indicative of careful political organizing among lesbians that resulted in a critical mass of individuals willing to take risks and engage in acts of literal public exposure to protest ongoing sexism as well as the invisibility of lesbians. At the same time, though, this act (and the media representation thereof) may have served to reinforce the objectification of women in the eyes of the spectators, and equally problematically, may have inadvertently played into the age-old heterosexual male fantasy of eroticized lesbian nudity. Female nudity in public spaces has traditionally been more socially acceptable in cultural products in Brazil than, for example, in the united States. This fact is easily evidenced by examining Brazilian advertisements, observing *Carnaval*, watching soap operas, or even taking a stroll on the beach. Nevertheless, to be fair, it is important to note that female public nudity on the *Avenida Paulista* would be deemed as socially unacceptable as it would be in Manhattan. Rarely is a male nude featured in popular culture, even in Brazilian cinema, but the female body is still a clichéd and exploited presence in a variety of public events. A more concrete example is the presence of female nudity in Brazilian *Carnaval*, perpetuated by all the samba schools and expected to be part of the spectacle.

Returning now to the role of popular mass media in the Parade, it is worth observing how the Parade reaffirms both the impact and the import of Brazilian visual culture. The 2002 edition provides a fascinating window into the complexities of this phenomenon, while demonstrating that the Pride Parade, while having borrowed many elements from the United States, is reconfigured as a distinctly Brazilian reality. A lesson in how Brazilian television (notably the *telenovela*, or Brazilian soap opera) strives to imitate reality affirms the opposite to also be true. Adorning the second float in the Parade were the actors José Wilker and Otávio Muller, who interpret the characters of Ariel and Tadeu, in the then extremely popular soap opera *Desejos de Mulher* (*What Women Desire*). Both of these actors, while playing the roles of gay characters, have asserted (on a number of occasions) their heterosexual orientation. As such, we cannot help but notice the double performance (or perhaps the performance within a performance) and the interesting irony of two self-labeled heterosexually oriented cast members of a popular Brazilian soap opera playing the roles of gay characters, parading (as the fictional characters they depict or as gay-friendly allies?) during the event. It is worthwhile to ponder, even briefly, the social dynamics of the reaction of the masses and the subsequent eruption of enthusiastic support: "The presence of the two actors in the float hosted by *G Magazine* raised a ruckus among the thousands of people that surrounded the float. The crazed crowd hailed the couple, elbowing one another to get closer to the actors. The mass confusion increased once the actors descended from their float. To try to take pictures of Wilker and Muller, fans pushed and shoved each other on the street, causing the actors to retreat back into their float."[21] [22] According to Marson, the actors had planned to film their final scenes of the soap opera during the Gay Pride Parade. In an ironic blurring of the lines between fiction and documentary, the crowd's rambunctiously enthusiastic reaction, to the point of potential violence against one another and/or the actors, prevented the final scenes from being filmed. The presence and mass appeal of such *novela* (soap opera) celebrities serve to reinforce the symptomatic rule of "exception" of the Pride Parade we have seen earlier. These actors are "portraying" LGBT people without identifying with sexual minorities or claiming their identities as such, a gesture quite similar to the *blocos do Carnaval*, which exist in all of Brazil, in which self-identified heterosexual men dress as women, but only as a *brincadeira* (i.e., joke or ludic performance).

A final note about the 2002 Parade bears consideration: The degree of presence (and absence) of political parties during the event. This assessment will help us to construct a more accurate portrait of the (ulterior) motives of the politicians and constituents who supported the Pride Parade and under which specific conditions. According to the Cotes, Leite, and Duran article, the *PT* (Partido dos Trabalhadores—Workers' Party—the party of Lula Inácio da Silva and Dilma Rousseff, past presidents of Brazil), was the only political organization to manifest itself in the Parade that year. This occurred despite the fact that the *APOGLBT SP* claimed to have invited preliminary candidates and council persons from a wide variety of political organizations. A statement from the president of the Parade Association, Roberto de Jesus, when interviewed in that article, alludes to the supposed non-partisan character of the Parade: "*CUT* [Unified Workers' Central], linked to the *PT*, was the only float representing a political party. In reality, the float was divided by members of the *CUT* and gay constituents of the *PT*. The first float is never driven by the *PT*; it just carries symbols of the association. We are nonpartisan."[23] The *Central Única dos Trabalhadores* (Central Workers Union), commonly known by the acronym *CUT*, is Brazil's most significant trade union organization. Established in São Bernardo do Campo, São Paulo, during the First National Congress of the Working Class in 1983, *CUT* was one of the key associations to challenge the military dictatorship of 1964–1985 during its final stages, calling for strikes in automobile factories throughout the São Paulo region and far beyond the confines of its capital. There is a significant link between Brazilian *Carnaval* and the Pride Parade, one worth mentioning. During *Carnaval*, a special order is issued that every school has to follow with their parade entries. Each school begins with the *comissão de frente* (vanguard commission), which is the first wing, made up of only ten to fifteen people, and they are the ones who introduce the *samba school* and set the mood for the rest of the floats in the Parade. These people have choreographed dances in elaborate costumes that usually relate a narrative. Following the *comissão de frente* is the first (and often considered the main) float of the samba school, called *abre-alas* (gate openers). Despite this attempt to deny the clear-cut relationship with the *PT*, as we have seen earlier, the Workers' Party has traditionally been the only political organization to participate in the Pride parades throughout the years, and as we should recall, was one of the initial organizers of the event prior to the existence of the *APOGLBT*.

As we continue to sharpen our focus on discourse analysis and both the symbolic and real implications of the use of language to construct the culture of the Pride Parade, we begin to see how *diversidade* was no longer being conceived as an optional but desirable feature. The didactic pleas for Brazilian citizens to incorporate diversity as part of a platform of human respect were quickly transforming to a much stronger stance, where the embracing of diversity was no longer a choice but an obligatory responsibility of citizenship in one of the world's most deeply multicultural countries. Marta Suplicy, mayor of São Paulo from 2001 to 2004, made a compelling opening speech with a lamentable choice of words, as follows: "In the first Parade, everybody looked at **us** in a **strange** way. Little by little, **respect** for **diversity** was **being imposed**" (emphasis mine).[24] This statement deserves careful analysis. First, the use of the object pronoun "us" is clearly a gesture toward inclusivity and does not consider the reality that a politician (even one progressive enough to propose civil unions) does not receive the same attention (or condescension) as the openly LGBT participants fighting to conquer human rights on their own behalf. Indeed, this assumed and declared inclusivity was in stark contrast to the Pride Parade the following year when Marta Suplicy remained distant from any aspect of the organization of the event, did not give any speeches (let alone participate in the opening remarks), nor did she appear in the main float. Thus, while a politician has the interstitial position to enable jumping back and forth into garnering support or revoking it in accordance with her political agenda, the LGBT community's fight to claim human rights is not a mere strategic stance (and much less a mutable circumstance) that might contradict itself in the ebb and flow of a sociopolitical system that oppresses them every day.

The phrase "in a strange way" is particularly problematic. While it is commendable that Suplicy finds joy and, to a certain extent, takes credit for the evolution of the Pride Parade over the course of its first six years, it is clear that she is seeking approval from heteronormative Brazilian constituents (the spectators rather than the participants) rather than one which would affirm the validity of LGBT citizens attempting to live ordinary lives in a society which represses and denies them basic human rights. While assuming the risk now of imposing my own North American interpretation upon contemporary Brazilian slang, I do not find it coincidental that although the term *estranho* in Portuguese denotes "strange" or "weird," it is also the word given in recent years to translate and/or critique the cultural imperialism implicit in the word *queer*. Until the advent of the coronavirus and arguably despite it, the use of the term *queer* is quite limited even in today's Brazil and is often considered offensive, not only for the pejorative nature of the term before it was exploited as an in-group "taking back" of power to attain positive affirmation, but also as it has dictated and regulated the academic discipline of LGBT studies in a non-U.S. context. The most revealing portion of Suplicy's phrase, and one that seems to indicate that her interest in accumulating gay votes may have surpassed her desire for gay rights, is the way in which she reads the employment (or, perhaps more fittingly, deployment) of diversity. Working to gradually achieve human rights by convincing the mainstream that their views may be homophobic and discriminatory in nature and results in the repression of a class of citizens is not the same process as imposing respect for diversity. To be sure, when it comes to attempting to change the mentality of the ethos of any patriarchal nation, the difference between demanding respect and commanding respect has much deeper repercussions than the semantics of diplomacy we may use to describe one's style of leadership. In a sense, then, the use of the verb "to impose" also removes agency from the citizens already marginalized from the political process, perceived as second class at best or not even citizens at worst, to empower themselves to "educate for diversity," as the slogan of the 2002 edition so proudly proclaimed.

Finally, the use of the verb "impose" in connection to either civil rights specifically or political culture in general is problematic when we recall Brazil's history of recent dictatorial regimes, the latest ending in 1985, only twelve years before the first Pride Parade took place in São Paulo. Indeed, staking out one's rights through insistence might be a worthwhile endeavor in the context of a discourse of citizenship, but it speaks nothing to the desire to educate others about the importance of claiming (and protecting) these rights for all citizens. One of the many photos and captions of the *Folha de São Paulo* article referred to earlier contains a quotation attributed to José Wilker, the soap opera actor who, as we recall, performed his portrayal as a gay character in the Parade. Referring to the massive protests and demonstrations occurring in Brazil in support of *abertura* (opening—the beginning of the return to democratization after dictatorship) and subsequent restoration of democracy in 1984, Wilker remarked: "I have only seen a demonstration of this magnitude during the marches for democracy in the 'Right to Vote Right Now' campaign."[25] Would the mayor of São Paulo *impose* democracy upon her constituents in 2002? Credibility for the politics of inclusion continued to erode in the seventh annual *Parada do Orgulho Gay*, held on June 22, 2003, with a momentous attendance of 1.3 million people, allowing it to claim the prestigious position as the third largest Pride Parade in the world, superseded only by San Francisco and Toronto. Nevertheless, this statistic is questionable since it seems that numbers were lower in both North American cities in 2003. In the case of Toronto, a definitive count of attendees was never determined, though official estimates in recent years have ranged from 500,000 to over 1 million for the entire Toronto Pride Week, and about 100,000 for the parade itself. The event is often touted as being one of the largest cultural festivals in North America. According to the San Francisco Pride Heritage website, there were reportedly 850,000 people attending the celebration.[26] In any case, the theme of São Paulo's Pride Parade that year, "*Construindo políticas homos-sexuais*" ("Building homosexual policies"), while maintaining the monolithic labels of "homosexual rights" in a "gay pride parade," emphasized the need for attention to political policies specific to the GLBT community. Though unnamed in the theme of the year and thus, deliberately or not, relegated to a second-tier class, *travestis* and transsexuals were far from invisible during this edition of the Parade, boasting, in fact, a float of their own. As tempting as it may be to view this gesture as a sign of the increasing visibility, hence validation, of transgender or transsexual persons, a more critical view may hold exactly the opposite to be true. Given that the "float of one's own" was not necessarily the space that the trans-identified participants had chosen but the one to which they were assigned, these individuals may have found themselves *floating* further away from mainstream (read, gay) marchers. This separation, whether intentional or inadvertent, perpetuates once again trans segregation and a potentially rather insidious exclusion from the poli-cies and politics that would guarantee them the same civil rights and freedom from discrimination their LGB counterparts clamored for. An astute observer may even view the designated float as a sort of jail for the most eccentric participants of the Pride Parade, an enclosed space where confined and com-modified exotics could be enjoyed especially, and exclusively, at a distance, much like the *desfile* (parade) of a samba school. Nevertheless, featuring a trans-identified float as one of the twenty-one parading that year was an important step forward.

Media coverage of the 2003 Gay Pride Parade was obsessively concerned with the manifestation and participation of political parties in general and Marta Suplicy's trajectory in particular. One of the reasons for this increased attention on local politics and politicians is undoubtedly attributed to a his-toric first: the *Prefeitura* (Mayor's Office) of São Paulo had its own float, in which two important figures, Marta Suplicy and José Genoino, the presi-dent of the *PT*, were critiqued, and in one amusing case discussed in the following, even mocked. Generating public discontent was a combination of two factors: The fact that Suplicy's civil unions bill remained stagnant in Congress, despite her promises to work to legislate it, and ignoring the Pride Parade Association's request for more concrete public policies, such as a community center with legal, medical, and psychological assistance specifically for GLBT citizens. In fact, the 2003 Parade marked seven years since Suplicy's civil unions bill was presented to the Senate, while she was acting in her role as federal deputy. Clearly, Suplicy showed concrete signs of either giving up the fight, even asserting that civil unions are no longer a necessary protection for LGBT citizens, for which she was criticized harshly. In a June 23, 2003 article published in the *Folha de São Paulo*, "Gay Parade Unites 800,000 and Is the Third Largest in the World,"[27] Suplicy was quoted as stating: " 'The Judiciary is already more advanced.

We have jurisprudence in almost everything. The [civil unions bill] project is already passé/outdated/outvoted. The world has already moved forward,' said the mayor in relation to the proposal that was one of the platforms that transformed her into the spokesperson of the gay community."[28] In addition to what many perceived as a blatant and insensitive denial of homophobia still rampant in everyday Brazilian society, it appears that much of the tension came from a perception of Suplicy's distantiation from her own pledges toward civil rights, symbolized by the fact that she had decided not to join the first float along with the Parade Association. Instead, and quite literally, she opted for her own vehicle of expression. The new president of the *APOGLBT*, Nelson Matias Pereira, perceived Suplicy's individuation from the float of the Parade organizers as a slap in the face, affirming that "I hope she was not apprehensive because of the things we asked of her. Just because we support her does not mean that we will not criticize her when necessary."[29]

Suplicy's gesture, in combination with other factors described before, may have prompted a *travesti* to critique Suplicy by performing and mocking her persona in that edition of the Parade. The *Folha de S. Paulo* article relates: "Another 'Marta' present in the Parade was the *travesti* Márcia Taylor. Dressed in a red suit, a blonde wig, and a crown, Taylor named herself 'the queen of taxes.' 'Next year, I will charge a tax to parade.' "[30]

As we can see, the 2003 Parade was marked by a series of internal conflicts, both within the Parade Association itself and within the discourse of the politicians who chose to participate, this time at arm's length. While Suplicy insinuated that Brazil was now a more progressive place and therefore no longer required anti-homophobia legislation, the national president of the *PT*, José Genoino, brought the proposal back to the forefront, stating: "With this demonstration, it is now time to vote on the [civil unions] project. This responsibility is not solely dependent on the government, but we will defend it [the bill]."[31] In addition, the former president of the Parade Association, Roberto de Jesus, lamented the choice of slogan, calling for a more inclusive politics that would unify all segments of the rainbow in a shared battle to claim universal civil rights for all sexual and gender minorities. But Roberto de Jesus was not necessarily referring to the missing "T" of the equation. In the same article published in the *Folha de S. Paulo*, de Jesus was quoted as saying: "That theme is outdated. We have to work with a common ground between all the segments that are political minorities."[32] The silence or even omission of trans-identified citizens continued to be exemplified in a statement issued by that year's president of *APOGLBT*, Nelson Matias Pereira: "The current Board has already announced that, in 2004, the theme will be dedicated to the elderly and adolescents,"[33] a promise he did indeed honor in the following year's edition, *"Temos família e orgulho"* ("We have family and pride").

The Eighth Pride Parade did not only focus on the family but also featured the return of the GLBT acronym, striving for more inclusivity and the Parade Association's hope that heteronormative Brazilian society had become, by 2004, successfully "educated" enough to have familiarized themselves with the meaning of the initials. Either way you slice it, with 1.8 million attendees according to the Parade organizers—and 1.5 million according to the Military Police—the 2004 edition reached historic proportions by becoming the largest Pride Parade in the world. This astronomical number far exceeds the New York City Pride Parade the prior year, which had nearly 1 million participants, as well as the Toronto Parade, with about 900,000 people in attendance. In fact, the São Paulo Pride Parade earned, in 2004, its rightful place in the *Guinness Book of World Records* in the category of largest Gay Pride Parade in the world. Though it was not the first time Brazil's economic center had hosted an event of this magnitude, it was a close second to the 2003 New Year's Day Celebration on *Paulista* Avenue, which drew 1.9 million people. Indeed, the sheer magnitude of the event qualified it as the most newsworthy Pride Parade to date. The physical logistics and geographic realities at stake to accommodate such large numbers were quite complex. For the first time, the Parade took over both sides of the *Avenida Paulista*. Also unprecedented and further demonstrating the ever-growing magnitude of the event, when the first of the twenty-five floats arrived at the end point of the Parade in the *Praça da República* (Plaza (or Square) of the Republic), the last few floats were still at the beginning of the *Avenida Paulista*, having yet to fire their own engines and begin their journey.

The qualitative dimensions of the *festa* (party) are also well worth discussing. The discourse of family was finally redefined that year, to call for expanded recognition of LGBT citizens from *within* the traditional family unit. This move represented a massive step forward from the prior conceptualization of affirmative family support conceived as straight-but-not-narrow heteronormative families that attended the spectacle from the sidelines in previous years. Mayor Suplicy, a candidate for reelection at the time of this edition of the Parade, was back in the business of making the opening speech, which quite interestingly was received with a fair amount of applause, as I personally noted during the introduction, despite the controversial veil of silence she maintained in the previous year's event. While the presentations did not exploit the discourse of family far enough—that is, there was no speech or public discussion about exploring and admitting alternative family structures, or redefining the family unit from a non-heteronormative perspective—Suplicy's speech echoed the desire to acknowledge that LGBT persons emerge from good traditional Brazilian families, which is a step forward but also tinged with a subtext of a potentially condescending *acontece até nas melhores famílias* ("It happens even in the best of families"). In her opening remarks, Suplicy, accompanied by her husband Luis Favre and once again by José Genoino, the national president of the *PT*, emphasized the enormity of the event, interestingly comparing it to labor union activities while helping to widen the discourse to applaud supportive family members of LGBT citizens: "The Gay Parade is the single event to unite the largest number of people in São Paulo, without having to conduct raffles or distribute prizes, like cars, [to draw people here]. . . . [This] shows the respect and the recognition that the city's inhabitants have for diversity and plurality. . . . Here [with us] are grandparents, children, and parents of homosexuals. [This event] is much more than a **religion**; it is an **option**. We have to continue to know more and more how to accept differences and give citizenship to people. . . . It is a beautiful party (emphasis mine)."[34,35] In a similar vein, Genoino publicly characterized the city of São Paulo as a "*seio acolhedor de todos os segmentos*" (literally, the "hospitable breast of every segment [of the population]").

Analyzing this rather fragmented and apparently unrehearsed speech reveals some problematic underpinnings when assessing Suplicy's simultaneous deployment of the discourse of family and that of citizenship as a means to empower sexual minorities, the segment of the population at the focal point of the event. The use of the verb "to give" citizenship to cast a wider net of liberated Brazilians is troubling in a number of ways. First, the idea of *providing* citizenship is both a patriarchal and a dictatorial gesture, not to mention populist, suggesting that the government's role should be to grant this wish of citizenship to a group of passive minorities rather than empowering them to stake out and to claim the rights to which they are entitled legislatively as tax-paying, contributing members of society. On a larger scale, of course, we are referring to the same rights and privileges that inherently belong to them as dignified human beings in any country. The image Suplicy portrays of doling out human rights both disempowers and infantilizes the sexual minorities who have been working tirelessly, both individually and collectively, to conquer them. Even more seriously objectionable is the fact that Suplicy displaces the focus of the battle; as we know, basic human rights were not and are not achieved by movements themselves but are, instead, concessions granted by politicians or by the State which legislates them. While Suplicy is clearly attempting to illustrate that the Pride Parade has become astronomically popular and that marchers, revelers, and onlookers alike are attending in increasing numbers and of their own free will, a second infantilization occurs, this time of the would-be allies of rights for LGBT citizens, with the presumption that citizens will not come to a protest unless the organizers hold a raffle to lure them into the event. She condescendingly applauds the fact that while there is no possibility of winning a free car, people still come, bringing along their friends and families. This unfortunate judgment is one that squarely and unfairly reduces the intentions of social justice–minded citizens of any orientation who may have an ethical or a philosophical reason to protest, whether in a labor movement or in the Gay Parade, to being moti-vated strictly by the carrot of consumer-driven reward.[36] Further problematic is Suplicy's flawed comparison to religion and her use of the term "option" in the same sentence, confusingly suggesting that religion is not an option but that the choice to forego church services, and instead attend a Gay Parade, is. It is worth noting that the Pride Parade traditionally occurs in São Paulo on a Sunday, unless the World Cup soccer tournament interferes, as it did in 2006 and again in 2014, forcing the Parade Association to move the festivi-ties to a Saturday, thus infuriating many of the city's finest hair stylists and salon owners who were unable to take off the busiest workday of the week in order to attend the Parade. Suplicy's implication that religion is obliga-tory and that attendance at the "beautiful party" is an optional activity in a country still rampant with homophobic and transphobic crimes is offensive at best and actually rather dangerous, especially when we consider her remarks in the context of a Brazilian nation that is both a secular state and a democ-racy.[37] The remarks she delivered also reflect Suplicy's blatant disregard for the multiplicity of identities of some of the participants in this edition of the Parade. Exercising their right to belong simultaneously to the LGBT com-munity while also participating in religious organizations, there was a small but vocal religious contingent present on that day, carrying signs that read: "*O Senhor é meu pastor e ele sabe que eu sou gay*" ("God is my shepherd, and he knows that I am gay").

Suplicy's critique of a society mobilized to participate only by capitalistic gain may have been symptomatic of the new directions and parameters the Parade Organization chose to adopt, as they witnessed the blossoming of their event to unprecedented numbers anywhere in the world. For example, it cost the Organization approximately R$400,000 (approximately US$180,000 by the day's standards) to coordinate the event in 2004, though it is important to acknowledge that R$150,000 (approximately US$70,000) of that figure came in the form of state subsidy and support from the Mayor's Office. Probable ulterior motives of campaigning reelection aside, the level of government support is significant and, in and of itself, cause for celebration. To maintain safety in what Suplicy declared that year to be "the safest Pride Parade in the world," 1,200 Military Police were contracted, along with 500 municipal security officers and 300 private security guards. Together with the intensify-ing national presence from all over Brazil, with 40% of the participants com-ing to São Paulo from other Brazilian cities, approximately 7% of attendance represented visitors from other countries, notably Argentina, Chile, and Hol-land.[38] Indeed, with such a mega-event on such a massive scale, opportunists would become increasingly more inventive in developing tactics to pocket the pink *real*. An article in the *Folha de S. Paulo*, quoted at length in the following, concludes as follows: "With an eye on the market niche of the parade-goers, the owner of the newsstand *Alfa*, on *Paulista* Avenue, adapted a sales scheme: She placed exclusively gay magazines in the window of her store."[39]

In examining the most widely circulated print media sources in São Paulo, and consequently those which have the greatest potential to shape public opinion, we can detect an interesting change in the tone of the press to appear more sympathetic to the plight of discrimination LGBT citizens experience, especially when we recall their portrayal as *irreverentes* just a few years earlier. In their article entitled "Gay Parade in SP is the Largest in the World: Festival Unites 1.5 Million People on Paulista Avenue,"[40] Viviane Raymundi and Jaqueline Falcão write: "Gays and lesbians who, on usual days do not feel the freedom to even embrace their same-sex companion on the street or to walk hand-in-hand, see the Parade as the ideal opportunity to let themselves go and exchange affections."[41] The issue of non-heteronormative public displays of affection is a serious one in Brazil, one that has resulted in homophobic slurs, beatings, and murders,[42] and, on the flip side of the coin, protests by the LGBT community to stage public kiss-ins. A particularly noteworthy event, the *Beijaço* (A Huge Hug & Kiss Combined), occurred in a major LGBT-friendly mall, the *Shopping Frei Caneca*. During this peaceful demonstration, approximately 2,000 people (primarily homosexual couples) kissed each other on the lips at the same time, and in harmony, to protest the fact that security expelled a same-sex male couple from the mall because they exchanged a kiss in the Food Court. The collective kiss took place at exactly the same time that Sunday when the couple was evicted from the shopping center. This staged kiss, a massive public display of affection, was particularly brave when we recall Roberto da Matta's *rua/casa* (public/private) dichotomy as it becomes completely subverted in this process, constituting a highly transgressive act according to the social norms of the Brazilian universe.[43]

In addition to its progressive internationalization, the 2004 Pride Parade began to see a dramatic increase in the degree of carnivalesque mood and activity. As Raymundi and Falcão note: "Transsexuals, drag queens and transgender persons designed special costumes for the party, ending up being a store window of color and creativity. Many people even asked to have their pictures taken with them."[44] In fact, a caption of one of the photos published in the article summarizes the mixture of politics and festivity quite well: "Paulista [Avenue] was taken by a crowd of marchers mixing militancy and Carnival."[45] The spectacle-like, carnivalesque atmosphere reaches significant proportions when we realize that the Mayor's Office actually provided an outdoor dressing room for the participants to put on their makeup and prepare themselves for their own unique performance. In an article published in the *Folha de S. Paulo* on June 14, 2004, titled "Gay Parade Brings Together 1.5 Million and Breaks Record: São Paulo Beats San Francisco and Hosts the

Largest Homosexual Event in the World, Organizers Affirm,"[46] the reporters note that "even the Mayor's Office built a dressing room in front of the Tri-anon Park so that people could make themselves pretty or doctor themselves up for the Parade."[47]

The composition of the twenty-four floats in the Parade could not resist the new wave of internationalization. In an anthropophagic fusion of local musical traditions, such as Bahian *axé music* with British and American imports, including techno music, the *trios elétricos* moved along slowly but at full volume, celebrating a global flavor while preserving uniquely Brazilian tunes to avoid total sell-out to cultures often perceived as "First World." The widening of musical traditions mirrored an expanding representation in both the collective and an individual sense. There was a much more diverse political presence, including militant members of *PT, PSTU,* who had participated in every Parade since its inception, encouraging the political discourse and content of the events, but also the *PSOL (Partido Socialismo e Liberdade)* The Party of Socialism and Freedom, a new group of *PT* dissidents, carrying a banner reading "*Livre expressão sexual*" ("Freedom of sexual expression") marked their presence. Perhaps not surprisingly, then, the specific discourse of GLBT civil rights, in 2004, becomes part of a much larger target to attain freedom of sexual expression for all Brazilian citizens. This goal would be equally true for the heterosexuals who attended the event. A perhaps unexpected demographic curiosity was the fact that this edition of the Pride Parade became a scene and a source for LGBT-friendly heterosexuals to make connections with like-minded people they could potentially be able to date. Raymundi and Falcão relate: "Those who support the gay movement generally attend the Parade to enjoy the festive atmosphere, but yesterday there were even people looking for other gay-friendly people—of the opposite sex. 'I want to see if I can find myself one,' said the unemployed 18 year-old Cibele de Almeida."[48]

Capitalizing upon the enormous turnout of the Pride Parade in 2004, the subsequent edition was reconfigured in an intriguing way: the Day of Pride was instantly expanded to the "*Mês do Orgulho GLBT* (GLBT Pride Month)," featuring a wide array of parallel activities hosted in the city throughout the entire month of June in commemoration of LGBT rights. With funding provided by the Ministry of Culture and the Health Ministry (STD and AIDS Prevention) and particular pressure to approve the Civil Unions Legislation, initially proposed in 1995 and by then held up in the National Congress for ten years, some 1.8 (according to the Military Police) to 2.5 million people (according to the Parade organizers) were declaring the slogan "*Parceria civil, já! Direitos iguais: nem mais, nem menos*" ("Civil Unions Now! Equal Rights: No more, no less") on May 29, 2005. In retrospect, it is important to note that same-sex civil unions were unanimously recognized by Brazil's Supreme Court (Senate Human Rights Committee) on May 24, 2012.

Media coverage of the event was extensive, and rather than repeating the pattern of a few articles appearing in São Paulo's mainstream newspapers, there were entire sections of newspapers devoted to the Pride Parade, containing series of reports as well as photojournalistic essays. For the purpose of our analysis of the representations of the Pride Parade in print media, I have chosen to focus here on the texts of eight particular pieces in three separate venues: *O Estado de São Paulo* (The State of São Paulo (daily newspaper)), the *Jornal @ Hora Online*, and *Folha de S. Paulo* (and its accompanying *Guia da Folha de S. Paulo*, the weekly supplement in the daily newspaper *Folha de São Paulo*). The reader might recall that I have opted to concentrate this analysis on those venues that have the widest available circulation in São Paulo due to the following factors: (1) The likelihood of influencing public opinion is much greater in media that is circulated for mass consumption; (2) Publications or articles that focus on LGBT issues are often for distribution among the LGBT community; hence, while a comparative study would certainly be an important undertaking in itself, their inclusion would have skewed the results of this research project; and (3) I am interested in examining mainstream hegemonic venues that purport to report on life in São Paulo for LGBT communities, therefore enabling me to identify and to interrogate those spaces where (mis)representation occurs.

Clearly, the primary focus of *O Estado de São Paulo* (The State of São Paulo (daily newspaper)) was political in nature. The article commented extensively on the opening speech given by the city's new mayor, José Serra. Its optimistic headline, "Gay Pride packs both sides of *Paulista* Avenue in SP: The Mayor of São Paulo (Brazilian Democratic Socialist Party) contended that the city 'has its arms and its mind open to differences and diversity and does not exercise discrimination,'"[49] was a mouthful in more ways than one. This liberal rhetoric was quickly neutralized in the same article by the president of the *APOGLBT*, Reinaldo Damião, denouncing discrimination against LGBT citizens and claiming that São Paulo was the Brazilian city to experience the highest degree of homophobic murders in the entire country. Damião's complaint was corroborated one year later by Luiz Mott, founder of the *Grupo Gay da Bahia* (Gay Group of Bahia), Brazil's first and still flourishing gay activist group. In a June 17, 2006 article appearing in the *Folha de SP*, "*SP tem maior número de mortes de homossexuais*" ("SP Has the Highest Number of Homosexual Assassinations [in Brazil]"), Mott contends the following: "São Paulo has the largest number of assassinations of homosexuals of any Brazilian state. According to the report, 'Murders of Homosexuals in Brazil,' issued by the Gay Group of Bahia, the average is 21 deaths each year. This number is worrisome. While São Paulo's population is large, homophobic crimes should not occur in any case."[50]

A discourse that portrays the Parade as a moment of openness and embracement of diversity contrasts sharply with the sobering reality of homophobic assassination occurring during the rest of the year. What is omitted from the article's assessment of São Paulo being Brazil's most homophobic city is the question of demographic proportionality. In other words, the ratio of homophobic hate crimes to overall population is not factored into the equation, consequently resulting in a dramatically inaccurate statistic. As Mott's report also contends (which both the president of the *APOGLBT* and the sensationalist article choose to ignore), "Besides São Paulo, our findings from the state of Pernambuco [on Brazil's northeastern coast] are of concern. There, the average is sixteen murders per year, but we must take into account that the population is six times smaller than that of São Paulo."[51] In fact, as the *Estado de São Paulo* points out, in the same article of May 25, 2005: "Hédio Silva Junior, the Secretary of the Department of Justice and the Defense of Citizenship, who participated in the Parade, confirmed that the government will soon announce a series of actions to help combat homophobic discrimination. According to him, since 2001, there is a special commission in his department designed to process complaints of this nature, having investigated 32 cases in that period [five years]."[52] While this figure may be more realistic, we must consider that there are cases left unreported, for a variety of reasons, and that the degree of impunity in a country where hate crimes legislation has not been approved is quite high. Mott notes in the same report that less than 10% of the criminals are sentenced. These factors may further skew the statistics examined earlier. In addition, we should exercise caution to not allow numbers, accurate or not, to dictate the degree of lenience toward any perpetrator of homophobic violence. While the number of assassinations is alarming regardless of which source we consult, it is almost a moot point on qualitative grounds. This is true, of course, if we believe in a universal value of basic human civil rights and social justice. As such, the ongoing controversy over the incidents of murder is rather irrelevant to the debate, given that the commission of any hate crime, let alone assassination, is one too many.

More prominent than the issue of criminalization of homophobia in this edition of the Parade was the specific fight for the implementation of the stagnant civil unions legislation. While the legislation was not designed to legalize marriage between same-sex partners, the initiative would legally recognize these unions, guaranteeing certain rights to homosexual couples, such as inheritance, custody, and other family benefits. The *Estado de São Paulo* nearly waxes poetic with its commentary: "The leaders of the movement are trying to use the event [this year's Pride Parade] to maximize their chances to parallel the civil rights legislation for same-sex couples to heterosexual couples, pulling it out of the closet drawer,"[53] reporting that the project, credited to Marta Suplicy, was currently paralyzed in the hands of Roberto Jefferson, a senator from Rio de Janeiro. The ultimate political goal of the event was to garner 1.2 million signatures on a petition to attempt to force the Congress to vote on the bill. The petition, whether or not it achieved the desired number of signatures, proved irrelevant, as further stumbling blocks, notably the conservative right constituted by dogmatic Catholics and Evangelical Christians, would continue to hinder the passage of the legislation. Thus it was not until May 2012 that the bill was approved by the Senate after an excruciating sixteen-year-long debate. Nevertheless, Brazil's judiciary moved toward legalizing same-sex marriages after state courts began allowing civil unions between homosexuals to be converted to full marriages in 2011 and 2012, with same-sex marriage becoming federally legal in 2013. However, religious and conservative groups staged a massive and well-organized protest in Brasília on June 1, 2011, to repeal the legislation, and continued large-scale opposition to same-sex marriage persists.

With the explosion of the Internet in Brazil came the proliferation of online news sources and agencies, of varied quality and reliability. One of the more comprehensive venues, the *Jornal @ Hora Online* posted an article, "*Parada Gay registra cerca de 2, 5 milhões de participantes*" ("Gay Parade Registers Close to 2.5 Million Participants") on May 30, 2005. Foreshadowing the more serious violence that would accompany subsequent parades, the article commented on the few cases of violence in 2005 that did not plague previous editions of the event, such as the theft of cellular phones and wallets occurring despite the presence of 1,200 security officers. The mixture of activism and festivity that had recently become a trademark of the event was appropriately balanced by political protest, likely because of the ten-year anniversary of Suplicy's civil unions legislation that would take an additional half-dozen years to see the light of day: "In spite of the festive nature of the Parade, which included thousands of drag queens and costumed participants, the protest was furtively political."[54] It is quite disconcerting that media sources have ignored the well-established fact that there is a strong political dimension in the activism of drag queens and costumed participants. We might benefit by deconstructing why media, and by extension, Brazilian collective consciousness, has deemed anti-political—or apolitical, at best—a manifestation with festive dimensions.

The most salient aspect of this article is the comments reportedly issued by ex-mayor Marta Suplicy and the then mayor José Serra, particularly with regard to the paralyzed civil unions bill. This time, Suplicy's literal position in the Parade was quite different. Of the twenty-four floats featuring NGOs; clubs and bars; and various other political, social, and religious organizations, Suplicy had accepted an invitation from one of São Paulo's most chic nightclubs, *The Week*, to party with its go-go boys and dance to nearly exclusively Americanized house, techno, dance, and disco music provided by the *Associação das Mulheres que Amam Mulheres* (*AMAM*), The Association of Women Who Love Women, though literally translating to "They Love (or Are Loving) Women." Suplicy's statements were as follows:

"I still do not know how my project has not been approved. The subject is so serious and pertinent that is already in jurisprudence in the country . . . the principal Brazilian courts created jurisprudence by granting in some lawsuits the same rights for same-sex couples that heterosexuals have with regard to inheritance, retirement benefits, and custody of children. Homosexuals and lesbians pay taxes and therefore must have the same rights as any other citizen."[55] While her remarks this time around, even off the cuff, were more articulate when compared to previous speeches I have already analyzed in this chapter, it is worth noting that, as evidenced in this passage, the politician defines the discourse of citizenship in purely economic terms, equating the fight for human rights with fiscal responsibility and obligations. For the first time, Suplicy also makes a perplexing distinction between "homosexuals" and "lesbians," reinforcing the divisive conception that "homosexuals" are assumed to be men, thus potentially also reinforcing male privilege, while women are to be classified in a separate category. It would be impossible to determine a "correct" reading of Suplicy's word choice. Nevertheless, this statement, while highly problematic, may be attributed to the particular emphasis placed on lesbian visibility in the 2005 edition of the Parade. In an article that specifically addresses this issue, "*Siameses usam roupas iguais em parada*" ("Siamese Twins Wear the Same Outfits in the Parade)," in the *Folha de S. Paulo* on May 30, 2005, Paulo Sampaio writes of the importance of lesbian visibility but also speaks to the divisive attitude of exclusivity: "The [female] President of the Association of Women who Love Women, the attorney Maria Stella Pires, 62 years old, prohibits a man from entering the float, saying: 'It's alright for the reporter to come in. The other guy can just wait outside. *AMAM* was founded on the necessity of creating lesbian visibility. So, if the float fills up with men, it's not going to work out. **I am not gay; I am a lesbian**" (emphasis mine).[56] As we can see from the re(actions) described earlier, even from within the trenches of the LGBT battlefield, the road is paved with traditional distinctions based on the machismo that has its origins in a markedly phallocentric universe.

It is worth noting that Mayor José Serra's speech was quoted quite differently in the *Jornal @ Hora Online* report than it was in the first article we examined from the *Estado de São Paulo*. In this second source, Serra was reported to have said: "São Paulo is open to different races and does not utter the word discrimination. São Paulo has its mind and arms open to diversity."[57] This version of the speech is far less inclusive than the one examined earlier. Clearly, his remarks signify that Serra believes the city does not endorse racial discrimination. However, it makes no reference to discrimination in any other way, much less on the basis of sexual orientation or gender identity. This statement is also symptomatic of a collective culture of denial wherein the "problem" or situation does not exist if the word is not uttered. Even more compelling is how the newspaper relates Serra's specific response to the issue of civil unions, obviously, as we have seen, at the core of the demonstration: "But Serra declined to respond when he was questioned by reporters whether or not he was in favor of civil unions between homosexuals and if he thought it was important for society and the family to accept gays. [He turned his back and did not respond.]"[58] Also quite revealing was the fact that Serra stayed for less than thirty minutes whereas the ex-mayor Suplicy, while still unclear whether or not she was planning to run for re-election in 2006, remained at the event for three hours.

A significant feature of Fabiane Leite's article in the *Folha de S. Paulo*, "*Parada defenderá a união civil entre gays*" ("Parade Will Defend Civil Unions between Gays") was that it appeared on May 23, 2005, one week in advance of the actual Pride Parade. With the exception of the blurb-like entries in the *Guia da Folha de S. Paulo* (the weekend calendar listing of city events on the cultural agenda for the week ahead), this marks the first time for a full-length feature piece to appear in mainstream Brazilian print media in anticipation of the event. This early coverage of the pending Parade was important for a number of reasons. First, it served as a reminder of the event itself, also educating the readership ahead of time that the focus in this edition was squarely placed on the issue of civil unions legislation. Second, it alerted the public to prepare food donations since there would be posts to collect imperishable goods at each of the stations designated for the collection of signatures on the petition to call for the approval of the Suplicy civil unions bill. Third, it served as an informative historical piece letting the reader know why the Parade follows the geographical trajectory it currently does. For example, Leite indicates that the march concludes in the *Praça da República* (Republic Square), where crowds gather and disperse because that is the site where "Edson Neris da Silva, one of the homosexual-symbols of the fight against discrimination was assassinated by skinheads in the year 2000."[59] The underlying tone of this phrase conveys a discourse of martyrdom, which, while well intended, has the unfortunate effect of stripping humanity from the victim, as the article portrays this person as a "symbol" or icon of the militancy of the movement itself. Nevertheless, it is a useful and important educational tool so that the readership may appreciate that the trajectory of the event, beginning on the *Avenida Paulista*, the financial center of Latin America, and ending in the *República*, is intentional and meaningful. A fourth advantage of publishing this piece in advance of the Parade was to inform the public that the Pride Parade was no longer being conceived as a one-day event but rather an integral part of a month-long agenda packed with activities in June to commemorate the newly inaugurated *Mês do Orgulho GLBT* (GLBT Pride Month). As the article points out, related events included a cycle of debates and lectures on AIDS, LGBT political activism, a film showing, a photo exhibition, a Gay Men's Chorus show, in addition to the regularly (annually) scheduled *Feira Cultural* (Cultural Fair). A fifth service that the press afforded to its community of readers by anticipating the event may at first seem quite superficial but is actually a very important contribution in the land of *Carnaval*. With the parameters of the Parade and its corresponding theme announced ahead of time, marchers and spectators alike would have the advantage of time to prepare their costumes to either support or mock (as the case may be) the civil unions legislation that was being called to the foreground of the discourse of citizenship in 2005.

A critical reading of Leite's article reveals an interesting intersection of interests and community solidarity reflected within the widening discourse of citizenship beyond the specific issues of GLBT rights. Leite interviewed the president of the Parade Organization, Reinaldo Pereira Damião, who summarized the official goals of the Parade as follows: "We want to transform each [canned food] donation and signature into a vote for the recognition of homosexuals as citizens and as an active protest against violence, inequality and any other form of racism in this country."[60] It is in 2005, then, that we begin to see a shift in the history of the Pride Parade, where the focus from civil rights of LGBT citizens is enlarged to raise social consciousness and combat any form of discrimination, violence, or sociopolitical inequality occurring in Brazil. This is an important marker of the transformative potential of the Pride Parade beyond the issues pertinent to sexual minorities. Nevertheless, it assumes the risk of quite possibly posing a distraction away from those central concerns and a consequent loss of focus about the specific reasons for the fight.

In the same article examined earlier, Damião was quoted as saying: "We consider the Parade to be a social movement. Neither the feminist movement nor the Landless Movement draws so many people to a public demonstration. *MST* organizes a march, but it does not have the support we do. In nearly ten years, we have changed mentalities. Today, any gay person, young or old, can come to the event without being exposed."[61] It is difficult to imagine that the same president issued these potentially divisive comments, and even more troubling, did so in the same interview for the same article. Apparently, the leadership of the Pride Parade had become just as obsessed with the quantitative aspects of the event as the print media trying to assess the huge discrepancies between the numbers reported by the Military Police and those of the Parade Organization itself. A reader may interpret this comparison as a nod to the *MST* in a quest for legitimation since the *MST* is presumed to be a legitimate social movement to which the LGBT Parade is comparing itself. However, I remain convinced to the contrary. This comparison between social movements may convey a certain elitism, and quite frankly, perpetuate inequality by parading the event as superior to the efforts of the *MST* marches which, unfortunately, have not been able to garner the same level of support

or scale of participation from Brazilian citizens. This affirmation, in my opinion, points to an extremely serious internal division in Brazilian social movements as a whole, constituting a lack of solidarity between leadership of such
organizations, resulting in the lack of recognition of the *MST* as something
that would be beneficial to society as a whole. The *latifúndio* (landlordism)
in Brazil, against which the *MST* is fighting, accumulates wealth and power,
while practicing discrimination against rural workers and leading to violence
in these areas. Implicit in this cultural reality is a profound sense of elitism,
which also plays out in the Pride Parade itself. In other words, legitimacy is
conferred by the elite few with the power to effect political change rather
than the masses who are demonstrating for such transformation to take place.

    The extensive coverage throughout the May 30, 2005 edition of the *Folha
de S. Paulo* includes numerous pages of some of the most insightful commentary yet to be written on this sociocultural phenomenon. As one may expect,
there are pieces of a repetitive political nature, hinting at Marta Suplicy's
ulterior motives for attending the event, pointing to T-shirts with the slogan *"Marta 2006"* circulating through the crowd. Also to be expected was
Suplicy's denial of this motivation, quoted in the caption of the article, "Gay
Parade Brings 1.8 Million to Paulista Avenue,"[62] as follows: " 'I am not going
to speak about that; I came here for another reason,'—Marta Suplicy, ex-
Mayor of São Paulo, denying that her presence in the Parade was to campaign
for the elections."[63] Far more interesting is the appearance of two stories that
comment on issues of lesbian identity, social inversion, gender ambiguity, the
role of the *novela* brasileira, and even provide some reflection on internalized
homophobia. *"Parada Gay tem ampla presença feminina"* ("Gay Parade Has
Ample Female Presence") by Laura Capriglione and Fernanda Mena opens
with a vocabulary lesson and then, four paragraphs later, incorporates the
term into its own language: "In Brazilian slang, *bolachas* [literally, cookies
or biscuits, as we shall see in chapter 4] are the lesbians. . . . The event that
brought together so many 'cookies' began in the afternoon, gathering on the
Paulista Avenue."[64] It is difficult to determine whether this discourse perpetuates stereotypical (and quite possibly pejorative) terms of self-definition,
especially when not employed by the "in-group," or if it aims instead to
educate the readership about the terminology circulating within the LGBT
community. In chapter 4, I conduct a much more detailed consideration of
lesbian linguistic codes and an analysis of LGBT language in general. As we
contemplate both of these possibilities, it is fascinating to examine the language the article uses to describe female presence at the event: "Motorcycle
chicks with leather jackets, sophisticated college professors, young students
or *dark* (perhaps rebellious) students, like Aline da Silveira Correa, 19 years
old, 'bisexual,' according to her own self-definition, with a piercing in her
bottom lip, flight attendant. 'We came here to show that we are not ashamed

to be free and happy.'"[65] One interpretation of this description may be that it is intended to illustrate the diversity of the female population attending the Parade in 2005, in both quantitative (stated in other parts of the article) and qualitative terms. A second possible reading is that it accentuates and exacerbates classist divisions among the attendees, all of whom happen to be women. There is also a romanticization of the "rebel," in this case with a cause, who is deemed as transgressive, with or without normative evaluation, since she marks her body with a piercing or chooses to adorn herself with leather. In a country with a bad track record for sexist stereotypes, flight attendants are still predominantly female and are expected to demonstrate effusive femininity in both uniform and gesture. A bisexual stewardess with a lip piercing may prove to be a challenging image for a general readership to digest.

A case in point is the recent underwear ads airing in Brazil in September 2011. The advertisements for the company "Hope" underwear featured a half-naked Gisele Bündchen, now forty years old and considered the second wealthiest supermodel in the world (after Kathy Ireland), confessing to her husband that she has crashed his car, maxed out his credit card (and hers, which belongs to him), and invited her mother to come stay with them. The voiceover suggests that the "correct" way to deliver such bad news is for the woman to strip to her tiny lingerie, delivering the news practically naked, using her charm and her body to avert confrontation or at least cushion the blow. Then the tagline "HOPE *ensina*" ("HOPE teaches") ensues. Fortunately, Brazilian consumers are beginning to take a stand against sexist stereotypes of women, such as portraying a model using her body to bypass the angry wrath of her husband, as evidenced by the fact that government officials from the *Secretariado da Mulher* (Ministry of Women's Rights) in Brasília released a statement denouncing the TV commercials after receiving numerous complaints from outraged viewers. Ultimately, the ad was deemed "sexist and offensive" and was subsequently banned by the Brazilian government, though it may be important to note that ex-president Rousseff did not release any official statements on the matter.

The article in question is pertinent for a number of reasons beyond its portrayal (and somewhat problematic characterization) of the presence of women in the 2005 edition of the Pride Parade. It is the first piece to break the silence about a significant sociopolitical rift, a battle—as it were—staged for an international audience on *Paulista* Avenue, arguably the center of commerce and banking in all of Latin America. The conflict over the symbolic space of the "postcard" of São Paulo is of dramatic proportions, as it juxtaposes the Pride Parade with the "March for Jesus" that occurred four days earlier on the same stretch of the *Paulista*. What appears is a subtext of didactic morality, alluding to cheap and abundant alcohol as both the mainstay of freedom and excess and, quite literally, consumerism to represent the Pride Parade while its virtual absence would come to signify the sober and somber presence of the religious right: "It [The Pride Parade] was a huge and festive party, fueled by liters and more liters of beer, fake whisky and cheap wine. A difference— and how!—when compared to the March for Jesus which occurred four days earlier on the same avenue, where alcohol, practically prohibited, was substituted for soda."[66] As the Pride Parade continues its transformation into a Dionysian winter *Carnaval*, the abusive consumption of alcohol increases along with it, casting the intoxicated (often to the point of serious illness) revelers in the role of self-destructive, hedonistic pleasure-seekers, consequently lubricating the task of discrimination that the conservative religious groups perform so well in solemn sobriety.

Capriglione and Mena's insightful article also breaks ground in hinting at the fact that the Pride Parade's atmosphere may be characterized as carnivalesque in more ways than one. In other words, while it is an enormously ludic and festive event, it also symbolizes the most important principles of Bakhtinian carnivalization, summarized concisely in Robert Stam's important work on Brazilian film and cultural criticism: Social inversion and gender ambiguity.[67] Reinforcing this observation is a homophobic yet thoughtful taxi driver, whose "real" occupation in stereotypical Brazilian popular culture may range from meteorologist to therapist to politician: "In the 'Orgy of the Inverts,' as a taxi driver irritated by the heavy traffic in the area of the Parade referred to it, all of the ironies about sexual roles played themselves out. While the gay men flooded the sidewalks of the Trianon Park, a group of girls on the corner of the *Casa Branca* public walk pretended to urinate on a tree trunk while standing on it. At their side, a male friend squatted to imitate the feminine way [of urinating]."[68] This anecdote, in addition to emphasizing festivity, mimicry, and social inversion—all properties of the carnivalesque, skillfully examined in Brazilian cultural context by scholar-writers like Affonso Romano de Sant'Anna—provides a glimpse of several more: The obsessive preoccupation with bodily fluids, particularly around the sexual organs; the combination of the lewd together with the ludic; and the appreciation for dark humor, often sophomoric and sexually explicit in nature.[69]

A second anecdote that exemplifies the *Carnaval* principle of inversion (and perversion) of social structures is an even bolder transgression of unadulterated sexual freedom, and at the same time, a disturbing and sobering subtext on the repression and secrecy that still abounds in daily life in Brazil and beyond: "The ATM machine at the *Banco Itaú* was transformed into a 'darkroom'—a dark room, in English, typical of gay clubs. 'I came to withdraw ten reais and ended up having sex [literally, in Brazilian slang, 'having a transaction'] with a guy,' related the publicist Mário (fictitious name), 35. The Bank sponsored the 'darkroom' of the Parade!, he joked."[70]

Most scholars would agree that the concept of the "dark room" is attributed to the English language, and the implication is one that would translate North American gay popular culture into a Brazilian context. Although the term is international and is identified with a Brazilian space as much as it is a U.S. one, the anecdote is loaded with symbolic value, from the implicit connection between capitalism and gay male American identity, to the reconfiguration of the closet into a public space where an automatic transaction occurs, literalizing the mechanical nature of the sex (trans)act(ion), to the subversive irreverence of transforming a prestigious and international institution of banking in the city of commerce into a "fast cash" withdrawal of a sexual service rendered on demand.

The influence of television and, in particular, of Brazilian soap operas begins to manifest much more powerfully in the 2005 edition of the Parade, blurring the boundaries between fiction and reality and entering into a fascinating realm where they are also inverted. This process gives further impetus to the carnivalization of social institutions increasingly at work during the event. In one of many photojournalistic captions, Capriglione and Mena feature young women costumed as actresses in current soap operas. But the power of these stars cannot be overestimated. The caption, which reads, "*As amigas Taís, Marina e Fernanda, para quem as meninas saíram do armário após novela*" ("Taís, Marina and Fernanda, friends who came out of the closet because of the soap opera's influence"), succinctly demonstrates the ability of primetime soap opera in Brazil to not only influence public opinion but also to inspire impressionable viewers to actually modify their own lives based on the role models they may be trying to emulate. But it would be a mistake to assume that, in Brazil, the most impressionable viewers are generally young people in the midst of figuring out how to fashion their lives. The article's interview with a sixty-two-year-old woman, attending the Parade for the first time, demonstrates the extraordinary ability of Brazilian television to empower its viewers if not actually prove life-changing: "If there are lesbians featured in primetime on the *Globo* network, if I pay my taxes and own my own nose, who is going to forbid me from coming [to the Parade] with my girlfriend?"[71]

Further evidence of the influence of the Brazilian *novela* occurs with the journalists' discussion of Bruno Gagliasso, a Brazilian sex idol and actor who played the role of a young man discovering and coming to terms with his homosexuality in the intensely popular soap opera *América*. At this rather offensive moment of the article, Capriglione and Mena would seem to assert, although perhaps with tongue-in-cheek, that the mystique of the Brazilian soap opera is such that it could potentially turn gay people straight: "Gagliasso portrayed the hetero moment of a group of 'cookies.' Hand in hand with their girlfriends, they suddenly forgot their partners when they found out that the hunk was hiding in a van nearby. With the shouts and screams of avid fans, they frantically searched for pieces of paper that they could use to get his autograph. After their mission was accomplished, they returned to holding the hands of their girlfriends."[72] While the journalists may have been attempting to exercise humor, or even suggest sexual fluidity, in their reference to this "straight moment" of lesbian women, it is irresponsible and unethical to suggest, in a homophobic climate where many still believe that sexual orientation is a lifestyle choice, that the girls, starstruck while *performing* their lesbianism, would suddenly lapse into a "hetero moment." This portrayal also reinforces the machista imaginary of compulsory heterosexuality, according to which a lesbian is only gay because she has not managed to find the "right man."

Nevertheless, as we have seen in our analysis of the Pride Parade of 2004, it was appearing ever clearer that the event was becoming less and less queer. The search for like-minded heterosexuals as potential dates and mates continued in the 2005 edition, representing both a widening of mainstream appeal and participation in the event as well as a significantly increased trend toward sexual objectification and commodification of literally millions of Brazilian bodies on display. This is particularly true and problematic when we consider the way in which the article uses language of "the hunt" to portray young, straight-identified men on the prowl for women. Even more disturbing is that the competition for the conquest was numbers driven, thus dehumanizing women in addition to their objectification: "Sporting baseball caps, loose pants, and T-shirts featuring rap stars, Edson Dias, 21, and ten metal worker friends, came from the extreme south (of the state of São Paulo) with a sole objective: To hunt women. 'Even though there are mostly lesbians who will not offer a single kiss, there are some lost goldmines there. At least I managed to score one,' he says. 'I scored three,' bragged 19 year-old Leandro Guimarães."[73] These images, of course, are agricultural metaphors which reflect a primitive world of *caçar e catar* ("to hunt and capture"). These notions precede modern culture, much like cultivating the earth, bringing the reader back to the moment when human beings hunted for their food in nature. The implication is, of course, very disturbing; that the male hunter collect and take his nourishment (*comida*), represented by the women he has conquered and placed into captivity during his journey, whether available or not, whether interested or disgusted.

Before proceeding to another critical year in the history of São Paulo's Pride Parade, it is worth referring to one more article, however briefly, for it illustrates both the work left to do in combatting homophobia and the sensitivity of a more mature journalistic enterprise for the mainstream *Folha de SP* that, along with the nine years of the existence of the event, had grown far more sophisticated in its portrayal. In his piece describing a "*Gay 'separatista' prefere festa à desfilar na parada*" ("Gay Male 'Separatist' Prefers to Party Instead of Parading"), journalist Paulo Sampaio ponders the problem of internalized homophobia within the gay male community: "The personal trainer Rogério Antônio da Silva . . . requested not to be associated with 'stereotypical faggots.' Silva self-identifies as 'a gay man with a hetero mind': He said that he regularly attends meetings of groups of car aficionados, that he likes radical sports and that he is a boxer. He says that few people know he is gay. Silva refused to pose for photos alongside the flamboyantly effeminate gays, stating that he did not want to be associated with 'those people' in any way. En route to a private champagne party, he said: 'Now that's my kind of place.'"[74] This statement reflects an attitude which permits and perpetuates a profound separation between socioeconomic classes, regardless of sexual orientation, in Brazilian culture. The rich do not recognize themselves in their less-privileged counterparts, even when they might have other affinities or links that might otherwise conjoin them and lead to solidarity.

The Pride Association commemorated its first decade of Parades with a month-long celebration that would culminate in the march of June 17, 2006, attracting three million participants. The slogan chosen for the year represents the organization's most aggressive stand against homophobia to date: "*Homofobia é crime! Direitos sexuais são direitos humanos*" ("Homophobia is a crime! Sexual rights are human rights"). Rallying for the approval of the ever-stagnant Law 122/06, a national bill to criminalize homophobic crime in Brazil similar to U.S. federal hate crimes legislation, the event was far more politicized than in prior years. While the private sponsorship by nightclubs and bars continued to encourage a festive climate, and despite the contention of the Parade organizers that the demonstration that year was more militant and less consumerist, the *Carnaval*-like characteristics persisted. The pre-Parade's *Feira Cultural*, now in its sixth edition, attracted approximately 100,000 visitors. Once again deemed to be the largest Pride Parade in the world, the sheer magnitude of the event, irrespective of its controversial politics, posed serious infrastructural problems surrounding the use of the *Avenida Paulista*. The *CET* (*Companhia de Engenharia de Tráfego*) (Traffic Engineering and Control) imposed restrictions in its "*Termo de Ajuste de Conduta*" (Conduct Adjustment Agreement), limiting the hours of the event, forbidding the construction of stages, and demanding that the Parade Association be responsible for cleaning all public spaces. The governmental agency imposed a fine of R$80,000 due to the alteration and the monitoring of traffic necessitated by the Parade route. Fortunately and somewhat ironically, the fines were counteracted by significant state support since it was now considered an official and permanent feature of the city's cultural calendar. While Nelson Matias Pereira publicly lamented the state having to assume the majority of the costs due to insufficient private sponsorship, I believe that the state's willingness to continue to sponsor the event is a meaningful statement in support not only of the ongoing success of the event itself but of the key goal of its sociopolitical agenda to take steps to eradicate homophobia.

Media coverage of the event centered on an issue that it had not encountered in previous editions of the Parade: a scheduling conflict between a World Cup match pitting Brazil against Australia. A clear indication that the national passion for soccer is also the most powerful unifying force resulted in the Parade's repositioning to Saturday to accommodate the game scheduled for Sunday. Clearly, this decision represents both the legendary Brazilian flexibility to *dar um jeitinho* (loosely translated as "finding a way around") as well as to endorse a "reality check" as to the nation's most pressing cultural priorities. But the switch provoked other problems. In her June 17, 2006 article, "Gay Parade tries to maintain its record today: Neither the World Cup soccer tournament nor the rainy forecast cast a cloud over the expectation of attracting two million people, continuing to be the largest in the world,"[75] Daniela Tófoli relates possible serious repercussions of the unprecedented switch from Sunday to Saturday, arguing that since Saturday was the busiest day for hair stylists, many loyal marchers were upset that they would not be able to participate in that year's edition. It is unclear whether there was legitimate concern over the impact the absence of salon employees would have on the overall numbers of attendees. Certainly, it is possible to interpret this comment as a subtle yet insidious homophobic remark that would restrict the profession to gay men, thus further perpetuating a common stereotype. Nevertheless, it is true that the Association was concerned about reduced attendance due to participants who had planned to attend but were hindered by Saturday work schedules.

As was the case in the previous year, *Folha de S. Paulo*, generally among the more progressive venues with respect to the Pride Parade, dominated the coverage of the event. The article entitled "Gay Parade resists the World Cup and breaks attendance record: According to the Military Police, two million people participated in the party, 200,000 more than last year"[76] summarized the interesting co-existence (and even conflation) of LGBT Pride with the often *machista* and deeply homophobic tradition of soccer in Brazil, a topic taken up expertly by João Silvério Trevisan's *Seis balas num buraco só: A crise do masculino*.[77] Noting the nationalism surrounding World Cup fever, the essay affirmed that "besides the kisses, an abundance of green and yellow [colors]. On T-shirts and within many floats, the colors of the national soccer team dominated the scene. The sixteenth float displayed hanging Brazilian flags, generating applause and screams from the crowd."[78] The reference to kisses alludes to an innovative official "mandate" that Pereira, the president of the Pride Association, issued for the public to kiss one another. Perhaps not surprisingly, though, the press interpreted this gesture as a license to perpetuate the stereotype of gay male promiscuity in particular. In the same article noted before, the unnamed journalist writes: "There was no shortage of people nor of kisses. Following Pereira's request, who at 2:10 p.m. shouted that the crowd should spend the whole afternoon kissing each other, couples did not waste any time at all. Paulo Ramos, 21, was calculating the number of kisses he exchanged even while the party was still well underway: 'I have already kissed eight [guys]. There are a lot of handsome men around here.'"[79]

A brewing crisis over space was far more serious than the confusion provoked by changing the day of the week. Critics contended that the event had seriously outgrown its space limitations and that consequently it was posing a threat to personal and collective security within an infrastructure that could not sustain the likes of three million people confined into the same space. While the Parade Organization fought tooth and nail to maintain São Paulo's postcard and commercial center as the site of protest and festivity, Mayor Gilberto Kassab bowed to pressures to relinquish the *Avenida Paulista* as the space where future Pride Parades would be held, promising that he would provide three suggestions for alternative parade routes within ninety days. As we shall see, the battle over maintaining the symbolic space of the *Paulista* for the Pride Parade, while genuinely fueled by infrastructural realities, is principally economic and ideological in nature. It is important to remember that the March of the Evangelical Christians (the March for Jesus) has also staked out the *Paulista*. After much negotiation, the Pride Parade Association announced that the sacred space of the *Paulista* would be designated and dedicated for the use of the Parade until 2020, ironically the year it would move online due to the pandemic.

Media depiction of the carnivalesque nature of the Parade takes some interesting and unexpected turns in 2006. It is worth considering the comments two interviewees made in regard to this issue, both quoted in the same article referred to before: (1) "It is impossible for a gay celebration **not** to end in *Carnaval*. We are festive people. But the purpose is not just to party. The objective is for society to notice us.—Tchaka Drag, 34 years old, who has participated since the first parade, in a moment of reflection,"[80] and (2) "Our proposal is to show during the light of day what the gay world is like at night.—Íkaro, 25 years old, performance artist participating in the parade every year."[81] These insights provide interesting perspectives on the idea of spectacle and performance, suggesting that there is a certain normalization of the evident carnivalization as an ordinary aspect of daily (or, as it were, nightly) life for many members of the LGBT community. Therefore, it is worth considering the argument that performing a parody of oppressive heteronormative life is the means by which queer-identified citizens transgress or subvert those very structures that repress them. Nevertheless, there is more to this than a rebellious and flamboyant slap on the face of the hegemony of heteronormativity. An equally important issue, one of (in)visibility, is at stake here. Bruno Paes Manso and Fabiano Rampazzo, columnists for the newspaper *Estadão* co-wrote an article on June 18, 2006: "Parade-Going Becomes Clubbing: With the theme Homophobia is a Crime, organizers wanted to maintain a politicized tone, but the tenth edition was an electronic party."[82] In it, they interview a group of middle-aged men who disagree with the notion that the Pride Parade is simply about costuming and makeup and hence argue against the exoticization of the carnivalization of the event. The men contend that the Pride Parade affords them a safe space to parade their identities (and part of that performance is dressing up), while forcing society to notice them for who they are without having to fear for their lives: " 'This is not a costume or a character; it is our lifestyle. Brazil must get more and more used to us,' said José Antonio Fonseca, 45 years old, who works in the tourism industry. His friends, the masked Márcio Almeida, 35 years old, and Eduardo Lima, 42, endorsed the choir. 'In other countries, people walk around like this without being labeled,' said Márcio."[83] This observation is fascinating in that it represents a consciousness that perceives self-costuming or dressing up in clothes as a means to attaining visibility of identity despite the dictates of a society that judges and represses with recourse to compulsory heterosexuality.

Opening with a colorful description of the abundance of costumes parading in the event that year, the article indicates (without commenting) that the vast majority of the icons being celebrated, parodied, or satirized are not national in nature at all but rather (sub-)products of the ongoing influence and valorization of North American, and in particular, Hollywood culture: "A large number of people dress up: Minnie Mouses, Batmans, Elvis Presleys, little angels, demons, traffic guards, people carrying their partners on leashes, the classic sailors, U.S. Marines, *travestis* masquerading as Cinderella and Marie Antoinette, with their breasts exposed. But the cowboy was one of the most popular costumes, inspired by the film *Brokeback Mountain*."[84] After painting this general picture of what the average North American might conceive as a massive X-rated Halloween party for adults, the journalists go on to observe that "*as lésbicas, no geral, usam as fantasias mais discretas*" ("lesbians, in general, use more discrete costumes"), suggesting the implicit male privilege built into this dynamic and leading us to theorize as to the reasons why women tended to opt for a more subtle performance. Certainly, an argument may be made that the hegemonic "performers" for this event are gay males, even in the cases where they are playing the roles of women, relegating lesbian women to invisibility or at least to the back of the stage. I find this to be a revealing reflection on the continuation of male privilege even (and, arguably, even more so) from within the ranks of the LGBT community. Of course, this is a question of occupation of public space, almost always more "masculine" in a *machista* society, one which also relegates discretion, linked to culturally laden notions of feminine beauty, as one of the socially constructed norms of being a woman.

An article appearing in the *Folha de S. Paulo* on June 16, 2006 reflects a new trend in the print media's interest on research about gay families and the degree of stability supposedly inherent in same-sex relationships. "'Gay family' is the mainstream in the São Paulo Parade: The majority of participants in [the] 2005 [Parade] had stable relationships, some including children, research shows. For the coordinator, the data help to combat the common belief that homosexual relationships are fragile and based on sexual desire,"[85] by Antônio Gois and Daniela Tófoli, helps to expand the trope of "family" beyond the earlier discourse that emphasized gay people within heteronormative families. In what I regard as a marked shift in consciousness, we finally begin to see evidence of some recognition of the possibilities of alternative family structures represented in mainstream print media sources. The article provides a comprehensive report of the findings of a research project that was conducted by an organization called *CLAM* (*Centro Latino-Americano em Sexualidade e Direitos Humanos*) (Latin American Center for Sexuality and HUman Rights) in partnership with the *APOGLBT-SP* and with the University of Cândido Mendes, USP (*Universidade de São Paulo*; the University of São Paulo), and *Unicamp* in Campinas.

To summarize the project, there were 973 participants in the sample. Among those individuals who declared themselves non-heterosexual, 45% said they were in a committed relationship or that they were dating. The majority of the relationships (37%) lasted less than one year, but the duration of the relationships increased with the age of the subjects in the sample. Of those forty years of age or older, 39% were living with the same partner for more than six years. Overall, the *CLAM*'s conclusions confirmed that some 14% of same-sex couples that attended the Parade in 2005 have children, and in 52% of those cases, the children are from a previous heterosexual marriage.

These results are quite interesting in and of themselves. However, the way that the coordinator of *CLAM* interprets the data is, in my view, extremely problematic and potentially dangerous. The article proceeds to quote Sérgio Carrara, the principal investigator of the *CLAM* Project: "These data indicate that stable relationships are a reality [among same-sex couples]. It is for that reason that we have to discuss the rights of this population."[86] While I agree with the spirit of the project and its intention to debunk the common discriminatory prejudices that would hold same-sex relationships to be fleeting, self-destructive, promiscuous in nature, or all of these, the report's bias has serious limitations in the continued battle for equality. Indeed, it is troubling to think that relationship "stability" should warrant or merit human rights more than individual human beings, straight or queer, in or out of committed relationships, long-term or not. My most serious reservation about the validity of the study is that it is rooted in both monogamy and, more disturbingly, in a patriarchal family structure that would hold longevity of relationships as more deserving of civil rights than a woman or a man who may choose to remain single or whose life circumstances (e.g., the death or loss of a partner) would prompt her to reevaluate assumptions about relationships. In my reading, the report would seem to indicate that the option to remain single or even to pursue a variety of love relationships in one's lifetime could potentially be grounds for treating those particular citizens as inferior, not on the basis of sexual orientation or gender identity, but on their marital status. This discourse is one which reflects, on no uncertain terms, a necessity for control over sexuality, accentuated when politics of the body become intimately (if not exclusively) related to a hegemonic vision of monogamy. In a Latin American cultural context that has historically held the institution of marriage and the family unit as among the most valued and validating socioeconomic structures, it seems that one's desire to remain single or, inversely, to form polyamorous relationships with the same, opposite, or both sexes is particularly stigmatized. Hence, as careful readers, it is prudent to remain apprehensive about any organization's efforts, whether inadvertent or intentional, to classify or judge the legitimacy of consensual adult relationships, even and perhaps especially one such as *CLAM*, invested in the promotion of human rights.

The article also provides a helpful window into the demographics of the Pride Parade from 2005, representing the first time that print media explored and reported on a calculated effort to ascertain the composition of the event other than the obsessively repetitive relating of the discrepancy in overall attendance numbers. Summarizing a survey conducted by *Datafolha*, a statistics-based appendage of the *Folha de S. Paulo* itself, of the heterosexually identified individuals who attended the Pride Parade in 2005, two-thirds were women. *Datafolha* interviewed 435 people, of which 46% self-identified as heterosexual. Of that 46% total figure, 66% were women. While I have some serious reservations about the small size of the sample in proportion to the enormous magnitude of the event, the decision of mainstream print media to analyze the demographics of the Parade (whether with skewed results or not) indicates a much higher level of sophistication and investment in its reporting on the event, and by extension, on the evolving issues surrounding LGBT civil rights in Brazil. On the other hand, an article published in the *Estadão* on June 18, 2006 described sobering results with its own single-question popular opinion survey. While the numbers of the sample were not revealed, the question *"A Parada Gay ajuda a combater o preconceito contra homossexuais?"* ("Does the Gay Parade help to combat discrimination against homosexuals?") yielded a result of 30.11% *SIM* versus 69.89% *NÃO*, suggesting to its readership to seriously consider its other headline on the same page in order to understand personal motivations and certain economic advantages to attending the event: "With tourists in town, nightclubs are packed full: The crowd who comes to the Parade wants to have a good time, consuming and making revenue for the city."[87]

Our journey through mainstream media representations of the LGBT Pride Parade in São Paulo is far from over. As we proceed to the next chapter, the reader will note an intensification of the issues I have presented thus far; notably, there are marked quantitative and qualitative increases in media coverage that would work to expand the discourse on citizenship, staking out diversity as emblematic of *brasilidade* while working to affirm that the LGBT Pride Parade is no longer exclusively about LGBT people but rather an exercise in democracy and inclusivity.

Chapter 2

Winter *Carnaval fora de época* (Off-Season Carnival)? Progression and Retrogression in São Paulo's LGBT Pride Parade (2007–2011)

The second cycle of Pride Parades in São Paulo would demonstrate amplification in every sense of the word, from attendance numbers, to intensified private sponsorship, to casting a wider net and enlarging the scope of social justice to march "*por um mundo sem machismo, racismo e homofobia!*" ("for a world without machismo, racism, and homophobia"). The eleventh edition of the GLBT Pride Month attracted 3.5 million attendees (including, importantly, 300,000 tourists)[1] and unprecedented partnerships with major private enterprises, such as the *Caixa Econômica Federal, Petrobrás, Ministérios da Cultura, do Turismo e do Esporte*, and *Embratur*, among other businesses and organizations.[2] Two minority social organizations joined the manifestation: the feminist pro-choice group *Católicas Pelo Direito de Decidir* (Catholics for the Right to Decide) and the *Rede Afro GLBT* (GLBT Afro Network) for Afro-Brazilian sexual minorities, further demonstrating the goal of embracing multiplicities of identities, of staking out membership in various categories at the same time and celebrating the ambiguity and diversity of intersectionality. The religious motif was particularly pertinent in 2007 since Pope Benedict XVI had made an appearance in Brazil one month earlier. Evangelical denominations like the *Igreja para Todos* and the *Comunidade Metropolitana* (Church for All and the Metropolitan Community Church) used the Parade as a publicity opportunity to build membership in their congregations. But, in typical carnivalesque fashion, the religious element of the Parade was irreverently mocked by a constituent that used papal costuming and ornaments to satirize the Catholic Church or symbolically transgress its rules and regulations. Julia Contier, in her article published in the *Estadão* on June 11, 2007, writes about the predominance of religious themes in the 2007 Parade: "Religion was the central motif in the Gay Parade: Pope's visit to Brazil inspired costumes and condom distribution: Event brought together people of all ages."[3] One activist-reveler, fifty-six-years-old José Ribeiro Fernandes, dressed in full papal gear, pleaded: "I am the pope of love. I refuse to die for not using condoms. Use condoms, my brothers."[4]

The eleventh edition also attracted a strong female presence, giving birth to a new tradition: The *Caminhada de Lésbicas e Bissexuais* (The Lesbian and Bisexual March), a separate and highly politicized march for and by the marginalized groups within the minority of the minority, giving significantly increased visibility to bisexuals and specifically non-heterosexual women in general. The Seventh *Feira Cultural* was moved from the *Largo do Arouche* to the *Vale do Anhangabaú* to accommodate more than 100 vendors and 150,000 participants. Gay Day in the *Hopi Hari* Amusement Park attracted 8,000 people, making it the single largest LGBT private event in the country.

Media coverage of the event praised the level of diversity and the practice of democracy but also introduced a new factor that would unfortunately become a growing problem in the last few editions of the Pride Parade: Violence and criminality. Dario Rigobelo's commentary in the June 11, 2007 edition of *Folha Online*, "*Em festa, verdadeiros 'donos' da cidade celebram Parada Gay*" ("Partying, the true 'owners' of the city celebrate Gay Pride") most clearly illustrates the definition of democracy purported by the media: "People from faraway neighborhoods of the city; the same people who enjoy other sunny Sundays to go for a walk in the Ibirapuera Park, to attend the games in the Morumbi stadium, to watch concerts [such as RBD and Ivete Sangalo]; in summary: The real democracy one experiences in an event like the Pride Parade of São Paulo is stimulating."[5] Indeed, the unprecedented range of diversity encompassed race, class, sexual orientation, gender identity, and even generational diversity to challenge a youth-oriented, plastic surgery–obsessed society that often equates beauty with youthfulness. As Julia Contier relates in her article appearing in the *Estadão* on June 11, 2007, aptly entitled: "*Religião foi o mote central da Parada Gay: Visita do papa no País inspirou figurinos e distribuição de camisinhas; evento reuniu pessoas de todas as idades*," referred to earlier: "Participation by the elderly was notable. Fifty-eight-year-old writer Ricardo Moura Aguieiros displayed a poster with the sweet message: 'Old people are also very good looking [literally, delicious].' 'Those who are elderly suffer a double form of discrimination. We live in a dictatorship of the beautiful and the young,' he related."[6] Even an eclectic diversity of musical traditions reigned in the Parade in 2007. Daia Oliver makes reference to the musical mixtures, in typical anthropophagic Brazilian style: "Parading down Consolation Street on a sunny afternoon, to the sounds of floats which mixed drag music, with Brazilian *axé* music, Xuxa's songs blending with progressive house music."[7]

The rather utopian vision of embracing democracy through diversity, however, was not necessarily celebrated or even appreciated by the Parade's participants themselves. Paulo Sampaio's "'I've never seen so many ugly people,' say regulars: Repeat participants complain about the eclecticism of the event,"[8] which appeared in the June 11, 2007 edition of the *Folha de S. Paulo*, illustrates that unabashed classism and prejudice based on socio-economic status and the superficiality of physical attractiveness, for many, triumphed over the desire for diversity or even democracy. Many of the comments of the spectators revealed shocking intolerance for the very diversity that the march had hoped to symbolize, not only in this eleventh edition of the Parade but deeply rooted within the foundational goals of the event itself: "Forgetting the unpartisan essence of the Parade, Rio photographer Mauro Scur, 32 years old, comments: 'As you see, here in São Paulo, the Parade is filled with a bunch of poor people from the periphery of the city. Over in Rio, we would say suburbanites.' This includes gays also. According to makeup artist Marcos Costa, 32, 'The beautiful ones [in the feminine] are prejudiced; they don't attend anymore. So, the Parade has taken a different direction.' "[9] The offensive elitism of the not-so-gentle men quoted earlier was echoed in the thoughts of other individuals Sampaio interviewed, including two reprehensible remarks so notorious that they unfortunately bear quoting here in their entirety: "Thirty year-old hair stylist Ronaldo Gomes, gets right to the point: 'The problem is the low buying power of the majority [of participants]. The people who attend are not necessarily and exactly ugly; at times, they are simply unkempt. Notice their hair, their skin.' "[10] Such condescension and narcissistic judgment of the "scene" of the Parade led one observer to even theorize and then speculate on a possible statistic of purportedly ugly people attending this year's edition of the event: "In an attempt to mathematically explain the phenomenon of 'the uglification of the Parade,' Edson's boyfriend [also an interviewee in the article], Carlos, from Cuba, guesses at a number: 'In the best-case scenario, 10% is the maximum percentage of good-looking people [at the Parade].' "[11] These comments are significant in that they reflect the construction of an image of the Pride Parade as a spectacle similar to televised representations of beauty. Every spectator is expected to submit herself to a model of the body that conforms to the dictatorship of beauty. The interviewee of this article clearly does not perceive that he is perpetuating an extremely repressive model of control over the body and around sexuality. To be beautiful, as argued before, it is necessary to be able to consume products, buy clothes, and seek treatments that homogenize bodies.

Violence and abuse unfolding with the Parade were directed both inward and outward. While the media had devoted limited attention to the abuse of alcohol and drugs in previous years of the event, the magnitude of the problem was such that it could no longer be ignored or denied. Daia Oliver paints the scene of the party as follows: "A bunch of 'participants' falling on the streets, the sidewalks, the gutters. I imagine the culprit was cheap wine

sold in plastic bottles."[12] A manipulative gesture of placing full culpability
on the quality of the alcoholic beverage rather than the quantity consumed
by the participants, thus ignoring accountability or personal responsibility,
is reminiscent of an article written about the Pride Parade of the previous
year, blaming the *vinho assassino*, the killer wine, for the high incidence of
illness due to excessive consumption of alcohol, as Bruno Paes Manso and
Fabiano Rampazzo report for the *Estadão* on June 18, 2006: "Parade turns
into Clubbing: With the theme 'Homophobia is a Crime,' organizers wanted
to maintain a politicized tone, but the tenth edition was an electronic party."[13]
Speaking of cheap wine is also a subtle way of separating the rich from the
poor, of emphasizing consumerism. Those who have the ability to pay more
supposedly behave better. This affirmation is absurd, of course, but undeni-
ably pertinent to the vision of a class-conscious context we are evaluating.

Physical violence against others was a particularly contentious point in a
Parade that Marta Suplicy once declared was the safest in the world.[14] While
the Parade Association attempted to downplay the number of attacks and
assaults occurring that day, the assessment of the print media told quite a
different story. According to an article which appeared in *S. Paulo Agora* on
June 11, 2007, "Chaos marks the record-breaking crowd at the Parade. The
most populous of the eleven editions of the gay party draws 3.5 million: An
over-crowded Paulista Avenue provoked shoving and pushing, in addition to
assaults and robberies";[15] there were fourteen first aid stations along the trajectory of the Parade route. At the post in front of the *MASP* (*Museu de Arte de
São Paulo*) (São Paulo Art Museum), traditionally the launching point of the
Parade, the medical team counted, in the beginning of the evening, more than
fifty patients, almost fifteen of whom were victims of physical aggression like
punches and stabbings. By the end of the afternoon, authorities had collected
eighteen stolen wallets, all empty. According to the Military Police, only four
individuals were arrested for assault or robbery. Among the recovered items
were a host of cellular phones and cameras. A section of the article was entitled "Police Station packed to limits: Reporters witnessed authorities telling
victims to look for other police stations or to file a crime report on the Internet,
alleging an overwhelming volume of incidents."[16] Perhaps to be expected,
none of the media sources that I consulted associated the growing violence
within the Pride Parade with the overall increase in violence in the city at large.

Police participation in that year of the Parade was particularly problematic
and polemical. A somewhat expected, if repetitive, conflict over the numbers
game was unusually disturbing in 2007, when the Military Police claimed,
rather anticlimactically, that they could not (or would not) count beyond the
figure of one million because that number represented the maximum capacity of the space relegated to the event. In the *Folha Online* article of June 10,
2007, "*Parada Gay bate recorde, dizem organizadores*" ("Gay Parade breaks

record, organizers say"), the Military Police is portrayed as exercising a potentially homophobic strategy of denial, in terms of both calculating numbers and suppressing the information obtained, ultimately refusing to release its numbers to the public that year: "This year, the Military Police stated that it would not release its calculations of the number of participants in the event. A representative of the Military Police stated that its calculations were customarily based on the number of individuals per square meter. In the case of an event like the Parade, whose participants constantly move from place to place, it is difficult to calculate the floating population. *Paulista* Avenue's capacity is 1 million, according to the Military Police."[17]

Debates over the degree of political activism vis-à-vis festivity continued well into the Parade's eleventh year. Daia Oliver makes a compelling observation about the limits of activism in the country known worldwide for hosting the greatest party on earth: "The Gay Parade is for everybody, as it should be. The level of militancy is perhaps not very strong, in spite of the slogan (on Saturday, a more politically 'conscious' lesbian march occurred on the same stretch of *Paulista* Avenue, drawing less than half of the numbers expected), but . . . is Brazil not the country of Carnival? The Parade, this 'other Carnival,' reaffirms the destiny to mix and meet."[18]

"*Homofobia mata! Por um Estado laico de fato!*" ("Homophobia kills! For a truly secular state!") was the slogan for the Twelfth Pride Parade, held on May 28, 2008, with some 3.4 million attendees. The focal point of the rally was, once again, to promote the approval of *Lei Federal 122/06* designed to criminalize homophobic prejudice, pressuring the Brazilian Senate to take long overdue action. This time, though, the strategy was clearly to endorse legislation free from religious influences. The *Prêmio Cidadania em Respeito à Diversidade* (Citizenship Prize to Honor Respect for Diversity) was awarded to the organizing committees of the Pride Parades of Moscow and Jerusalem, for their courage in overcoming repression by their respective governments and moving forward with their plans despite oppressive conservative and fundamentalist forces. Already an international event in 2008, attracting approximately 327,000 tourists, 5% of whom came from other countries, the São Paulo Pride Parade Association continued to globalize in a very specific way, deliberately situating itself in respect to similar worldwide parades, as activists representing both the Parades in Moscow and Jerusalem traveled to São Paulo to represent their contingents and collect their well-deserved prizes. In an agreement demonstrating solidarity well beyond national borders, both Moscow and Jerusalem were declared "*Paradas-Irmãs*" ("Sister Parades") to the São Paulo phenomenon.

The twelfth annual event was historic for the Pride Organization's decision to ban the sponsorship of nightclubs and bars, thus excluding what were typically the most festive and celebratory floats on display. This intentional strategy to reinvest activist fervor into an event which had become, in the eyes of many, just an excuse to throw a big party, occurred for the first time since the third edition of the Parade in 1999. Nevertheless, there was no shortage of *trios elétricos*, as twenty-one floats of NGOs, community sites, and governmental organizations paraded throughout the day. State sponsorship continued by the *Caixa Econômica Federal* banking institution and also *Petrobrás*, mixing with government support from the Ministry of Tourism, which constructed its own float in the Parade with the new *Ministra*, Marta Suplicy, at the helm, as well as the usual financing provided by the *Prefeitura* (Mayor's Office). Significantly, the Military Police offered record-high security for the event, including 1,000 military police members, 300 civil officers, and 320 private security guards, and two tele-centers to immediately register police reports of occurring crimes. Also ready for action were thirty mobile first-aid units, forty-six doctors, fifty-five nurses, and three supporting hospitals, contributing eighty hospital beds. This large-scale relief effort at hand likely reflects a concerted response to the media's portrayals of violence, apparently justified, in the previous year's event.[19]

Mainstream media coverage in 2008 reflected the changing dynamics of the Pride Parade, ever more concerned with economic benefit and the infinite possibilities of financial gain, as well as some of the internal contradictions within its own organizing forces. An Internet source posted on May 25, 2008 from *UOL Online* (similar to AOL in the United States), *"Parada gay leva milhões a pedir por mudanças no Brasil"* ("Gay Parade brings millions to ask for changes in Brazil") by Cláudia Fontoura, pointed out a marked change in Suplicy's public discourse. Assuming her new role as minister of tourism, Suplicy exhibited shameless ambition to utilize the event for economic purposes, namely as a tool to bring in more tourist dollars. In Fontoura's article, Suplicy was quoted as saying: "This is the kind of diversity that the country wants, the diversity that we have in order to grow as a country seeking out a niche in international gay tourism."[20] As such, and rather disturbingly, the discourse centered on human rights took a back seat to the new concept of diversification—of proceeds from the event. But if unfettered economic interests were to reign in a Parade made possible essentially due to corporate sponsorship, the Pride Association was carefully scrutinizing where LGBT Brazilians were spending their money and the degree of homophobic discrimination existing in national commerce. According to Fontoura's article, "Research specialists said last year that gays in Brazil earn above-average income and spend more money on leisure activities, but the Federation of Commerce in São Paulo states that 40% of gays, lesbians, bisexuals, and transgendered people suffer discrimination as consumers."[21] The article further clarifies the Pride Association's cooperation and endorsement with this initiative to situate the buying power of the pink *real*, investing money where it is welcome and in venues free of any form of discrimination, homophobic or otherwise: "The Association also supports the plans of the Federation of Commerce to certify businesses and service providers who show evidence of respecting diversity of race, ethnic origins, disabilities, and sexual orientation."[22] An article expressly devoted to the protection of the rights of consumers offered more clarity on this important economic initiative. The piece appeared in the *Estado de São Paulo* on May 26, 2008, "*Fecomércio-SP quer criar Selo Diversidade*" (Federation of Commerce and Services of São Paulo wants to create Stamp of Diversidade), and emphasized the following disturbing numbers while clarifying the process the Pride Association planned to follow to assure that LGBT citizens were deliberately rewarding businesses who did not discriminate against them: "40% of LGBT consumers experience discrimination in the sectors of commerce and service industries. According to a study released yesterday by São Paulo's Federation of Commerce, 60% of those who experienced bad customer service do not return to the place where they made the original purchase. Of those 60%, 30% report the abuse to consumer protection services. The organization wants to create, together with the NGO *APOGLBT SP*, the Diversity Stamp, a certification designed to recognize those businesses that value diversity of consumers."[23]

Clearly, though, elitist discrimination was not only occurring in the shopping centers but much more visibly and insidiously on the streets of São Paulo. According to a report issued by the Mayor's Office, in just the first quarter of 2008, from January to April, there were ninety-eight registered cases of homophobic violence. As alarming as this number sounds, we must realize that the statistic is likely a gross underestimation since many such cases go unreported in Brazil, in part because of intimidation and threats experienced by the victims, but also due to an overall perception (and an unfortunately correct one) of impunity in the vast majority of cases filed. The recognition of increasing homophobic violence not only in São Paulo but also in Brazil overall was likely the principal reason to explain why the Parade Association suspended the floats of bars and night clubs, resulting in a more solemn demonstration and an elevated political consciousness. It is for this reason that headlines like Claudia Silveira's "Gay Parade gains in numbers and economizes in glitter: Scarcity of drag queens and costumed people made for a less colorful party. Final numbers will be released today" (*S. Paulo Agora*, May 26, 2008)[24] became the norm in this unusual edition of the event. Symbolic of an increased political consciousness, perhaps at the expense of a good amount of hype of festivity, was the inclusion of the final float of the Parade, a tribute to the victims of homophobic and AIDS-phobic violence. The last float, decorated with the red AIDS ribbon against a large white strip, passed by with nobody inside.

While the incidents of homophobic violence were indisputably rising in Brazil, it is important to counterbalance this reality by acknowledging the efforts of the national government. Former president Luiz Inácio da Silva (Lula) authored a new project "*Brasil sem Homofobia*" ("Brazil without Homophobia"), which effectively sponsored over 300 LGBT events solely in 2007, including parades, conferences, seminars, film and theater festivals, sporting events, and other activities. The program was systematically dismantled in 2016 by pastor and politician Ezequiel Teixeira. The 2008 Pride Parade was an exercise not only in combatting homophobia but in demonstrating the excesses and self-abuse of internalized homophobia, with at least 500 participants injured through self-indulgence of alcohol and drugs according to Vivian Masutti's article in *S. Paulo Agora* on May 26, 2008: "Festival brings confusion, robberies and alcohol abuse: Crowds invade space designated as a medical post. At least 500 people were treated. Twenty robberies were registered."[25]

That year, the Pride Association lost credibility in its stubborn insistence to continue the numbers game against the Military Police, claiming on its website that five million people had attended the event in 2008.[26] But at the end of the day, the Association revoked the number for further consideration. The Military Police had its own share of clashing with the public in 2008, forcing the critical observer to question the true degree of both democracy and diversity in light of its aggressions. At 7:30 p.m., the Military Police used pepper gas to disperse the crowds on Consolação Street, despite the fact that they were not engaging in any kind of civil disobedience other than outstaying their welcome into the hours of the early evening. Earlier in the day, the police arrested four trade unionists belonging to the association *Conlutas* (*Coordenação Nacional de Lutas*) National Coordination of Struggles; allegedly, thirty members of that group attempted to enter the Parade line-up against the permission of the *APOGLBT SP*. According to the police, the individuals were accused to have been interfering in the passage of the Parade. The conflict escalated when the Pride Association confirmed that the group's participation had indeed not been approved. Journalists seized the opportunity to report on this impasse, and with good reason, given that the practice of both democracy and the valorization of diversity have become a rhetorical platform of the Pride Association's principal goals. Daniela Arrais and Luis Kawaguti, writing for the *Folha de São Paulo*, on May 26, 2008, relate the conflict in their story: "*Direção da Parada Gay barra carro de central sindical*" ("Leadership of Gay Parade bans trade union float"): "José Maria de Almeida, President of *Conlutas*, denies [that they had irregular documentation], claiming that the float was legally approved. 'What that [Pride] Association does is to commercially exploit this demonstration. They cut deals with hotels, businesses, and shops, making a profit from this. They know we are against that type of thing,' he said. Alexandre Santos [2008 Parade Association President] claimed that Almeida's accusation did not make sense."[27]

As tempting as it may be to discredit the would-be rebels, the astute observer and critic must recognize the *real* possibility that the Pride Association may indeed have been in the business of making quite a lot of *cents*.[28]

The Thirteenth LGBT Pride Month, held in June 2009, attracted some 3.1 million attendees and sported a reordering of the acronym to include the "L" segment before the "G," in conformity with the international political movement to promote lesbian visibility first, resisting the patriarchal tendency to equate gayness with maleness. Therefore, while the transposition of just two letters may seem minor in nature, the symbolic representation of this gesture, particularly in a strikingly *machista* society, is paramount.

The bad luck of number "13," however, would haunt the June 14, 2009 edition of the Pride Parade, which was marked by a sharp increase in homophobic violence, assault, and theft. In an ironic twist on the slogan of *"Pela isonomia dos direitos"* ("For equality of rights"), an unprecedented terrorist attack at the end of the Parade would confirm that protection from homophobia and the guarantee of equal rights under the law were more urgently needed than ever. For the first time, an act of terrorism occurred at the end of the Parade, when someone threw a home-made bomb, seriously injuring more than twenty people. As if this incident were not enough, the sad day was also marked by the assassination of a gay activist and the gay bashing of a seventeen-year-old boy. In light of the serious crimes committed during that edition of the Pride Parade, the *Programa Brasil Sem Homofobia* of the *Secretaria Especial dos Direitos Humanos da Presidência da República* (Brazil without Homophobia Program, affiliated with the Special Bureau of Human Rights of the Presidency of the Republic of Brazil) released a sobering official statement about one week after the event, on June 22, 2009: "Unfortunately, the day in which more than 3.1 million people took to the streets to demand respect for differences ended in a tragic way. . . . The National Congress has still not come to any consensus about the law which criminalizes homophobia. The bomb set off on *Vieira de Carvalho* Street, which injured more than twenty people, the beating of a 17 year-old young man on *Frei Caneca* Street, and the murder of Marcelo Barros on *Araújo* Street reinforce the urgent necessity to include crimes motivated by intolerance in the Brazilian legislation."[29] A word or two is necessary to contextualize not only the violent crimes committed but also their geographic and symbolic spaces. For example, *Frei Caneca* Street is widely known by many *paulistanos*, heterosexual or LGBT, as a "safe space" for LGBT-friendly commerce and socialization. Though unsuccessful, there was a movement, since 2008, to declare *Rua Frei Caneca* (aptly nicknamed *Gay Caneca*) the first official LGBT street in Brazil. In addition to hosting the LGBT-oriented mall *Shopping Frei Caneca*, which attracts and caters mainly to the gay male consumer, the street, just off the *Avenida Paulista*, was home to the NGO *Casarão Brasil*, Brazil's first LGBT community center, which initially proposed the *Gay Caneca* baptism but itself has since dissolved. The *Rua Vieira de Carvalho* constitutes, for many, the heart of LGBT night clubs and bars. The fact that the crimes were committed in the very neighborhoods that are considered central to LGBT life in São Paulo is a chilling display of the necessity of legislative action to condemn homophobic hate crimes even as additional attacks and murders inevitably occur.

Perhaps lulled into a false sense of security by the limited episodes of violent crime in previous parades, or perhaps due to a reduction in state support of the event, the sharp increases in assaults and robberies in the 2009 edition of the Parade was due, at least in part, to the significant reduction of security personnel assigned to monitor the Parade. The journalist Monica Cardoso and her colleagues reported the staggering numbers in an article published on June 15, 2009 in *O Estadão*: "Gay Parade experiences chaos and fights: Military Police should suggest changes for next year."[30] As far as robberies are concerned, 120 wallets were found in just three locations. By 4:00 p.m. that afternoon, sixty medical emergencies were registered, predominantly sixteen- and seventeen-year-old victims of alcohol poisoning. Even the Parade Association admitted, in this article, that there was a marked increase in the number of physical altercations and assaults during this edition of the Parade. In addition to an increase in the usual occurrences of theft of wallets, cell phones, and digital cameras, a man was assaulted at gunpoint in broad daylight in the middle of *Avenida Paulista*. The article relates the incident as follows: "The 30 year-old businessman Fernando Tabatino was attacked in the middle of Paulista Avenue. 'A group of four people approached me, placed the gun on my stomach and demanded my wallet.'"[31]

Nevertheless, the most devastating aspect of the article had nothing to do with the commission of larger numbers of physical violence. Instead, the most serious problem was the structural violence of the piece itself, which committed a grave injustice in its inaccurate coverage of the terrorist bomb incident. Shockingly, the crime was not linked to either terrorism generally or to homophobia specifically: "During the dispersion of the Parade, some participants continued to party on *Dr. Vieira de Carvalho* Street in the neighborhood of *Santa Cecília*, around 10:00 p.m. Annoyed by the noise, a resident threw a homemade bomb down upon the group. According to the Military Police, thirty people were wounded."[32] In an astounding display of insensitivity at best or blatant homophobia at worst, the fact that the journalists depicted the perpetrator of such a violent crime as simply a neighbor who was upset with excessive noise at 10:00 p.m., deciding to express his objection to the revelers by bombing them, is an inexcusably irresponsible act of misreporting. The severe downplay of the magnitude of the event, minimizing the realities of an overtly homophobic terrorist act, calls into question the ethics of responsible journalism. In a similar story, appearing in the June 15, 2009 edition of the *Diário de São Paulo*, journalist Dani Costa relates the apathy and implicit inequality of the police investigation of an openly gay teacher's murder becoming a focal point of the protest for many marchers in the Parade: "Right after the opening float began its journey, friends of the teacher José Carlos de Siqueira, murdered eight days ago in Suzano, carried signs to protest against the manner in which police authorities have been treating the crime. 'They stopped investigating the case as they normally would when they discovered that he was gay,' said Priscila Lucena, a secretary and the victim's sister-in-law."[33]

While there were twenty *trios elétricos* parading in 2009, the Pride Parade Association continued its stance to keep the night clubs and bars out, re-emphasizing the political militancy of the demonstration. But Daniel Bergamasco's June 15, 2009 article in the *Folha de S. Paulo* insinuates another possible interpretation for this omission—the imposition of enormous fees for such floats to participate in the Parade. In the column "In the absence of night club floats, politics advance in São Paulo's Gay Parade: Trade unions and organizations in defense of the environment and health utilize the event to spread their ideas and attract new members," Bergamasco writes: "It was the first time in many years that, amidst complaints about the entrance fee of 10 thousand *reais*—approximately US$4,500.00—for floats to participate in the Parade, not a single night club participated in the event."[34][35] While we may not find an adequate or definitive reason to account for the total absence of these floats, it is worth investigating possible motives that caused this decision. In other words, does this absence signify increased political activism or is it merely a consequence of economic hardship imposed by a greedy Parade Association? Another way to interpret this situation may be that, in the attempt to exercise "real" democracy, the Association may have decided that it could not ban the entrance of floats from the nighttime entertainment industry. However, it may have strategically (ab)used its right to (over)charge these businesses, intentionally assessing cost-prohibitive fees to deter their participation.

Bergamasco's article also points out the relatively recent trend to generalize the discourse of protest for change in Brazil, well above and beyond the specific call for LGBT rights, noting the active presence of environmentalists, race relations activists, church organizations, labor unions, and even proponents of new legislation to ban smoking in the state. Some of the new floats included a group of members from the *Central Única dos Trabalhadores* (*CUT*), mentioned earlier in this chapter, and the trade unions of nurses (*Seesp*), telemarketers (*Sintratel*), and teachers (*Apeoesp*). A few religious organizations marked their presence with a very clear stance against the perception that the "gay lifestyle" revolves around bars and clubs, waging war against these potentially damaging stereotypes but also exercising their

own form of repression in virtually condemning an important constituency
in the LGBT community. As Bergamasco writes, "The New Hope Christian
congregation called for militancy on the ground, with many representatives
and posters. 'We are here to show that [being] gay is not just about clubbing
but also spirituality,' said Esdraz Xavier, an assistant pastor of the church."[36]

This edition of the Parade, in addition to being the most violent, was also
the most overtly militant, with phrases like "Did you know that same-sex
couples have 37 fewer rights than the others [their heterosexual counter-
parts]?"[37] prominently displayed in the front of each of the twenty floats.
Additionally, the Association put an ambitious goal into place to obtain at
least one million electronic signatures before the end of the Parade to send a
petition to the National Congress, as well as the president of Brazil, the Federal Supreme Court, and the Superior Court of Justice. With some cause for
optimism as the then-governor of São Paulo, José Serra, switched his political
views to defend the passage of civil unions between same-sex partners, Marty
Suplicy, the minister of tourism, was portrayed, perhaps for the first time
in the print media, as far more pessimistic, as we see in Monica Cardoso's
article quoted earlier: "Immediately after Serra [the governor] and Kassab
[the mayor] left, . . . former Mayor Marta Suplicy appeared with short hair
and a leopard-skin blouse. She posed for a few pictures with spectators and
then joined the second float to enter Paulista Avenue. She did not stop dancing to the sounds of 'The Age of Aquarius' and other classics from the 70s
and 80s. 'The situation has worsened for homosexuals in Brazil,' she said.
'Crimes have increased and the situation in Congress has not been favorable.
In spite of the big party, we are witnessing an ever more difficult reality.' "[38]
While it is perplexing to explain the incongruence between the portrayal of
Suplicy's incessant dancing, on the one hand, and her grave pessimism on the
current state of affairs for LGBT Brazilian citizens, it is perhaps indicative
of a cultural context that would insist that the party must go on, even if or
precisely because there is little to celebrate.

The Fourteenth Pride Parade (June 6, 2010) continued the persistent plea
to *"Vote contra a homofobia: defenda a cidadania"* ("Vote against homophobia: Defend citizenship"). It is impossible not to notice the rapidly increasing
internationalization of the event and its financial impact on the economy of
São Paulo. Of the 3.3 million in attendance, approximately 400,000 were
identified as tourists, accounting for the movement of between R$180 mil-
lion and R$190 million. Despite being election year in Brazil, it is interesting
to note that there was comparatively very little campaigning. Violence and
crime were significantly lower in this edition of the Parade, and punishment for the homophobic violence in the 2009 Parade was strictly enforced.
According to the *APOGLBT SP*, there were a total of eight assaults, three of
which were robberies and five were altercations. Though I find this statistic

quite difficult to believe, the Pride Association continued to insist that "it is worth reiterating that the LGBT Pride Parade of São Paulo is considered by public security officials to be the most peaceful event of such a large magnitude in the State."[39] Armed with a semblance of an intelligence unit, the *Delegacia de Crimes Raciais e Delitos de Intolerância* (*DECRADI*—Police Station for Race-Related Crimes and Incidents of Intolerance) mapped out a list of groups they deemed likely to perpetuate hate crimes or terrorist acts and readied its constituents to prosecute the would-be offenders to the full extent of the law. This unit was also responsible for the identification and imprisonment of all the members involved in the neo-Nazi group to which the bomb attack at the end of the 2009 Parade was attributed.

Of the eighteen *trios elétricos* parading that year, four were strictly devoted to ending discrimination and violence and to raising the self-esteem of LGBT persons. The sixth float was particularly notable, as it dedicated itself to two groups who often suffer double discrimination: *os ursos* (*gays gordinhos e peludos*, often translated literally to "bears" in the English-speaking gay male community) and elderly LGBT citizens. The tenth float, interestingly denominated *Gol contra a homofobia* (Scoring a goal against homophobia (soccer metaphor, of course)), called the public's attention to an issue rarely acknowledged in mainstream Brazilian cultural representations: Prejudice and discrimination on the soccer field. According to the Pride Association, this float "communicated the message that the sport is, above anything else, a means of conviviality and that the diversity of fans and athletes must be respected and expected to live in harmony with one another."[40] In a sport whose tradition is deeply ingrained with patriarchal and *machista* values,[41] the specificity and boldness of this message were particularly necessary and, frankly, a revolutionary contribution to the political activism of the demonstration. The eighteenth and final car was, much like the final float in the 2009 Parade, the most somber and sobering of all, carrying 198 colored and numbered crosses to symbolize each homophobic assassination that occurred in the year 2009. The Parade Association went on public record to state: "This [number] means that Brazil has the highest number of fatal homophobic crimes in the world, making the approval of the bill to criminalize homophobia the most important demand of the Brazilian movement right now."[42] [43]

The controversial debates over the degree to which the Pride Parade may be labeled a huge carnivalesque party rather than a call to militant political action continued to be waged in 2010. The final sentence of an official statement, released by Alexandre Santos, president of *APOGLBT SP*, and Manoel Zanini, general coordinator of the Fourteenth *Mês do Orgulho LGBT de SP*, reads as follows: "We conclude with the definitive position that, in no circumstance whatsoever, do we support the incorrect characterization of the demonstration through the **carnivalization** of its identity or the creation of private entities that would encourage elitist participation through social seg-regation of the demonstrators" (emphasis mine).[44] A careful analysis of this statement brings us to at least four conclusions: (1) The Parade organizers are evidently not interested in perpetuating the festive atmosphere of past demonstrations and are attempting to replace the ludic quality of the event with serious sociopolitical intention and manifestation to provoke and promote national change, as if the ludic were opposed to the critical and the festive were the opposite of political militancy; (2) The tenet of diversity must be the cornerstone of such demonstrations; (3) The Parade must be characterized by true democratization, and any attempts to ban participation based on social or political differences will not be tolerated; and (4) Each of the previous observations, from rejecting intolerance, to the repression of festivity (vis-à-vis the banning of representation by floats commanded by nightclubs and bars), to the enforcement of the "seriousness" of the event and monitoring its popularization all contradict, in ironic but concrete ways, the very diversity of opinion and freedom of democracy that the Pride Association had desperately attempted to espouse. It is interesting to note the extreme level of resistance to the universe of laughter, which, as Bakhtin has shown us, is blessed with the agency to question and even the power to transform.[45] In a speech delivered at the opening of the Thirteenth Pride Parade on June 14, 2009 and published approximately two months before the 2010 Parade, on April 17, "The Place of the LGBT: Ladies and Gentlemen, the people you are witnessing marching down *Paulista* Avenue on [June] 14th, are the second-class citizens of our Republic,"[46] Pride Association president Alexandre Santos compared the fight for LGBT civil rights to the abolition of slavery, blaming the stereotype of Brazilian *cordialidade* (cordiality, congeniality, or gentility) for the untenable delays in delivering basic human rights. Also, now that the Pride Parade had earned international visibility, Santos tried to use the tactic of shame and embarrassment in the eyes of other nations to encourage Brazilian citizens to join the international movement to defend LGBT rights:

Instead of commemorating a legislative success, we return to the streets to appeal again to the good sense of the Brazilian State, to the characteristic delays that Brazil champions, after being one of the last countries in the world to abolish slavery. Foreigners that are following the news of the largest parade in the world must be confused, for they do not understand how it is possible that a country which permits and even finances a demonstration like this one, can also be one of the countries to have the highest number of assassinations of homosexuals in the world and where there is no legislation whatsoever that can curb homophobic [hate] crimes.

My dear friends, I am going to try to explain. We are the country of cordiality. A country that, for many centuries, treated its black people as if they were added on, in spite of being slaves, and as long as they were not disobedient. A country where, still today, the maid is treated like a family member, until the day comes when, with difficulty, she asks for her workers' rights. It is the same thing with gays, lesbians, bisexuals, *travestis* and transsexuals. We are all very well seen and useful, as long as we put ourselves in the places designated for us, without demanding our rights.[47]

This speech laments not only the *cordialidade* of which many a Brazilian sociologist has written, most notably Sérgio Buarque de Hollanda, but also the remnants of the hierarchies and the rigid categories espoused in positivism, where everyone is expected to stay in his or her allotted space to maintain the structures perceived as necessary to allow order and progress to flourish. But at what expense? Another way to pose the problem in a more contemporary sense might be to ask how to get around getting around the law. Sociologist Lívia Barbosa famously defined *o jeitinho brasileiro* (the Brazilian art of circumnavigating the law to find "a way around" a problem, resolving it creatively and not necessarily through legal means), for many at the heart of *brasilidade* just as much as cordiality, as "*a arte de ser mais igual que os outros*" ("The art of being more equal than others").[48] How, then, can equality be cultivated, let alone democracy, in a nation where Roberto da Matta's celebrated phrase, "*Você sabe com quem está falando?*" ("Do you have any idea to whom you are speaking?"), antagonizes any true attempt at equality of the relative value of citizenship.[49] This problematic perspective is also quite visible in various middle-class discourses in Brazil, who fight for *privileges* (defined as exclusive and directed to just one particular group), rather than *rights*, which would, in principle, belong to all.

YEAR FIFTEEN: SOCIAL INVERSIONS AND STRATEGIC SUBVERSIONS

The edition of the São Paulo LGBT Pride Parade occurring on June 26, 2011 was the most numerous yet, and, quite paradoxically, the most peaceful and polemical at the same time. With the recently won gay civil unions approved by the Brazilian Supreme Court (*Supremo Tribunal Federal*) on May 5, 2011, just weeks before the Parade, it would be important to see how "necessary" the event would be in the eyes of Brazilian citizens. After all, the state-sanctioned ability to form stable unions and families was one of the most important battles in the fight for civil rights and had finally been conquered. Media sources reported that between 4 and 4.5 million people attended the Parade, proving that the tradition was alive and well and that the battle to continue to end homophobia in Brazil intensified even further. Fascinating developments occurred this year, moments that would remind us that, despite globalization, Brazil is also very much still the land of *Carnaval*, of internal contradictions and of social inversions. The "players" on both sides of the field, as it were, would no longer be so visibly (m)aligned. For example, the *Igreja Cristã Evangelho Para Todos* (Evangelical Christian Church for All), an Evangelical Christian congregation in São Paulo, distributed pamphlets throughout Paulista Avenue, reading, "*Para Deus somos todos iguais. Amor não é pecado*" ("In the eyes of God, all of us are equal. Love is not a sin"). The pastor of the congregation, Silvio Pompeu, was interviewed in the *Folha de S. Paulo* on June 27, 2011: "'We just want people to respect what Jesus Christ said two thousand years ago, that everyone should love one another.' According to the pastor, the Church has existed since 2001 and receives nearly 180 people on the day of worship, every Thursday."[50] Another Evangelical Christian organization, the *Igreja da Comunidade Metropolitana*, performed a collective commitment ceremony with ten same-sex couples (six male couples and four female couples) in the wake of the Supreme Court's unanimous decision to approve same-sex civil unions, attracting a crowd of 300 people to the event, according to Ricardo Gallo's article, "*Casamento coletivo com 10 gays reúne 300 pessoas em SP*" (Group Marriage Ceremony for 10 gay people in São Paulo draws an attendance of 300 people) (*Folha.com*, June 25, 2011).

Nevertheless, this institution was not the only traditional antagonist of LGBT rights that would join the ranks of the 2011 Pride Parade. Quite surprisingly, a group of forty young skinheads and punkers, identifying as the *Ação Antifascista* (AntiFascism Alliance), marched during the Pride Parade, displaying a sign reading "*Punks e skinheads contra a homofobia*" ("Punks and skinheads against homophobia"). Given that the increasing numbers of homophobic crimes committed in central São Paulo had been attributed to skinhead groups, the most recent attack at the *Paraíso* station of the subway on July 3, 2011, summarized in an article appearing in the *Estadão* on July 4, 2011: "Skinhead accused of the bombing in 2009 Gay Parade commits another hate crime,"[51] the Military Police detained the group when they arrived at the event but later released them when they learned that the protesters were marching in favor of diversity. Cristina Moreno de Castro ("*Skinheads também participam de Parada Gay*," "Skinheads also participate in Gay Parade," *Folha.com*, June 26, 2011) interviewed one of the organizers of the group, twenty-nine-year-old openly gay Danilo Henrique, who said that this was the first time that the group had participated in the Parade: "The goal is to demystify the idea that all skinheads are homophobic. The Gay Parade should serve as a platform for all demands and not just to show the pride of being gay."[52] A second member of the group, eighteen-year-old Bruno Cavalcante, identifying as straight, told the reporter that the group is against any kind of prejudice, stating, "The media says that we are homophobic, but not all of us are. We are not,' he says. He affirms that they [skinheads] are also victims of intolerance."[53]

As if the support of an Evangelical Christian group and the alliance of skinheads against homophobia were not enough evidence of the potential for social transformation, or merely another case of social inversion, the *APOGLBT*'s slogan for the 2011 Parade, "*Amai-vos uns aos outros: basta de homofobia!*" ("Thou shalt love one another: Put an end to homophobia"), controversially adapted and subverted Biblical discourse to call an end to discrimination against LGBT Brazilian citizens.

The most polemic part of this edition of the Parade was the HIV/AIDS prevention campaign, where posters depicting homoeroticized Catholic saints in vulnerable sexual positions, with the phrase "*Nem Santo te protege: Use camisinha*" ("Not even a saint can protect you: Use a condom"), filled the medians of the *Avenida Paulista* throughout the entire trajectory of the Parade.

HETERO PRIDE: THE STAKES OF COMING OUT STRAIGHT

There is another story that must be told as this chapter unfolds to its conclusion, a subversive scenario which reinforces the arguments I have made earlier about the principles of social inversion in a Brazilian carnivalesque context. Depending on one's perspective, countering or paralleling the presence of the LGBT Pride Parade was the invention of the *Parada do Orgulho Hétero*, the Heterosexual Pride Parade, in 2007. Media coverage of the emergence of the event was initially relegated to an "*Extra: Notícias Bizarro*" ("Extra: Bizarre News") section of *O Globo* on June 17, 2007, in the form of a brief headline and two short sentences: "*S. Paulo faz parada do orgulho hétero mas só atrai 50 gatos pingados*" ("São Paulo hosts Hetero Pride but only attracts fifty stalwarts"). *Gato pingado* is a colloquial expression, which translates literally to "drunk cat" but is a depreciative term which implies numeric inferiority or insignificance of substance, or virtual irrelevance. The editorial opens with the sarcastic "*É cada coisa*," which translates loosely to "The strangest things happen," and reads with a touch of irony and a connotation of abnormality. The brief text of the article is as follows: "One week after bringing together more than 3 million gays and gay-friendly allies, Paulista Avenue, in São Paulo, once again became the stage for another protest of a sexual character: A group of nearly fifty people realized the First Heterosexual Pride Parade in front of the São Paulo Art Museum (*MASP*)."[54] The location is not accidental, of course, since the meeting ground mimics the traditional starting point of the LGBT Pride Parade, in front of *MASP*. It is interesting and productive to assess both the irony of the event itself in addition to the way it was portrayed in mainstream media. If, by 2007, the LGBT Pride Parade had become a normative feature of the city's annual calendar, then it is enlightening to consider that efforts to return São Paulo to heteronormativity would be viewed or construed in a depreciative manner as "bizarre." What we are seeing here, portrayed in mainstream Brazilian journalism, is the denormalization of heteronormativity, or perhaps more accurately, the normalization of the queer. In the country of *Carnaval*, the abundance of social inversions leads to a high degree of contradictions and paradox, even to the point, one may say, of subverting any initial attempts at subversion.

Nevertheless, what began as a group of stray cats not to be taken seriously and with no tangible impact on Brazilian mentality or collective consciousness had evolved into a serious ploy on the part of Evangelical Brazilian politicians who, in 2011, effectively campaigned for the establishment of the Hetero Pride Day as a permanent feature of São Paulo's cultural agenda. The initiative evolved, in 2008, to become the "*Segunda Parada do Orgulho Hétero e Simpatizantes de São Paulo*," translating roughly to the "Second Straight and Straight-Friendly Pride Parade of São Paulo." Organized by a middle-class family residing in the suburbs of São Paulo, the goal was to consistently hold the event on the first Sunday following the LGBT Pride Parade. While the news was not disseminated widely and certainly not taken seriously by the mainstream readership, both queer and straight readers of the *Folha de S. Paulo Online* expressed general outrage and condemnation of the "movement" upon reading Sérgio Ripardo's May 21, 2008 article, "*SP terá 2a Parada Hétero no Masp, no dia 1*" ("São Paulo will have Second Hetero Parade at MASP, on June 1"). It is worth considering whether the condemnation and fierce criticism may be read as *heterophobic* in nature, or perhaps be indicative of a certain intolerance of normativity, especially given that "straight-friendly" allies were welcome to join the event. Or is the initiative merely an attempt to mock, through mimicry, or to belittle the importance of the Brazilian civil rights movement for LGBT equality?

The young organizer of the event, twenty-year-old Cristiano Vicente, an English teacher majoring in graphic design, was quoted in the article mentioned before: "The Straight Pride Parade is not an affront against gays. We do not want to offend anybody. We reject any homophobic comments in our *Orkut* community."[55] Vicente claims that the Hetero Parade defends freedom of expression and that, since its inception, he has been the victim of attacks and harsh criticism by gay and straight people alike. Might this condemnation reflect prejudice or intolerance toward a part of diversity known as "normativity,"[56] or is it merely a reassertion and affirmation of equality in the face of so many movements and organizations that have tried to deny it? The platform of the Hetero Parade is one that believes in sexual freedom and pride, hence the slogan "*Muitos são, poucos se orgulham*" ("There are many [heterosexuals], but few are proud"). What we see here, I believe, is an ironic and potentially dangerous social inversion which would uphold, with some degree of truth, that the LGBT Pride Parade, having become the "normative" (hence hegemonic) *festa*, now dominates the scene and the stage, relegating all other interest groups to marginalization. Whether we agree with it or not, the inverted slogan is a brilliant appropriation, since it plays with the concept of *minority* (a few), of *majority* (many), and of *pride*, all of which are central elements to the motifs of every Pride Parade that has occurred in Brazil. Hence, the resignification of "straight pride" as a response, in Bakhtinian terms, to the LGBT Pride Parade which had become the active hegemonic center subject to subversion by the far right.[57]

On the other hand, what makes such a potentially absurd movement dangerous to the slow but ongoing development of civil rights for LGBT Brazilians is its appropriation and manipulation by Evangelical Brazilian politicians. Appearing in the online newspaper *Estadão.com.br* on June 22, 2011, was the headline: "São Paulo City Council attempts to create Hetero Pride Day, jamming the daily agenda: With the support of Evangelical constituents, Carlos Apolinário insisted upon emergency vote."[58] Diego Zanchetta, journalist for the *Estado de S. Paulo*, writes as follows: "Four days before the Gay Parade, one of the largest events in the city, the São Paulo City Council approved this Wednesday, (June) 22nd, the inclusion on its agenda of the project that creates Heterosexual Pride Day, which will proceed to a second discussion and a vote."[59] Though it was eventually overturned and erased from the Calendar of City Events, there was a good chance that the project would have been successful, since it was backed firmly by Evangelical Christian leaders and resulted in twenty-eight council members voting in support of its passage. It is clear that the politician who wrote the text of the bill, Carlos Apolinário, himself an Evangelical Christian, was focusing his energies on reacting to the space conflict discussed earlier in this chapter since Apolinário had protested for the past three years that the Gay Parade was being held on Paulista Avenue. Zanchetta writes in the article referenced before: "Apolinário promises to obstruct any city council project under consideration if his proposal is not put forward for a vote. 'They removed the March for Jesus from Paulista Avenue and let the gays stay, that's absurd! I am not against the gays, I am against the place of their event,' he argued."[60] There is no doubt that Apolinário is hell-bent on retribution. Further, as we know, the absurdity of Apolinário's statement cuts much deeper than the issue of space and exhibits distress with the positive affirmation that the Avenue symbolically confers.

The larger concern in 2011, however, was the paralysis of the political process that such a self-righteous bill generated. This stagnation was particularly dangerous, given the fact that serious initiatives, such as the passage of *PLC 122/06*, an anti-homophobic hate crimes bill, which had an expiration date of December 2011, though later extended, to be considered or else find itself *"definitivamente arquivado pelo Congresso"* (permanently closed by Congress), a Brazilian political euphemism used to describe the fate of a piece of legislation that dies a permanent death. Ultimately, in the case of *PLC 122/06*, the bill that would have made illegal any form of discrimination or violence due to one's sexual orientation and/or gender identity, 2013 was a decisive year for LGBT Brazilians. The human rights bill that had been stalled by fundamentalist religious groups for twelve years finally went to a vote in December 2013, with disastrous results for LGBT Brazilian citizens: twenty-nine senators voted against it, only twelve in favor, and two abstained. An undeniable victory for anti-LGBT prejudice in Brazil, LGBT Brazilians, murdered at increasing rates, continued to enjoy for years to come no federal protection against discrimination or violence on the basis of their identity. To make matters worse, the defeat created significant pessimism for the future since it also erased the concepts of sexual orientation and gender identity from a review of protected classes of citizens under Brazil's penal code.

"CIVILIDADE É A DIVERSIDADE. SÃO PAULO, PORTANTO, É MAIS GAY DO QUE EVANGÉLICA" ("CIVILITY IS DIVERSITY. SÃO PAULO, THEREFORE, IS MORE GAY THAN IT IS EVANGELICAL")

The quotation in the heading is attributed to journalist and community activist Gilberto Dimenstein, who in his June 24, 2011 editorial column, "*São Paulo é mais gay ou evangélica?*" (Is São Paulo more gay than evangelical or vice-versa?) coherently describes the conflict between the LGBT community and the Evangelical Christians by succinctly comparing the LGBT Pride Parade with the March for Jesus. Dimenstein argues the fact that the former does not desire to take away anybody's rights (even those of fundamentalist Christians), while the Evangelical March for Jesus argues against LGBT rights and therefore against diversity. He proceeds to write that gays speak from a platform of happiness and joy, while the Evangelical marchers are filled with anger and consequently attack diverse segments of society, the most recent target being the *STF* (*Supremo Tribuno Federal*), the Brazilian Supreme Court. The final portion of the editorial is worth quoting in its entirety, for it summarizes the compass of one of the world's most diverse and multicultural cities—heading firmly toward liberation: "Behind the scenes of the Gay Parade, there are no political or partisan schemes. In the Evangelical Parade, there is a relationship which mixes religion with elections; this is clear if we look at the number of politicians in leadership positions marching in the parade. And this is not to mention many characters who, if they do not have accounts to settle with God, they certainly do with the Justice of mortals, having been accused of fraudulent financial practices. I have nothing against the right of Evangelical Christians to have the right to march. Quite the contrary, actually. But I prefer the happiness of the gays, who want happiness for everyone. Including the Evangelical Christians."[61]

The state of journalistic representations of LGBT social movements in Brazil reflects the very ambiguity that characterizes the contradictory nature of queer life in a Brazilian context, and by extension, the contradictions that seem to manifest themselves in any critical assessment of *brasilidade*. On the one hand, articles like *"União entre dois homens consumada em cartório surpreende moradores de Manhuaçu"* (Union between two men consummated in a notary public surprises residents of Manhuaçu), published in Minas Gerais on March 23, 2012, attempt to objectively balance the controversy over same-sex marriage, while dignifying LGBT citizens, and thus empowering them with respect and the courage to resist social injustices and live their own lives and loves without seeking the approval of others, especially not the government. On the other hand, both those who clamor for LGBT rights and freedom from persecution and those whose (c)overt discrimination would condemn sexual and gender identities to death, are empowered by articles like the following one, published on *Folha.com* on April 4, 2012: "Source claims that Assassination of Homosexuals Reached a New Record in 2011."[62] In this brief piece, journalist Aguirre Talento highlights the fact that, according to research conducted by the *Grupo Gay da Bahia*, 266 Brazilian LGBT citizens were murdered in 2011. Furthermore, the article predicted that a new record will be reached by the end of 2012, since there were already 106 murders registered in just the first three months of 2012.[63] Unfortunately, this prediction has come to fruition, with the 2012 calendar year closing with a record high of 388 assassinations of LGBT Brazilians, 312 murdered in 2013, 326 brutally assassinated in 2014, 318 members of the LGBT+ community executed in 2015, 343 perished in 2016 at the hateful hands of others, 445 individuals massacred in 2017, 420 documented assassinations in 2018, and 329 homicides in 2019.

Indeed, it is long overdue to ask a series of difficult and controversial questions. What is the effect of such news on public opinion, and what degree of ethical responsibility do media sources in Brazil have for reporting such findings? Luiz Mott was quoted in the article as follows: "Greater visibility of homosexuals—stimulated by the gay pride parades and by the presence of gay and *travesti* characters in Brazilian soap operas—provokes more homophobic aggression."[64] Somewhat ironically, then, do we not run the risk of instigating and even sanctioning further violent crime to occur when media outlets report that they are growing at such alarming rates? Without responsible denunciation of these crimes, the realities of impunity, and the lack of any anti-hate crimes legislation until the Brazilian Supreme Court's 8–3 ruling of June 13, 2019 to criminalize homophobia and transphobia, would it not be logical (though disturbing) to assess whether those who commit homophobic acts, fueled in their mission by growing numbers, may wish to maintain Brazil's reputation as a place where LGBT citizens are not welcome and are in grave danger of losing their lives? Can we not conclude, even, that a machista and patriarchal perspective might argue for the attaining of a new record high in each subsequent year? Hence, the question of media reporting (and how such journalistic accounts are carried out) takes center stage when we ultimately question the pros and the cons of the increasing visibility of the LGBT Pride Parade, the largest of its kind on the planet hosted by the champion of homophobic murder. What is at stake in coming out in a highly visible form(at)? What are the connections between invisibility and the closet? Is it less dangerous to simply exist in the world without proclaiming identity politics of any kind, or does this gesture risk the erasure of difference and promote further intolerance? Activists and academics must come together to ask these challenging questions, not only for the sake of philosophical inquiry and stimulating intellectual discussion, but in the urgent interest of basic survival and self-preservation in the context of ever-increasing assassination of openly LGBT citizens. Staying invisible may be a form of cultural resistance in contemporary times, when the images of the media bombard our senses and defuse our militancy into strategies of marketing.

As we conclude this portion of our queerly contradictory journey into the paradoxes surrounding the world's largest Pride Parade, it is worthwhile to pay particular attention to an astute observation by film studies and gender theory scholar Denilson Lopes arguing, in his ground-breaking essay, "*Por uma nova invisibilidade*" ("For a New Invisibility"), that remaining invisible, in the context of a hostile environment where one's life itself may be in grave jeopardy, may also constitute a strategic way to stay alive. This is not necessarily a discourse of returning to the closet, but rather an opportunity to assert one's minority identity in situations and contexts where it is safe to declare one's authentic self. Lopes also implies that the media machine not only manipulates knowledge but tends to dehumanize its subjects in its quest for collective representation and massive spectacularization, thus endangering those who may choose to identify as part of a minority group. At this juncture, it is worth quoting Lopes at length:

> Invisibility often used to have a negative meaning within a politics of identities; perhaps now, however, it can mean something different. To become invisible in a society ruled by media where everything and everyone are or want to be as visible as possible, including more and more LGBT representations, invisibility can serve as a means of differentiation marked by pauses and subtlety. Which does not mean to escape nor to hide oneself from reality. Rather, it is a strategy functioning within the corrosive power of the simulacrum, of the excess of images. Disappearance may become a form of living. Disappearance positions itself constantly in tension with appearance and the politics of *outing*. . . . How to disappear? It is not only a question of knowing how to deal with public image

as in the case of pop stars and politicians. It is something broader and common. Invisibility has less to do with a romantic fascination for the marginalized than it has with the formation of a subjectivity. . . . I would argue in favor of invisibility. Now silence is able to return without necessarily meaning death. Defending invisibility does not mean to return to the *closet* but rather to increase subtlety and decrease confrontation in our strategies in light of the increasing conservatism of discourses of visibility. . . . The politics of confrontation was won by the right. The politics of identity has been used more and more and successfully by narrow fundamentalisms, be they nationalistic or religious. Where a confrontation, a fight, is expected, disappearing only to reappear ahead of the opponent in some other place, in some other form, may be a solution.[65]

The present chapter ends here, at a critical and contradictory historical moment of the LGBT social rights movement in Brazil, but the story continues to unfold in a multitude of ambivalent ways. In the following chapter, I analyze media representations of more recent versions of the Parade, jumping on and off the streets and into smartphone applications. What roles do electronic social platforms and new media play in a global environment where "fake news" and manipulation have influenced how cultural phenomena are portrayed to fulfill homophobic, transphobic, and racist ideological and political agendas insidiously perpetuating hegemonic privileges of patriarchy and white superiority while claiming to speak in favor of diversity?

I observe eagerly and worriedly as the Parade continues to intensify year after year. For so do the violent murders of the LGBT citizens who courageously and proudly march within them, whether on the streets or in isolation at home, quarantined for fear of but nonetheless unprotected from the world outside whose dangers pose (in)visible but lethal threats.

Chapter 3

WhatsZapping the LGBT Pride Parade of São Paulo: Fake News and the (Ab)uses of Social Media Platforms in Digital Brazil (2012–2020)

"Sejamos o pesadelo dos que querem roubar nossa Democracia."
("Let us be the nightmare for those who wish to rob us of our Democracy.")

—Slogan from the Twenty-fourth LGBT Pride Parade of São Paulo

APOLGBT SP Manifesto, June 14, 2020

Democratization manifests itself not only in calls for collective participation and spectatorship of each edition of the *Parada de Orgulho LGBT+ de São Paulo* but also in the Organization's annual call to create the thematic catch phrases each year and even the text of the respective manifesto, the widely publicized *justificativas*. The Board of the *APOLGBT SP* meets to determine these mottos every year but takes into account public opinion of fellow *internautas* (internet users) who are also stakeholders in the LGBT civil rights movement in Brazil. A post from February 14, 2019 illustrates this goal for collaboration with constituents: "The Board of the Association has already met to consider possible slogans but would also like to know from Internet users who participate in our LGBTI+ movement. We remind you that the slogan is a phrase that expresses our feeling in an international context, determined in consultation with partners, NGOs, and activists/militants who are involved in the LGBT+ Social Movement."[1] Unique to the 2019 call for participation is the inclusion of the "I" (representing Intersex). No prior editions of the Parade have given visibility to this contingent, and the I returns to the closet of invisibility in 2020, when for the first time in its nearly twenty-five-year history, "Q" (representing queer) finally makes its way into representation of subjectivities, though as coronavirus would require, only virtually.

This chapter examines the continued development of the largest Pride Parade in the world, focusing our attention to the past eight years of how media representations invent or prevent imaginaries around this massive sociopolitical cultural event. As Jean Wyllys has reminded us in his recent interview that opens the U.S. Network for Democracy in Brazil's "Dialogues for Democracy/*Diálogos pela democracia*," new global tendencies to manipulate the Internet as a tool to perpetuate a confluence of "fake news" (a phenomenon whose internationality in scope and dimension is represented by the use of the still-hegemonic English language even in Portuguese), "*desinformação*" (disinformation), and "*pós-verdade*" (post-truth), complicated of course by political repercussions of Trump's election to the U.S. Presidency in 2016, the emergence of "Brexit" that same year, and the rise of Bolsonaro and his election in 2018. With the emergence of conspiracy theories and denials of major international historical events (such as slavery in the Americas or the Holocaust in Europe), the international LGBTQ movement did not escape wide-scale manipulation at the hands of new social media outlets.

The year 2018 marked a key moment in malicious misinformation propagated by social media networks, prompting the *APOGLBT SP* to prominently display the following message in the virtual edition of its May 2018 newsletter: "*Vai ter Parada SIM!*" "Yes, there will be a Parade [this year]!" (see figure 3.1) in which the organization relates that the Pride Parade will indeed occur despite the claims of untrustworthy "fake news" sources to the contrary, alleging that the infamous truckers' strike of that time was responsible for making it impossible for the floats to ride. The *comunicado* (memorandum) also refers to, though vaguely and without revealing the identity of perpetrators, recent years when similar attempts to disseminate misinformation also took place. Strangely, though, the article takes a curious anti-democratic turn when it points out that the Parade is a private event and therefore those responsible for creating falsehoods about it could be sued for damages that may occur as a result of engaging in such intentional acts of deception.

Another example of the impact of misinformation and the organization's attempts to dismantle it, strive for damage control and call out "fake news" already circulating online is the widespread sharing of a visual image that allegedly appeared in a Twitter account called "@EqualLuv4All." Though it was posted on April 1, 2017, its origins can be traced back to a 4chan misinformation campaign from 2016. April Fools' joke or not, it would be foolish to minimize the impact of deceptively attributing pedophilia (i.e., pedosexuals) to the LGBT movement. According to a Reuters e-mail interview with LGBT News published on May 29, 2020: "A poor Photoshop attempt . . . this image is all over the internet with different names attached to it, various age groups, etc. We are against any and all forms of Pedophilia obviously. Whoever is spreading these images are trolls and haters trying to give the LGBT community a bad name. We meet them often in our inbox and comments." The language used in this attempt to undo damage caused by the homophobic post is problematic even as it tries to set the record straight, so to speak, and

Figure 3.1. Ad Campaign Launched by the *Associação da Parada do Orgulho LGBT de São Paulo (APOLGBT SP)* to Combat Fake News and Social Media Sources Maliciously Claiming that São Paulo's Twenty-Second Annual Pride Parade of June 3, 2018 Would Be Canceled due to the Truck Drivers' Strike.

rectify the misinformation. Calling the hackers "trolls" and "haters," though colloquially acceptable, minimizes the fact that the individuals involved deliberately committed a dangerous crime of manipulation and misrepresentation that knows no borders thanks to the powerful dissemination of the Internet at its disposal, one that could potentially lead to higher indices of homophobic assaults. Giving "the LGBT community a bad name" is too general and generalizing to make a valid point about "community," reinforcing also a view of "the community" in monolithic terms, a common practice with serious consequences that negates diversity within LGBTQ communities, a tendency I highlight in the first two chapters looking at media representations of São Paulo's LGBT Pride Parade. Finally, the frequency of such a (mal) practice is diminished by the statement indicating, "We meet them often in our inbox and comments," as if the repetition of the perpetuation of these crimes should simply be brushed off without accountability or responsibility for the numerous (though invisible) damages they may cause.

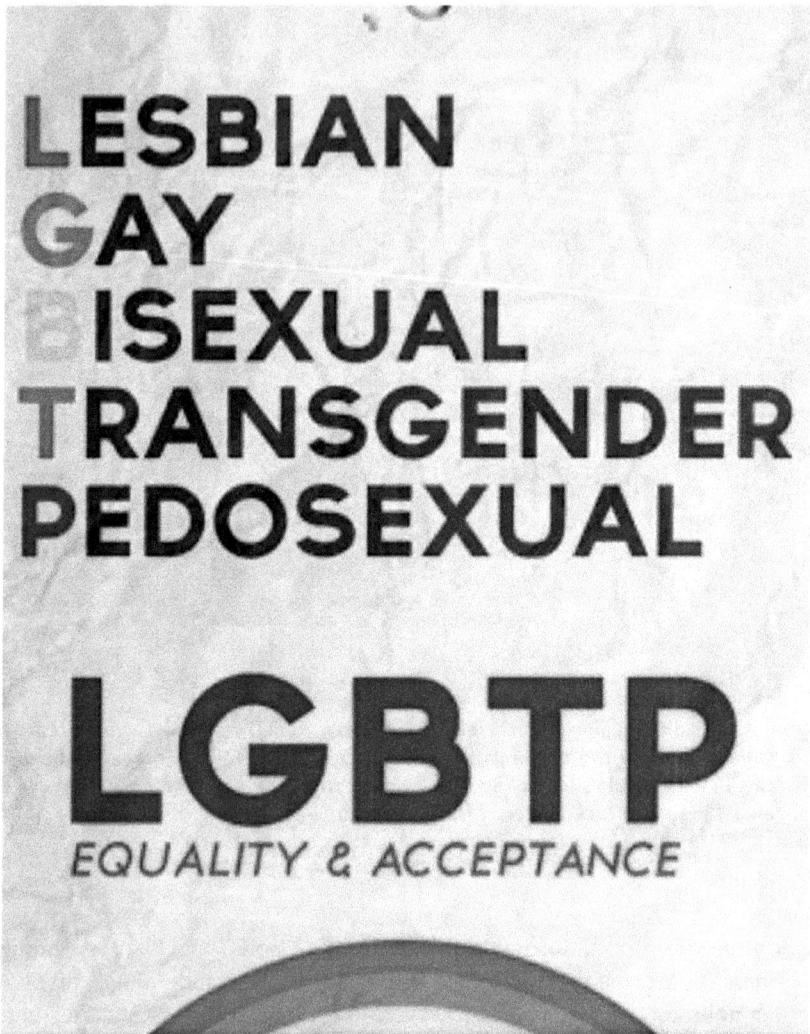

Figure 3.2. "Alert: The Inclusion of the 'P,' for Pedophiles, in LGBT Is Fake News" (*APOLGBT SP* Virtual Newsletter, July 19, 2018). Translation by author.

In any case, it is clear that this hate campaign gone viral reached Brazilian algorithms long before the Reuters fact check process was published in 2020. The July 2018 edition of the *APOLGBT SP* virtual Newsletter cites the poster but places a red "X" through it to deny its veracity, pointing out the "new normal" of new media campaigns that attempt to claim LGBT equality movements as falsely accepting of psychiatric disorders and conditions, such as pedophilia. It also points out what neither the Reuters piece nor the statement from LGBT News does not: The inherent danger of a hate campaign that is actually quite sophisticated in its conception and therefore insidious in its criminality: "Some of the sources associating the 'P' with 'LGBT' are so well written that they even led to dissemination of the slogan 'Love knows no age'" (see figure 3.2).[2]

Perhaps the most remarkable thing about the Pride Parade of 2012 was its sheer magnitude. Though the 2006 edition of the Parade was inscribed in the *Guinness Book of World Records* as the largest in the world, 2012, with its slogan "Homophobia has a cure: Education and Criminalization,"[3] would host 4.5 million participants, according to the organizers, and, in a report from the *Observatório do Turismo* (Tourism Observatory), would have the largest international contingents from Peru, the United States, Holland, and Argentina. The demographics of the event that year would comprise a diversity of sexual orientations, with just over half (55.8%) of the participants outing themselves as gay, 31.9% self-identifying as heterosexual, and 12.4% self-declared bisexuals. Curiously, the demographic report did not take gender identity into consideration, and there is consequently no statistical information of cisgender, transgender, or gender non-conforming/non-binary individuals attending the event. When asked if they had experienced discrimination on the basis of homophobia, the majority of respondents said no (66.1%) while a significant minority (33.9%) noted that they had personally suffered homophobia in public spaces (23.6%), shopping malls and restaurants being the most common locations (14.6% and 12.4%, respectively).

The seventeenth edition of the Pride Parade took place on June 2, 2013. Its slogan, "Back to the closet, never again! Unity and Awareness in the fight against homophobia,"[4] ironically illustrated the continued discrepancy in numbers, and though it included seventeen floats, the event was inarguably significantly smaller in attendance than the year prior. Official *APOLGBT SP* organizers claimed an attendance of 3.5 million, while the Military Police documented merely 600,000 participants. The eighteenth edition, on May 4, 2014, proclaimed: "A successful country is a nation without homolesbotransphobia. No More Deaths! Criminalization Now!"[5] With attention turned to fighting for federal protections on the basis of gender identities, the only other significant thing that year which gives us a window into Brazilian cultural traditions is the modification of the date expressly because of the 2014 World Cup in June. The nineteenth edition, on June 7, 2015, was united by a slogan reminiscent of Lady Gaga's smash single from 2011, "Born This Way": "I was born like this, I grew up like this, and I will always be like this. Respect me!"[6] while the twentieth anniversary of the phenomenon, held on May 29, 2016 was particularly pertinent for its fight for equality on the basis of gender identity: "Gender Identity Protections Now! Everyone Together Against Transphobia."[7] In the year 2016, for the first time, transsexual and *travesti* rights were hailed as the central theme of the Parade. While there is evidence to substantiate a direct effect on the outcome of the legislation that occurred two years later, it is quite possible that centralizing the effort for trans rights led to the Brazilian Supreme Court's 2018 federal law to end the classification of transsexuality as a psychiatric disease while also approving that use of "social names" for trans Brazilian citizens without the need to undergo gender confirmation surgery. On June 18, 2017, São Paulo celebrated the twenty-first edition of the event with the motto "Regardless of Our Beliefs, No Religion is Law. Together for a Secular State."[8] The Brazilian Tourism Board estimated that there were three million participants and that hotels in the area of the event and all of downtown São Paulo had reached 90% occupancy, representing an infusion of R$2.4 million per day during the weekend of the twenty-first edition. The increase in tourism may be attributable, at least in part, to the hospitality efforts of a campaign and companion pamphlet released at the end of 2016 titled "Hints on How to Provide Good Service to LGBT Tourists."[9]

June 3, 2018 witnessed the twenty-second edition of the Pride Parade with the slogan "Power to LGBTI+: Our Vote, Our Voice!"[10] clearly energized by the 2018 elections, and with the *APOLGBT SP*'s expectation of 5.5 million participants. Similar to the slogan from 2010, when elections and political representation returned as the primary themes for the Parade, with eighteen floats featuring star-studded LGBT personalities such as Drag Queen Tchaka, Pablo Vittar, Preta Gil, Mulher Pepita, and Lia Clark. The absence of the letter "Q" whether to designate "queer" or "questioning" silently speaks volumes about the resistance to the term "queer" despite the North American–inspired characteristics that came to (stereo)typify the event since its opening in 1997. However, it is worth noting that the inclusion of the letter "I" and the "plus" sign (+) appeared for the first time in the history of self-representation of the Pride Parade, making visible intersex and other minority (queer?) identities not included in or encompassed by the LGBT designation. In honor of the Stonewall uprising and clearly in anticipation of and competition for the following year's tribute to its fiftieth anniversary, TV Brasil launched a twenty-five-minute documentary, entitled *A Maior Parada do Mundo* (*The Biggest Parade in the World*), on June 28, known in Brazil (at least that particular year) as the *Dia Internacional do Orgulho LGBTI+* (International LGBTI+ Pride Day) before the "I" would again disappear into invisibility in the 2019 edition. There is a rather disconcerting paradox that reflects a disconnection between Brazilian cultural values and beliefs and the right-wing homotransphobic president that would be elected that year. According to surveys conducted by the respected research institute *Datafolha*, commissioned by *TV Globo* together with the *Folha de S. Paulo* on October 24 and 25 and released to the general public one day before the election, on October 27, 2018, popular opinion reflected that 74% of Brazilians believed that homosexuality should be accepted in society. Though the survey had a limited demographic composition, it had a margin of error of 2% and a level of confidence of 95%, counting on the participation of only 9,173 Brazilian citizens in 341 municipalities across the entire country. The questions it posed were quite unambiguous in nature. Topics treated on the questionnaire ranged from disparity in women's wages, to Afro-Brazilian rights, to the right to bear arms. On the specific topic of homosexuality, the survey asked participants to declare whether or not they agreed with the statement "Homosexuality should be accepted by society" ("*A homossexualidade deve ser aceita por toda a sociedade*"); 74% were in agreement, 18% self-aligned with the category "Homosexuality should be discouraged in society" ("*A homosssexualidade deve ser desencorajada por toda a sociedade*"), and 8% marked "*Não sabe*" (Do not know).

"Fifty Years of Stonewall: Our Achievements, Our Pride to be LGBT+"[11] brands the twenty-third edition of the Parade on June 23, 2019. The irony of the renewed invisibility of the "I," as indicated before, tells a story in its very omission, especially considering that this is the annual Brazilian event that purports to celebrate and elevate diversity in all its manifestations. Coming full circle in its recognition of Stonewall and by extension the U.S. civil rights movement, the continued absence of "Q" (whether representing "queer" or "questioning") exemplifies the ongoing resistance to adopting or adapting "queer" in a Brazilian context, something we shall see beginning to occur without open dialogue or inquiry in the Pride Parade that coronavirus forced off the streets and online for virtual consumption and participation in 2020. For the first time in the event's history, the 2019 edition was broadcast live by the cable channel GNT and featured on eight YouTube channels. According to data from YouTube, 40 million people watched the Parade online. After twenty-three years in existence, the São Paulo Pride Parade would finally gain recognition as the newest member of "InterPride," an international network of pride parades and festivals throughout the world, founded in Boston in 1982, also credited with creating and promoting World Pride. As the first Latin American city to join the ranks of membership, despite being declared the largest LGBT Pride Parade on the planet since the 2002 designation in the Guinness Book of World Records, São Paulo was to be added to a long list of LGBT-positive cities like Toronto, Madrid, London, Oslo, Las Vegas, Rome, and New York. Curiously, however, upon examination of InterPride's official website listing 356 members from 56 countries, updated on May 16, 2020, no Brazilian Pride organization appears on the list. In fact, with a handful of organizations just from Southeastern Massachusetts (the Cape Cod region) alone, the only two Portuguese-speaking organizations listed in InterPride's database are in Portugal, the *Associação ILGA Portugal* (in Lisbon) and the *Associação Para o Planeamento da Família* (in Faro), respectively. In fact,

Brazil is nowhere on the radar for hosting a future World Pride, with Copenhagen slated to host in 2021; Sydney in 2023; and tentatively Austin, Texas, or Rome in 2025; Orlando, Florida, in 2026; and Boston in 2030.[12]

Media coverage of the 2019 *Parada de Orgulho LGBT de São Paulo* was unremarkable except for the acknowledgment of evidence of steep (and expected) decline in LGBT rights in a Bolsonaro presidency, whether in mainstream venues or in LGBT-specific sources. NBC's "Out & Proud" series featured a piece entitled "Brazil's Largest City Draws Hundreds of Thousands for Pride March," where the very title tells the story of a Pride Parade downgraded in attendees to become "one of the world's biggest pride parades." The somber mood of the festival to decry the self-declared openly "proud homophobe," that is, Bolsonaro, was accentuated by studies that illustrated the difficulty of accepting a gay child. The article rehashes well-known claims that Bolsonaro has stated he would rather have a dead son than a gay son and the moment in April 2019 when he told reporters that Brazil "cannot be a country of the gay world, of gay tourism." At the same time the Pride Parade would lament Brazil's deep turn to the right, it would paradoxically celebrate the Brazilian Supreme Court's June 13, 2019 decision to criminalize discrimination against LGBT citizens, to which Bolsonaro retorted that Brazilian employers would be even less inclined to hire LGBT employees than before the hate crimes bill passed because, as the article relates, "they could be taken to court if they make a joke."

Other sources, among them the *Rio Times*, claimed that the 2019 event would see a 12% increase in international tourists despite (and in spite of) Bolsonaro's criticism of LGBT tourism. Statistically, this prediction proved to be true, exemplifying the paradoxical power of conservative thought to attract more rather than less spectators to protest it. According to sources representing the Board of Tourism and the Mayor's Office in São Paulo, an influx of R$403 million in the Brazilian economy was attributable to the event, representing a 40% increase over the R$288 million spent in the 2018 edition of the event. While the organizers' expectation of 5.5 million participants did not come to fruition, there were 3 million people confirmed to have attended the Parade, celebrating a "collective" same-sex marriage ceremony and the presence of local and international stars that would include Mel C, former member of the "Spice Girls."

LGBT-oriented media sources were generally not as hopeful and even less celebratory, such as the *APOGLBT SP*'s dissemination of a report showing that 92.3% of the 143 Brazilian citizens who experienced a hate crime or act of violence on the basis of their sexual orientation or gender identity between December 18, 2017 and December 27, 2018, neglected to report this abuse to authorities. The study, prepared by the non-profit startup *TODXS* founded in 2016, illustrates "Institutionalized LGBTI+-phobia and a lack of readiness to accommodate and deal with acts of oppression that this population experiences. The LGBTI+ person is afraid to report the crime, for fear of suffering more violence and ends up not denouncing the abuse because of a lack of support in terms of political power."[13]

We arrive, finally and apprehensively, to the present moment. June 14, 2020 marked the twenty-fourth edition of the Parade and its first virtual variation, with the following Che Guevara-inspired slogan: "Let's Be the Nightmare for those who would want to Steal our Democracy."[14] Urging spectators to *Participe da primeira parada virtual de Orgulho LGBT de São Paulo!* (Take part in the First Virtual LGBT Pride Parade of São Paulo!), the event was twice rescheduled due to COVID-19. It was originally transferred to November 22, conflicting with the weekend of the *Dia Nacional de Zumbi e da Consciência Negra* (Brazil's National Day of Black Consciousness and Afro-Brazilian Awareness) (November 20, 2020), originally created in 2003 and instituted as a federal holiday in 2011, now observed with state decrees in nearly 1,000 cities throughout Brazil. As a result of this perceived "conflict" and necessary sensitivity toward the global Black Lives Matter movement, though the intersectionality of the Parade's scope could perhaps not be any more pertinent to the day, the Parade was moved to November 29 only to be canceled altogether with an official announcement issued on July 24, 2020 on all official social media outlets of the *APOLGBT SP*: "The SP LGBT Pride Association and City Hall cancels the event for this year due to the pandemic. The NGO continues with the Parade Solidarity Project and announces that in 2021 the SP Parade will take place on June 6th."[15] According to journalist Fabrício Viana, the objectives of the Solidarity Project include: to help LGBT Brazilian citizens in distress, to distribute basic supplies, hygiene kits, and masks, in addition to promoting online dialogues and debates in collaboration with more than 180 pro-democracy anti-homotransphobic, anti-racist organizations in Brazil.

The virtual format of the event opened the doors to a much larger-scale global sponsorship of the online version of the Parade, occurring over the course of eight hours. Though one might think that the magnitude of the event would have been larger than ever, accommodating internationally mandated quarantines and allowing participation to occur from homes and living rooms instead of the *Avenida Paulista*, initial counts revealed that attendance on the YouTube platforms and *Dia Estúdio* (News Day) may have been much smaller than expected, the latter confirming 30,000 people connected at some point during the schedule of events. At the same time, a host of international corporations flocked to participate in the event, widening substantially its commercialization and amplifying its global partnerships. In addition to well-deserved credit acknowledging the NGO *APOLGBT SP* as the sole organizer and the financial support of São Paulo Governor and Mayor's Offices, the most generous co-sponsors include Burger King, which in 2010 was acquired by 3G of Brazil in a deal worth US$3.26 billion and was listed in official media communications as master sponsor ("*patrocinador master*"). Two further co-sponsors include the Dutch Amstel Lager and the U.S.-based Uber. Avon (headquartered in the United Kingdom) is noted as an additional co-sponsor with lower-scale support from Jean Paul Gaultier (France), Rainbow Doritos (Mexico), and Zendesk (the United States) and supplemental participation from Natura, Netflix, The Body Shop, Tinder, Universal Music, Bradesco, among others.

Claudia Garcia, president of the *APOLGBT*, launched the festivities stating rather ironically, "We are occupying this space of virtual expression. You are here participating in the Parade right now. We are making our voices heard. Our theme for this year is democracy, precisely because of everything that is happening. Imagine yourselves on Paulista Avenue. We are going to shout for democracy, against homophobia, against racism!"[16] This statement forces us to evaluate to what extent public expressions of protest or demonstration are democratically possible when observers are following from the safety and comfort of their homes instead of actively displacing themselves in order to gather collectively, organizing in solidarity on the streets for the right to be heard. How does one exercise democratic freedom while "occupying a space" online, symbolizing at its best an act of imagined solidarity based on creative visualization or even magical thinking while not confronting the reality that a contagious virus has spoken far louder than any combination of voices that would either register support for LGBT liberation and equality or express disdain for these communities? How does the terror of cross-contamination literally relegate the spectator to keep safely behind closet doors for fear of being a contagion or of becoming contaminated? What about the millions of Brazilian citizens who may not have access to sufficient broadband to be able to watch the Parade online? Is it a more democratic exercise of citizenship to afford expensive hi-tech devices and smartphones than to gather the few reais necessary to take a bus to and from the financial capital of Brazil to march for democracy? Fabrício Viana, the journalist responsible for the official online publications and communications of the *APOLGBT SP*, is a voice that appears in all the written archives of the NGO and is therefore cited extensively in the bibliography of this book. He records the *justificativa* (rationale) for the 2020 manifesto, writing: "On the surface we seem to be a democracy, but our words and practices do not reflect the theory. What we are seeing in Brazil is a police force that kills (and dies) more than anywhere else in the world, marches and protests being repressed, accusations without evidence, and a resurgence of dictatorship sympathizers."[17]

Thelma Assis, anesthesiologist from Limão, São Paulo, became a celebrity after winning the competition for the twentieth season of Big Brother Brazil's 2020 (BBB20) edition, highlighting the intersectionality between LGBT rights and the continued struggle for the equal treatment of Afro-Brazilian women, stating: "There are various intersections with the LGBT community that have to do with my own life story. These are extremely important alliances we have to use to unite to expose an extremely discriminatory society. I identify with Marielle [Franco], the black woman from the *favelas* (slums) that has to fight for her respect."[18] It is worth noting that Assis's success and popularity were not based on her medical skills or accomplishments that would defeat the odds of marginalization for being born an Afro-Brazilian women in São Paulo's *periferia* (ghettos). The superpower that distinguished Thelma Assis, as it turns out, was an extraordinary aptitude for dancing *samba*.

I am interested here in the paradoxical quest for revering ideals of democracy given the lack of any actual measured response, whether with words or any perceivable body language, to heed the *APOLGBT* director's call or the Thelma Assis's pleas for intersectionality. The "new normal" imposed upon human thoughts and behaviors may serve as a catalyst for lack of reciprocity and a move toward greater invisibility. To be clear, I am not challenging here the necessity of quarantine to adapt to and to combat dangerous public health circumstances that warrant self-protection and defense of others. But the consequential reality of being met by silence and anonymity that technology enables while clamoring for the continuation of democratic traditions in an increasingly conservative right-wing Brazilian milieu is a metaphor that speaks louder than any human protest or movement has the power to decry. What are the next steps in a fragile young Brazilian democracy that is literally condemned to masking itself as a prerequisite for accessing the freedom to speak and to act? Will a global pandemic that has already laid bare profound institutional racism and classism also widen gaps in access to citizens deprived of resources on the basis of the devastatingly undemocratic reality "on the ground"? Is this not reminiscent of Lívia Barbosa's definition of *jeitinho brasileiro* that all are equal but some are more equal than others? And if the masks come down and the virus relents, will homolesbotransphobia of contamination and the fascist perpetuation of gender ideology used to justify woeful discrimination on the basis of difference shed its virus more actively, continuing to thrive in a post-COVID quotidian? Or, as sources seem to corroborate at this time, will Brazil's health care professionals exercising their perceived responsibility to test vaccines developed in Russia, in China, or from the United States, be among the first to block the continuation of the virus with their very bodies so that multinational pharmaceutical companies can, once again, reap the benefits of neo-colonization and post-COVID coloniality—one that does not extract wealth like the traditional model but that alters and allocates health. How do we thank or think of the bodies of "volunteers" in the Global South who are flexing their democratic muscles to contain, sustain, and neutralize the virus in their own collective cells? Will the families and friends of these (s)heroes be the first to access vaccinations that could have potentially cost them their lives? Or will global economic markets and political arrangements encourage distribution patterns that would offer protection to the "First World" first and then recirculate uncontaminated air to the rest?

Chapter 4

Looking Them Up (and Down): What (Homo)sexuality Means in Brazilian Reference Works

Puta /ˈpu.ta/
A whore, a prostitute.
A cis-woman who likes sex or just happens to be caught up while doing it.
A transwoman, period. A lesbian woman, according to cis-men.
A disqualifying adjective—either the woman has or has not engaged in sex.
What we desperately try not to be.
A threat.

Ironically, in some Brazilian cities *puta* is also an intensifier meaning *huge*, *impressive*,
   or *impactful*.
Uma puta festa, a hell of a party.
Uma puta mulher, a great woman.

A magnitude of anger.
Tô puta! I am pissed off!

You, me, them, us.
Para o movimento de putas no Brasil e em todo mundo.
   —Aline Fantinatti, "An Analysis of *Puta Dei 6*: A Sex Worker-led Platform for
       Social and Political Transformation," MA Thesis, Utrecht, 2019

Much like the chapters dedicated to analyzing and assessing the (f)utility of language to create a conflicted idea of utopian freedom in a carnivalesque atmosphere where extreme violence invades those idyllic spaces, this chapter takes up similar ethical and theoretical considerations. At the core of our analysis are the following dilemmas: How do we define, understand, or problematize the relationship between reference-type manuals (whether didactic or satiric in nature) on sexual culture and the development of *popular* notions of both mainstream and diverse or divergent homosexualities in present-day popular culture? How may we understand the paradoxical positioning of viewing encyclopedic and therefore hegemonic sources under a critical lens informed by queer theory? Finally, is it possible to utilize the inherent limit-lessness of queer theory to examine and critique the reference genre, the most finite (and confined) of all literary genres? To help address these specific theoretical questions, I examine three contemporary controversial literary releases in Brazil, all "passing" as reference books or, more precisely, as instruction manuals. These texts have staked out their right to be "politically incorrect" and attempt—rhetorically at least—to inscribe themselves as infor-mational yet subversive "manuals" that pertain to sexuality and to talking about sexual themes in a Brazilian context.

The first is *Manual do Podólatra Amador: Aventuras & leituras de um tarado por pés*, which I loosely translate as *Manual of an Amateur Foot Fetishist: Adventures and Readings of a Man Obsessed with Feet*, written by Glauco Mattoso, published in 1986, and re-released in a new amplified edi-tion in 2006. At no point in the work does the protagonist self-identify as gay, straight, or bisexual. In fact, he chooses not to label his orientation altogether, projecting himself in the role of foot fetishist regardless of the gender of the individual who becomes the object of his desire. While an attraction toward women is never articulated in Mattoso's highly homoerotic poetry, the genre which constitutes the bulk of his impressive corpus, it is a significant com-ponent in both the development of the *Manual of an Amateur Foot Fetishist*, which he labels as his "sexual autobiography," and the *Aventuras de Glau-comix, o Podólatra (The Adventures of Glaucomics, the Foot Fetishist)*, the comic-book adaptation written four years later. Mattoso's development of the Japanese-Brazilian character of Sílvia serves as an interesting example of fetishism that is not confined to a particular gender and may therefore echo the voice of a pansexual protagonist seeking a sexual partner who transcends membership to a singular gender identity.

While the text is critically acclaimed by a select few,[1] it serves as merely a footnote of an "outrageous" poet's eccentricity to other critics, who continue to designate it as "marginal," applying normative labels such as "the most bizarre book in the history of Brazilian erotic literature." Even the sparse criticism that exists, in the form of David William Foster's assessment of Mattoso's piece, which appeared in *Cultural Diversity in Latin American Literature*, is preoccupied with exploring various levels of outrageousness, both with respect to Mattoso's themes and his "unrepentant, unmediated" style of expression. Foster points to the liberalization of the "carnivalization" of sexual signifiers evident in Mattoso's autobiography. In addition, Foster alludes to the fundamental sense of "symbolic humiliation" within the realm of sadomasochism, by which Mattoso infers the need to separate real physi-cal suffering from sexual (role-)play. Foster essentially contends that the work's fetishistic obsession with feet reasserts the "outrageous" nature of the text. This critic, therefore, is not convinced that Mattoso has succeeded in depathologizing the revisionist eroticism that he proposes. In his concluding remarks, Foster maintains that the *Manual do Podólatra Amador* succeeds in its "degendering of erotic pleasure, in its rejection of sex as masculine or feminine role playing" (71). Hence, I contend that this text is queer in its very nature.

An alternative reading that Butterman offers in the book *Perversions on Parade: Brazilian Literature of Transgression and Postmodern Anti-Aesthetics in Glauco Mattoso* observes that the "transgressive" themes of fetishism and sadomasochism—while interesting in and of themselves—are actually symbolic of a much larger and far more complex enterprise that Mattoso sought to undertake. The *Manual* successfully served some read-ers as an excellent *desabafo*, an outlet and possible affirmation of their own sexual desires as different from the proscribed hetero and, equally oppressive, homonormative phallocentric (in the literal sense of compulsory genital-oriented) discourses. Going further than simply expanding the landscape of sexual diversity beyond the obsessive motif of penetration, the tired trope of active and passive distinctions that still characterize much of popular notions of sexuality in Latin American contexts, Mattoso's pseudo-autobiographical discourse follows the sexual conquests and misadventures of a narrator who, between the lines (underneath and on top of them), manages to denounce and debunk sexual and physical violence in a society (in this case, the mega-lopolis of São Paulo, Brazil) inundated with hypocritical sexual, and more specifically, homosexual mores.

Ultimately, one of the most radical goals of Mattoso's project is to mock monolithic notions of "heterosexuality," in its singular form, and play with alternate constructions of masculinities and femininities. Of course, this ten-dency occurs quite frequently in queer writing. However, the queerness of Mattoso's enterprise is demonstrated more precisely in rejecting stereotypic sex roles and even eroding the erotic power of the phallus, thereby satirizing and subverting a hegemonic construction of conventional homosexuality. The only normalization that Mattoso's literary universe purports to accomplish is to establish the valorization of sexual fetishes while simultaneously uphold-ing their supposed "perversity." As such, the *Manual do Podólatra Amador*, as is the case with much of Mattoso's work, is engaged in a productively con-tradictory process of depathologizing sexual "deviance" while, at the same time, praising the transformative political power of perversity.

Mattoso's *Manual* is indeed instructive in a variety of ways. In it, he objectifies the erotically charged foot (stepping in, as it were, for the phal-lus) to decenter a phallogocentric culture of sexual expression, to degender eroticism, and to depathologize fetishistic sexual behaviors. In this process of assuming and glorifying sexual practices historically viewed as perverse, the author symbolically uses humiliation and degradation to denounce the realities of physical torture and violence toward minority sexualities in contemporary Brazilian culture. The *Manual* teaches its readers to embrace more versatile and fluid conceptualizations of sexualities. Destabilizing the binary roles of "the sex act" leads to the radicalization of the subject who, from the standpoint of the margins, articulates a subversive voice of social critique. The resulting performance is that of an artist unjustly denied recognition simply on the basis of his own out-rage-ousness. For an in-depth discussion of Glauco Mattoso's revisionist eroticism, I would like to refer the reader to chapter five of *Perversions on Parade: Brazilian Literature of Transgression and Postmodern Anti-Aesthetics* (181–230).

A second reference work is one which I place at the heart of the questions raised at the beginning of this chapter. *Aurélia: A Dicionária da Língua Afiada* (*The Dictionary of the Sharp Tongue*), in literal translation to English, or alternatively and more colorfully, *The Dictionary of the Slick [or perhaps Sassy] Tongue*), was released in May 2006, on the eve of the Tenth Annual *Parada de Orgulho LGBT* in São Paulo and, of course, marketed precisely for this occasion. As the reader shall recall, the previous three chapters performed a detailed analysis of media representations of this significant sociopolitical event and that 2006 was a pivotal year for this record-breaking phenomenon. This deceptively succinct volume of 143 pages contains terms and phrases from all regions of Brazil and nearly the entire Lusophone world, including Portugal, Cape Verde, Angola, Mozambique, and even the islands of São Tomé e Príncipe. The book begins with a sort of pseudo-disclaimer, one whose validity or even sincerity we shall evaluate in the pages to come: "This dictionary does not have the pretension of being politically correct. Many of the terms are dirty and pejorative and may be offensive to certain people or groups. If that is the case, we recommend that this reading be interrupted immediately" (5).[2]

The *Dicionária*'s co-authors, Angelo Vip and Fred Libi, are two gay white males whose authorship is semi-closeted behind the literary privilege of the tradition of utilizing pseudonyms. In the introduction to the text, the reader discovers that "the work is the product of ten years of research by Angelo Vip [pseudonym of the journalist Vitor Angelo] and of Fred Libi" (10),[3] later revealing further that "Fred Libi prefers not to identify himself, defining himself in the work as a 'gay man from birth who sought refuge in his studies to try to understand a world that treated him with hostility'" (32).[4] Much in the tradition of Mattoso's anti-traditional *Manual*, the work claims to invoke a "politically incorrect" and irreverent spirit using a single, simple, but highly problematic grammatical strategy: the feminization of canonical, mainstream reference icons. This process is clearly present, for example, in the gender reassignment of *Aurélio*, one of the fathers of the Brazilian dictionary industry, equivalent perhaps to *Merriam-Webster* in the Anglophone world, to its new queer incarnation of *Aurélia*. There are multiple and multivalent meanings of *Aurélia* in Brazilian slang, the most significant of which are highlighted in the dictionary itself): *Aurélia*: "(1). Nosy faggot who is quite fluent in the language of *bajubá*, swearing to know everything; (2). Philological, lexicological, eloquent faggot . . . loquacious and extremely amusing; (3). Rich faggot, owner of an island, who fearlessly buys her husbands; (4). My ass: Expression used to designate indignation, denial or disdain" (21).[5]

Further evidence of both the political gesture and the ludic playfulness of gender inversion is the reassignment of the *Editora do Bispo*, the actual publisher of the text, having transitioned to *Editora **da Bispa***, appearing on the book's front cover as well as its title page. Even the preface of the book has been transformed into *A Prefácia*," which features a highly pompous and pseudo-pedantic introduction by Dr. A. Jaccourd, a supposedly renowned Saussaurean linguist from the University of São Paulo, whose very image is mocked with a drawing featuring a profile of a bearded, suited professor reading an unlabeled document in an armchair, surrounded by shelves of tomes (only two of which are inscribed with incomplete and barely readable titles, fragments of which are unsurprisingly noted in English), an obsolete typewriter and a large fluffy teddy bear on his lap. The professor's wall is adorned by an enormous portrait of Carmen Miranda.

I argue that the playful manipulation of language, quite common in both Latin American and Latinx contexts, may actually have serious social and political consequences. The danger of this entertaining and liberating piece resides in its own grammar. Our closer examination will soon reveal that the text, rather than subverting heteronormative linguistic and, more specifically, semantic patterns, often serves to reinforce a hegemonic and monolithic view of homosexuality inscribed with racist, classist and, at times, even misogynist undertones. For instance, the definition of *bofe* (bofe = butch or macho man often considering himself heterosexual if he sexually "dominates" another man) reads *Homem heterossexual ou homossexual ativo* (homem heterossexual = straight man homossexual ativo = the "top" or partner who penetrates the *bicha* (bottom or passive) partner), thereby perpetuating the now-ancient binary and often homophobic dichotomy of "active" versus "passive," of top = straight versus bottom = gay, reinforcing the roles of the so-called *bofe* and the *bicha* rather than inscribing them with new—and less oppressive if not more diverse—potentialities. To be fair, though, it is important to recognize that these dichotomous designations are still in frequent use today, and certainly not exclusively in Brazil (or elsewhere in Latin America, for that matter).

As innovative as it is problematic, the *Dicionária* was not the first tongue-in-cheek resource to publish an encyclopedic compilation of Brazilian Portuguese terms and phrases associated with homosexuality. A clear precedent is Orocil Pedreira Santos Júnior's *Bichonário: um dicionário gay*, published in Salvador da Bahia at the end of 1996 and containing approximately 750 entries. The term *bichonário* is a humorous euphemism referring, of course, to the noun *bicha*, defined before. The reference text appears to be aesthetically packaged more seriously, as it were, than the *Dicionária*, featuring a brief preface by Marta Suplicy, at that time federal deputy of the *Partido dos Trabalhadores* (*PT*), the Workers' Party, and credited with the professional designation of "sexologist" at the end of the preface. The invitation for the preface is not surprising, given that the book received cultural and financial support from a variety of local (Salvador) political organizations connected to progressive political parties associated with the *PT*, such as the *Central Única dos Trabalhadores* (*CUT*). The reader may recall that in chapters 1 and 2, I comment extensively on Marta Suplicy's contradictory political discourses and interviews during the first fifteen years of the *Parada de Orgulho LGBT de São Paulo*.

While the *Dicionária*'s illustrations, as we shall see, are considerably ludic in nature, the *Bichonário* features in its pages eighteen artistic representations of eroticism and sensuality throughout centuries of Western art, mostly Italian and German in origin, including black-and-white reproductions of internationally celebrated paintings by Michelangelo, Botticeli, Pietro Perugino, Brozino Agnolo, Antony van Dyck, Ticiano, Luca Signorelli, Parmigiano Francesco Mazzola, Orazio Gentileschi, Rafael, Jacopo Tintoretto, Giovanni Luttri, Andrea Mantegna, Bartholomeus Spranger, Albecht Durer, and Joseph Heintz. Also interspersed throughout the text are apparently random quotations and excerpts attributed to a wide variety of internationally renowned writers and philosophers, such as Marcel Proust, Simone de Beauvoir, Erasmus of Rotterdam, Fyodor Dostoevsky, Dante, the Marquis du Sade, and even Albert Einstein. In the majority of cases, these citations emphasize the importance of freedom, harmony, laughter (even if ironic), self-knowledge, and love. The inclusion of an excerpt from an occasional Brazilian poet, such as Carlos Drummond de Andrade, João da Cruz e Sousa, the poet-musician Caetano Veloso, and the activist-journalist João Silvério Trevisan, is paramount in a work that claims to take pride in the Brazilian creative ingenuity for developing colorful neologisms and the rich malleability of the Portuguese language while constantly gazing north to Europe to praise cultural and artistic manifestations of eroticism in foreign sources.

This brochure-style guide, unlike the *Dicionária*, also features a pragmatic and overtly sociopolitical intention to involve the reader in learning more about LGBT topics and even in joining activities and events designed for this community. The appendix marked *Dicas* ("Hints") includes lists of cultural artifacts, a bibliography of scholarly works, gay or gay-friendly bars, clubs, saunas, and hotels throughout Brazil, local and national political organizations in Salvador and beyond, Brazilian beaches, landmarks, and locations for cruising, and even a single travel agency, curiously located in Curitiba. These lists, while somewhat useful and well-intended, are also arguably discriminatory, inadvertently or not. For example, the first category features a succinct list of some eight *filmes* (movies), appearing in alphabetical order by title in Portuguese: "The Adventures of Priscilla, Queen of the Desert," "Wedding Banquet," "Philadelphia," "Male Prostitutes," "Strawberry and Chocolate," "The Priest," "Orlando," and "Boys in the Band." This "master list" precedes a subsequent separate list of eight additional "Lesbian Movies," the title of the category itself appearing in English, followed by a virtually unknown list of obscure films in Portuguese translation: "Soulmates," "Love and Human Remains," "Even Cowgirls Get Sad," "The Perfect Pair," "Serving in Silence," "Sister My Sister," "Only Them," and "A Bed for Three." This gesture, while potentially useful, is problematic in various ways. In fact, the categorical separation itself is rather disappointing. First, a reader would logically interpret the list of *filmes* retrospectively as gay male-themed since it occurs independently from "Lesbian Movies." This reference appears to be "the" hegemonic list, not only because of its placement as first but also because the films included are distinguished from films that are exclusively "lesbian" in nature. Clearly, there are films on the first list of eight that develop motifs around bisexual characters and others that are trans-themed and involve gender identity rather than portraying sexual orientation. Another problem is that the first list of *filmes* includes feature-length productions from Australia, Cuba, and Great Britain, in addition to the United States. The second list of "Lesbian Movies," on the contrary, features titles that are largely unknown, if not entirely invisible, to the average spectator, symptomatic too of the erasure of women. This discrepancy is certainly not unique to the *Bichonário*. In patriarchal societies, homosexuality has been read—and is often still interpreted—as gay male-focused, resulting in the marginalization of other sexual minorities, in particular of lesbian identities. Nevertheless, it is problematic for a reference work of any caliber to perpetuate a system which, even from within the LGBT community, categorically omits women during its task to record and refer the reader to cultural products that supposedly mark or represent all sexual and gender identity minorities.

At the current time, the *Dicionária* is one of the most complete reference guides on the topic of LGBT language in the Lusophone world, with 143 pages and 1,300 entries, at a special price of R$24 (approximately US$11.00 at the time it was published), which is both affordable and symbolic, for the number represents the figure of the deer in the *Jogo do Bicho*, whose image also adorns each of the page numbers of the text. The image of the *veado*, the deer, is significant in the context of contemporary Brazilian popular culture. The deer was born in the Brazilian "animal lottery" game, a technically illegal but widely disseminated gambling game. In Brazil, the number twenty-four is associated with homosexuals due to the number representing the deer. The word *viado* (an intentional misspelling of *veado*) was adopted as a slang term to signify a homosexual, perhaps because of its docile features or graceful femininity, but one which generally carries pejorative connotations. We shall return to the image of the deer in the second half of this chapter, as we explore some of the key illustrations in the work.

The antagonistic reaction to the news of the release of the highly imagina-tive *Dicionária* meant that the work would almost never come into existence. The publisher and authors were threatened with potential lawsuits from the widow of Aurélio Buarque de Hollanda, who died in 1989, and *A Positivo*, which publishes *Aurélio*. Capitalism was mixed with implicit homophobia, both displayed under the guise of a legal desire to protect the brand. André Caldeira, marketing director for the publisher, argued: "I would take all the appropriate legal measures to defend the brand. I want to make it very clear that this action does not constitute homophobia. It's about protecting a trade-mark." According to Caldeira, it would be a "misrepresentation of the name." "They are grabbing a free ride on a very important institution."[6]

Ivan Junqueira, a member of the distinguished *Academia Brasileira de Letras* (Brazilian Academy of Letters), was even more outraged, stating: "It is interesting that a Dictionary of gay expressions exists in Brazil. I just think that they took the joke too far and really let us down. *Aurélio* is a Brazilian institution."[7] Implicit in Junqueira's assessment is the unstated but inferred belief that institutions to protect civil rights and cultural diversity are less important in Brazil than the legal rights of a powerful family who tried to impede the release of the *Dicionária*. To be fair, though, the opposition to the work may have been prompted by its objection to appropriating a canonical "brand" to publish a piece on sexual themes and vocabulary (and not neces-sarily homosexuality specifically), provoking a negative aesthetic judgment based on a hegemonic and classist view of topics considered "low culture," thus contaminating what has traditionally been conceived as a marker of dis-tinction and sophistication.

At the end of the day, then, the threats of a possible lawsuit were dropped, and the attempts of the family of the late philologist Aurélio Buarque de Holanda to halt the launching of the text proved unsuccessful. The proper name *Aurélio* had already been *dicionarizado* as an adjective long before the *Dicionária* had come into being. Therefore, the term itself had been popularized and resignified, already connoting multiple meanings before the *Dicionária* was published. *Aurélia, a Dicionáia da língua afiada* finally emerged in mainstream booksellers in the city of São Paulo, barely escaping censorship on the supposed basis of copyright violations.

When pondering the power of such texts to shape popular ideas about minority sexualities, another important question to consider is their degree of feasibility. Is a "manual" of this nature a viable resource—comedic or not, serious or satiric—to describe or outline a sexual culture so diverse and contradictory? A significant work in cultural anthropology, Richard G. Parker's *Beneath the Equator: Cultures of Desire, Male Homosexuality, and Emerging Gay Communities in Brazil* confirms that "the essence of gay identity" cannot be found when examining homosexuality in Brazil in contemporary Brazil. Indeed, there is astounding complexity involved when undertaking any study of Brazilian homosexualities, as a result of a multitude of factors of change brought about by redemocratization; the neoliberal restructuring of post-*Abertura* Brazilian life; and the appropriation of international gay styles, music, clothing fashions, and symbols. This combination of numerous influences on modern queer *brasilidade*, if you will, has led Parker to conclude the following: "The fragmentation in what was once perceived as a relatively monolithic gay community has become apparent, as a growing cacophony of diverse gay, lesbian, bisexual, queer and transgender voices have loudly announced themselves—and any pretense to a unified gay or lesbian identity has increasingly slipped away" (229).

Given the difficulty if not impossibility of monolithically characterizing "the gay community" as a consolidated entity anywhere in the world, we can only imagine the challenges involved in attempting to define any unified sense of "gay and lesbian language." In 1979, sociolinguists Julia Penelope and S.J. Wolfe wrote that the following:

> Any discussion involving the use of such phrases as "gay community," "gay slang," or "gayspeak" is bound to be misleading, because two of its implications are false: first, that there is a homogeneous community composed of Lesbians and gay males, that shares a common culture or system of values, goals, perceptions, and experience; and second, that this gay community shares a common language.

We must not overlook that there are, of course, additional layers of ambiguity inherent in Brazilian sexual semantics; for instance, the theorization of the complex conceptualizations of the terms *brincadeira* and *sacanagem* in the context of Brazilian sexual play and innocent child play. The Portuguese verb *brincar* and its noun forms *brincadeira* and *brinquedo* convey the sense of "to play" or "playfulness" or "toy." The term is multi-faceted and psychoanalytically rich, most importantly because it blurs boundaries between the innocent child-like playfulness and the sexual play or bedroom experimentation that may occur, while one's "playing" coincides with sexual development. As a point of comparison, this highly charged, multivalent term, when it appears in *A Dicionária*, is entirely stripped both of its innocence and of its playfulness. According to this source, the term is given merely two synonymous meanings: *transar* and *foder*, "to engage in sexual intercourse and to fuck."

With the objective of explaining the highly problematic term of *sacanagem* in contemporary Brazilian popular culture, some of Richard Parker's earlier work has attempted to define its many angles, most notably his groundbreaking study from 1991, *Bodies, Pleasures, and Passions: Sexual Culture in Contemporary Brazil*. However, in order to hear the voice of the "native informant," especially when it speaks so comprehensively of the innuendos and multiple meanings of slang and idiomatic expressions, I now refer our attention to a fourth "reference-style book," which, while space constraints do not allow detailed evaluation in this chapter, is useful to expand our perspectives on the multiplicity of *sacanagem*: Glauco Mattoso's *Dicionarinho do Palavrão & Correlatos: inglês—português, português—inglês*, published in 1990. In it, Mattoso relates at least four distinct conceptions of the term. The first category includes, among other similar adjectives, "depravity, lasciviousness, libidinousness, debauchery, filth, lewdness, lust, and smuttiness." This is sexual *sacanagem* at its most refinely base. An alternative meaning, sub-classified as *mau caráter/patifaria* (bad character/shamelessness), includes the words "rascality, double-cross, low blow, dirty trick, and dirty work," therefore exploiting the term for its lack of playfulness and, instead, denoting deception, deceit, structural violence, and corruption that the term *sacanagem* may also imply in other contexts. A third set of meanings is categorized as *literatura de sacanagem*, which includes, according to Mattoso's conception, "JO [jack-off] literature, written pornography, and rough stuff" (170–1).

Returning now to the gender question raised earlier, I would like to examine more closely the utility or futility of the process whereby words and phrases are feminized to attain a subversive effect. Does such a superficial transformation actually "queer" the text at all? In his astoundingly still relevant 1941 text "The Language of Homosexuality: An American Glossary," Gershon Legman wrote the following:

> A very common usage in the speech of male homosexuals is the substitution of feminine pronouns and titles for properly masculine ones. Male homosexuals use the terms *she, her, hers, Miss, Mother,* and *girl* (almost never "woman") in referring to themselves and each other, where one might expect "he," "him," "his," "Mr," "Father," and "man" (or "boy"). This usage is sometimes rather confusingly carried over to references to heterosexuals, though an overtone, in such cases of jocularity or mild contempt usually serves to mark the heterosexuality of the person referred to. (Legman, 1155; Cameron & Kulick, 82)

I think it is important to quote the entire definition/usage of the article "*a*," which, naturally, is the first term to appear in the *Dicionária*: "In the gay world, the feminine definite article often precedes common masculine nouns, such that the noun itself is also transformed, if possible, to a feminine form, therefore creating a neologism" (16).[8] Interviews with drag queens related in a March 7, 2007 article in the *Folha de S. Paulo* entitled "*São Paulo vira*

capital do 'gay carão' " ("São Paulo becomes the capital of the 'gay snob'")
clearly confirm that this phenomenon of queer Brazilian subculture is still
very much in vogue today, from popular drag icons Divina Núbia to Paulette
Pink to Silvetty Montilla. In their comments in the following, attempting to
define the term *bicha carão* and this figure's notoriety in contemporary São
Paulo, one cannot help but notice the consistent use of the feminine terms to
refer to this "class" of gay men. The emphasis in the original text is my own,
meant to point out the feminization of nouns, virtually untranslatable in the
English version in the following:

> For Paulette Pink, the "snob" is eternally lonely and miserable. "Deep inside, they
> are insecure, full of an inferiority complex. For that reason, they create this façade
> of being gorgeous girls, who don't need anyone else, but the reality is that they
> are ridiculous and needy. Faggot, take off your high heels," she instigates. Silvetty
> Montilla reveals the false glamour of the category of gay men. "The snob will
> never give a penny. They spend the entire night drinking water or sipping just one
> drink, and they return home all alone. They need to be more humble." According
> to Divina Núbia: "They are not very prudent in the saunas. They refuse to wear
> flip-flops. They cause a stink if there is one brand of beer missing in the bar.
> They turn away, making a nasty glance, when someone who is not of their level
> dares to flirt with them. They prefer to share a three-bedroom apartment in a chic
> neighborhood with eight other faggots than to live in 'downtown decadence.'"[9]

The *Dicionária* defines the term *carão* as "*pose* (pretentious); *esnobação*
(snobbery); *presunção*" (presumptuousness) (40). My analysis will attempt
to show that the class-conscious *bicha-carão* is not only present in but dominates the discourse of the *Dicionária* itself, a character type who, despite his
own marginalization as gay, often engages in classist, racist, and misogynist
judgments leading to discrimination. As the same article in the *Folha de S.
Paulo* contends, "São Paulo is the Brazilian capital of the 'gay snob,'" claim
the most well-traveled drag queens in the city. In slang, '*carão*' means
affected, snobbish, and blasé. She sees herself as unique, superior. She does
not walk, She parades. . . . **she despises poor people, black people, and
Brazilians from the northeast. She humiliates waiters, doormen, security
guards, maids**" (emphasis mine).[10]

Of course, there are serious problems associated with this ironic process of
feminization. Inverted language proved to be embarrassing for U.S. activists
when the gay liberation movements began to form in the 1950s and 1960s,
indicative of the assimilationist model of the academic discipline of "gay and
lesbian studies" during its incipient stages. This perspective paralleled the
strategies of the political movement of the day, holding that gays and lesbians are productive, "normal," tax-paying citizens just like their heterosexual
counterparts, whether or not they fulfill any of the "flamboyant" stereotypes

attributed to them (the latter generally discouraged). Perhaps this reaction, in a specifically Brazilian context, may be attributed to a combination of social class differential and the universal, almost archetypal presence of the *bicha carão*. As Deborah Cameron and Don Kulick write, in their 2003 book on *Language and Sexuality*: "The fact that the inversions and much of the vocabulary were predominantly employed by homosexuals who were either **working-class** or **upper-class** made such language even more unacceptable to the middle-class gay men and lesbians who were struggling to create a new social role, and win mainstream tolerance and acceptance of homosexuality" (83; emphasis mine).

The gender play discussed earlier brings us to another problem: Exploiting the feminization of words to exhibit queer language does not represent how lesbians use language. In fact, this process may ironically result in the exclusion and oppression of women, particularly those of homosexual orientation. According to sociolinguistics scholar Julia Penelope, "The slang that writers insisted was homosexual slang was *male* homosexual slang; lesbians did not use it. In other words, they were at once both too (gentle)manly and too womanly to want to talk about sex or take 'flamboyant' liberty with pronouns" (86). Cameron and Kulick pose a rather disturbing paradox, presenting the following contradiction: "Affirming lesbian identity and increasing the cultural visibility of lesbianism were major preoccupations for activists in the 1980s. So why was there no concerted attempt to show that lesbians too had a language of their own? Are lesbians different from gay men in this respect, and, if so, what explains the difference?" (96). In other words, why do lesbian women, in general, not engage in gender crossing as a resource for signaling non-heterosexual identity? I would argue that the simple gesture of asking this question may inadvertently invoke a discourse of masculinist privilege—although of the homosexual persuasion—that would coerce women to conform to typically—or, more precisely, stereotypically—male conventions, even at the most basic level of language. We must recognize that as linguists have confirmed over the course of various decades "linguistic gender inversion, for particular historical and cultural reasons, has become iconic of **male** homosexuality" (89; emphasis mine). Indeed, in a patriarchal system where sexism is perceptibly when not insidiously reinforced with the very language we use to communicate, imprisoning words within the confines of binary structures and dualistic dichotomies, it would seem that any question that would implicitly or overtly attempt to draw a gender divide between "male" language and "female" language would inevitably default to a masculinist discourse, either by domination or by comparison, and is therefore doomed to failure. It is for this reason, in part, that North American feminists began, around 1979, to engage in alternate orthographies of the term "women" to disentangle the female gender from its implicit connection to "(-)men."

Vicki Nogle's groundbreaking essay, "Lesbianfeminist Rhetoric as a Social Movement," was one of the first pieces to both colloquialize and dissociate the term, which she re-semanticizes as "wimmin." Other feminists in the era joined this mission to assert agency for self-definition, creating various alternate spellings of "woman," the most common of which is "womyn." Around the same time, Louie Crew proposed an alternative reading on the effects and consequences of feminizing parts of speech as part of "gayspeak," arguing that cross-gender identification does not parody or mock women, but is used as an instrument to defy heterosexual culture and restore a sense of pride in this difference, which, in his view, defines as feminine all males who do not desire sexual intercourse with a woman. Nevertheless, women of any sexual orientation pay the price for the perpetuation of misogynist stereotypes, intentional or not. It is fair to mention that even the genesis of the term "gayspeak," first used in the late 1970s and widely attributed to Joseph J. Hayes, in his pioneering article of the same title, where he intentionally excludes women from the analysis, with the following dismissive disclaimer placed in a footnote: "Although I refer in several places to the language of both gay men and women, I am speaking primarily about gay *men*. My experience in the lesbian community is not sufficient to delineate a special dialect among gay women" (Footnote 3, 319). Nowhere in his research does Hayes grapple with the question of why such a study may not exist or the implications of this invisibility for women of any sexual orientation.

Deliberate exclusion and consequently the silencing of lesbian linguistic codes is also a significant shortcoming of the *Dicionária*. Unfortunately, erasure of cultural representations of homosexual women is exacerbated by an even more serious problem. Due to gross generalizations, we often encounter moments when the language borders—intentionally or not—on misogyny and even homophobia. In an interview with the book's co-author published in the *Folha de S. Paulo* on May 29, 2006, Angelo Vip claims that the merits of his encyclopedic source go well beyond that of merely a reference work, asserting the problematic observation that there may actually be a linkage between "gayspeak" in Brazil and the "way" that heterosexual women speak: "Besides the cataloguing of gay expressions, the book may be useful in helping parents understand what their children are saying. And also so masculine straight men may be able to better understand the phrases used by their girlfriends, since many [straight] women speak like gay men."[11] If there is no gender-crossing "gayspeak" per se (i.e., language that unites gay men and lesbian women), can one propose a linkage between gay male speech and straight female speech? If so, what are the implications of tracing this connection? Do gay men, in the process of "succumbing" to feminized language, end up losing their masculinity along the way? If this is the case, in a process whereby gay men surrender their privileges and obligations as card-carrying *machões*, does their collective speech truly become incompre-hensible or at least irrelevant to a straight male audience? The underlying question that continues to linger, without any apparent resolution, is the fol-lowing: Where, if anywhere, do gay women fit into this project of linguistic re-gendering? During an interview with co-author Fred Libi, I asked if he thought the content of the *Dicionária* privileged gay male identity. His brief response was quite revealing: "*Sim, é que as sapas não fazem tanto humor quanto as bibas . . . Elas são mais sérias.*" While it is nearly impossible to provide a translation of the statement, due to the use of Brazilian slang, the response reads roughly: "Yes, it does, because lesbos are not as funny as fags. They [the women] are more serious." This reflection, on the relative lack of seriousness of gay-identified men and therefore the potential to exploit humor as a strategy for resistance, is an interesting, if troubling, admission that gay women and their language are intentionally excluded or, worse, made invis-ible in the pages of a text that claims to (re)present the *universo gay* (back cover), politically incorrectly or not.

These provocative questions lead us to a larger and entirely ironic final question: Is this admittedly politically incorrect LGBT dictionary an inad-vertently, if not internalized, homophobic text? In order to appreciate the significance of this question, I would like to evaluate an additional comment made by Angelo Vip, critically examine certain specific terms and phrases that are cited in the pages of the *Dicionária* and how they are defined. Then I will carefully study the illustrations that adorn its pages, and finally, evalu-ate whether or not this question is unique or bears special applicability to a specifically Brazilian context. To do so, I will briefly consider the body of work that has emerged mainly in a North American context surrounding the language of "gayspeak."

Let us first consider an important passage that reveals the central premise of Didier Eribon's *Insult and the Making of the Gay Self*: "Historically speak-ing, the repression of homosexuality has nourished the determination toward self-expression. But inversely, that expression has shaped itself to the modes of thought that despised it. My attempt here is to study the imbrication of gay speech and homophobic discourse" (7). One of the motivations for Eribon's project is reflected in a comment like the following one made by Angelo Vip: "Producing a politically correct gay book would not be interesting at all. And also, to have to be labeled as 'gay' is a lousy thing. It's *viado*, it's *bicha* [Brazil-ian slang terms for "faggot," and, more specifically, the passive, or "bottom" partner in the sexual act of anal intercourse]. Many groups insist on calling this 'homosexuality,' which is annoying."[12] While the term "homosexuality" is often criticized as too medicalized or sanitized, or perhaps even too formal in a Brazilian context, the aggressive rejection of its usage may in itself be con-strued as homophobic. This implicit homophobia seems to resonate throughout the pages of the *Dicionária*. There are various instances, in both verbiage and graphic illustrations, in which queers become the object of ridicule and condescension. A clear example of this occurs in the definition of the term *piti*, which the authors conceive as follows: "*Nervosismo, histeria, ataque de bichice*" (106; "Nervousness, neurotic behavior, hysteria, a faggot attack"). A second example is the definition of the phrase, "*ataque epilésbico*" ("epilesbian attack"), which, according to the *Dicionária*, refers to the *nervosismo das lésbicas e à vontade de fazer um barraco em público* (the neurotic nature of lesbians and to the desire to make a scene in a public space). Alternatively, in its second definition, the phrase connotes a supposedly characteristic "lesbian" epileptic attack, exploited for its nationalistic slant: "*Atitude petulante das sapas em pedir ao DJ para tocar MPB durante uma festa animada e chique*" (21; "The compulsion of dykes to ask the DJ to play Brazilian Popular Music during a fun and *chic* party").

Due to space constraints, I have chosen only a handful of specific terms and expressions from the *Dicionária*, with the hope of illustrating more concretely the problems and issues I have raised earlier. If this text aims to attain the status of a reference resource, while at the same time valorizing both the inventiveness and the humor of the phrases that abound in its pages, it is worthwhile to ponder to what degree is LGBT language being "refereed" from a source that claims to speak for such communities. At the same time, if a liberating premise of social justice and embracement of queer creativity is at the core of such a project, the critical reader must ethically engage in the analysis of the messages that certain "definitions" convey. Is it acceptable, for example, to legitimate sexism, racism, and/or classism while embracing a celebration of queer language? For example, the term "*África*," recognized in the text as a regionalism within the state of São Paulo, is defined as"*cansativo; chato; difícil*" (17; "Cumbersome; annoying; difficult"). This definition would certainly point to both a regional and quite possibly racist bias within the lexicon of the *paulista* LGBT community. What are the classist and racist implications in a definition wherein an entire continent is read as tiresome, weary, and bothersome? Striving for further clarity, though receiving greater complexity, I devised an informal questionnaire to "test" the accuracy and validity of the *Dicionária*'s terms at the *Feira Cultural* on May 22, 2008, an event which immediately proceeds the *Parada de Orgulho LGBT de São Paulo* (see Appendix for the content of the questionnaire). One of my findings is that not a single respondent of any sexual orientation or gender identity "correctly" defined the term *África* in accordance with the text's description. A significant majority of blank responses were the most common, followed by *não sei* or *desconheço* (I don't know or I am unfamiliar) in second place, *negro, ou referente ao universo negro* (Black or referring to the Afro-Brazilian universe) in third place, a reference to *continente sub-desenvolvido* (underdeveloped continent), and, finally, a singular *país* (country).

A second revealing example is the offensive manner in which the text defines the expression *bi-curious*: "A type of queeny faggot who tries to pass for bisexual on the Internet because one time, in a particularly exaggerated affected moment, she rubbed up against her fag hag [or perhaps 'fruit fly' in more contemporary urban American slang] beginning to feel a little hetero" (32).[13] Homophobic slurs aside, which are actually hard to discard in a description as blatantly insulting as this one, essentially denies the possibility of the existence of bisexual orientation. Laden with homophobia as it is with biphobia, the "definition," likely meant to be humorous, is also extremely sexist. Why is it that the "bi-curious" persona mocked in the description is automatically gendered as male and the "friend" is gendered and sexualized as a heterosexual female? The implication is that there is no such thing as a bisexual, implying that men who have sex with men and occasionally with women are fooling themselves. Besides these problems, clearly "bi-curious," while taken from its original English-language form (since it is not translated in the text), has a significantly different meaning in a North American context. Contemporary U.S. slang ascribes meaning to the expression as an individual (of any sexual orientation and/or gender identity) who is willing or curious to investigate his or her own sexuality, discovering the possibility of feeling attracted to members of both sexes. The online *Urban Dictionary*, for example, defines "bi-curious" in the following degendered, non-judgmental way: "(1). One who is interested in bisexuality as a potential life style or self-ID. (2). One who wishes to explore their capacity for a bisexual or same-sex relationship." At this juncture, it is important to note that I do not mean to conflate the more sex positivity-valued connotation of "bi-curious" with prejudicial notions or beliefs (North American or otherwise, from within the LGBT community or not) about the category of "bisexuality" itself. It would be dangerously inaccurate to presuppose public acceptance or even affirmation of this category of sexual orientation, for its existence remains contentious, its validity constantly challenged by straight people and gay people alike. Nevertheless, this offensive appropriation of the expression in a Brazilian context, besides its explicit sexism and homophobia, may perhaps be read as a counter-attack to the cultural imperialism of American English in contemporary Brazilian culture. This is especially possible given Brazil's history of ambivalent reactions to U.S. cultural modes and forms, which have alternated (and often negotiated a tightrope) between fascination for the foreign, for "First World" cultural products and simultaneous disdain for their imposition and influence on Brazilian markets.

An example of the (mis)uses of LGBT language occurs with the problematic conceptualizations of the phrase *Bicha-pão-com-ovo*: " 'Bread and egg fag' [derogatory, used in São Paulo]: 1. Culturally impoverished homosexual; (2). Expression referring to faggots who do not have financial resources to dine out and bring an egg sandwich to eat on the trip back home from the clubs; (3). Refers to a morally bankrupt faggot with no scruples, without dignity and with character flaws" (31).[14, 15] The expression, on no uncertain terms, reflects discrimination and marginalization of lower social classes regardless of sexual orientation (e.g., other individuals self-identified as gay may employ the term to insult someone else of the same orientation but of an "inferior" class). Even more problematic is the connection or conflation of socioeconomic conditions with moral character judgment. The expression maintains the normative judgment that would hold that not only do poor gay people exist, but, by virtue of being poor, they somehow inherently lack basic moral values. Attaining cultural sophistication, whatever that may mean, is not even a remote possibility for the *bicha-pão-com-ovo*, who is perceived to be bankrupt of dignity or versed with "proper" culture.

Phrases or terms that refer to women, in the *Dicionária*, are often imbued with sexism and racism as well, not to mention a degree of homophobia that is perhaps more covert than in the passages which generally refer to gay men (which, as one may expect, occupy the vast majority, at least 90%, of the text's entries). *Coronel* (Colonel), defined as "*Lésbica independente e mais velha, que sustenta a amante*" (44; "Older, financially independent lesbian who supports her lover"), may be read as a critique of patriarchy or, at the least, an interesting role inversion in a sexist society. Unfortunately, though, the masculinity portrayed here is of a "military" nature, stereotypically gendering the older member of the lesbian couple as more "mannish" in nature (hence, the allusion to coronel), and assuming the patriarchal role of provider for her younger partner, complying with a sort of paternalism so prevalent within a *machista* consciousness.

The few other terms that refer (or infer) femininity are often sophomoric in nature and sexist in implications. One example is the use of the phrase *Jogar o picumã*: "To throw smut/grime [literally, coal dust]; to cheat or swindle: To turn one's head, flipping hair from one side to the other, just like blondes do, but in a slightly more intelligent way and with the intent to belittle or to ignore someone" (75).[16] It does not take a brunette to realize that this definition is a blatantly stereotypical attack targeting the supposed stupidity of women with blonde hair. This parenthetical analogy, "just like blondes do," is doubly objectionable, for it reflects cultural imperialism in that it borrows from English-language sources while also expressing a certain degree of misogyny, even if veiled in humor. While there is no shortage of interesting and disturbing examples of the perpetuation of homophobic, sexist, racist, and classist stereotypes in the *Dicionária*, I would like to turn our attention now to examine the most recurrent of the approximately fifty illustrations in the book.

The animal imagery, in particular, is quite fascinating. Symbolic representations of the *veado* (the deer), whose connection to the *bicha* I discussed earlier in this chapter, occur on nearly every page of the book. A miniature print of a deer, perhaps also meant to represent exquisite femininity, gracefully and elegantly prances over the numbers placed at the bottom of almost every page. One of the most provocative of these images is the one present on the last quarter of page 100. The hunt scene depicted is quite an unusual one: The deer that is evidently prey is standing still or "sitting pretty." The immobility is portrayed as a permanent state of existence since the animal is missing hooves. Directly behind the deer's backside is a target or a "bull's-eye" diagram, which also looks suspiciously like a finger or thumb print. A question mark is located above the deer's head as if to demonstrate curiosity, surprise, or perhaps given a more metaphorical reading, self-questioning. The image on page 136 seems, similarly, to be a promotion for deer hunting season. In both cases, the "feminized," if passive, homosexual male is depicted as the sitting target of inevitable "masculine" (*bofe*) aggression, frozen in place and totally submissive to a destiny where he will inevitably become nourishment (*comida*) for the hunter's sexual gratification.

A reindeer bearing gifts hanging from its antlers adorns the second half of page 112. The drawing evokes festivity, as the deer's antlers seem to be equated with a Christmas tree, displaying a series of ornaments, including a stylized Wonder Woman bag, the popular superhero figure offensively Brazilianized in the *Dicionária* as "*bicha multimídia performática e sissi*" (136; "Multimedia sissy fag who likes to perform"). The remaining prized possessions of the *viado* are depicted as a cuddly teddy bear, infantilizing the figure of the *bicha-viado*, and a pair of pants connected to an antler with a hanger, quite likely designer jeans connoting materialism and perhaps even uniformity in the objects that are revered as essential to the deer's very survival.

The portrait of an elegant *gato* or *gata* (literally, a cat, but also Brazilian slang for a handsome man or woman) appears on page 63. But this attractive, elegant animal is cross-sectioned and segmented, much like in the drawings one might find in a traditional Brazilian *churrascaria*, depicting the process whereby a cow is divided and apportioned for food (again, *comida*), each section labeled for consumption. The labels on the cat's body are as follows: "Fixed idea" (*ideia fixa*) on top of the animal's head, "Jealousy" (*ciúmes*) emanating from his mouth, *perversão* located in the region of its hind leg, *ego* on the underbelly, *charme* in the back region underneath the *azia* ("heartburn"), which labels the tail. There are two additional portions that also deserve mention: First, there are *neuras* diagrammed all over the cat's top coat, literally referring to nerves or the nervous system but also popularized in Brazilian slang as one who is neurotic in action or overthinks. The front legs are labeled with the capitalized letters "D & G," alluding to *Dolce & Gabbana*, no doubt to symbolize the world of expensive (designer) fashion Italian accessories. That portion of the cat's body is labeled as *espaço reservado para publicidade* ("Space reserved for advertising"). Clearly, our cat model literally possesses a modeling contract, along with a huge ego, a one-track mind that is fueled by jealousy and is graced with equal doses of perversity, charm, and heartburn.

Finally, the affectionate couple of zebras appearing early in the text (on page 11) seem to be innocent and platonic in nature. After all, in a book about sex and sexuality, the fact that the animals are not engaged in intercourse could be indicative that the relationship *deu zebra*, Brazilian Portuguese slang for *não deu certo* (i.e., "it did not work out").

In addition to the animal imagery that roams through the pages of this work, there are numerous references to queer popular culture icons, all of which are foreign to Brazilian soil, comprised primarily of Hollywood divas and heart throbs, both male and female. Most of these images reflect a large degree of cultural and linguistic imperialism, classism, and racism. When there are titles placed on books, they invariably appear in English (with the exception of the illustration for *gilete*, used to designate a bisexual man who cuts both ways, so to speak). The most celebrated icons are exclusively white and predominantly female, from Marilyn Monroe, to Marlene Dietrich, to Carmen Miranda, to Wonder Woman. Nevertheless, an exaggeratedly muscled Superman does make a cameo appearance on page 43, bursting proudly out of a wardrobe and about to take flight. Indeed, there are numerous instances of such cultural references, the most notable ones occurring on pages 23, 43, 56, 71, 90, 123, 124, and 139.

The third most common type of illustration in the *Dicionária* is based on a commodification and exoticization of difference and diversity. The entirety of page 33, for example, is devoted to the faux-Egyptian art with what appear to be pseudo-hieroglyphics displayed on a papyrus curtain in the background. The drawing resembles (a mockery of) ancient works of erotic art that one might find in a museum. The story depicted, however, could not be more contemporary. An androgynous person is sitting down and masturbating a male figure, who in turn appears to be dominating the other with an outstretched arm holding down the partner's head. The skin color variation between them is quite obvious: the darker skinned person, who could be male or female or transgender, is "servicing" the lighter skinned man, who stares proudly and indifferently straight ahead (not glancing down at the partner who is pleasuring him, whether by force or by choice). The image on page 76 similarly romanticizes sexual contact between two apparently indigenous men embracing one another, though there is only one penis among them.

The remaining images are focused on caricatural representations of transgender people, the eccentricities of queer sexualities, including multiple stereotypical references to sadomasochism in both gay male and lesbian contexts, though I do question if the BDSM portrayed between women, because it is so unimaginative, simply repeats trite heterosexual male fantasies of two women in competitive erotic situations. Illustrations of this nature occur on pages 89, 94, 97, 108–9, and 115. The depiction of the "gay sailors" does not escape caricatural representation in the *Dicionária*, as a two-page drawing depicts two white, handsome, effeminate sailors on a ship, in which their "effeminacy" is clearly marked through gesture and posture; namely, by the way they are poised and holding their bodies. One of the sailors is checking out the other's back while his neighbor gazes out to sea to watch the sun set on the horizon. Both men are wearing nothing but shoes, their sailor's hats, and provocative bathing suits, one with a cougar print, each exposing an ass cheek. An unusually configured and loaded gun appears on the opposite page, unbeknownst to our sailors, its shaft twisted upward, erect like a pipe and shooting darts of hearts in their direction.

As critical readers, it is worthwhile to ponder whether the images and illustrations, the majority of which were described earlier, serve to enrich or detract from the book's intention to provide a comprehensive yet tongue-in-cheek reference-"style" guide to LGBT language in Luso-Brazilian cultural contexts. To what extent does the caricatural reinforcement of gender-based stereotypes, in a work that proudly proclaims itself to be politically incorrect, carnivalize, parody, satirize, and thus subvert the discrimination it seeks to represent? On the other hand, do the explicit references to sexism, classism, homophobia, and racism that inform the images reflect a text that is intentionally (at worst) or inadvertently (at best) perpetuating and thus validating social injustices that are born and propagated through such images? I would argue that the *Dicionária* ambiguously and ambitiously does both, forging a literary universe where self-deprecation is both valued and mocked, where the profane (and profanity) of repressed and oppressed minorities is articulated loudly and proudly in the pages of a colorful and humorous text. As such, much like in the North American queer movement's strategic gesture to disempower voices of oppression by taking the "sting" out of derogatory words like "faggot" and "dyke," subsequently adopting them in an in-group context and adapting them in new cultural contexts, one might argue that the *Dicionária* empowers sexual and gender identity minorities by repossessing the terms that are employed against them and resignifying them in lewd and ludic ways. A clear example of this is the use of *"bicha"* or its abbreviated *"bi"* in an affectionate rather than pejorative sense when two gay-identified men are speaking to each other or about one another. We can observe a similar process occurring with the reappropriation of terms like *"nega"* (in the feminine) or *"negão"* (in the masculine), which romantically involved partners, of any sexual orientation and arguably of any race, use as terms of endearment for one another. At the same time, we may contend that using humor to categorically reinforce the stereotypical labeling that often leads to discrimination does LGBT communities a great disservice.

An extensive interview with the co-authors of the *Dicionária* reveals mixed intentions with regard to these issues. When I asked Fred Libi how questions around racism and classism were acknowledged or treated in the text, he responded: "We never tried to be politically correct. By the way, that [PC] is a North American invention that never really caught on here [in Brazil]; it is a stereotypical and authoritarian idea of ethics. . . . [We wanted to embrace] irony above all else!" This praise for irony is coupled with a performative strategy involving the deployment of humor as a site of resistance or even a coping mechanism to encourage Brazilians to accept homosexuality, viewing "seriousness" as the ultimate enemy to accomplishing this goal:

> As I mentioned before, everything in Brazil has a tendency to turn into a big *Carnaval*, but this also has its positive side. On Sunday, during the Pride Parade, I arrived quite late; the floats had already passed by, and I was on the corner of *Paulista* and *Consolação*, watching the people go by. What I saw was a party of teenagers, young boys 14, 15, 16 years old, having a good time. I think that the road to acceptance is through diversion and fun, but that, under the guise that we Brazilians don't take anything seriously, the inversion of values and the consequent cannibalization of any movement gradually contributes to a change in mentality and in behavior. And this young generation is appearing, showing and accepting themselves much more than five or ten years ago.
>
> —Fred Libi

I find Libi's reflection powerful and useful, for it recalls and reinforces the paradoxes discussed in chapters 1 and 2 about the unnecessarily polemical relationship between political activism and collective festivity. During my analysis of mainstream media representation of the LGBT Pride Parade of São Paulo, we observed a demonstrable increase in the media's association with the event and *Carnaval*, resulting in a rather reactionary decision on the part of the Parade Commission to mandate the exclusion of social and festive features of the LGBT community, such as occasionally banning the floats of bars and nightclubs, to create more "serious" militancy, relevance, and purposefulness of the demonstration. As we have seen, though, in a Brazilian context, it is a mistake and often even counterproductive to dismiss the political nature of humor itself as a powerful means to cultural resistance, and it is naive to dissociate the militancy of protest or demonstration from the ludic or parodic inversion of social roles that the carnivalesque fosters. In fact, coupled with the earlier observation that playfulness with language is the creative impetus for the genesis of much of the phrases and expressions recorded in the *Dicionária*, though with the troubling exclusion of women's voices from the universe of humor, seriousness is, in classic carnivalesque fashion, relegated to inferiority in this discourse, one which is consistently equated with the conventional, the normative, the proscribed social roles that LGBT language portends to subvert or reinvent. Humor ushers in subversive Bakhtinian laughter to indirectly critique or mock and thereby "invert and cannibalize" (as Libi put it) movements, deploying the power to transform oppressive sociopolitical structures and move collective consciousness toward acceptance, even self-acceptance as Libi implies with his description of the young teenagers earlier.

I would like to consider the linguistic foundations for what makes the development of queer language rather unique in a Brazilian context, different from "gayspeak" or variations thereof that have often been associated with other cultures. *Bajubá* (or *pajubá*) is a "coded" language, at one time employed exclusively by *travestis* as a means of in-group communication to warn one another of potential threats from clients, the police, or other external forces. This formerly secretive language has since been adopted and adapted by mainstream gay male communities in Brazil, though the *Dicionária* falsely attributes contemporary use of the language to all sexual and gender identity minorities. While it is not within the scope of this chapter to study the sociolinguistic features of *bajubá*, making for a monograph in its own right, it is important to point out both its origins in and adaptations to contemporary Brazilian Portuguese lexicon since many of its terms and phrases abound in the *Dicionária*.

Brazilian *travestis* have an extensive slang vocabulary, which Don Kulick documented in his groundbreaking 1998 work *Travesti: Sex, Gender and Culture among Brazilian Transgendered Prostitutes*, discussed in detail in the two chapters to follow. The reader will recall, though, as we have seen in the preceding chapter, the Brazilian soap opera has significant power to shape opinions of the spectators, whose own *brasilidade* may be questioned and reimagined as a result of this influence. The same sociocultural phenomenon applies to the adoption of *bajubá*, when the scriptwriter of a popular television *novela* in the mid-1990s introduced its viewers to a sassy female character who integrated the language into her daily speech, soon becoming popularized and imitated by largely middle-class gay Brazilians. The use of *bajubá* (alternatively known as *pajubá*) reflects important interconnections between religion, race, sexuality, and gender in Brazil. The language takes its origins from *Yoruba*, of Western Africa, having arrived in Brazil during the slave trade. To this day, there exists extensive religious terminology that form the language around the Afro-Brazilian syncretic religion of *candomblé*, which itself has been mystified and exoticized (and often marginalized) by mainstream Brazilian Catholicism and variants of Evangelical Christianity.

It is also pertinent to chart the flow or direction of the sociolect as it eventually reached "mainstream" status, remembering that it did not originate from the LGBT community, for it represents an interesting trajectory of a marginalized "secret" language employed by a specific subgroup of male-to-female sex workers evolving into mainstream use by the hegemonic center of sexual minorities, in this case gay men in Brazil. Perhaps the most significant contribution of the *Dicionária*, then, is the cataloging of specific ways in which typical *bajubá* expressions have entered into the homosexual male lexicon and been adapted (or one may say, appropriated, perhaps even in the imperialistic sense of the term) to Brazilian gay slang. This commodification of a coded language, which initially emerged as a survival mechanism, surely represents a gesture of preservation of a language born in the cradle of self-preservation. At the same time, we cannot overlook the implications of linguistic codes being utilized for commercial purposes, and in this case, for the palate of male homonormative Brazilians (often, e.g., to the exclusion of women of any sexual orientation). In a future study devoted specifically to *bajubá*, it would be worthwhile to acknowledge, and then of course, to trace the evolution of a coded oral language that, while it served and continues to serve to exclude those who do not speak it, has since enriched Brazilian Portuguese with significant creative potential for aesthetic development and increased malleability. A reference like the *Dicionária*, as problematic as it may be for the host of reasons enumerated before, has made an important contribution in this regard.

Well-known Brazilian screenwriter Hilton Lacerda, who directed *Tatuagem* (2013) among other feature-length films we shall examine in chapter 7, summarizes the value of such a text as follows: "*Bajubá* is the language utilized in the circles of *umbanda* and *candomblé*, adopted by the 'pre-op travestis' (literally, in *bajubá*, 'the pipe vaginas'), that made the language popular, recreating it and grafting within it life experiences and tongues that are present in the *Dicionária*. A combination of creativity and adaptation of the Yoruba language from West Africa with the velocity of the speech patterns of the marginalized was developed for self-defense and attack. These expressions invaded the gay universe and finally opened into the world like a creative and abundant waterfall."[17] If, as Lacerda maintains, the secret is out of the closet and this colorful "coded" language now finds itself at the centerpiece of contemporary Brazilian Portuguese slang, losing its status as an instrument of self-preservation, which tools, if any, have Brazilian *travestis* reinvented to form linguistic safety networks? After all, there is no evidence to suggest that *travestis* are suffering less discrimination than in previous years. In fact, statistics clearly show the opposite trend, that they are being harassed and murdered in record numbers.[18]

Indeed, the transition from the margins to the center of hegemonic discourse (whether heteronormative or homonormative in identification) brings out new problems that require our critical attention, both from the perspective of political activism for promoting social justice and in the ways in which we approach supposedly "LGBT" or "queer" discourses. As we see in the specific case of *bajubá*, as well as the case of various other modalities and nationalities of "gayspeak" or queer language, these discourses are not the sole property or prerogative of queer-identified people. Much of "gayspeak," in this country and in others, has gradually been appropriated and absorbed into mainstream heterosexual popular culture, resulting in words and phrases that have lost their distinction on the basis of the speaker's own sexual orientation. In other words, I would argue that language functions similar to the ways in which "peripheral" cultural products such as fashion trends and culinary equipment become "centered" and commodified for mainstream consumption. As such, terminology that may have begun in the "gay ghetto," once it begins to circulate beyond its own borders, often bleeds into heteronormative discourses of slang, particularly in rural areas, a process whereby cultural reappropriation takes place. While some may interpret this adaptation as a sign of the decreasing marginalization and valorizing of the minority populations who have created a "coded" language, we must bear in mind that this invented "gayspeak" or similar manifestations of it came about with the explicit purpose and desire to *not* be understood outside their circles. Therefore, this cultural assimilation process also results in a decodification of "secret" language codes of queer minorities, who historically (and even presently) take refuge precisely in a lack of mutual intelligibility as a means for community self-protection or even self-preservation in a discriminatory homophobic or transphobic society. As Cameron and Kulick contend: "The problem . . . with even the most recent and innovative work on gay and lesbian language . . . is that it still remains invested in the idea that 'queer language' is somehow necessarily linked to queer (i.e., non-heterosexual) identities" (102).

As we have noted, the co-authors of the *Dicionária* have expressed their opposition to the usage of the term "homosexual" when referring to gay men. Instead, they have noted, as have countless others, a distinct preference for the multivariate and polysemantic *bicha* in its place. Somewhat ironically, the term "homosexual" becomes construed as almost pejorative in the context of queer subjectivities, for it is a term born in patriarchal language that classifies and clumps together sexual minorities and has historically been accompanied or manipulated to exist in association with the stigma of medicalization, or worse, of pathologization. Of course, in common usage, the term also denotes (and often alludes exclusively to) sexual behavior, thus not revealing (or caring to reveal) anything about the lives and loves of the individuals who are labeled as such. Considerably less research has been done in Brazil on whether the use of the term "homosexual" is also objectionable to non-LGBT popular opinion, as it is for LGBT organizations who have invented terms like *homoafetividade*, *homoparentalidade*, and *Homocultura*, still currently in usage, for example, in the active and notable *Associação Brasileira de Estudos da Homocultura* (*ABEH*).

Writing in 1981 about the usage of the noun "homosexual" in a U.S. context, James W. Chesebro cites numerous studies that corroborate the fact that popular American opinion at the time "have suggested that the label *homosexual* has more impact than the actual existence of a homosexual person," the term itself generating "overtly negative behavioral and attitudinal responses" (xi). A particularly notable example of one of these studies is Rodney G. Karr's "Homosexual Labeling and the Male Role," which found that interactions of groups of men were "significantly altered when the group believed a homosexual man to be present. The same man was perceived as having a number of significantly different characteristics, depending on whether or not he was labeled homosexual" (10). Furthermore, the study found that high levels of homophobia were virtually inextricable from group perceptions of gender identity, or degree of "masculinity," hinting at the likelihood that internalized homophobia may also be at play: "Apparently, the impact the homosexual label has is intertwined with expectations inherent in the male role. If an individual is perceived as homosexual, there is a general move to devalue him and to maintain social distance—perhaps an avoidance of guilt by association" (10).

Clamoring to reclaim their own identities apart from proscribed categories that would otherwise exclude or inferiorize them, LGB members of various societies have adopted and adapted "gayspeak" to assert their agency for self-identification as well as to shield its members with a codified language that, at once, deepened a sense of in-group community while excluding those of heterosexual orientation from understanding and thus defending a non-heteronormative universe from penetration and possible discrimination. The goal to maintain self-protection is so paramount in the research around contemporary U.S. "gayspeak" that linguists like Joseph J. Hayes have argued that "as certain words or phrases pass into general usage or become generally familiar, some gays must develop new phrases or employ more arcane synonyms, in order to maintain secrecy. They are always on stage and usually on guard" (47). An interesting example is the universal "in-group" rejection of the term "homosexual" illustrated in a 1978 survey of a sample of lesbian and gay male professionals who attended that year's Gay Action Caucus of the Speech Communication Association. In the study, twenty respondents answered the questionnaire, representing a 41% participation rate. While it is important to acknowledge certain limitations of the study, such as the fact that it was administered solely among researchers in the same academic association, this fact does not invalidate its findings, particularly in reference to the various means of self-labeling discussed. Across the board, the survey found that all respondents, rejecting the term "homosexual," actively chose to classify themselves as "gay" or "lesbian." Though the sample was relatively small and highly restricted to a specific population, the results are worth quoting in detail:

> More than half the males either used the same or similar constructs to describe both homosexual and gay, or they stated that they saw no difference. In contrast, only one third of the women failed to make a distinction between homosexual and gay—or, as most added, lesbian. Males tended to describe homosexual and gay in more sexual terms than did females. . . . Women, however, used almost no patently sexual terms, except for the standard sexual labels that were also used by men, e.g., "gay," "dyke," "lesbian," "homosexual," etc. The actual terms women used were more complex and made more distinctions between homosexual and gay-lesbian. (21)
>
> —Joseph J. Hayes

Returning now to our discussion of the *Dicionária*, this distinction may shed more light on the nature of the authors' perceived "seriousness" of lesbian language, across national boundaries. If, in the sample discussed earlier, the lesbian respondents were able to present "more complete, more integrated pictures of themselves" (26) in comparison to their gay male counterparts, we may conclude that the rejection of the term "homosexuality" may go deeper for women than the obvious and historically repetitive tendency to equate gayness with maleness. It seems clear that gay male respondents have internalized far more the cognitive aspects of "sex acts" by deploying terms like "hot," "gorgeous, "trade, "hunky, "size queen," "well-hung" (21), and others to reject compulsory heteronormativity and possibly even stereotypical notions of homosexual sex by owning the positions, as it were, proudly and prominently. On the other hand, the fact that the majority of women who took the survey did not choose to define themselves within the labels or parameters of sexuality does not necessarily point to their collective "seriousness" but rather to a much more sophisticated breadth and depth of definitions, thereby prompting Jandt and Darsey to argue that lesbian women tend to "release themselves from the oppression of their own limited definition of themselves" (26), unlike their gay male counterparts, whose language has as its foundations often superficial and almost always sexualized self-constructs.

In one of the pioneering essays on "gayspeak," Joseph J. Hayes takes up the controversial question of how cohesive "gay language" is in an American context, reinforcing the sexist male-centered divide between gay men and lesbians that Julia Penelope and others have addressed before him. While he purportedly agrees with Penelope's contention that "in our [Western] culture, men are the coiners and users of slang; thus gay slang is a male domain. It is designed for the expressive needs of men, not women, who have no use for it," he rebukes the claim that the language and culture of gay males is, as

Penelope has argued, "a distorted imitation of the dominant society that condemns and oppresses them, the macho male hetero hegemony" (39). Instead, he notes, with some condescension, that most of these terms were borrowed from "underworld and criminal groups—thieves, addicts, prostitutes" (such as "trick" and "rough trade") and that many terms for sex acts for both men *and* women were borrowed from heterosexual males. Hayes's interpretation suggests the limits of any language system that is born inside the patriarchy, no matter how subversive or transgressive its reordering, resemanticization, or regendering may be at the hands of minorities. Ultimately, he vilifies the existence of gay slang rather than praising it for its creativity and the possibility of liberation, arguing that "the mere existence of a gay slang is one of the factors that holds homosexuals to conform to corrupt social values and prevents them from pressing ahead into a political existence based on their *own* lives, not as a distorted reflection of others" (39). This conclusion, though it discriminates against prostitutes and other members of the so-called underworld, offers convincing insight on the dangers of appropriation of existing words and terms from within the patriarchy. The implication here is that no matter how they are reappropriated or subverted, transfigured, or transformed, their usage still ultimately and inescapably restricts queer subjectivities from successfully unlabeling their "selves," making it virtually impossible to undo the naming imposed from external sources that has generated such negative (self-)judgment. At the same time, and somewhat paradoxically, Hayes places value on "reclaiming and flaunting the worst terms of abuse—dyke and faggot—and give them *their* meanings" (40). These conflictual arguments would later parallel the eventual reconfiguration of "queer" in academia as a positive affirmation of difference and antinormativity and the still active debates existing today in academe and among political activists on the merits of the preservation of identitarian politics to avoid erasure of minorities vis-à-vis freedom from the established patterns of static identities, which may impede the potential for psychosexual human development and creativity.

Roughly two years after the publication of the *Dicionária*, on May 22, 2008, I set out to interview random passersby attending the *Feira Cultural* preceding the actual Pride Parade that year. My ultimate goal, of course, was to test the validity of the source across lines of differences based on gender identity and expression, race, sexual orientation, and socioeconomic class. As such, I devised a *Queer-stionário*, which included a sampling of thirty-two vocabulary terms pulled from the book, with special emphasis on terms pertaining to multiple constituencies of the LGBT demographics but also the inclusion of words that represent or identify specific segments of the population; that is, slang allegedly used to describe lesbians, gay men, bisexual men and women, and transgender people. I asked each respondent to provide a written definition of all the terms on the questionnaire or as many as they knew. Of the thirty-two terms I had selected, approximately eleven alluded specifically to gay men (*Beth Faria, bi, biba, bicha, bicha-bofe, bicha-pão-com-ovo, bicha-wallpaper, bofe, Helen(inh)a, Irene, Viptimização*), seven to lesbian women (*Ataque epilésbico, bolacha, boot, coronel, Homossex-uellen, Lesbian chic, sapa(tão)*), two to bisexuals of either orientation (*bi, bi-curious*), three were attributed to *bajubá*, purportedly the language of Bra-zilian *travestis* (*Aquendar, Aurélia, Mona*), and six were neutral or universal to LGBT language in Brazil (*Baba-ovo, bas-fond, Ebó mal despachado, Emma Thompson, Jogar o picumã, piti*). While recognizing a series of limita-tions of such a study, including the relatively small sample size—I received eighteen completed responses—in addition to the fact that the survey con-tained isolated terms, taken completely out of their context, the fact that I was asking respondents to provide written definitions of terms that are generally employed orally, and the geographic bias toward a massive urban megalopo-lis like São Paulo, I figured it would be a productive way to begin to see if and how LGBT-identified Brazilians use the language of the *Dicionária*. The reader will note that the complete survey appears in the Appendix at the end of the book. One of the most revealing and repetitive responses was actually framed as a question: "What does 'queer' refer to?" one respondent asked. Another asked: "What is the 'Q' in the acronym of GLBTQ?" This question, one which I had hoped to provoke with the actual title of the survey, is indica-tive of the lack of relevance that the very term "queer" may hold in contem-porary popular Brazilian society outside academic discourses. As discussed elsewhere in this book, popular attitudes toward the term "queer" are often negative, and not necessarily for the same reasons as they are with North American LGBT citizens. Though some may still find the term too offensive to transcend its original pejorative denotation, many Brazilians perceive the term as completely foreign to a national context, not simply because the term is in English but precisely *because* of the use of English, which activists and scholars alike have accused of bearing a culturally imperialistic bent or even part of a veiled agenda to Americanize or Europeanize the ways in which Brazilians think about or construct theoretical formulations around sexual orientation and gender identity.

While the sample was admittedly too small to arrive at any definitive con-clusions, I think it is worth some attention for the preliminary glimpse it gives us in determining whether or not random terms pulled from the *Dicionária* are in the popular lexicon among members of the LGBT community in São Paulo. Of the eighteen respondents who actually completed the entire quiz, three self-identified as transsexual women (two black, *afro-descendente*, and one white), one as a heterosexual female (*afro-descendente*), one as a bisex-ual female (white), six as lesbian (three white and three *afro-descendente*), and five as gay men (four white and one Japanese-Brazilian). Three of the respondents, one female and two males, all self-identifying as white, denied belonging to any sexual orientation or gender identity classification, conceiving themselves as *sem rótulo* (without a label) in the case of one male and one female respondent and *não classificável* (unclassifiable) in the case of the other male. Given the national and international prestige of the LGBT Pride Parade in São Paulo, the geographical diversity of the respondents provided a natural factor of diversification. In other words, of the eighteen surveys completed, three respondents reported they were born in Salvador da Bahia (two lesbian women and one of the men who preferred not to be classified); two transsexual women (both "M to F," male to female), both from Teresina in Piauí; a gay white male from Brasília; a gay white male from Rio de Janeiro; a gay Asian male from Céu Azul, Paraná (in southern Brazil), a trans female (male to female) who preferred not to reveal her origin; and the nine remaining respondents from São Paulo of mixed ethnicity.

PRELIMINARY RESULTS: WHOSE LANGUAGE DOES THE *DICIONÁRIA* SPEAK?

Despite my assumptions to the contrary, there was an abundance of terms in addition to *África* where definitions were either unknown entirely (in the vast majority of cases) or did not correspond to the purported meanings highlighted in the *Dicionária*. In fact, the only demonstrable familiarity included the following six terms (out of the possible thirty-two), though by no means were meanings ascribed to them in a uniform or even consistent fashion:

1. *Bi*: The ambiguous and multivariant *bi* was defined as an abbreviation for "*bissexual*" by ten respondents, with definitions ranging from the most common "bisexual" and the more colorful *gostar de meninos e meninas* ("to like boys and girls"), *dupla sexualidade* ("double sexuality"), and *transa com os todos* ("has sex with everyone"). The term was defined as an abbreviation for *bicha* by three respondents (two of whom self-identified as trans females and one as lesbian), defined as *duvidoso* (doubtful or suspicious) by a self-identified gay man, and most explicitly by one who identifies herself as bisexual, in the following way: *quem está se descobrindo e sempre diz que é bissexual* ("One who is discovering himself/herself and always claims to be bisexual"). Not a single respondent indicated the double meaning that the *Dicionária* presents. The remaining three respondents, all women of mixed orientation, left the item blank.

2. *Bi-curious*: Left blank by over half (ten) of the eighteen respondents, this term yielded multiple variance of meanings. Of the eight respondents who commented on the term, a gay man interpreted the phrase as one which *se*

refere à curiosidade inerente ao bissexual em relação ao sexo ("refers to the curiosity inherent to the bisexual in relation to sex"), two gay men conceived the term as *heterossexual interessado em experimentar relações homossexuais eventuais* ("a heterosexual interested in eventually trying out homosexual relationships"), two gay men defined it as *não assumido* ("not out of the closet") or *pessoa em dúvida enquanto sua sexualidade* ("a person who is confused about his/her sexuality"), an openly lesbian woman wrote, *tem vontade mas não tem coragem* ("one who has the desire but not the courage"), and two lesbian respondents wrote, literally if not amusingly, *bissexuais curiosos* ("curious bisexuals"), which may also evidence an unfamiliarity with the term as it is employed in the English language.

3. *Bicha*: Initially, I had predicted this to be the most indisputable term on the survey, one that I mistakenly had thought would have been identified in a similar way by all respondents. Surprisingly, it was the one term that received the highest number of responses, having generated only one blank response. Seven responses indicated that the term was synonymous with "gay," five responses highlighted more specifically gender expression as being the differentiating factor in identifying the "type" of gay man the term encapsulates, such as *efeminado ao extremo* ("effeminate to the extreme") or *passivo*. Two respondents associated the term with flamboyance or extravagance, such as *quem gosta de se mostrar gay* ("one who likes to show off being gay") or *gay escrachado* (more or less translated as a "dishy or campy gay man"). Two respondents identified the term as a "pejorative" or "offensive" means to describe a gay man. Finally, one respondent associated ambiguity with the term, understanding it to mean *gay ou travesti*.

4. *Bofe*: Three respondents equated an aesthetic dimension with the term, associating it, respectively, with *homem gostoso* ("sexy man"), *homem atraente* ("attractive man"), and *homem lindo* ("beautiful man"), with no mention of sexual orientation at all. Two respondents believed that this is the term used to complete the coupling, as *o homem para as bichas* ("the man for the *bichas*") and *garotão namorado de bicha* ("hunky boyfriend of a *bicha*"), clearly a reflection based as strongly on gender identity as it is on sexual orientation. Two respondents defined the term as alluding to a straight man: *heterossexual ou machão—straight*. Two respondents equated the term with, quite simply, *homem*. One lesbian respondent equated the term with *machão* or *machona*, indicative that in her conception, *bofe* may be used to designate an accentuated sense of performative masculinity in either a man or a woman. One respondent defined the term by his perspective of what it is not: *gay não-afeminado* ("non-effeminate gay man"). One respondent attributed physical strength to the term; that is,

homem muito forte ("very strong man"). One respondent recorded *menino novo* ("young man"), therefore ascribing a connection between maleness and youth in his perception of the term. One respondent noted that this is the term used to designate a *homossexual com características masculinas mais definidas* ("homosexual with more well defined masculine traits"), and the remaining four surveys were left blank.

5. *Mona*: The reader may recall that, according to the co-authors of the *Dicionária*, this term is derived from *bajubá*, the language of the *travestis* described earlier in this chapter. In the text, the term is defined as follows: "*O termo originalmente designa mulher, mas é frequentemente usado para denominar homossexual masculino*" (92), meaning that the term was originally employed to designate a woman but has changed and frequently now denotes male homosexual. Four respondents wrote *mulher* ("woman"), one of which specified this woman's orientation to be *geralmente heterossexual* ("generally heterosexual"). Four questionnaires conceived the term as synonymous with *bicha* or *gay afeminado*, respectively. Two respondents attributed age to it, defining the word as *viado velho* (roughly, "old fag") and *gay velho*. One respondent wrote *travesti*, and still another defined the term as *amiga*, which literally means "female friend," of course, but is also defined in the *Dicionária* as *amiga gay* (19). The remaining six surveys were left blank.

6. *Sapa(tão)*: Six respondents defined the term as a synonym for *lésbica*. Three respondents indicated a gendered differential from other lesbians, believing that the term designates, in particular, a *lésbica masculinizada* ("masculinized lesbian"), *mulher que gosta de mulher e não é feminina* ("woman who likes women and is not feminine"), or *lésbica com característica mais masculina* ("lesbian with more masculine characteristics"). Two respondents recorded *mulher homossexual* or *gay mulher*. It is worth noting that two self-identified lesbian respondents did not note sexual orientation at all but rather connected to socially constructed gender expression, defining the term as equivalent to a *mulher masculina* or *mulher macho*. Finally, five respondents left this term on the survey blank.

PRELIMINARY CONCLUSIONS

While recognizing various limitations of this study, such as the ones mentioned earlier, I believe it still sheds light on challenging the very notion that a common LGBT language exists in Brazil, even one that would predominate in a specified region. While there is some degree of consensus on the meaning of a particular word or expression, there is no substantial consistency on the interpretations of denotations in any of the terms the survey tests, including

those that have, in countless anthropological sources and ethnographic studies, been ascribed uniform or unambiguous meanings. In the majority of
cases, respondents who self-identify as lesbian seem to overlook questions
of sexual orientation altogether and instead construct meaning based on gender expression or identity, as we have seen with the use of the term *sapa* or
sapatão (literally, "big shoe").

In reference to the terms *bi* and *bicurious*, whether respondents comprehend
it as an abbreviation for *bicha* or *bissexual*, not a single response included
both possible meanings, though a significant majority equated the abbreviation with *bissexual*. Clearly, there are nearly as many different interpretations
of the term as there are questionnaires completed. However, a larger number
of male respondents than female respondents attributed negative judgment to
the term, believing that the word connotes a sense of cowardice, closetedness,
and/or confusion, given the implication that the person so labeled is actually
gay but unwilling to accept that fact. In general, female respondents seemed
to equate either a more positive affirmation with the term, emphasizing courage or even a sense of pride in the process of self-discovery of one's sexual
orientation. At the very least, women's responses lacked normative judgment
that the term evidently connoted for male respondents. Though I did not
ask the leading question of whether respondents believed bisexuality to be
a legitimate category of sexual orientation, I find it quite revealing that of
the eight respondents who addressed the term, only three seemed to endorse
bisexuality as a valid category of identity, whereas the remaining respondents
stated or implied that the individual who self-labels as bisexual is truly either
homosexual or heterosexual and, in reality, attempting "to pass" as bisexual,
for a variety of possible reasons.

In the case of *bicha*, unlike *sapa(-tão)*, there was no ambivalence at all
about the identity category being synonymous with gay male, but there was
some difference of opinion on whether the term is considered offensive or
objective. A significant majority of the respondents who defined the term,
regardless of their own orientation, found it to be imbued with traits of
effeminacy and/or flamboyance. This perception fulfills the conventional
heteronormative stereotype of "faggot," whether or not the term has been
reclaimed by gay men who, in traditional Brazilian society, would consider
themselves as "bottom" or *passivo* since they engage in the "feminized" role
as being penetrated or dominated by their *bofe*. Only one respondent did not
attach any gender expression or identity to this term, and that same respondent, self-reporting as transgender (male to female), ascribed multiplicity to
the word, as being indicative of either a gay man or a *travesti*.

The term *bofe* yielded fascinating results. In a vast majority of definitions,
we can see a positive value judgment made on the qualities or attributes of
the *machão*, whether they are reported in terms of physical beauty, strength,

young age, or in absence of the frequently perceived inferior qualities of the feminized, scandalous, flamboyant *bicha*. Half of the respondents (seven out of fourteen completed surveys) did not include sexual orientation at all as part of the definition. In fact, two gay males alluded specifically to the fact that the *bofe* is straight or heterosexual. In one case, the *bofe* is recognized for male-gendered characteristics (masculinity) regardless of gender, such as in the case where a woman can be *bofe* if she is *machona*, perhaps parallel-ing a North American construct of *butch*. In the case of the Brazilian variety of "gayspeak," the orientation of the *machona* may be either homosexual or heterosexual.

The word *mona* was the only term borrowed from *bajubá* that received a fair amount of recognition among the respondents. While one-third (six) of the surveys were left blank, there was an equal split on how many respondents gendered the term as referring to a "man" while half alluded to "woman." In all cases of the former, the "men" were described as effeminate or *bichas*. In two additional cases, the men were not only feminized but old age was also attributed to them, a trait not recorded in the *Dicionária*'s definition of the term. In all cases where the definition was gendered as female, there were no aesthetic or physical characteristics included in that designation, and only one respondent who believed the term referred to women who are generally heterosexual in orientation.

As we have seen, the allegedly self-referential language of references such as the *Dicionária* and the *Bichonário*, while rich and colorful and certainly creative, does not necessarily represent LGBT Brazilians who supposedly speak this language. Nevertheless, these works function to both catalog terms and expressions that characterize "gayspeak" or LGBT language in a par-ticularly Brazilian context, and in the case of the *Dicionária*, in a Lusophone linguistic universe that spills well over the geographical borders of Brazil and enters into Europe, Africa, and Asia. Finding this resource to be limited and limiting in its ability to capture the nuances of LGBT language in the daily experience of LGBT Brazilians does not, by any means, invalidate or even diminish the value of such a resource. On the contrary, it proves that LGBT language in Brazil is even richer than scholars had previously thought, for its universe is filled with far more ambiguity than the "gayspeak" we have examined in the context of the English language. Amidst such extraordinary variance, there is one certainty that this resource reveals to be true—its mal-leability. At the end of the day, we must acknowledge that human language of any stripe, whether ascribed to LGBT populations or not, whether as ambigu-ous as that found in Brazil or more consistent in the context of the United States, is a breathing, living organism that is as dynamic and flexible as the speakers who utter the words and phrases that constitute it, regardless of the sexual orientation or gender identity of the speaker.

Chapter 5

Translating Trans in Brazilian Culture

Language is an excellent point of departure to continue our journey as we begin to conceptualize how trans Brazilians are defined in academic circles since, in Foucauldian fashion, terms codify and serve to police identities not central to hegemonic rules and roles of sexual and gender normativity. Before presenting a very brief and general description of the terms that are critical to an understanding of gender variance in a Brazilian context, we must keep in mind that each and every one of these terms forms a contestatory site and their very definition and conceptualization comes from within a patriarchal society. Therefore, I would like to qualify this section of the chapter by clearly stating that the terms examined here take their origin from a heteronormative and often highly *machista* mentality, one that is certainly not exclusive to Brazil, though the object of this study. How these concepts may have become internalized and the ways in which these labels have been rejected or discarded by trans individuals themselves is of significant importance, a matter I will take up in a different section of this chapter. The core of chapters 5 and 6 shall engage in a critical reflection on the representations of *travesti* identities and lives in two non-governmental organizations, *S.O.S. Dignity* and *The Red Umbrella Fund*, aiming to provide medical support and legal assistance, along with traveling photographic exhibitions and other cultural interventions to attempt to speak for, and in support of, *travesti* sex workers in contemporary Brazil and beyond.

Namaste's *Invisible Lives: The Erasure of Transsexual and Transgendered People*, published in 2000, provides one of the most succinct yet comprehensive definitions of the term "transgender," conceived as follows: "The word 'transgender' is an umbrella term used to refer to all individuals who live outside of normative sex/gender relations—that is, individuals whose gendered self-presentation (evidenced through dress, mannerisms, and even physiology) does not correspond to the behaviors habitually associated with the members of their biological sex" (1). To briefly deconstruct Namaste's excellent yet problematic definition, I applaud her use of the adverb "habitually' (which could have been very easily substituted with the more expected "traditionally") because it connotes the perception of the viewer, the outsider who is experiencing the presence of an individual whose self-presentation does not adhere to what the observer "habitually" encounters. Nevertheless, Namaste's conceptualization is troubling in that it seems to reduce the object of her own study, the "transgender" individual, to a series of behavioral and physiological traits that are superficial at best (i.e., attire, gestures), thus simplifying the psychological complexity of gender ambivalence into a category that one may potentially label, with derogatory intentions or not, as "transsexual" or "cross-dresser." Namaste goes on to describe the identities subsumed, in her view, by the big T label: "Cross-dressers, or individuals who wear the clothes associated with the 'opposite' sex, often for erotic gratification; drag queens, or men who usually live and identify as gay men, but who perform as female impersonators in gay male bars and leisure spaces; and transsexuals, or individuals who take hormones and who may undergo surgery to align their biological sexes with their genders" (1). Reading Namaste might occasion the danger of essentializing these sub-categories as follows: cross-dresser = trans for sexual pleasure; drag queens = entertainer or performer; and transsexual = not in an ambivalent, fluid space of betweenness but instead on a mission, as it were, to "align their biological sexes with their genders." Namaste's conceptualization is helpful to demonstrate the diversity within individuals who may be gender variant but is dangerously simplistic in its unambiguous assertion of what each "label" means or represents. Even as she stakes out her own identity as male-to-female transsexual, Namaste falls into the trap of romanticizing the very differences that she criticizes academics of perpetuating. Somewhat ironically, she uses a highly sophisticated theoretical apparatus to argue that the academic enterprise robs transgender individuals of their dignity (and often deprives them of their humanity) because of a refusal to look at the details of everyday life, of lived experience, of the objects they study. Namaste defines the transgendered subject as a body in excess, too complicated to be decoded, and hence unwittingly romanticizes the impenetrability of this difference: "But our lives and our bodies are made up of more than gender and identity, more than a theory that justifies our very existence, more than mere performance, more than the interesting remark that we expose how gender works. Our lives and our bodies are much more complicated, and much less glamorous, than all that" (1). While it is clear that Namaste is emphasizing the complexity of transgender bodies and lives, her relegation of them as "more than" locates them in excess of categorization, thus running the risk of enacting her very real criticism that becomes a central part of her overall thesis: "I argue that transsexuals are continually and per-petually *erased* in the cultural and institutional world" (2). To be fair, later in her work, Namaste makes much more concrete definitional divisions between the identities studied in her earlier chapter, arguing, for example, that it is nearly impossible, in Anglo-American academic debates on "transgendered people," to hear the dissenting voices of individuals who claim transsexual rather than transgendered identities. In a similar vein, she asserts that the experiences of heterosexual transsexuals are also erased from "the language of Anglo-American lesbian and gay theory and politics" (62–63). These are compelling statements that remain unresolved in Namaste's work but may receive a quite different hearing in a Brazilian cultural context. While very recent scholarship has tried to disconnect *travesti*, as an identity, from sex work, as an occupation, most Brazilian intellectuals—whether academic or activist—believe the identity to be indissociable from the occupation, a mat-ter to which we shall return later in this chapter. Namaste comes closest to the reality of *travesti* in a Brazilian context when she examines the invisibility of what she terms "street transsexuals," the most marginalized class of trans-gendered citizens. The reasons Namaste alleges for this continued erasure, paradoxically, at the hands of American transsexual activists themselves, are relegated, by Namaste, exclusively to the issue of socioeconomic class: "If the everyday lives of street transsexuals are not mentioned (let alone exam-ined), the visions of community elaborated by American transsexual activ-ists will reflect professional and middle-class biases" (66). Issues of race, religious conceptions of prostitution, and other factors are, ironically, all but erased from Namaste's rather reductive analysis.

This chapter is about the cultural representation of trans Brazilians. How-ever, it is equally invested in grappling with the ethics of representation as the scholar-activist embarks on a dangerous journey to tell stories on behalf of but not substituting for minority populations and individuals. Lack of owner-ship in the specificity of multiple trans* identities may very well disqualify a writer, no matter the intentions, from authority to speak. I can share my own profound apprehension in seeing this chapter in print after years of struggling with how to ethically and responsibly write about one of the most vulnerable communities in the world, Brazilian *travestis*, without inadvertently commit-ting further violence against the marginalized population I feel responsible to write about. How does one balance or mitigate the risks of perpetuating objectification, romanticization, dehumanization, or even deification of the very populations that we strive to destigmatize? Incrementally increasing risk is the fact that photographs, unlike names in an oral history account, cannot strip the identities of their models. How does activism through photography as a performative mechanism humanize folx who have suffered in the flesh (heart and soul) the consequences of marginalization that a heteropatriarchal society repeatedly perpetuates? There are a number of turns our story may take at this point, including silence or censorship, but I argue that maintaining or reinforcing invisibility is not a viable option to combat continued violence in the world's most openly transphobic society.

We can learn much about the work of ethnographers and anthropologists who live and work among the communities they study. But we gather so much more from the experiences of the minorities their contributions bring to light and to print. Inequalities based on race, class, gender, and sexuality in queer studies are both the landmine and the G-spot for the researcher who navigates and negotiates subjectivities, including their own, through the process of gathering, synthesizing, and analyzing narratives. Heather Love reminds us that "because of structures of race and class inequality, and their imbrication in desire and sexual practice, it is impossible to steer clear of the . . . visceral entanglements between researchers and the subjects they study . . . one can simply navigate it with awareness" (36). In her research on the "racialized erotics" of women in prison, Jessica Fields writes about the inevitability of finding herself deeply drawn into a nexus of "violence, pleasure, affirmation and exploitation" (75), ultimately postulating a "complex personhood" that Kadji Amin skillfully deconstructs in his work *Disturbing Attachments: Genet, Modern Pederasty and Queer History*. The issue of ethical representation does not have a resolution or offer any comfortable finality. In the face of a decision on whether to risk including marginalized voices in his research or to eliminate for fear of how the scholar may inadvertently (re)construct or (mis)represent these voices, E. Patrick Johnson (2019) reminds us of what is at stake in this ethical quandary when he writes about African American queer women from the South as a gay black man:

> I believe that the benefits of the research far outweigh the potential pitfalls, for to not conduct this research based *simply* on the fact that I am a man would be to fall prey to what the late performance ethnographer Dwight Conquergood called the "skeptic's cop-out," a pitfall of ethnographic research that retreats to quietism, paralysis, and cynicism based on "difference." According to Conquergood, "this position is the most morally reprehensible on his moral map of performative stances toward the other . . . because the 'skeptic's cop-out' forecloses dialogue altogether." (55)

CONNECTING THE "T" IN LGBT
IN A BRAZILIAN CONTEXT

It is important to note that, while self-definitions of *travestis* are based on ambiguous criteria and characteristics of a fluid sense of gender—such as, for example, the versatility in active and passive sex roles—the representations constructed by male to female transsexuals about their condition affirm a model of a defined and rigid gender, in which the separation between the masculine and the feminine is clearly marked. MTF (male to female) transsexuals deny any erotic potential of their masculine sex organ; they do not accept using their penis to achieve pleasure because, in their perspective, women do not have a penis. For that reason, they profoundly desire gender confirming surgery. In their explanations and justifications, MTF transsexuals seem to deny ambiguity, the principal characteristic that constructs and defines *travestis*.[1]

—Benedetti 2005, 114

Turning now to contemporary Brazil, we learn that both activists and academics consider an additional category of group identity under the umbrella of "transgender." Social anthropologist Marcos Benedetti's 2005 study *Toda Feita: O corpo e o gênero das travestis* (*All Dolled Up: Body and Gender of Travestis*) provides somewhat more textured but equally problematic definitional categories of *travesti, transformista, transexual*, and *transgênero* (18–19). To paraphrase the differences between the terms here, Benedetti argues that the primary distinguishing factor between these identities can be found not only in the body, much like Namaste proposes, in its forms and its uses, but also in social practices and social relations. Transsexuals are defined, in Benedetti's view, as the group that has gone all the way, one might say, permanently transforming their bodies, without which action they would suffer severe social and personal adjustment issues. *Transformistas* (or crossdressers), Benedetti affirms, undergo "light interventions" that may be rapidly suppressed or reversed, donning the clothing and assuming a "feminine identity" only on specific occasions, not spending his daily existence, unlike his transsexual and *travesti* counterparts, in women's clothes. Definitional precision becomes considerably more vague when Benedetti arrives at the category of *travesti*. Due to the importance of the distinction and the specificity of the terms used to conceive it, I have maintained the definition in its original Portuguese. What appears here is my own translation into English: "It is necessary to point out that the category of *travesti* is subsumed under the category of *transsexual*, since the latter is recent and still has a limited presence in the universe in question, functioning much more as self-identification than through attribution, perhaps through the psychiatric (medical) logic that constructs and defines it" (Benedetti 2005, 18).[2] This statement is as important for what it asserts as it is for what it omits. Benedetti's attempt to move the discussion of identitarian politics beyond physiological realities and into a realm that questions the language of modern medicine, attempting to position and placate such minority identities, is an intriguing and convincing one. However, his conflation between transsexual and *travesti* is erroneous in a number of ways, not the least of which is that, unlike transsexuals, *travestis* typically maintain their male sex organs in addition to transforming their bodies (through hormone intake, silicone, etc.) so that the feminine physiological traits also become pronounced in their male-identified bodies (if only for the presence of a penis and testicles that is not surgically removed). The implications of this truly *trans* state of existence between sexes (female body, manners, and gestures with male sex organs), without intending to romanticize or exoticize it, is one aspect that distinguishes transsexual psychobiology from that of the *travesti*. Additionally, a person who self-identifies as transsexual and decides to undergo gender confirming surgery is moving from one fixed "sex" to another: from male to female, or from female to male. The self-identified *travesti*, on the other hand, is born "male" and chooses to experience a sociocultural and physiological transition to female while maintaining her male sex organs (which, in effect, may or may not become impotent or compromised in the process of hormone therapies). This liminal space guarantees a certain amount of flexibility for the *travesti* who clearly self-identifies as a woman. In an experience of sexual intercourse, she can and is often penetrated by the (always) male sex partner, but (s)he may also assume the "active" role in penetrating other men. Anthropologist Don Kulick's discovery that *travestis* feel the ability of males in both penetrating and receiving the penis prompted him to conclude that this capacity gives them a sexual flexibility that "allows them access to the entire spectrum of sexed and gendered behavior and subjectivities. They may be born and will subsequently die men, but the 'flexibility of the male genitals permits males to construct themselves as feminine' " (Kulick, 193). While Kulick's rather utopian assertion is theoretically a fascinating one, carrying serious implications for the rethinking of "trans" in a far more holistic and integrated context, it seems to contradict quite markedly the experience of *travestis* as corroborated by both Benedetti and Barry Michael Wolfe, president and founder of the NGO *S.O.S. Dignidade*, now part of the *Instituto Cultural Barong*, which we study in the next chapter.

During his analysis, Benedetti (2005) highlights other "types" that constitute the Brazilian trans universe, including *gay, viado, bicha, bichaboy, traveca, caminhoneira, bofe, maricona,* and *marica* (19, 56, 87–88), providing ample evidence that the author is projecting views that some *travestis* also share, the fusion of gender identity and sexual orientation (29, 99, 120). Of course, this controversial conflation of sexual and gender identity is certainly not unique to a Brazilian context. An interview with *The Advocate*'s Gabriel Rotello reveals a belief in a parallel existence between sexual minorities and gender variant individuals: "I increasingly believe that I am transgendered. What's more, I believe that if you are lesbian or gay or bisexual, you are too. And I believe that an emerging definition of all gay people as transgendered is the wave of the future" (Namaste, 61).

This position may hold some political truth if we were to assume that the members of the LGBT communities are natural allies and that the progress of rights and social integration for transgender individuals will advance more profitably through an alignment with a lesbian and gay political agenda, an issue we will explore later in this chapter. For now, suffice it to say that it is clear that gender and sexuality are not one and the same but that they nevertheless intersect in significant ways. In her 1992 essay, "Of Catamites and Kings: Reflections on Butch, Gender, and Boundaries," Gayle Rubin cautioned lesbian feminists to not be hostile toward transsexuals, noting a great deal of common ground between butch lesbians and FTM transsexuals: "A woman who has been respected, admired, and loved as a butch may suddenly be despised, rejected, and hounded when she starts a sex change. . . . Lesbian communities were built by sex and gender refugees; the lesbian world should not create new rationales for sex and gender persecution" (475, 477). These assertions, clearly made in the interest of attaining political unity for LGBT as a social movement, also have complex implications theoretically, urging academics and activists alike to seriously reconsider the conceptual walls that language (or our collective use thereof) has constructed to separate gender identity from sexual orientation.

The question of language, even (or especially) the use of a gendered article, is a matter of significant debate for scholars and activists alike who study the daily lives of Brazilian *travestis*. According to all consecrated dictionary sources in Brazil, the term *travesti* is a masculine one (represented by the Portuguese definite article *o*), simply by virtue of the fact that (s)he is biologically and physiologically male at birth, attributable to the presence of male sex organs. In recent years and increasingly so, scholars have made a strong argument to reassign the gender of the article to the feminine *a*, Benedetti being among the first to make a case. Very early in his study, Benedetti explains the clear but multi-faceted rationale for this choice, attributed to both the need to value and respect the process of feminization that *travestis* undergo as they transform their bodies, as well as the political validation that would guarantee respect for the choice to consciously construct femininity despite contradictory physiological traits. As Susan Stryker (2008) notes in *Transgender History*: "One's gender identity could perhaps best be described as how one feels about being referred to by a particular pronoun" (13). As such, the adoption of *a travesti* becomes a symbol for personal freedom and the quest for societal acceptance of such transformation. An academic study that refers to *travesti* in the feminine may seem an inconsequential detail; nevertheless, as sociolinguists have affirmed, grammar is deeply ingrained in culture. Truly, a renewed conceptualization of *travesti* life in the feminine is more groundbreaking than it might, at first, appear to be. As Stryker writes, "Changes in language structure usually happen very slowly and pronouns are among the linguistic elements most resistant to change" (22).

Language and its ability to transform social reality are indeed at the heart of Benedetti's analysis, for he argues quite convincingly that the body of the *travesti* is, in itself, a system of **language**: "The body of *travestis* is, above all, a language. It is in the body and through the body that the meanings of feminine and masculine become concretized, conferring to the person his/her social qualities. It is in the body that *travestis* produce themselves as subjects" (2005, 55).[3] Indeed, a review of the literature available on the anthropological studies of "trans Brazil" (see Benedetti 2005, 30–34 for a brief but comprehensive discussion) reveals a dearth of any significant published studies on the language (in the sense of both *linguagem* and *língua*; that is, both systems of language and a "secret" language composed of codified and encrypted words and phrases) of *travestis*; that is, *bajubá*, a topic explored in the previous chapter.

Benedetti is one of the first social anthropologists to examine, for example, the language codes that would legitimate violence within (and not merely external to) the universe of *travestis*. As one might expect, though, the instances of self-induced violence and even mutilation are often attributed to repression and various forms of violence at the hands of the police, including imprisonment and public humiliation, rape, and assault while in jail (Benedetti 2005, 64–67). Many of Benedetti's informants reported that in the 1970s and 1980s, *travestis*, fearing arrest and then a much worse fate behind bars, would customarily slit their wrists as the police approached them, obliging the authorities to bring the victims to the hospital rather than the police station. Similar practices occurred within the jails, so that gender variant individuals would be sent to hospitals, considered far more receptive than jail cells. As we have seen in the introduction, police brutality of both sexual minorities and gender variant Brazilians is, unfortunately, a long-established pattern that continues to the present day.

What is most pertinent to our discussion now is the adoption or perhaps adaptation of violence within the *travesti* culture as a means of risk management, controlling or regulating the degree of violence that would otherwise be experienced if the victims had not engaged in self-mutilation. For some anthropologists, this self-mutilation has evolved to a culturally symbolic level of import that would perhaps be equivalent to the earning of wounds in a battleground and is resignified, either by the *travestis* themselves, by anthropologists, or both, as a marker of survival and courage, preventing the perhaps life-threatening violence that may have occurred (and has often happened) otherwise. As such, perhaps ironically or perhaps quite fittingly, depending upon one's own preconceptions of "masculinity" and "femininity," one might argue that there is a degree of performative bravado among *travestis*, who historically have internalized aggression, often read in a patriarchal context as hyper-masculinist behavior, to proudly display their self-inflicted wounds as signs of both courage and *esperteza*, street-smartness, employed to evade a much worse fate. Benedetti goes so far as to contend that the scars of self-induced violence, when read as acts of perseverance while faced with the potential for greater harm, may be responsible for the proliferation of tattoos throughout today's population of Brazilian *travestis*. While certainly worth careful consideration, the assertion that recent forms of marking one's body is a response to violence or read as an inheritance of self-mutilation is an unwise argument to make. The contemporary appeal and abundance of tattoos are much more emblematic these days of youth culture and, in fact, a characteristic of mass popular culture in general. To what extent tattoos may be read as self-mutilation is a controversial point, especially in the context of contemporary aesthetic codes, which empower tattoos as a form of body art, as markers of individuality, or deliberately staking out alternative forms of subjectivity. Indeed, one may argue that, in a context where tattoos have become, to a certain extent, normative means of expressing individuality, those who choose to remain "unmarked" may perhaps be interpreted as nonconformist within a mainstream culture where one's markers of body language is, quite literally, a unique projection of the performance of subjectivity.

There are other ways in which Benedetti reads the bodies of *travestis* as language, such as the use of clothing. The anthropologist engages in a fascinating discussion of performative use of attire to arrive at a *montagem* that constructs a presentation of a "feminine quality" that would be "sufficiently convincing," from the point of view of the *travestis*. This process, he writes, represents one of the first strategies to create visibility of the desire for transformation and also the routine importance of the daily ritual of spending hours in preparation to become the *modelo da noite*, literally, "the model of the night."[4] While I agree with the importance of the process of transformation described, I worry that Benedetti, as so many scholars before and after him, and with the best of intentions, falls into the all-too-common trap of glamorizing the body of the *travesti*, assuming, for example, that the average object of his research would have the money to spend on choosing and/or the time to agonize over the perfect outfit for the evening ahead. There is also a hint of a theory of deception, which I find more disturbing. When Benedetti reconstructs the daily lives of *travestis*, he does not take sufficient care to avoid terms like "convincing" and "manipulation," thus playing into, consciously or not, Namaste's criticism of the academic that would distort quotidian reality for trans individuals, in this case accentuating the theory that the model of the night has something to hide and plans her hours plotting how she can deceptively manipulate her appearance to convince others (even if these "others" are themselves *travestis*) of their adopted/adapted femininity. At the same time, and hence the complexity of this study, there is abundant ethnographic evidence to support the extreme degree of rivalry among Brazilian *travestis*, competing against one another to attain a higher degree of "femininity" in their newly (re)constructed bodies. As such, one cannot help but remark on the rather paradoxical intensity of patriarchy-laden masculinist competition among *travestis*, competing with each other not on the size of one's penis but on the degree of perceived "femininity" one is able to attain in this transformation process. Consequently, among the *travestis* Benedetti has interviewed, there are phrases that demonstrate both the rivalry at play and the judgmental terms *travestis* often use to classify degrees of success or failure in the level of "femininity" attained. The term *toda feita*, for example, is read as the highest compliment possible since the use of silicone and quite possibly plastic surgery have resulted in the development of feminine curves. Those *travestis* relegated to failure in the realm of femininity are classified as *toda plastificada*, indicative of low-quality or badly administered applications that have resulted in exaggerated features which compromise the "harmony" of the *travesti*'s body (Benedetti 2005, 86). Indeed, there are numerous ways in which Benedetti's *travesti* informants express intense competition with one another, sometimes provoking violence. We will look at some of these struggles as we approach the central discussion of this chapter, on how *travestis* perceive themselves in relation to each other. This chapter has been preoccupied with language among *travestis* in the Portuguese denotation of *linguagem*. The reader shall recall that extensive discussion and theoretical analysis of *bajubá*, *bate*, or *bate bate* (the language of the *travestis*, in the sense of *língua*) was presented in chapter 4.

One of the most valuable aspects of Benedetti's analysis is his brief discussion of the vast array of performative *personae* that many of his informants conveyed to him. In his necessary disclaimer to invent fictitious names in place of the real names of the individuals he has interviewed to produce his study, Benedetti notes that "many informants have more than one feminine (code)name, generally employed with situational logic. They may have one or more names in their roles as prostitutes; a different artistic name for shows and parades; and, also, their *nome de batismo*" (49). At the expense of linking situational (and pragmatic) realities to theoretical considerations, I think it is important to point out how this performative multiplicity, or heteronomy of assumed identities, serves as a fascinating concretization of the post-identitarian existence of *travestis* while reflecting the complexities of ambiguity in their daily lives.

THE (NEARLY) INESCAPABLE LINK: IS DEFINITIONAL CONCEPTUALIZATION CAPABLE OF RESISTING EXOTIC COMMODIFICATION?

Whether as academics, as activists, or attempting to serve in a dual role as both, it is critical, from an ethical standpoint, that we acknowledge our own positionality and the limits and boundaries of our research. This is necessary to not only call attention to our own implicit biases and preconceptions about the subjects that inevitably become objects of our study but, perhaps even more importantly, to avoid unintentional perpetuation of stereotypes and moralistic judgment about *travestis* in the body of our own work. Even the most well-intentioned researcher runs the risk of succumbing to paternalistic or unrealistic portrayals when attempting to describe life on the ground for Brazilian *travestis*. For example, in Benedetti's text, discussed extensively earlier, there are a number of pitfalls for us to examine. This part of the chapter is meant to serve as constructive criticism of such problems as well as a platform for my own discussion of the activities of the non-governmental agency SOS Dignity discussed in chapter 6.

First and foremost, as researchers invested in the lives of what is arguably the most stereotyped and discriminated class of people in the contemporary Western world, we must take particular care to address the issue of diversity within and among *travestis*, resisting the urge to reduce or simplify such complexity in any way. In Benedetti's ethnographic profile, the only concrete differentiating factor for a generally homogenous group of *travestis* is that some obtain more money than others through sex work. Otherwise, he claims, besides varying difference in access to financial opportunities, the group as a whole possesses similar levels of education and moral and aesthetic values. Therefore, he renders the collectivity of his informants as "homogeneous" (Benedetti 2005, 41). The assertion of sameness among any group, but especially one constituted by severely stigmatized people, is a dangerous one to make, particularly given the reality that socioeconomic class and access to resources, whether in the form of good nutrition or good makeup, is a factor that promotes significant differences in cultural attitudes as well as "moral and aesthetic values." In other words, we can identify a shortcoming in a reductive statement like "It is about a pattern that varies very little. Some obtain more money as prostitutes than others. . . . The mentality is, however, quite homogeneous" (41).[5] Clearly, this perspective is somewhat naïve. Financial access should not, of course, be exaggerated, but it is an issue that can result, due to clothing, access to cell phones and other accessories (or lack thereof) in an in-group perception of a *travesti* that is *toda feita* as opposed to her *toda plastificada* counterpart, or in essence, and in the language of the *travestis*, the difference between success and failure not only in the assumed occupation but in the sense of belonging to the group or exclusion from it. In the context of repression of diversity among transgender (TG) and trans-sexual (TS) populations, it is worth noting Namaste's remarks on the division within TS and TG communities, especially when it comes to issues of socio-economic class and the degree of access afforded to individuals classified as marginal by the very institutions supposedly created to serve and assist them.

Namaste writes: "The refusal of services and the conditional acceptance criteria of many social service agencies exclude the most marginal individuals
among transsexual and transgendered people: those who are seropositive,
prostitutes, in prison, poor, young, and/or homeless. This division within TS/
TG communities is remarkable. . . . *Attention to the refusal of services must
recognize that this exclusion is most noteworthy in the case of transsexual
prostitutes*" (189; author's use of italics preserved). While Namaste's own
ethnographic work concerns the experience of trans-identified citizens in
Canada, I believe it bears relevance in a transnational sense, most especially
a Judeo-Christian context that deems prostitution to be immoral and, in most
cases, criminal, whether or not the secular state condemns or condones it.

In my research, I have found that there are a variety of ways in which
Benedetti and any scholar or activist treating the lives of transgender Brazilians, myself included, run the risk of inadvertently distorting or inaccurately
portraying the populations we are working so hard to de-stigmatize and with
the very best of intentions. Among the most common are as follows:

1. **Fetishization**. Benedetti (2005) fixates rather obsessively on the hands
   and the finger nails of *travestis* as they are getting ready (*montagem*) to
   become *toda feita*. His lengthy description of the treatment of nails is
   interesting but quite unnecessary (55–56). Similarly, the focus on the eyes,
   and more importantly, the gaze, finds Benedetti (2005) making such out-
   landish statements as "The eyes of the *travestis* are not merely characterized only through the use of cosmetic products, but there is an investment
   in transforming the expression of the look, turning it more objective, more
   confused and lost, more delicate, almost innocent and defenseless" (58).
2. **Paternalism**. When describing the details of his interaction with informants, Benedetti (2005) writes: "One of the first characteristics to jump
   out at me is the extreme degree of economic difficulty of some *travestis*.
   As a result and at times, some of them saw in me a possible solution for
   the oppression and the scarcity that plagued their daily lives" (46–47).
   I would like to refer the reader to chapter 6 for an in-depth discussion of
   this problem, where I examine the photographic work of a notable Brazilian NGO, "SOS Dignity."
3. **Moralism**. The didactic or normative tone rarely appears in Benedetti's
   analysis, which tries to maintain neutrality and objectivity at all times.
   It is precisely for this reason that it is especially noteworthy on the rare
   occasions when a moralistic tone does occur in his work. A particular
   instance is when the anthropologist is discussing the patterns of everyday
   violence in the lives of his *travesti* informants. He maintains objectivity
   until the following assertion, one which I find disconcerting: "Besides,
   the very practices of bodily transformation that they carry out constitute

acts of violence since they produce pain and suffering" (Benedetti 2005, 47). To equate the necessary pain involved in the transition from one sex to another with an act of violence seems to betray the very fabric of Bene- detti's overall goal to sensitize the reader to the fact that these changes are inherent to the subjective identities reconstructed by the subjects for whom he demonstrates compassion.

4. **Vampirization**. As if *travestis* do not suffer enough persecution and dis- crimination in their everyday lives, and often to the point of dehumanization, Benedetti (2005) makes a point of drawing parallels between the *mundo da noite* and the Romantic conceptualization of darkness that encompasses this threatening, if not forbidden, space: "I learned very quickly that the vast majority of *travestis* have nocturnal habits and expose themselves very little to natural light since they generally sleep by day" (43).

5. **Trendy scholarship**. The scholar acknowledges how academic work on trans issues has become *da moda* (fashionable) in the 1990s, especially in North America, thus further fetishizing the lives of the population he hopes to demystify (28).

6. **Excessive generalizations**. There are many moments where this tendency occurs in Benedetti's work, but I have chosen to highlight the most appar- ently innocent of them: "The tweezers (to pluck eyebrows) is a basic instrument of any and every *travesti*, and it is nearly impossible to find one who does not carry this tool in her purse" (2005, 59).

7. **The use of *travestis* to exoticize and idealize ambiguity**. As part of his concluding remarks, Benedetti (2005) writes, quite compellingly but also disconcertingly, that "*Travestis* live the experience of gender as an artificial game that is possible to recreate. For that reason, they create a particular feminine, with ambiguous values. A feminine that constructs and defines itself in relation to the masculine. A feminine that is, at times, masculine. They live, in essence, an ambiguous gender, erased, without limitations or rigid separations" (132). The issue of ambiguity is one that is paramount to this book, in each of its constitutive chapters, but for the time being, let us consider the words of one who defines herself as a transsexual activist. Returning full circle to Namaste: "Our lives and our bodies are . . . more than the interesting remark that we expose how gen- der works" (1). Benedetti's exoticized conceptualizations cast *travestis* in the role of providing the magical key to unlock biological sexes as they confront and enter into dialogue with social constructions of masculinity and femininity. This hypothesis is interesting and is worth considering with some depth (as we have and will continue to do), but it also runs the risk of appropriating the lives of transgendered people to theorize about social relations of gender with little regard for the routine violence that encompasses daily existence.

SELF-REFLECTION: SOCIAL CONSTRUCTIONS
OF MASCULINITY AND FEMININITY
AMONG BRAZILIAN *TRAVESTIS*

Earlier in this chapter, we have seen how masculinist competition or rivalry between *travestis* to transform into the most **naturally** "feminine" is a central preoccupation for Benedetti's informants. Indeed, *machismo* among *travestis* would seem to indicate an interesting paradox where *travestis* collectively perpetuate patriarchal hierarchies and territorial divisions within their own communities and even when choosing a mate (Benedetti 2005, 67, 69, 116–7, 119–23). These cultural realities would suggest that the romanticized vision of the *travesti* as one who possesses a peculiarly or uniquely high level of consciousness and is able to cultivate ambiguity in her daily life is a faulty notion based on exoticizing difference. In fact, Benedetti was quite surprised to find extreme conformity and classism within a community marginalized for being **different** (2005, 72, 116, 117). Thus, the anthropologist investing *travestis* (or at least his informants) with the power and even the desire to "fabricate their own subjectivities," or what we might otherwise call agency, is seriously called into question when we are in the midst of communities that are both highly conformist and competitive.

The enlightened third gender hypothesis, which is meant to place transgendered individuals on a pedestal of respect, also serves to dehumanize them and their life on the ground. In fact, as Benedetti notes in his work, there is a very high incidence of internalized (in addition to externalized) homophobia among *travestis*. In his interview with informants reacting to the fact that Rogéria had undergone gender confirmation surgery to transform her penis into a vagina, her colleagues stated that just because she now possesses a vagina does not mean that Rogéria is more of a woman. The responses were aggressively homophobic in nature, ranging from Gabrielle's comment that "when I saw her and her new vagina, I thought she was very beautiful and chic, but she is not a woman. She is a faggot. A big fat faggot just like us" (Benedetti 2005, 108). Sissi's remarks were quite similar, revealing a grave sense of internalized homophobia, not to mention low self-esteem: "**She** [Rogéria] is very beautiful, but **he** is a whore. A faggot in the way he speaks and he cries and shouts like a fag, in a way that no real woman would do. I think that the question of your being more or less feminine is in everyone's head" (Benedetti 2005, 108–9; translation and emphasis mine). I venture to say that in this context, *bicha* may actually be translated as an effeminate gay man in opposition to a "real woman" or even strict normative conformity to an ideal of a "third gender." I would argue that the level of homophobia and rigid gender conformity among some *travestis* is so high that it often results in acts of violence, particularly against closeted gay male clients who are, quite fascinatingly, judged as failed *travestis* because they did not have the courage to transform themselves into real "women." I would like to offer an alternative interpretation: Is it not the case that these queer subjects perceived and judged by their peers as inferior or even inauthentic in the new gender category they are expected to perform did not reach their potential to claim membership in their conformity to the gender non-conforming community they had hoped (and transformed themselves) to join? In the language of the *travestis*, male clients are separated into two categories: *as maricona* and *os homes*. The first category is typified by males who assume a masculine appearance (and constitute themselves as male) but prefer to be the passive partner (the "bottom") in their sexual relationships with *travestis*. According to Benedetti's informants, the *maricona*, feminized and made singular in the common vernacular, are despised and often viewed as "false *travestis*." Generally, these clients belong to a higher socioeconomic class, are older men with traditional heteronormative families. Quoting Benedetti (2005), "Precisely because they are identified with a feminine position within this logic of gender values, these clients 'deserve' to be exploited, according to the *travestis*. They are frequently the most common victims of the assaults and robberies, the blackmail, committed by some *travestis*" (124).[6] In this sense, then, homosexuality is clearly associated with gender inversion. Of course, these observations reveal many disturbing attitudes, including the conflation of sex and gender, the serious potential for homophobia, both internalized and conscious, and a deeply ingrained sense of misogyny upon attributing to the feminine a sense of vulnerability, weakness, and deserved victimization. As Namaste reminds us, these assigned roles are not exclusive to heteronormative models for "elements of femaleness and femininity are highly regulated within gay male consumer culture" (10). Nevertheless, even as we examine conformity to socially constructed gender norms of "masculinity" and "femininity," Cáel M. Keegan points out a larger theoretical question that shines light on the fissures between queer and transgender studies: the fact that queer theory emphasizes deconstruction/failure of cis or "normative" subjects while trans* studies make their centerpiece precisely the opposite: reconstruction and recovery (Keegan, 394): "Feminist queer studies' emphasis on antinormativity (i.e,. 'perversion') as a kind of disciplinary political impetus overlooks the problem that many transgender people seek to live their lives as 'real' and 'normal' men and women" (395). Still, as we come full circle to addressing the necessary complexity involved in studying the particularities of Brazilian *travesti* cultures, we must be keenly aware that *travesti* bodies resist even North American trans* academic scholarship to classify or compartmentalize them, for they are neither "failed" men or "reconstructed" women but instead occupy the interstitial spaces between, among, and beyond the dualistic structure that would stake no claims for "perversity" in antinormativity nor any static or stationary positionality as "real and normal men and women."

According to Benedetti's interpretation of the *machismo* of *travestis* (though he does not label their behavior as such, as I do here), there is a serious conflation of gender identity with sexual orientation, resulting in the following belief: "Among the *travestis* . . . all people (whether they be anatomically men or women) that experience sexual desire for men are automatically situated in the feminine pole. The husband of the *travestis* must, therefore, be situated in the extreme opposite pole. He must be a man with a penis . . . the larger, the more virile . . . the essence of the masculine according to this point of view, capable of satisfying the desires of those men and women who crave him (sexually)" (Benedetti, 121–22). These patriarchal and clearly *machista* and misogynistic attitudes translate quite interestingly into the dynamics of the sexual relationships and partnerships that Benedetti follows in his study. The question of who wears the pants in the relationship yielded interesting results. For those *travestis* maintaining sexual relationships with "masculinized" men, the vast majority were the ones economically supporting their husbands (Benedetti 2005, 122), who are expected to remain loyal and monogamous at all times. As Benedetti writes, "The husbands of the *travestis* must be faithful. Betrayals, especially those committed with other *travestis*, are considered abominable and subject to revenge, including the use of violence" (2005, 123). As such, the *defesa da honra* (Defense of Honor), legal in heteronormative Brazil until the 1988 New Constitution, permitting the husband to kill both an adulterous wife and her male lover (but not the inverse) still applies informally in the *travesti/bofe* union.

The introduction of this book begins our general examination of the social and political movements in Brazil to combat homophobia, but we must also take a careful look at transphobia, a far less-studied area with significant battles yet to be waged. LGBT Brazilian citizens have recently begun to witness promising developments in trans rights that have manifested themselves into legislative processes. As a result, more legal protections are beginning to be implemented, in no small part due to activism to combat transphobia in Brazil. The recent federal legislation to permit Brazilian citizens to choose their own social names and have legal documents modified to reflect this and the retraction of gender identity disorder as a pathology are two major victories to illustrate this.

The next chapter will focus directly on a related but far more contentious topic: the relationship between art (specifically photography) and political activism in the ongoing battle to legitimate the lives and livelihoods of Brazilian *travestis*.

Chapter 6

Tracing the Trenches of the *Travesti* Travesty: Trans Photography and Artivism in Brazil

How many words is a picture truly worth? Are collections of photographs enough to inform, change minds, alter mentalities, and combat prejudices? Or do images simply reify the objectification of the subject-turned-object at the hands of both technology (the camera itself) and the gaze of the photographer who selects the angles, zooms in and out, the background objects to include or exclude, and the foreground to accentuate or to manipulate? What follows is a selection of photographs I took in June 2011 in downtown Rio de Janeiro's *Cinelândia* neighborhood.[1] My own gaze focuses on the public square's big blue phone booths, known in Brazilian slang as *orelhões* (or big ears), since they are shaped like the human body part alluded to. Much like in the United States and many other nations, public phone stations are almost antiquated in a society where mobile phone usage is at the height of its popularity (as is the case, e.g., with the relatively recent invention of the "smart phone," the tool that I used to take the photographs which follow). Within the spacious enclosures of the downtown *orelhão*, I found myself completely inundated with both color and black-and-white posters containing advertisements for *travesti* (active and/or passive) sex workers. At the expense of unfairly generalizing the "ambience" of the neighborhood in which these phone booths appear, I feel it is safe to state that, in comparison to other neighborhoods in Rio, *Cinelândia* is populated by bohemian night clubs, porn theaters, and shops, and has a reputation for a higher level of violence, allegedly brought about by drug use and prostitution. Many of Rio's prized architectural landmarks are also located in this large open public space, such as the *Odeon* Theatre and the historic and magnificent *Teatro Municipal*, both of which attract tourists and residents alike. I do not think that it would be going too far to suggest that *travesti* sex workers, with all the occupational risks assumed, may well have negotiated a "safe space" to announce and to

advertise their services. After all, the posters seem to have become a permanent feature to decorate the interior spaces of these phone booths, as we shall
see. If there were serious moral objections to the virtual collage of advertisements that adorn the *orelhões*, then surely police authorities would have taken
the liberty of removing them (or would have been instructed to do so). At the
same time, we must exercise special care to not make any claim to the effect
that these spaces of apparent tolerance are actually safe simply because they
exist publicly. Namaste's generalization about the relative lack of safety with
respect to spaces inhabited by sex workers rings especially true in an urban
Brazilian context: "Regarding incidents of violence, most TS/TG prostitutes
work in an area with a much higher frequency of criminal acts than the gay
village" (151). As such, one must acknowledge that the degree of risk for the
most stigmatized class of Brazilians is much higher than for members of the
gay or lesbian community, for while Brazil continues to experience an eruption of homophobic violence in the streets, LGB citizens may circulate more
freely and with relatively more safety in "ordinary" public spaces designated
as gay, lesbian, or bisexual, such as businesses, restaurants, theaters, bars,
clubs, and other establishments. It is worth acknowledging that *travestis* do
not necessarily find a haven or even refuge in LGB-owned or gay-friendly
establishments and have often found themselves in jeopardy in spaces designated as "safe" for the LGBT community, judged harshly for their "difference" as trans, their involvement in sex work, or both.

   With phone numbers prominently displayed in each of the poster advertisements, as we shall see in the following, some choose to hide their eyes or their
entire faces while other *travesti* sex workers display their bodies (as well as
their faces) in all their feminine glamour and glory. The first photograph in
the following, which I have labeled figure 6.1, shows a variety of sex workers, mostly racialized as white or lighter-skinned, including the presence of a
token *michê* (gay male prostitute) among the menu of choices for the caller
to order without registering a trace to the personal or mobile phone; hence,
the relative anonymity of the public phone booth. Women and children
shared this public space, demonstrating that it is not reserved exclusively
for sex work. In the image it is also possible to see the repetition of identical
ads, often one on top of the other or in very close proximity to each other.
Among the images, there is a flyer focused on "Marcela's services," featuring
a provocative black-and-white photo with the center of attention placed on
her silicone-induced breasts and her hand caressing her erect and enormous
penis. The bolded caption "*Ativíssima*" may be translated into English as
"an aggressive top" (but, notably, in the feminine form). Her poster ad also
promises "total privacy," noting that she is from the city of São Paulo and
is a *verdadeira cavalona*, a true or real prostitute. Interestingly, though, the
slang term *cavalona* is the feminine equivalent of *cavalão*, which literally

Figure 6.1.   Photo Taken by Author at *Cinelândia* **in Rio de Janeiro, June 2011.**

means "big horse" but is used in contemporary Brazilian Portuguese to refer to a person whose sexual genitalia is well developed, or, as we might say in English, "well-endowed."

Another ad introduces us to "Aline," who is offering her services as sexually versatile (active and passive), has measured her penis to be 22 centimeters long (though the sex organ remains out of view from the advertisement), and accentuates her *bundona*, "big butt," which, according to Brazilian stereotypes about feminine attractiveness, is considered nirvana to "straight men" who find pleasure engaging in heteronormative anal penetration with a "straight female" sex partner. Aline claims to work alone, makes sure to emphasize the fact that she is blonde and voluptuous (*seios fartos* literally means "generous breasts"), characterizes herself as warm and affectionate (*carinhosa*), and makes sure her potential clients know that she provides her services in a commercial downtown building where they may take the liberty to go right up to her office (*sobe direto*). Finally, she includes both her cell phone and her residential line for clients to reach her more readily.

"Andreia," also featured in figure 6.1, exaggerates the size of her *bundona* and creates an ambient blue aura or boundary around her black-and-white photograph. It is clear that Andreia's forte is role-playing and that she markets herself as a versatile (top and bottom) dominatrix (*dominadora*), quite likely advertising her skills or penchant for BDSM. "Taissa's" objectified image depicts her as sexually versatile. Her photograph exemplifies physical diversity among *travestis* and that clients demand all shapes and sizes, since she is likely to be construed as *gordinha* (chubby) by her potential clients.

In the most detailed poster in language, and yet the most reserved in appearance, "Pamella's" face has been whitened out and is impossible to perceive. The appearance of the silicone-induced breasts seems to be the centerpiece of this photograph, as Pamella uses her hand to clearly accentuate her chemically constructed breasts. The pose also centers on the sensual feminine curves of Pamella's body. Importantly, the most operative term she uses to package herself is the word "Woman," to be taken as her most prominent feature, since the term immediately follows her first name. This gesture is in stark contrast to her colleagues (or rather, her rivals), who almost exclusively use the term *travesti* to accompany the first name. Pamella characterizes herself as "blonde, delicious, and perfumed" (*loira, gostosa, cheirosa*). She also advertises her big breasts, thick thighs, and well-sculpted physique and wants her potential clients to know that she is attractive, sexy, and very sensual. In contrast to the other *travestis* pictured thus far, Pamella gives her mobile phone number first, followed by the land line, communicating either a readiness or wider availability, a sense of professionalism, or both.

"Layla" advertises her young age (twenty-two years old), her sexual versatility, and her blondeness and attests to the fact that (in large letters) the photo is actually real. This compelling disclaimer may lead the viewer to doubt the "veracity" of the pictorial representations of other *travestis* who may be offering their services under false pretenses or using photographs that do not actually correspond to their actual physical appearance. Alternatively, this strategy may simply be Layla's way to overcome the competition, using her youthfulness and her *authenticity*, as it were, as her primary selling points. The phrase *adorando troca/troca* literally means "adoring back and forth exchange" but may also be interpreted as "flip fuck," an enjoyment of swinging, or versatility of sexual positions in anal intercourse.

Finally, we are introduced to a voluptuous Melissa, whose description seems to synthesize many of the desired traits emphasized by her *travesti* counterparts, from versatility, to blondeness, to big breasts, to an affectionate nature, to attending to her clients with exclusivity, to being the object of a true photograph. Nevertheless, Melissa (or her photographer, perhaps her pimp) has decided to place a black band over her eyes to conceal them. Unlike Pamella, however, the rest of Melissa's face is revealed to the camera, which accentuates sensual curves and delicately polished fingernails holding onto a large, clearly phallic tree in a bucolic, park-like setting. It goes without saying that these sex workers almost uniformly racialize themselves as white to the point of fabricating Aryan blonde models for their male clients' sexual consumption and gratification, a tendency that corroborates David Brookshaw's *branqueamento* thesis at all socioeconomic levels of Brazilian society.

MIGRATING MARKETS: THE PROFESSIONALIZATION OF *TRAVESTIS* IN THE NEW MILLENNIUM

The long-standing and typically automatic association of *travestis* with prostitution is gradually changing. Two years prior to the new legislation that would increase protections to transgender individuals in Brazil, discussed from a legal standpoint in chapter 1, progressive journals and newspapers were beginning to follow stories of *travestis* who had not "succumbed" to prostitution, despite great temptation to do so (such is the standard discourse of these articles, as we shall see) and acquired the skills to enter the mainstream workforce, abandoning a life on the streets. This stepping stone to a more progressive representation of alternative occupations and choices for *travestis* is precisely just that: a step in the direction toward acceptance of gender variance and de-stigmatization/de-eroticization of the body of the *travesti*. Nevertheless, implicit in this trajectory is the deeply ingrained (if unconscious) didactic and even moralistic rejection of prostitution as a viable or valid career option for *travestis* (or anyone else, for that matter), despite the fact that sex work is technically legal in Brazil.

A clear example of this new attempt to integrate the *travesti* into mainstream career pathways is the centerpiece article featured on the cover of the May 2008 (Number 10) edition of the popular monthly magazine *Brasileiros: A Revista Mensal de Reportagens* (Brazilians: A Monthly Newsmagazine), published by *Brasileiros Editora* in São Paulo, with a circulation of 30,000 copies per edition. The front cover features a thirty-five-year-old photogenic and attractive *travesti*, dressed in professional attire (see figure 6.2 in the following). The headline states *"Além da calçada"* ("Beyond the Sidewalk"). Written by Leonardo Fuhrmann, with photographs by Heloísa Ballarini, the subtitle reads as follows: "Her name is Bruna Bianchi, she has a degree in Business and owns a driving school. Bruna, actually Daniel, is a *travesti* [note usage of masculine indefinite article, *"um"*] and must constantly fight to avoid falling into prostitution."[2] Poor writing aside, the language of the subtitle of the article is offensive in two very important ways. First, it seems to sensationalize the gender-fuck inherent in this transformation, stating that Bruna is actually Daniel dressed as a woman. Second, the use of the masculine indefinite article before the term *travesti* reinforces re-masculinization of the gender identity of Bruna, even though she has transitioned far away from her days as Daniel. Nevertheless, the article succeeds in its attempts to validate those relatively

Beyond the sidewalk

Brasileiros: A Revista Mensal de Reportagens
Published by Brasileiros Editora
May 2008, Number 10

Figures 6.2. Cover of *Brasileiros: A revista mensal de reportagens* (Brazilians: A Monthly News Magazine) (May 2008, Number 10).

few *travestis* who have had the gumption and the education to enter "normal" or "normative" careers despite being constantly lured into sex work. The patronizing tone of this successful conversion from a naturally deviant path is repeated in the article, making heroines of its subjects, for they have had the discipline to resist a life of prostitution. At the same time, the article makes a point of showing that their experiences are not shared by the majority of their *travesti* counterparts, who have not had the strength to resist the "urge" or "compulsion" of prostitution. The article conveys the unsubstantiated statistic that 83% of *travestis* earn their living entirely from sex work.[3]

The first phrase of the article unnecessarily repeats the text on the cover but displays a slightly lesser degree of ignorance: "They [the subject pronoun in the masculine or the feminine] are *travestis*. They were born men, self-identify as women, and they face serious struggles to avoid falling into prostitution" (37).[4] At the beginning of the article, the reader is presented with a black-and-white photo of a *travesti* named Cláudia with the following caption underneath her photograph: "The money she accumulated while working as a prostitute enabled Cláudia to open her own business—today, she works with computer software in the medical field" (36).[5] Indeed, this is the only moment that the reporter does not seem to vilify prostitution, if only because it provided the financial stability to allow Cláudia to pursue another (read: respectable) profession. The reporter's interview with Cláudia reveals that she had accumulated the means to purchase her own house and a business by prostituting herself for five years on the streets of Milan. Importantly, Cláudia relates that life as a prostitute was easier in those days because the competition used to be less intense: "At the time [I lived and worked in Italy], there was less competition on the streets of Europe, but there are not a lot of [*travestis*] who plan and desire to leave that life" (41).[6]

Indeed, the issue of monetary compensation is a complex one. In an interview with Bruna's childhood friend Simone de Oliveira Cruz, a *travesti* that Bruna hired to work at her driving school she weighs the pros and cons of taking on a job that pays one-third of the salary she earned while working as a prostitute: "In the beginning, I only came to work for Bruna because she needed me, but I continued to work as a prostitute at the same time. On the street, I was earning three times more than I make here, but I don't miss it. I've been working at the driving school for three years now. I am less exposed, and I live a more secure life" (41).[7]

Another image, "Tábata," portrays a rather sterile or even feigned happiness, approaching the type of pose one might find in a high school yearbook photo. The close proximity of the model's face (the close-up of the camera) seems to suggest that something is being hidden. There is a peculiar and quite staged bend of the head and a distinct focus on the model's chest and above. The tilt of the head may suggest that this person is attempting to make the viewer believe that she is more self-confident than she actually is.

The photograph of "Alessandra" is quite different from the previous two examined before. It is clear from the photo that the object of the camera is passionately speaking to an audience of one or more people. The gaze is from behind one of the audience members, permitting viewers to participate in the experience of what is being witnessed. The long hair of the woman in the foreground as well as the model's right hand in movement (as indicated by its blurriness) indicates that the person is not concerned about looking into the camera and is going about her work, in contrast to the clearly posed shots. The model seems to be narrating or perhaps giving a testimonial. The hands also show openness, and the star-shaped clasp may be read as strength or certainty of conviction. The background focus of the camera captures a parallel star traced on the chalkboard directly behind the speaker.

Then we see "Mariana" surrounded by paperwork, showing that the model is driven, empowered in her bureaucratic role, and has something substantial to offer to the mainstream marketplace. The picture seems posed, focusing on the interaction between the jewelry and the hair, assuming a staged air of mainstream "femininity," coupled by a facial gesticulation of satisfaction or happiness. The low-cut dress demonstrating cleavage may or may not detract from the professional appearance of the model, depending upon the perspective of the viewer.

"Moa" represents the first time in the article that the viewer receives a full-bodied picture. The object of the camera appears far more serious, perhaps even stern. She seems to be en route to a professional engagement and is therefore not interested in being photographed. The elegance of a well-dressed woman, in good physical shape, demonstrates sensuality (via cleavage and curves of the legs), while it is clear that she means business. As such, she holds her bag confidently in the right hand. The use of black sunglasses may perhaps be read to demonstrate that there are multiple layers to the model's personality or, quite possibly, indicate the concealment of secrets.

The presence of a grandmotherly appearance represented by "Kátia" displays a woman who is older than her counterparts (in the previous pictures described), strong, but worn or tired. The flowered blouse connotes femininity, but the jewelry is not ostensibly glamorous and likely not intentionally placed on "for the camera." The cross she is wearing may be a symbol of religious conviction but may also represent an inclination for compassion or love. This model may be wearing some makeup, but she does not seem overly prepared for the camera. Her hair is "picked up" for ease and daily comfort and reflects unpretentiousness and a total lack of vanity.

The photo of Cláudia shows her striking a pose that seems to demonstrate satisfaction or happiness. Unlike the previous photos discussed so far, the photographer gives the viewer a glimpse into the comforts of the model's home life, opening us up to her abode (rather than remaining at the work place). She is tugging or clutching a pillow, which may demonstrate hardship or insecurity. The fact that she is sitting on what appears to be a bed may sexualize the photograph somewhat. Her large jewelry demonstrates strength or self-confidence, and the crossed legs show that she might be holding back a little. One leg is pulled back and she has a heeled shoe on her foot, which conveys a sense of professionalism, of formality, even amidst the comforts of her home.

"Phedra" is clearly portrayed as an older woman who seems to be in a highly contemplative, meditative pose. The pinky nail under her lip may suggest regret or simply that she is lost in thought, pondering a serious matter or perhaps reflecting on a memory. Cultural notions of femininity are cut almost completely from the photograph because there is only a close-up of the model's face. Even the hair is cut out from the majority of the picture. Finally, "Claudia Wonder," perhaps similar in age to the previous model, appears far more confident, driven, and direct. The black colors of the hat and the hair demonstrate a possibility for passionate engagement. The lipstick is lighter than her lip line, which has the effect of caging her lips in black. It seems the last two pictures seem to contemplate how these particular models have framed and/or altered their age.

Going back to the magazine cover, it depicts "Bruna" as an attractive woman, who is seemingly content. The close-up of the model's face seems somewhat uncharacteristic when compared to normal conventions of facial shots on other magazine covers. The bright red lipstick evokes conventional

femininity and the colors are warm, the hair natural, the makeup not over-
done. She is wearing a suit jacket, giving an air of sophistication. One may
read her crossed arms as indicative of strength. The colors of the handbag,
however, do not combine well with the colors of her suit, possibly serving
to challenge conventions. The gaze of the photographer is clearly on the
face of the model, with the hand positioned as if to hold something back,
accentuating the bag and its buckled strap, which lends more strength to the
model, while possibly suggesting that she is tightening up (e.g., her body, her
finances, her privacy).

S.O.S. DIGNITY: *PROJETO NOME DELAS*: HUMAN
RIGHTS VIA ART: SEX WORK, WORK ETHIC,
AND THE ETHICS AND AESTHETICS
OF REPRESENTATION

The final sections of the chapter share the ethical concerns and imperatives
raised in Viviane Namaste's work on *Sex Change, Social Change*—"By
integrating the lives of transsexual prostitutes, prisoners, and drug users into
public discussions of transsexuality in feminist communities, we can imagine forms of political action that make the questions of poverty a political
priority" (Namaste 2005, 267)—but I am also interested in breaking through
the stereotype that would hold sex work as the only viable form of gain-
ful employment for Brazilian *travestis*. One of the most salient criticisms
Namaste launches in her book is the need to acknowledge and integrate the
daily lives of transsexual (or transgender) prostitutes into our theoretical
considerations and challenges in academic theory beyond political activism.
Critiquing a feminist framework that is based on what she names "the values
and experiences of certain white, Western, middle-class women," reminiscent of much of the theoretical and creative work of a generation of scholar-
activists like Gloria Anzaldúa, Namaste writes: "By integrating the lives of
transsexual prostitutes, prisoners, and drug users into public discussions of
transsexuality in feminist communities, we can imagine forms of political
action that make questions of poverty a political priority" (2005, 267). She
eventually argues a point that the founders of NGOs like "S.O.S. Dignity"
hold to their very core: To combat discrimination against the population that
is most severely marginalized or collectively targeted for hatred and abuse
is to make, as Namaste concludes, "broader links concerning the regulation
of marginalized people," taking issues of individual human rights to a level
where human communities and social movements are viewed as collective
entities to improve injustices on a universal scale. Giving attention to the lives
and the work of *travestis*, however, does not give license to exoticizing or

romanticizing their existence. Organizations like S.O.S. Dignity, which strive
to "humanize" or bring integrity to individuals through photography, tread a
fine line between exploitation and objectification within the purported goal
of humanization. For even if the camera does not eroticize their images and
even if no genitalia is exposed, the subjects are still transformed into objects
of both the camera itself and the ambivalent intentions of the middle-class,
white, Scottish male attorney who is photographing them with the intent of
recovering, or perhaps attempting to uncover, personal dignity. I am left to
wonder how much of this gesture is consciously or otherwise motivated by
a voyeuristic fascination with "these people" (as Barry Michael Wolfe put it
in our interview together). The simultaneous creative arts outreach and legal
work of an organization like S.O.S. Dignity bring us squarely into the center
of the debate between objectification/exploitation through the camera versus
normalization by de-eroticizing sex workers with the attempt to restore their
humanity/dignity as individuals. But do these photos project sensual poses or
familiar faces? This is particularly important in a climate where many *travestis* are rejected by their families, expelled from their homes, and begin work
as prostitutes as early as age 12, some preparing themselves (and transforming their bodies) in preparation to work in Europe, where they hope to make
enough money to better their financial situation.

My research shows that S.O.S. Dignity represents the troubled relationship between art and politics as much as it zeroes in on the necessary link
between academic (scholarly) work and sociopolitical activism. We must,
therefore, take particular care in assessing the lives and the experiences of a
population that is especially vulnerable to commodification and imperialism.
The eroticized Brazilian body is a traveling exhibit, once inserted in a global
spectacularization, masquerading its carnival carnality abroad. This myth is
one of the most dangerous stereotypes of all: that these sexualized and sexually adept multigendered exotic Latinxs exist to be used as objects of satisfaction. In its list of goals and objectives, S.O.S. Dignity, founded in 2005,
defines *travestis* as "People who were born men and present themselves as
women," subsequently identifying this population as "the single most marginalized group in Brazil." The description continues as follows: "*Travestis*
are vulnerable to exploitation by clients, pimps and traffickers, not to mention
arbitrary violence from police, organized crime, and the general public." It
defines *travestis'* subculture as "pre-political," meaning below the level of
protection of both local and international law, concluding that "Effectively,
their plight does not reach the agenda of law enforcement agencies and NGOs
dealing with human trafficking and slavery. Consequently, attempts to attack
exploitation and trafficking through political or legal action tend to result in
further suffering by the victims." Finally, I examine the political ramifica-
tions of the fact that the photographic exhibitions to date have been at least

partially sponsored and funded by Brazilian government AIDS organizations. In fact, the vast majority of the photos I have selected for brief analysis
are excerpted from the collection entitled "Expressions of a Hidden City,"
exhibited in June 2007 at the Gallery of the *Conjunto Nacional* in São Paulo.
Co-sponsors of the exposition included various São Paulo Municipal AIDS
and Human Rights Programs, the AIDS Program of the State of São Paulo,
the AIDS News Agency, and the *Instituto Cultural Barong*, a Brazilian STD-
AIDS Prevention/Education NGO.

Before we begin our analysis of the photographs themselves, it is worthwhile to consider Barry Michael Wolfe's own conceptualization of the term/
category of identity called *travesti*. Wolfe generously agreed to conduct an
interview with me in English, which I conducted at his home in São Paulo
on June 25, 2008. During our conversation, Wolfe characterized *travestis* as
follows: "Although anthropologists might disagree, and unlike in the States
and the UK, *travestis* don't consider themselves women. They consider themselves as men and women in the same person. But they present themselves as
women. They don't want to **be** women. They don't want to have operations;
they want to keep their penises. In English, we define a concept by what it
is not. They're not drag [queens] because they can't dress up as men and go
about their business as men during the day. They're not transsexuals because
they don't believe they were born in the wrong body. They don't want to
become women. So they are essentially androgynous, intrinsically androgynous." This statement is rather fascinating in that it conflicts, quite substantially, with the claims and opinions of scholars, particularly ethnographers
and cultural anthropologists, who often insist that the attempts at "feminization" equate to the desire to become a woman. Wolfe's conceptualization here
appears to echo, to some extent, Judith Butler's well-known assertion that
"identifications are multiple and contestatory" (Butler, 1993, 99), therefore
arguing for the productivity of androgyny, as it were, or at least the fluidity
of unfixed and malleable performances of gender that tend to ambivalently
conflict with each other. In fact, some queer theorists might argue that it is
precisely and perhaps even only within this ambivalence, within the "androgyny" of multiple identifications, that liberation from hegemonic and heteronormative classifications of gender identity confers value to gender variation.
Nevertheless, I remain concerned as to whether or not SOS Dignity falls into
the category Namaste elucidates as follows: "Indeed, transsexual and transgendered people and characters have become objects of fascination. . . . Critical theory and activism must consider the extent to which these inscriptions
of TS/TG people are complicit with the virtual erasure of transsexual bodies
and lives. More often than not, cultural representations about transgendered
phenomena have nothing whatsoever to do with the everyday lives of transsexuals and transvestites, especially the lives of prostitutes, immigrants, and

the working poor" (270). In other words, to what extent does the collection of photographs inadvertently, and perhaps ironically, dehumanize its subjects by re-objectifying them, if only to cast them in a different, supposedly more "human" light?

I believe it is an indisputable fact that the intention of SOS Dignity, in essence to humanize the most stigmatized and misunderstood population in Brazil, is a noble and admirable one. Nevertheless, it is worthwhile to evaluate whether the medium of photography might be the best way to attain these goals. What follows are a series of questions and critiques that are designed not to mitigate or minimize the significant positive impact that such an organization has made historically and continues to achieve in the current civil rights movement. Rather, I am interested here in the theoretical considerations of the role of photography as a discourse of political activism in comparison to other cultural representations and media I have examined in this book. As we have seen, each medium, including the present book which attempts to represent such cultural representations, has its own limitations, its inevitable shortcomings, its particular pitfalls that by no means invalidates or minimizes the invaluable contributions these entities have made to the LGBT movement in Brazil. Nevertheless, I feel it is an ethically important exercise to problematize these discourses, including a virtuous and even altruistic NGO like SOS Dignity, to understand the ways in which the "language" of each of these narratives limits or polices the potential for a richer impact on the lives of the individuals they work so hard to protect and to improve.

A careful analysis of the "SOS Dignity Action Plan," last updated on July 22, 2009, may help to illuminate if not begin to alleviate some of these ethical concerns. Most of my preoccupations stemming from this document involve the use of language, unintentionally I believe, to reify or reinforce certain generalizations and assumptions that may risk perpetuating the marginalization of this community. The first issue, to my mind, is the NGO's exclusive definition of the term *travesti* as "transgender sex worker." As we have seen in the preceding pages, there is a nascent but increasingly visible degree of acceptance of alternative occupations and professions for *travestis*, since 17% (according to government statistics) as opposed to 5% (according to my interview with Wolfe) have already entered the official or formal job market. The very definition of *travesti* on the NGO's mission statement must be modified if, indeed, one of its primary goals as stated is "to create employment opportunities outside prostitution."

The use of the term "underworld" to refer to the workplace of *travestis* is a potentially problematic term that might romanticize or perhaps even vilify the dangers of the downtown city streets at night. As far as semantics is concerned, the choice to conflate *transvestites* (or cross-dressers) and *transgender people* with *travestis* as identical in nature is erroneous, as we have seen earlier, and potentially dangerous. In the section of the "Action Plan," which discusses advocacy and the raising of awareness of human trafficking and pedophilia, the document reads: "Silicone pumping . . . is a staple of many transvestites' lives, especially those who engage in sex work. Some transvestites become specialists, known as *bombadeiras* (literally 'pumpers'), in pumping unsterilized, industrial silicone into the bodies of other transgender people."

At this point, two content-related critiques are warranted: the harsh (if unfair) criticism of other "Transgender NGOs" in Brazil and a portrayal of mixed intentions at best or total inefficiency at worst comes across in my reading of the following statement: "Transgender NGOs (which are often run by former or working pimps and traffickers) do very little practical individual level human rights work in Brazil in general and almost zero in the largest city, São Paulo." Calling on the assistance and the experience of one who has lived as a trafficker or even a pimp, therefore having not only seen but participated in the sexual exploitation of the individuals whom they have essentially sold into slavery is, of course, highly controversial. However, it is damaging and, of course, discriminatory to directly and uniformly undermine potentially competent individuals who have quite literally been in the "field" in a previous phase of their lives. Such a statement runs the risk of creating animosity and a sense of competition or rivalry among other organizations that may be invested in the very same or similar goals of curtailing human trafficking and sexual exploitation. SOS Dignity might be more effective, in my view, if the organization were to take special care not to belittle either the intentions or the actions of other entities investing time and energy to assist the very same populations.

Finally, while it is important to be clear (and certainly not to deny or even understate) the important connection between sex workers and the transmission of HIV/AIDS, I worry that the text of the "Action Plan" may have gone too far in its assertion that "as demonstrated in the 'Our Story' section of www.sosdignity.org, 2,000 transgender [sex] professionals in one Brazilian city generate hundreds of thousands of potential HIV transmissions to women every year." I wonder if this statistic may be (mis)read to suggest that sex work and its links to sexually transmitted diseases is exclusively, or even primarily, grounded in the city of São Paulo. Further, I think it is worth considering the validity of this statistic, which only shows part of the story by casting the spotlight on "heterosexually" identified men on the "down low," contracting *travestis* for their services and potentially contracting HIV and bringing it home to their unknowing (and innocent) wives or girlfriends. This is particularly disturbing because the "Action Plan" highlights only the hegemonic group or category of people, thus reifying a heteronormative view of the individuals who may become victimized, essentially relegating sexual minorities to invisibility at the same time as it seems to cast *travestis* as the predominant group of workers spreading the HIV virus to the traditional *paulistano* household. My concern, therefore, is whether the language of this "Action Plan," a document that is used to generate further sponsorship and funding from supportive individuals and organizations, may inadvertently deepen transphobia, discrimination, and fear.

As we turn now to an analysis of the photographs in Wolfe's collection, I notice a commonly repeated pattern. Figures 6.3–6.9 display curvaceous bodies with angles that serve to profile beauty, femininity, and sensuality.

Figures 6.3–6.9. Photos from Barry Michael Wolfe's Exhibit *Expressions of the Hidden City*, June 2020. *Conjunto Nacional de São Paulo.*

Figures 6.3–6.9. (Continued)

Figures 6.3–6.9.   (Continued)

There is an apparently posed sense of happiness or satisfaction on the faces of each of these models. The tight clothing clearly demonstrates well-endowed physical attributes, often big bosoms and small blouses. The gaze is uniformly alluring, inviting, enticing, while still exhibiting individual characteristics of difference. At first glance the photographs reveal both non-specific moments as well as possible milestones (a prom, a graduation from a vocational/career school, a group clad in matching uniforms at a high school Team Spirit Day) all categorized in the vernacular genre of photography. The color photographs seem to depict the normal lives of typical, Latinx young women in their sexual prime, tagged as Brazilian by the telltale green and yellow garb seen in one of the snapshots. Terry Barrett writes in his book *Criticizing Photographs* (fourth edition): "Their [queer theorists'] analyses disclose complicated cultural strategies that attempt to regulate sexual behavior by defining notions of what is normal and deviant in order to repress those who challenge sexual norms or who do not conform to socially privileged gender roles of straight men and women" (201). Taking a closer look, we see the females could be transgender women with "travesti" in the cover bylines as a major contributing clue along with a certain, subtle penchant for what is commonly referred to as "extra," which I noted in the heaved breasts and contoured makeup of several of the images, none of which specifically "out" or confirm their gender identity as trans or cis women. In terms of ethical photography, while the images may convey healthy, relaxed, and genuinely happy young adults in safe living spaces and homes, this naive view clashes with the reality of violence on the streets. In interpreting these images and the bright, alert and fresh faces, we sense a positive support center or group for these young individuals where they are able to exist without fear outside of the all-too-prevalent street work trajectory for young trans women. Some of these photos represent subjects who appear to be in their prime of a long, happy life. This notion is juxtaposed, of course, with the sobering reality that, as of 2018, the average life expectancy for *travestis* and transexual Brazilians is 35 years old (Antunes 2013) compared with the Brazilian population in general, which is 74.9 years old (*IGBE* 2013). In their 2018 dossier on "Murders and Violence against Travestis and Trans People in Brazil," statistics from the National Association of Travestis and Transsexuals (*ANTRA*) and the Brazilian Institute of Trans Education (*IBTE*) indicate that 60.5% of the homicide victims are between seventeen and twenty-nine years old. Most of the models in these photographs would end up as victims of murder, HIV/AIDS, or drug overdose.

One of the many paradoxes we find in this powerful collection of photographs helps to guide us on a slippery slope and paradoxical path where the ethics of representation becomes the centerpiece of a theoretical battleground that continues to be staged upon trans bodies, a triangular space where empowered subjectivities come into conflict with imposed objectivities (vis-à-vis the objectifications that both the camera and the photographer perpetuate) and the role of the spectator constituting meaning from the work of art. The images that follow poignantly portray the complexity of the work of an activist artist (artivist) like Barry Michael Wolfe. Many of the models cast in the photographs, such as Bia from Belém do Pará in northern Brazil, reflect an exponential widening of not only the stigma of living with HIV/AIDS (Bia ultimately died of the disease at the age of nineteen) but also what black feminist critic Patricia Hill Collins brands "the matrix of domination" in which there occurs a multiple layering of discriminations that intersectionally overlap, leading to a deeper marginalization and stigmatization. In Bia's specific case, there are at least five levels or "layers" of discrimination that her mere existence represents for a Brazilian viewer. In addition to being a trans woman, Bia is a *retirante nordestina*, an immigrant from Brazil's impoverished north and northeast to an economically more prosperous megalopolis like São Paulo or Rio de Janeiro, or Porto Alegre in southeastern or southern Brazil. She is also the vulnerable victim of the structural violence of poverty in a deeply class-conscious and classist society, with a dark-skinned body in a country where racial discrimination and institutionalized anti-black racism unfortunately finds one of the most protected harbors in the Western world. Additionally, Bia is a victim of a stigmatized virus that would eventually lead to her death caused by HIV/AIDS at the young age of nineteen.

While I acknowledge the critical importance of giving name(s) to the victimization of Brazil's most vulnerable citizens, the objects of the camera are also subjects, empowered with the agency to accept or reject the terms of the "contract" under which their faces and bodies transform into viewable objects for consumption and capital. At this theoretical juncture, Pierre Bourdieau's work on multiple spectatorships reminds us of the multiplicities of motives and intentionality of all the actors in this process. For example, it may be useful to assess the degree to which *travestis* who are sex workers may agree to pose for the camera, as models of idealized feminine beauty that they can then utilize to exercise or enhance performance of their profession. Although there is no question that violence occurs as a result of stigmatization of the individuals objectified by the camera, the photographer's intent is to "sell" their humanity, human dignity, whereas the hope of the model may very well be to sell her work (including her body/beauty), while she develops or adds to a portfolio that she may use to attract clients. For this reason, it is incumbent upon the critic-observer to carefully distinguish between how they are viewing the photos while not discounting the agency of those who chose to participate in the project, self-empowered with new photographs they may use to sell their image, whether to future clients or to an estranged family, or even to foster self-confidence while receiving positive attention and successfully performing their own idealized notions of femininity. These are all possible narratives that may clash with how the critic or even the photographer may perceive or analyze the "life" of the photographic images extending beyond the lives of the individuals who ultimately chose to contribute to the project. This perspective not only forces the spectator to view sex work as a "legitimate" client-building recruitment activity like any other position in sales and marketing but also resists the discourse of moralization of conventional work ethic often reserved for work regarded as "suitable" in a cis-centric heteropatriarchal context, one that judges, denies, and shames prostitution as viable or valuable work.

Figure 6.3 represents relationships between two women who are clearly posing for the camera. This may be indicative of friendships but, due to the high degree of eroticism in the sensual poses, the photographs may also play into stereotypes, somewhat ironically, of heterosexual male "girl-on-girl" sexual fantasies. Simultaneously, as noted earlier, this is the kind of sex that sells in heteronormative circles. Therefore, the models may be consciously and conscientiously exploiting that narrative for their own economic gain, something which in the vast majority of these scenarios represents and equates to financial survival.

Figures 6.5–6.7 clearly show the *travesti* sex workers to be in movement, working or "in their element" (that is, on the streets), perhaps reflecting a bit more honesty and disclosure about the ambience of their assumed professions. The model in the middle of figure 6.7 distinguishes herself quite significantly from the other photographs in the collection. She seems to portray more depth than her counterparts, is more grounded and reflects a certain degree of comfort in her own skin. While the earlier photographs cast models who seem to feel compelled to portray an image for the camera, this particular model seems far more raw due to the absence of glitter. The sense of "femininity" appears to emanate from inside the person, in stark contrast to the images of plastered models preceding this one.

The photographs displayed in figure 6.10 come from a special collection of Wolfe's work, "Portraits of a Trans Marriage." While the series contains about a dozen photos, I have chosen just three to display here, due to space constraints. What is different about these family portraits, other than the fact that the objects are not displayed alone and in erotic poses we have become accustomed to seeing in most instances, is that the parents are present,

Figure 6.10.   Photo from Barry Michael Wolfe's Collection Titled *Retratos de um casamento trans* **(Portraits of a Trans Marriage), 2008.**

appearing proud and happy, and the gender identity of the individuals in the union is irrelevant to the sanctity and the joy of the momentous occasion of union portrayed and celebrated in these photographs.

OVER THE RAINBOW AND UNDER
"THE RED UMBRELLA FUND"

With the proliferation of NGOs designed to assist and advocate for the rights of sex workers internationally, it is worth turning our attention to an organization that models a more inclusive (and paradoxically exclusive) infrastructure based on self-determination of sex workers since its founding in 2012. Awarding 157 grants to sex worker-led groups between 2012 and 2018, the Red Umbrella Fund bills itself as "the first global fund *by* and *for* sex workers" (italics not mine). Funding is provided by a number of partners. The 2019 cycle, for example, had the following organizations among its sponsors: American Jewish World Service, the Dutch Ministry of Foreign Affairs, the Gates Foundation, Mama Cash, the Oak Foundation, and Open Society Foundations, among other individual donors not published on their website.

To evaluate submitted entries to its call for grant applications, its Program Advisory Committee (PAC) is comprised of a peer review panel led by sex workers from the entire world. Its International Steering Committee, whose function is to approve the final selection proposed by the PAC, includes a majority of sex workers among its membership. In its 2019 Application Guidelines, the Red Umbrella Fund not only requires that groups or networks who apply be led by sex workers but holds as prerequisites that each applicant "recognise that sex work is work" and must concretely demonstrate interest in "contributing to building and strengthening the sex workers' movement." Its funding sources are available exclusively to "sex worker-led organisations and networks that are based in any country, registered or unregistered, and led by people of all sexual orientations and gender identities." With the epidemic invisibility of sex workers in the very organizations or groups existing to advocate for their rights, the Red Umbrella Fund will not consider applications from any group or network that does not possess a democratic majority of sex workers who are working for the benefit and with representation of and for sex workers. As such, the criteria for eligibility state that "at least 60% of the decision-making body must be sex workers. This composition may include former and current sex workers, but with at least an aspiration to include current sex workers. An additional parameter for consideration is that at least 60% of the "spokespeople" of the organization must be sex workers by profession, with at least 33% of staff members self-defined sex workers as well. With its taboo-breaking repetition of the words "sex workers" occurring on nearly every line of the application instructions, the Red Umbrella Fund clearly breaks silences by insisting that applicants demonstrate that sex workers themselves must be "at the heart of the design, implementation, and evaluation of programmes" and also clearly stipulating that academic research or individual requests are not considered for funding. With grants ranging from €8,000 to €80,000 for a period of two years, The Red Umbrella Fund anticipated awarding approximately twenty-eight grants in 2019, extending support to networks and groups located in at least thirty-one countries. What is revolutionary about this organization is its refusal to "buy into" conventional discourses that see sex workers as victims or, at best, its attempt to speak for or on behalf of sex work professionals.

Though it lacks the specificity of trans sex workers, one may ask if this type of model is workable in a Brazilian context where transgender sex workers are the most vulnerable segment of the population. The answer is a resounding "yes." Although prostitution is legal in Brazil, and the country's Labor Department added sex work to the official *Classificação Brasileira de Ocupações*, making it possible for sex workers to contribute to retirement accounts and receive social security benefits via *Brazilian National Institute for Social Security (INSS)* upon their retirement, the social stigmatization of sex workers continues to dissuade them from signing up for these benefits on the basis of their occupation. In 2018, for example, approximately 30% of sex workers declared their profession when they enrolled in *INSS*. Anthropologist Maria Isabel Zanzotti de Oliveira explains the problem of (self-)stigmatization in a March 2020 interview with Brazilian news source *TAB*: "Despite being a legalized profession that is included in the registry of existent occupations in Brazil, to self-declare as a sex worker brings so much discomfort that few have the courage to transcend the stigma. However, informality is what is practiced in labor markets, resulting in a lack of rights and safety measures, even for those who have spent a good part of their lives practicing the profession. This is a similar scenario, therefore, of many informal workers in various sectors of the Brazilian work force" (translation mine).[8] [9]

Since 2012, activist Leila Barreto, who proudly and publicly stakes her identity as a *Filha da Puta* (literally, Daughter of a Whore) in all capital letters, is the daughter of Lourdes Barreto, a prominent founder of the sex workers activism movement in Brazil, the Brazilian Network of Prostitutes (*Rede Brasileira de Prostitutas*). Barreto is the founder of an annual event called *Puta Dei*, now taking place throughout many cities in Brazil parallel to International Sex Workers' Day, which the global sex worker community commemorates on June 2 of every year. Studying this sociopolitical event brings us to fascinating conclusions about the roles of language in the creation and proliferation of this cultural moment appearing every year on the Brazilian calendar. The multiplicities of meanings of the terms *Puta Dei* represent a movement that is as specifically Brazilian as it is global in nature, recalling and echoing back to the sociolinguistic "conversations" in chapter 4 of this book. More specifically, *dei* is a Brazilianization of the English term "day," highlighting the well-known prestige of the English language in Brazil, especially when pertaining to social movements. One example is the use of "Black Pride" alternating in mainstream Brazilian Portuguese with the *movimento negro*. However, in Portuguese, *dei* is the first-person preterite form of the verb *dar*, which while meaning "to give" in English also carries particularly Brazilian denotations of the passive partner in the sexual exchange (i.e., the "bottom" who literally gives to the active partner who "eats"). At the same time, *dê*, which is phonetically identical to *dei*, is the imperative (command) form instructing another to "give" of oneself, such as in an act of generosity in an interpersonal transaction, sexual or otherwise. (Code-)switching back and forth between English and Portuguese, in contemporary American slang, *Dei*, also generally capitalized, signifies "goddess," with origins in deity. In 2017, the *Urban Dictionary* defined "Dei" as follows: "She may seem cold at first but warms up once you get to know her. . . . If by chance you begin to develop feelings for a Dei, let her know quickly because many guys will want her. . . . Many Deis may be insecure, so treat her with some god damn respect." This colloquial definition is, of course, repugnantly filled with misogynist, sexist, heteronormative, and cis-normative implications as it points to "her" insecurity, the objectification of the "goddess" to be possessed before other (men) begin to "want" her, female frigidity, and a total lack of agency as she falls to male ownership. But it is also revealing when we reflect on the "god-like" representation of the sex worker who gives pleasure to others who hire "her" for that purpose, remaining emotionally inaccessible while desirable to other "guys."

Finally, it almost goes without saying that *Opus Dei* (Latin for "The Work of God") opens a new set of denotations for the ludic and lewd *Puta Dei*'s (serious) play on language.

CONCLUSIONS: TRANSPHOBIA, THE DISCOURSE OF CITIZENSHIP, AND THE TROUBLED RELATIONSHIP BETWEEN LGB AND T COMMUNITIES

The phenomenon of transphobia and its violent malevolence, with particularly serious consequences for FTM individuals, is articulated quite well in Viviane K. Namaste's (2000), *Invisible Lives: The Erasure of Transsexual and Transgendered People*:

> If gender ambiguity is habitually resolved within a masculinist frame of reference, then genetic males who live as women will be among those most at risk

for assault. Simply put, within Western societies, it is easier for females to pass as men than for males to pass as women. Ethnographic research on gender confirms this hypothesis: In Holly Devor's study of "gender-blending" females, she notes that several of the women she interviewed felt free enough to walk down dimly lit streets late at night, given that they were perceived to be men. Furthermore, many genetic females can live full-time as men without plastic surgery and/or male hormones. Conversely, many genetic males need to take female hormones in order to pass successfully as women. (145)

The discourse of citizenship, which, as we have seen in chapters 1–3 with our detailed investigation of the relatively brief but remarkably lively history of the LGBT Pride Parade of São Paulo, is a marker of both identity politics and the movement to conquer the right to a level of social justice. Such hard-earned equality would no longer allow mainstream heteronormative or homonormative hegemonies to relegate trans-identified individuals and communities to secondary citizen status, in the best-case scenario, if not deem them sub-human altogether. Namaste's work also illuminates the discourse of citizenship and how legal institutions erase the existence of transgendered citizens from acknowledged participation in society, mainstream or otherwise: "The sexed production of bodies produces only men and women. Transsexuals do not, and cannot exist, from a legal standpoint. . . . Transsexuals are produced through erasure to the extent that civil status and juridical identity foreclose transsexual possibilities, authorizing only nontranssexual men and women as citizens" (263).

Finally, this scholar's work, though it addresses transgendered sex workers in Canada specifically, effectively highlights, in a more general sense, the troubled relationship between L/G and T communities and individuals: "Transsexuals and transgendered people are perhaps better aligned with prostitute activists than with lesbians and gay men. Systemic and institutionalized discrimination against prostitutes impedes and prevents their access to health care and thus the ability of many transsexuals to live their bodies as they choose" (269).

All of the previous conclusions collectively lead us down a path that would clearly argue for not only a much more visible inclusion of the "T" in the "LGBT" classification but also for legitimizing the existence and the contributions of trans individuals within both the movement itself and society at large. To my mind, responsible legislation to guarantee inclusivity must be paralleled by ethical cultural representations of the communities that continue to be marginalized and stigmatized.

Chapters 1–3 have primarily examined journalistic discourse to analyze changing media representations of the LGBT Pride Parade in São Paulo over the course of its first twenty-three years of existence. Chapter 4 analyzed the linguistic codes of the dictionary or reference manual. This chapter considers the use of photography and other "artivistic" projects as both a language and a tool to illuminate representations of *travestis*. The first section, including figure 6.1, contains photographs from my own collection and reflects how *travesti* sex workers represent themselves, their work, and their services. The emphasis is predominantly, though not unanimously, placed on sexual versatility, blonde-haired, light-skinned physical traits (i.e., racialized as white), voluptuous "feminine" curves, affectionate behavior, and potent sensuality. The models featured in the following section and represented by the magazine cover in figure 6.2 are the subjects/objects of a mainstream popular magazine article, which tries to salvage *travestis* from sex work, with all the patriarchal paternalism I mean to imply by the term *salvage*. The essay also makes a compelling attempt to disconnect transgender identity from prostitution, displaying the accomplishments and successes of *travestis* who have entered the formal marketplace. Figures 6.3–6.9, from Barry Michael Wolfe's SOS Dignity collection, are particularly useful in that they display a wide variety of portrayals, ranging from facial and upper body snapshots, which exhibit the objectification of curvaceous, sensual bodies with alluring, enticing gestures we have seen ad nauseam, to the relationships between *travesti* colleagues and friends, if only in the imagination of the photographer, to the more precise but equally eroticized portrayal of sex workers in movement, in their work environment, and on the streets.

The images represented in figures 6.3–6.7 and 6.10 are the ones that give me the most hope for the possibility of attaining a more ethical portrayal of the daily lives of *travestis*, transcending the sensual poses and the erotic sexualization of their bodies. The two first models in figure 6.7 are clearly engaged in activities beyond sex work, exhibiting multiplicities of identities, which move beyond the reinforcement of an objectified existence, meant solely to satisfy the sexual whims of their clients. The inclusion of a guitar and reading material (though the viewer is not privy to the text the model is reading) reflect much more humane and human portrayals of the subjects, even as they succumb to become objects of the camera. The last model in the same figure is perhaps the quintessential antagonist to Benedetti's notion of *toda feita*, for she exudes a sense of comfort and a level of depth, even with her gaze, marking a presence that is not adorned or complemented by the glitter or glamour so characteristic of her counterparts. Finally, the three family members in figure 6.10 disrupt the framed solitary confinement of the majority of the models photographed, inviting the viewer to a wedding ceremony between two individuals of ambiguous (and, more importantly, irrelevant) gender identity, with a proud parent adorning each of the newlyweds. By the same token, and paradoxically, the conventionality of the marriage ceremony itself, if viewed in a queer light, may be evaluated as one whose ceremony mimics the heteronormative institution of marriage to such an extent that the performance commits a serious injustice to queer subjectivities, especially those deeply invested in attaining antinormativity.

Chapter 7

(For)getting Far Away from Home: Cinematic Representations of Twenty-First-Century (LGB)Trans Brazil

Exile places you in the category of migrant. My biggest difficulty in exile is the question of language because I am a man who adores speaking Portuguese. I know that the Portuguese language was imposed by the colonizer. The Portuguese language is the colonizer within me. This is my contradiction. I love the language the colonizer gave me because it is from within this language that I take action against colonization. It is also because of this language that I engage in the work of decolonization. The work of decolonization is also linguistic work.

—Jean Wyllys, *"Diálogos pela Democracia,"* Episode 1.

The U.S. Network for Democracy in Brazil, July 2, 2020

This chapter continues to build on our study of visual cultures in contemporary Brazil, examining seven LGBT-themed feature-length film productions and three shorts released during the first two decades of the twenty-first century to illuminate the pathways of queer diaspora for the LGBT Brazilian protagonists who choose (or are forced) to leave Brazil in search of broader acceptance for their very physical, emotional, and/or spiritual survival. Without taking limited space here to rehash the plot summaries of any of the films examined herein, available elsewhere, this chapter takes up the major motifs that these films collectively explore, centering on the (im)migration process of Brazilians outside Brazil. The following are the films we shall explore in this chapter. The reader should keep in mind that this is a selective list and that a more comprehensive, though incomplete, filmography may be found at the end of the book for additional reference or analysis.

FEATURE-LENGTH FILMS CONSIDERED IN THIS CHAPTER:

"Dois perdidos numa noite suja" (José Joffily, 2002)
"Madame satã" (Karim Aïnouz, 2002)
"Do começo ao fim" (Aluizio Abranches, 2009)
"Tatuagem" (Hilton Lacerda, 2013)
"Do lado de fora" (Alexandre Carvalho & Maitê Romão, 2014)
"Praia do futuro" (Karim Aïnouz, 2014)
"Hoje eu quero voltar sozinho" (Daniel Ribeiro, 2014)

SHORTS (CURTAS) EXAMINED IN THIS CHAPTER:

"Hoje eu não quero voltar sozinho" (Daniel Ribeiro, 2010)
"Meu jogador favorito" (Adriano Oliveira & Guilherme Luka, 2018)
"Depois daquela festa" (Caio Scot, 2019)

Figure 7.1.   Chart of Films Studied in Chapter 7.

CINEMATIC REPRESENTATIONS OF CONTEMPORARY LGBT BRAZIL (2001–2019)

A focus on the cultural representations of Brazilians moving through geographical, existential, and identitarian displacement necessarily addresses the motif of fleeing "home" in order to reinscribe and reconstruct what I would like to call "quome," a progressive transition to "queer home(s)" of their own invention. To mark this nonlinear and often conflicted internal journey toward liberation and away from patriarchal imposition, the protagonists we shall meet in this chapter forge queer utopias, create alternative families and communities while depathologizing and "normalizing" their own psychosexual development—whether gay, lesbian, bisexual, transgender, *travesti*, or transsexual in nature. Paradoxically, I argue that their function in the majority of the films I analyze here is to intentionally displace the attention of the spectator from seeking/staking out minority gender identities and sexual orientations as the central motifs of the narrative—resisting the word *problems*—to other social taboos, which may include but also divert from gender and sexuality. Specifically, I will critically assess the creation of the *utopia do cu* in the film *Tatuagem* (Hilton Lacerda 2013), contrasting cinematic creations of fictitious lands with spectacularization in the fantasy worlds of *Madame Satã* (Karim Aïnouz 2002), turning to the construction of a performative identity in queer flux as a response to and a protest of discrimination based on the intersectionalities of anti-black racism, homophobia, and transphobia. The chapter contrasts the more concrete "grounded" displacement in *Dois perdidos numa noite suja* (José Joffily 2002), *Praia do futuro*

(Karim Aïnouz 2014), and other films from this period, effectively "queering" the utopian American/European dream of *trans-brasilidade* abroad.

As a cultural studies critic interested in how language (dis)empowers the development of alternate subjectivities, I find myself (un)thinking, (de)constructing, and (re)inventing the term *pertencer*, to belong, *pertencimento* (belonging). The ephemeral condition of one's process of "be-longing" may also represent a state of being in "longing," of embracing *saudade* and, perhaps paradoxically, liberation that comes from the (im)permanence of moving from one cycle/circle to another. Many of the characters we shall meet in these films join a journey (whether internal or collective) to simultaneously embrace the ambiguity of queer affect *as* fluidity of moving *on* without necessarily enduring trauma or loss of beginnings or endings in relationship(s) to others or their selves or themselves. This exercise in linguistic intercomprehension in times of virtual density/destiny to the point of intercomprehensibility (and I mean "virtual" in its multiple denotations) finds a particular resonance in a post-pandemic global reality where communication is literally compressed into digital squares and virtual boxes within a community that builds its very existence and even nurtures itself through the screens of the hi-tech devices of individuals. What impact does this "new normal" have on human cognitive powers and patterns to distinguish "physical" reality from "virtual" representations of spaces no longer limited or dictated by geographic sites or synchronous time (zones)? Or to ask a similar question in a different way, can quome-seekers reconfigure Zoom breakout rooms as communal coming-out spaces to literally and figuratively break out of conventional modes of time and space? I offer this chapter to interrogate how contemporary Brazilian film carves out audiovisual spaces for the spectator to take uncharted steps forward to move through and away from home, even if that movement is merely to suspend, if only for a fleeting moment, an inevitable journey back home, a "queer return" as Afro-Canadian scholar Rinaldo Walcott might argue, though that "re-turn" home is actually not, nor can it ever constitute the same foundations once home transforms to *quome*. To what extent do Brazilian LGBT protagonists reinvest in Gloria Anzaldúa's spiritual universe wherein psyches departing from biological homes actively cultivate dis-location in order to reterritorialize the queer (or some might argue, pre-queer) subject in newly refurbished, deconstructed, or even dis-integrated homes? As we examine character development in Brazilian cinema to understand an epistemological shift in focus which would depart from where they *live* to engage in a process of leaving *as* living, we must temper this trope of moving far away from home to determine if it is nourishing enough to forget the lands and lives that we leave, or at least forgive their murderous impact on queer psyches who move away *as* an avenue to attain their very survival. Whether by choice or by coercion, I explore in these pages the processes whereby main characters in Brazilian cinema partake on a journey to rediscover or rebuild metaphorical, metaphysical "homes" in diaspora, *quomes* that exist outside material manifestations, new refuges which do not necessarily equate to real estate. Among many questions that emerge in this journey of character development are as follows: To what extent do (homo)normative theoretical discourses on migration paradoxically bent on seeking queerness end up actually reinforcing binary dichotomies from within pre-established or internalized limitations of the protagonists in movement? I deconstruct the traditional trope of the drama and trauma of the divided self, conventional duality that would suspend and up-end exiles to have one foot firmly entrenched in Brazil, even as its toes point to departure, and the other firmly en route to foreign locales. What does it mean to simultaneously seek membership, *pertencer*, in adopted shelters, refuges as temporary as they are pathways for ephemeral passage one (dis)place(ment) to the next, while remaining and perhaps even perpetually (be) longing for "assigned" homes one had to flee to be free? These are some of the larger ontological questions I raise as we (re)view the capacity of contemporary Brazilian film to represent LGBT+-identified primary characters who find themselves, or actually exile their *selves*, to the queer uncertainty of geographical (and existential) flux.

These larger philosophical questions coalesce to a specific concern at the heart of this chapter: What are the techniques that contemporary Brazilian cinema employs to represent themes around queer Brazil? To answer this question, I propose investigating how cultural representations of Brazilian diaspora and geographical adaptation and displacement in feature films dialogue with queer diasporas, which I reiterate here, though in a more reductive fashion, as the motif of leaving home in order to traverse to new home(s), spiritual or geographical *quomes*, of one's own volition.

Because Hilton Lacerda's *Tatuagem* (2103) is a meta-cinematographic treasure of much larger magnitude that I am able to treat in these shared pages devoted to assessing a compilation of feature-length films, a deeply textured film that creates parallel universes and story lines in simultaneous co-development, this fascinating piece could very well be the subject of an entire monograph. For our purposes in this chapter, the mega meta-cinematic structure of films within films causes the kind of displacement that frees queer movement to take place while resisting any attempt to placate or to fix it in time or space. The theatrical construction of *a utopia do cu* ("the utopia of the asshole") at the heart of counter-discourse of a film not only about political dictatorship but also about the psychological dictatorships we allow in our selves, such as (self-)repression based on perceptions of heteropatriarchally imposed identities, represents an allegorical escape from harsh authoritarian realities of punishment, censorship, torture of various kinds, be they physical, psychological, or spiritual. The paradoxically named "*Chão das Estrelas*" (literally, "Floor of Stars") theater troupe's performative (re)creation of performative lands blend "fiction and philosophy" to forge and merge parallel, surreal planes of reality with quantum physics, ultimately transforming Recife specifically and (Northeastern) Brazil more generally into fictionalized universes, where any singular reality is contested and ultimately rejected in order to attain a liberated existence for each character-member of the troupe and for the community as a whole. The alternative (read: diverse and democratic) planes that this anthropophagic (bowel) movement instigates results in translinguistic and intercomprehensive features in the performances of the *Chão das Estrelas* troupe in *Tatuagem*: The figure of the Sun (*Sol*) speaks her lines in Spanish but carries the French name Paulette and is largely responsible for the homonym of *Tem cu, tem cu, tem cu*, an enthusi-*ass*-tic embracing of diversity and democracy for all assholes, since no two are exactly alike, corresponds to the English "Thank you, thank you, thank you." The Brazilian accent finds expression in the tongue that resists placement between the teeth that chew out the dictatorship, anthropophagically resisting the phoneme "th" and by extension the sound of "the." I interpret this performance as a subversive rejection of essentialism or a critique of the false nature of monoli*th*ic *th*oughts, identities, or realities that either do not fit in a Brazilian context or are too restrictive at the expense of other creative modalities or means of democratic expression on the "back burners" of creative minds who would ultimately be condemned to silence, whether the spectator interprets the *cu* as erotic (asshole), derogatory or dirty (asshole), or scatological (shitty) in nature. Democracy and freedom in *Tatuagem* and by extension in dictatorial Brazil are represented by *a utopia do cu*, the asshole being the ultimate equalizing force (i.e., quoting from the performance: "Even the illustrious President has one . . . perhaps even God . . . [in which case] *cu* is our only salvation").

The theatrical movements that are so integral to expelling (literally, shitting out) dis-integrating "reality" imposed under dictatorship are also illustrated by the lives of the protagonists who characterize the effects of such transformative (bowel) movements on daily lives. The young soldier Arlindo's (nicknamed Fininha) move from a conservative, heteropatriarchal home traces the young man's coming out process from a tiny female-dominated kitchen (no doubt to emphasize traditionally gendered divisions of labor) in a modest home in rural Pernambuco, to the camera's gradual dislocation from the kitchen, revealing his presence in the *sala de estar*, a living room which literally and figuratively enables him to occupy more space, to live and to stretch his subjectivities, as it were, and ultimately to gather psychic strength to move away from his humble origins. Fininha's journey takes him to Recife, the capital, where he ultimately meets and falls in love with Clécio

(Irandhir Santos), a gay father married to Deusa (which translates literally to "Goddess"), a straight woman portrayed by Sylvia Prado, raising their son Tuco (Deyvid Queiroz de Morais) together. Fininha's (Jesuíta Barbosa) psychological transformation in the capital unmasks his desires and subjectivities, making impossible a return "home" on the same plane of prior existence. Returning home to find it is no longer home for him in a psychic or emotional way that makes sense for his own self-discovery process, Fininha makes a final decision to permanently stay in Recife and continue life with the family he chooses rather than his biological one.

Similar triangular trajectories occur in other feature-length Brazilian films in the early 2000s. José Joffily's *Dois perdidos numa noite suja* (2002) unfolds a trajectory in which the characters undergo a circularity of circulation from Brazil (São Paulo) to the United States (New York) but ultimately re-route back to Brazil. Paco's escape from an oppressive, homophobic father in Brazil is as compelling as Tonho's escape from poverty and a life of misery. In a process of self-displacement and distantiation (or de-territorialization, recalling Anzaldúa), one to which I shall return later, the protagonists explode the monolithic myth and fallacy of the (singular) "American dream." The film *Do começo ao fim* (Aluízio Abranches 2009) takes the spectator on a journey from Rio de Janeiro to Moscow and then back to Rio again. Karim Aïnouz's *Praia do futuro* brings us from Northeastern Brazil (Fortaleza, Ceará) to Berlin, Germany, bringing as a central conflict an ardent desire to return to Brazil while ultimately arriving at the decision to stay in Berlin, whose imaginary is represented as a space of freedom for the discovery of sexuality not only for the main character but to all who traverse this legendarily liberating site. In Daniel Ribeiro's *Hoje eu quero voltar sozinho* (2014), Leonardo's (Ghilherme Lobo) desire and intent to live and study abroad conflict with the wishes and insecurities of an overprotective mother, as her fear for his well-being abroad as a blind person forbids this wish from realization. Léo's desire to leave Brazil is fueled by his conviction, as a result of his own process of maturation, that his own perceived limitations are not the barrier to attaining this goal but rather a homophobic and ableist society that infantilizes and disempowers its citizens who happen to be different, or in Léo's specific case, gay and blind. The film's brilliant strategy to equate the trait of (homo) sexuality as congenital or genetic infers that being gay is as much an option as it is for one to choose to be blind, or pick the colors of one's eyes, whether functional or not. In *Madame Satã*, as we shall soon see, the viewer is treated to an exuberant and colorful escape into a world of fantasy and spectacle as a response to discrimination on the basis of intersectional black racism and homophobia.

Much like in *Tatuagem*, the construction of performative identity and *transformismo* or drag performances, though they do not necessarily correlate to trans identification, is associated with fascination for the exotic, for Orientalizing difference. This tendency manifests itself in a stereotypical association of gay men with the foreign and the exotic, accenting and accentuating the "othering" of gay male characters. This is inarguably the case in a Brazilian context, and LGBT-themed Brazilian films seem to be invested in a process of subverting, undoing, or even queering stereotypical renderings on how Brazilians are "read" both abroad and within Brazil. In *Praia do Futuro* (Karim Aïnouz 2014), for example, there is the memorable scene of the bartender in Berlin (Natascha Paulick) who states that "Everyone says that Brazilians are always very happy." This comment serves as a counterpoint to the protagonist Donato's (Wagner Moura) own emotional experience at that time, for it is uttered at a moment of profound anguish as the main character struggles with his decision to return to Brazil, the news of his mother's death, and the dilemma of whether to fulfill his obligation to loyalty to his family by returning to Brazil or to continue to pursue his own happiness abroad. In *Tatuagem*, the repetition of the well-known joke, *Brasil é o país do futuro* ("Brazil is the country of the future") without (read: while censoring) the second part of the popular saying, *e sempre será* ("and it will always be"), is illustrative of the contradictory degrees of hope and disillusionment in the film itself and in the psychosocial development of its protagonists.

An example of a feature-length film that commits nearly every imaginable stereotype is *Do lado de fora* (Alexandre Carvalho & Maitê Romão 2014), which takes place during (and between) two consecutive years of the LGBT Pride Parade in São Paulo, by this time already legendary for being the largest of its kind in the world. With its contrived but a well-meaning "afterschool special" message that bonds a group of family and friends who witness or experience an act of homophobia immediately after the Pride Parade, a young non-binary teenager proposes a "pact" among the cast in which they all agree to come out at the following year's Pride Parade. With some actual footage of LGBT Pride Parades in the past as its only redeeming feature, this film perpetuates a host of stereotypes based on race, class, sexual orientation, and gender identity. To begin, all of the principal characters, with the possible exception of legendary drag queen Silvetty Montilla, who hilariously plays a straight conservative "mother-in-law" to a protagonist's (pregnant) wife, are white. Roger, the handsome, straight-acting (and on the down low) married man played by heartthrob André Bankoff about to become a father for the first time, is won over (like a trophy *bofe* heterosexual) by Mauro's Uncle Vicente (Marcello Airoldi), who helps Roger patch up the wounds from the homophobic attack he suffered while at the Parade. The understanding, empathetic gay uncle helps young Mauro (Luis Fernando Vaz) contend with but makes no efforts whatsoever to educate his Pentecostal parents who on more than one occasion attempt to exorcize the demons from Mauro's head, a facile but pointed critique of religious fundamentalism in Brazil and its effects on members of the LGBT community. The only black character in the film is not a Brazilian at all but a Parisian businessman, who ultimately lures Vicente to work in France and never speaks a word of Portuguese while conducting business in Brazil. The use of French extends also to social gatherings, hinting at the cultural superiority and prestige of the language. During an important business dinner, Vicente begs his best friend, the "fruit fly" Marília (Titi Müller), to pretend to be his wife and introduces her, in French of course, as such at the dinner. Other than revealing a fluent use of French at the dinner and using it to embarrass a nervous Vicente, we learn nothing about this character, her occupation, her aspirations, even her identity. In fact, she is completely invisible and irrelevant as a human being other than her role to play the "beard" for an evening. Even the lesbian couple depicted in the film is stereotypical: Lipstick lesbian Raquel (Fernanda Viacava) is a business partner to her overzealous political activist partner Jane (Tânia Granussi) who, when not working in the clothing store with Raquel, is busy updating her blog to chronicle violence and stigmatization of LGBT Brazilians in São Paulo, at one point threatening Mauro with outing after filming his first private drag performance and his parents' horrific homotransphobic reaction to it. Ultimately, the only successful character in the film is Uncle Vicente, who accepts a job offer that involves moving to Paris. It is unclear if Roger would ultimately join him after the baby is born, though his symbolic unmasking of his costumed self at the Pride Parade one year later may be interpreted as a gesture of coming out to leave his marriage (and child) and join Vicente in France.

Mauro's undefined sexuality and gender identity mark him as the only "queer" character of the film; and if this is indeed the case, his buffoonery and immaturity throughout the film, though providing moments of comic relief, do not speak well for the development of a character who is "othered" by difference. One of the only other characters in the films studied here who arguably exhibits "queerness" is Paco/Rita (Débora Falabella) in Joffilly's "*Dois perdidos numa noite suja*" (2002), a loose cinematic adaptation of Plínio Marcos's daring neo-Naturalistic play of the same name written at the height of Brazilian military dictatorship, in 1966. The piece depicts Brazil's most vulnerable populations, stigmatized by socioeconomic class as well as sexual orientation and gender identity, trying to survive a bleak existence in dark times. Paco, who was biologically born female and whose birth name is Rita, experiences a gender identity in flux, characterized by fits of internalized anger and anguished self-questioning. Though ignored by other film critics, I argue that the ambiguity of Paco's identity is a major plot point of the film. The cinematographic representation of Paco's inner chaos translates to the confusion of the spectator/viewer, forcing the audience to come to terms with our own frustration of being part of a society that pushes individuals into rigid categories of identification, externally imposed rather than internally innate. We can perhaps compare this with Paulette's (Rodrigo García) reaction when she is mistakenly referred to a "Paulinho" in *Tatuagem*, where a dead name in the masculine evokes a viscerally angry reaction when it is inadvertently used to address her. Paco's in-betweenness and queerness also extends to Paco's profoundly ambivalent relationship with Tonho (Roberto Bontempo): Is it romantic in nature? Do they merely (co-)exist as roommates? Is the "glue" economic in nature, borne out of necessity for survival in a hostile (and expensive) foreign (First) world? The film successfully oscillates between these layers of friendship, never fixing the relationship into anything one-dimensional in nature. While sexual attraction is often clear, love is questionable.

The queerness of the love relationship between the two half-brothers in *Do começo ao fim* (Aluizio Abranches 2009) begins as playful and turns romantic. The spectator is expected to equate the sexual and emotional intimacy between the siblings, Thomás (Rafael Cardoso) and Francisco (João Gabriel Vasconcellos), as "gay." This assumption begs a series of questions from the viewer about the nature of the relationship between the two men. Can they possibly be soulmates where sex is just one factor of intimate connection? Thomás's "heterosexual" sex affair in Russia while competing at the Olympics, though secondary to the overall plot structure of the film, would seem to underscore this. In spite of the viewer's expectation or prejudice, the character can no longer be conceived/labeled as exclusively gay. Another interpetation that emerges from the development of this relationship, though it is born of wealthy white male privilege, is the distinct possibility that the characters fell in love with each other when they were very young and before any recognition of being gay or self-labeling as gay. As we shall see, this motif also occurs in Daniel Ribeiro's 2010 touching short film, *Hoje eu não quero voltar sozinho*. Still, the film has serious problems of both a political and an aesthetic nature. Classism is a non-issue only because it does not exist in the homogeneous, completely "whitened" Brazil of *Do começo ao fim*. Literally everything, human, alive, or inert, is draped in bright white hues: All the characters, the entirety of the house itself, the overexposed lighting of the photography. In fact, the entire film appears as if it were drenched in sunlight, blinding the spectator to viewing Brazil as an ethnically diverse democracy. The family portrayed in the film lives in a contemporary, well-designed home, within a bubble of sports cars, Mac computers, and a swimming pool. Throughout the film, there is not only a lack of conflict in the inner workings of the life of a wealthy *carioca* family, but the evolving love relationship is as insular as it is intimate. The majority of the scenes occur in internal spaces, inside the parents' house, inside the hospital where their mother worked as a doctor, or around family members or close family friends. This perceived "safety" of the private, confined home, where anything is permitted to occur and social norms are not rigidly enforced as usual, contrasts sharply with the inexistent public world on the invisible outside, also blinding the spectators and even the characters of this film. As Da Matta has famously noted, Brazilian social realities differ substantially from within the privacy of the home than they do in the public space/imaginary of the street.[1]

But the film is daring in other ways as it takes up taboos that transcend (homo)sexuality. How is incest "gendered" in Brazil and, by extension, in Western societies? If the male half-brother protagonists were replaced with female characters, would intimacy between them still be read as incest? Also, would the average viewer perceive two sisters as lesbian characters? Or would the spectator construe the older sister as the nurturer of her baby doll younger sister, authorizing and even expecting nurturing scenes of touch, warmth, and affection between them? Why is intimacy between two brothers in love read as "gay" and further "unmasculine," as if heterosexual love were a prerequisite to attain masculinity? If the characters were brother and sister, the taboo would have been around procreation/reproduction, but would this have been equally unacceptable or more scandalous in a heteronormative context? In the end, both homosexuality and incest go hand in hand in *Do começo ao fim*, persuading spectators that the gayness of the characters is not what is objectionable but rather their incestuous relationship. Nevertheless, this component of their relationship is also construed as totally natural, even organic, raising political and ethical questions from the perspective of LGBT rights. If the possibility for procreation is the biological "risk" of incest for heterosexual siblings, is the film successful in representing the incestuous relationship between two half-brothers as acceptable once and if the viewer is able to move beyond homophobic judgments or prejudice? Finally, would the director have assumed a higher risk for public rejection had he cast the two brothers to be offspring of the same parents (and not just sons of the same mother)?

The relationship between Konrad (Clemens Schick) and Donato (Wagner Moura), the two main characters in the Brazilian-German co-production of *Praia do futuro* (Karim Aïnouz 2014), is rooted in circumstances around the drowning death of a loved one, Konrad's partner, while visiting Brazil. Intimacy develops concurrently with the grief process while the protagonist works through the literal and metaphorical drowning of love. Donato's apparent sexual fluidity/versatility varies depending on the geographic locations/sites of his dual existence. For instance, I am interested in why he self-identifies as *ativo* (a top) in Brazil and *passivo* (a bottom) after he moves to reside in Germany. One of the most creative and poignant motifs of this film is its seamless work in the resignification of heteronormative superheroes reincarnated as the two gay male characters in *Praia do futuro*. The film also makes multiple references to "Aquaman's" protection of his younger brother (Donato's younger brother) and Konrad's association as an invincible "Speed Racer," metaphorically serving to empower but also to "masculinize" the two main characters. In fact, both Donato and Konrad are characterized as obsessed with images and symbols of idealized masculinity; that is, lifeguard/protector/savior (Donato, "giver of life") or Konrad's fascination and excellent prowess with motorcycles. Both characters are stereotypically heteronormative males while also conforming to homonormative constructions around idealized gay masculinity: muscled, young, handsome, virile. The cinematography of *Praia do futuro* reinforces (hetero)conventional codes of masculinity: the quiet, calm, and silent scenes mirror the fact that the two male characters do not communicate with one another about their relationship. In fact, verbal communication does not seem to play a role in the development of their intimacy, dominated by sexual attraction and erotic impulses. In a patriarchal context, men who communicate with one another about intimacy are often perceived to be "feminized." The relationship between Donato and Konrad is as troubled as it is ambiguous in nature. Ultimately, it is difficult for the viewer to determine the degree and at times even the extent of intimacy between them. The spectator does not witness a gradual and typical (heteronormative) "falling in love" between the two protagonists. Long drawn-out pauses, awkward silences, and sparse and unsentimental dialogues characterize the pained interaction between the two characters. The words "I love you" are never uttered by either of the two lovers. As such, the viewer is compelled to either imagine these developments occurring "behind the scenes" or remain unconvinced that the relationship is indeed a loving one when voyeuristically observed, regardless of the sexual orientation of the spectator. It is entirely possible, then, that Donato may not perceive himself as "gay" per se but rather as MSM (a man who has sex with men) but without emotional affect (that is, the risk or the ability to fall in love). Though their sexual relationship is passionate, exchanging words is not part of their love connection, though movement and physical activities, like dancing, diving, motorcycling, and hiking together reveal their affection for one another. The film concretizes the clichéd "actions speak louder than words."

An ambiguous reading of intimacy in the portrayal of same-sex male relationships in particular characterizes the majority of such relationships throughout the universe of nearly all the films we examine in this chapter. From *Tatuagem* to *Madame Satã*, to *Dois perdidos numa noite suja*, the expression of emotional and sexual affection alternates between romantic kissing, penetration, to physical dominance and submission, wrestling, and even physical and emotional abuse. I argue that these multivalent "outlets" for sexual expression are modulated by degrees of internalized homophobia

residing within the psyches and the bodies of the characters who suffer marginalization on the basis of their sexual orientation and/or gender identity.
Perhaps symptomatic of both the wholescale homophobia that exists in the
universes that these Brazilian films are contesting and critiquing, it is worth
noting that in the movie theater screening of *Praia do Futuro*, many spectators walked out when the first "gay scene" was shown after having their
expectations adjusted when they saw two heartthrobs for the price of one on
the screen—kissing one another.

In *Praia do Futuro*, Nature is queered in that the water imagery is inverted,
perhaps also being a metaphor for a Brazil that seems calm and even paradisi-
acal on the surface but is actually dangerous and deadly deep within (literally,
under the surface). The foreign tourist comes to Brazil for a tropical/utopian
escape from Europe but actually loses his life under the turbulent waves of
the sea. Also, as a professional lifeguard, the ocean Donato once viewed with
admiration and even prowess is reconstructed as a dangerous "current" from
which the character is charged with protecting potential victims. The loss
of a life to the sea then comes to represent both fear of his profession as a
failed lifeguard and the motif of cowardice, developed later in the film with
Konrad's taunting of Donato's decision to return to Brazil. This moment in
the film reinforces the (loss of) masculine codes around bravery. In general,
though it is rendered as a turbulent and dangerous force of nature in *Praia
do Futuro*, water is an archetype for change, for rebirth, for fluidity, and for
transformation: "But you know that everything is dangerous in this endless
sea." This vision contrasts sharply with the imagery of water in *Tatuagem*,
representative of blossoming sexuality, fluidity and freedom, rebirth and
transformation. The beach the characters visit in Berlin has no water. As a
result, there is no danger of drowning, including in any perceived opportunities for transformation or navigating fluidity (of decisions, of identity,
of sexuality, etc.). The safety of landlocked protection, therefore, symbolically limits potential for growth, and I interpret this as cinematographic
reinforcement that the characters are always protected by nature, enclosed
in aquarium-like scenes surrounded by the sea but sheltered from its
un-*man*-ageable *men*ace—and grounded from its infinite possibilities. At the
same time as we view the act of fleeing to Berlin as a response to a denial
mechanism to not have to cope with trauma, the imaginary of the big city is
also clear in the film, where the trope of loneliness, of being anonymous in
a big city and unable to establish relationships, is a consequence of running
away to a large impersonal urban space like Berlin. Hence, the relativity of
equating freedom with happiness, a poignant motif in the film.

The films I have selected to examine in this chapter, I argue, possess an
affinity and a common strategy: To queer not only childhood and adulthood
relationships but also the conventional (Aristotelian) notion of cinematic

narration. For example, the queer portrayal of male same-sex relationships occurs in many of the films through questioning and problematizing monogamy as the only or even the best way to conduct a relationship. *Tatuagem* contrasts Clécio's jealousy and patriarchal notions of ownership and possession of Fininha with the latter's clarification, in critical disagreement with Clécio's claims that "We have no contract," thus suggesting an open relationship. At the same time, Clécio's character development as both a "queer" father and husband in a heterosexual marriage raising a child also begins to "queer" the very notion of fatherhood itself, opening the doors for renewed relationships and improvements of relations with other members of the family. In both *Do começo ao fim* and the short film *Eu não quero voltar sozinho*, there is a queer utopian vision that forbids adults from forming part of the landscape of the film, enabling the young characters with the power to boundlessly shape their own relationships. In other words, there are no guardians to impose "morality," conditions, or heteropatriarchal structures that would make it very difficult (if not impossible) for the children to forge their own self-identity. In *Do começo ao fim*, the biological mother of the brothers (Júlia Lemmertz) consciously chooses not to interfere in the budding intimacy (and the consummation of that love) between her two sons. Similarly, in a frank conversation with the father of one of the boys (Jean Pierre Noher), it is clear that love is the issue and that it is to be celebrated rather than regulated. Such narratives provide revisionist readings and reconstructions of childhood with queer potential for liberation beyond how both sexuality and emotional intimacy are inhibited by regulatory "adult" mechanisms to control it. In two short pieces, *Meu jogador favorito* (Gui Luka, nine minutes, 2018) and *Depois daquela festa* (Caio Scot, fifteen minutes, 2019), there is an inversion of the social roles of "adult" and "child" in two completely different ways. In the latter, Léo (Lucas Drummond) catches his father (Charles Fricks), who strategically remains nameless in the short piece, kissing at a party another man (Alcemar Viera), who we later discover to be the father's boyfriend. The dramatic tension revolves and evolves around how to "confront" his father to tell him not only that he knows he is gay but that he loves his father and simply wants him to be happy. Léo's best friend Carol (Mel Carvalho) takes the lead in walking Léo through this process, ultimately leading to a poignant final scene in which the son embraces his father in acceptance and the roles of parenting are temporarily reversed. In *Meu jogador favorito*, the foreshadowing occurs in the very first scenes, as the spectator immediately spots the word *viado* as graffiti on the wall of a soccer field. Gustavo (Raphael Machado) suffers an unrelenting crush on his soccer mate Eduardo (Marcelo Ronqui), leading to an emotional implosion on the soccer field and a confession to his object of desire that is happily met with joy and not anger. Despite very little character development, other than the *machista* gestures and words that the two main characters use to assert their "masculinity" over their homosexuality, Gustavo's exceedingly brief conversation with his father is the most poignant. While watching a soccer match on the television and cursing the players correspondingly, Gustavo dares to ask his (once again, nameless, but in this case also faceless) father (Valdeci Gonçalves) if it is possible for a soccer player to be gay. The camera focuses on the father's shapely legs and bare feet, perhaps indicating that he too is (or was) a soccer player in his heyday, never moving its angle above the legs. While continuing to watch the match and clearly attending to his son with divided attention, the father abruptly states: "Pay attention, son! Soccer is only for *machos*," clearly translating as both males in the biological discourse of *macho* and *fêmea* and "real men" according to the perverse logic and rigid gender roles of *machismo*.

QUEERING TRAUMA WHILE ANXIOUSLY AWAITING TRAGEDY TO COME (OUT) TO PASS

The proscribed Aristotelian formula of narration, whether cinematic or otherwise, is completely disregarded in a film like *Do começo ao fim*, where there is no conflict, even at moments when the spectator expects there to be problems. The mother chooses not to impede the incestuous relationship between her children. The expectation that the mother's death would cause friction or conflict is debunked, ultimately intensifying the bond between the two brothers. What would have happened had the mother survived? Is the death of the biological mother (who gave birth to both of the protagonists) responsible for increasing the intimacy between the two brothers? The incest motif in the film mirrors the reality created that there is practically no meaningful interaction with the outside world, highlighting the insularity of the two main characters, and suggesting that they are part of the "perfect family" untouched and unhinged by external influences that would censor or censure their relationship in any way.

Similarly, in the short film *Hoje eu não quero voltar sozinho*, there is no conflict where the viewer may have expected it to occur. Quite simply, the film is about the normalization of being gay. The plot is surprisingly uneventful despite what would conventionally be portrayed (and often has) as a dramatic moment or crisis. We could perhaps construe this strategy as a pedagogical tool to show how announcement or revelation of one's "difference" is completely normal in a society that truly sees diversity in a positive light. Alternatively, we can read this lack of friction as part and parcel of a utopian vision of the world where human differences do not provoke conflicts or elicit crises but are rather non-events at worst or celebrated at best. The feature-length film, based on the short version, takes the naturalization of Léo and Gabriel's sexuality to a utopian peak of naturalization, where the coming out process is minimized or diminished in both its intensity and difficulty.

Aesthetically, the slow movement or the reduced velocity of the plot development in many of the feature-length films I discuss here moves the consciousness of the spectator to a queer sense of time.[2] *Praia do Futuro* is an excellent example of this technique, where velocity of movement is diminished even to the extent of slow motion at the end of the film. The long, sustained final scene in the film shows the characters riding their motorbikes into the unforeseeable and unrecordable distance. The creation of queer utopias in place of heteropatriarchal dystopic realities is one of the techniques that bond and bind these films into a similar trajectory: A childhood world safe from adult intervention, insularity, and protection from the potentially hostile outside world, and in the specific cases of *Madame Satã* and *Tatuagem* explored later, meta-cinematic performances, which belie spectacularization and carnivalization as escape valves from dystopic realities. As we have seen thus far, Brazilian filmmakers employ the strategy of depathologization and "normalization" of homosexuality while diverting focus onto other taboos or societal "problems" judged as more egregious in a patriarchal context. In the *longa* "*Hoje quero voltar sozinho*," Léo is bullied more for being blind than he is for being gay. The process whereby coming out as gay and "coming out" as blind run parallel to one another. The comparative inference here is that the genetic characteristic/trait of sexuality is as much of an option as it is for one to choose to be blind. Blatant racism, classism such as when the family is denied entrance to the "High Life" Club, and misogyny, especially the treatment of prostitutes, are the most serious offenses in *Madame Satã*. Poverty and its intersections with other forms of marginality is the main "problem" in *Dois perdidos numa noite suja*. It is no secret that Paco's homelessness, while unjust, is more easily faced as a boy than as a girl, commenting on female vulnerability in a position of poverty. Even Paco reveals himself to be conditioned to associate strength and perseverance with maleness and virility, hence *machismo*. Traditional notions of family are reconfigured in these films as estranged holders of birth identities and circumstances but turned down and away in favor of choosing and constructing new communities. For instance, Paco's elusive past, decrying a powerfully negative relationship with his father, is never staged and therefore is rejected or cast aside just as the transphobic response to a child's coming out would be withdrawal or rejection.

In addition to fleeing heteronormative impositions, many of the protagonists in the films I study also denounce or at least interrogate homonormativity. Examples abound throughout the films I study here. Ambiguous gender agreement in "*Dois perdidos numa noite suja*": Paco, though renouncing the assigned name/identification of "Rita," often responds "*Obrigada*"

("Thanks") in the feminine. Inversion of gender roles is a common occurrence in this film. Tonho oscillates in his treatment of Paco—sometimes like a boy, when he is physically abusing Paco. Paco becomes a stereotypically machista male during moments when he teases and accuses Tonho of being a *bicha* and insists that he must have been raped in prison (in a *machista* logic, implying the loss of his masculinity). Obsession with assigned gender roles is also handled and well developed in this film. One example is Tonho's persistence and insistence on having to know Paco's assigned birth name ("Rita") in order to continue a relationship. In *Hoje eu quero voltar sozinho*, heteronormativity is called into question in the scenes where Giovana (Tess Amorim) is "slut-shaming" the female colleague and also the false assumptions of Gabriel's (Fábio Audi) straightness.

I have chosen these LGBT-themed films not only for their "queer" content but also because of their compelling representations of deeply and rigidly proscribed gender roles. There is the overt symbolism of Tonho wielding of a gun, the traditional symbol of male phallus/masculinist aggression, which he uses to force Paco to undress at the end of the film and the trauma that this inflicts on Paco (calling into question the seriousness of the problem of transphobia and the potential for tyranny of the cisgender male). The metaphor of the expensive and fashionable boots that Paco insists on purchasing evokes materialism, status-consciousness, grounding, and protection from the ground (literally and figuratively), while also recalling images of oppression and violence under dictatorship and authoritarianism, stamping out or stepping on would-be protesters. As we have seen in chapter 4, the image of the *bota* is also suggestive of the possible lesbianism but certainly the internal confusion of Paco's character, though she denies it, in a *homonormative* context where *bota* is a slang term (*gíria*) used to classify lesbians from within the lesbian community in Brazil as opposed to the often derogatory *sapatão*. From a gendered perspective, the bright red boot represents fetishism, in the erotic/sexualized sense, and consumerism. Paco constantly repeats the price of the boots, US$500, almost as if he could reaffirm himself and through his capacity to be economically successful, especially in comparison and arguably in competition with Tonho. Paco views the attainment of money as the ultimate goal of every successful *man*. In other words, every action, including practicing prostitution, dealing drugs, and violence, is justified by the final result, symbolized here by the buying power to acquire those flashy boots. In order to buy such an expensive commodity, Paco sees himself as closer to achieving "the American dream" than Tonho ever was. When Paco returns home and shows (off) his boots to Tonho, a series of conflicts emerge. Paco repeatedly asks Tonho what he thinks of the boots, eliciting an erotic response and confessions about how turned on he has become watching Paco model the boots. Paco teases Tonho relentlessly with the boots that are at once "feminine" (their red glossy lipstick color and the vinyl material) and "masculine" (chains and heavy soles, similar to a military boot), mirroring the character's own androgyny. Ultimately, Paco turns down Tonho's sexual advances, bringing the tension between the two protagonists to its climax. Because the amount Paco paid for these boots is exactly the sum Tonho needs to buy a return ticket to Brazil (at this point, Tonho has already accepted the failure of his dream of the American dream), the brand new shiny boots represent Paco's momentary success and Tonho's failure at the same time. Tonho does not have the resources to go back to Brazil or the love for Paco to entice him to stay in the United States. Paco, on the other hand, deceives himself to believe he has "made it" in the consumerist logic of the American dream, satisfying himself with a material product since love with Tonho does not feel possible or even desirable. Once the boots walk onto the scene as a provocative though inanimate character, there is no turning back on the (delusions of) attaining the American dream. The desire to consume more and more with the momentary adrenaline rush of feeling empowered, experiencing success in a foreign "First World," justifies the value of any risk that the characters take to experience this sensation, though short-lived, legally sanctioned or not.

In *Hoje eu quero voltar sozinho*, attraction is decentered from physical appearance, due to Léo's blindness, and reconfigured as an internal characteristic of interior or intrinsic beauty. The film sensitively explores blindness in a variety of ways, transcending but also including the physicality of possessing eyes that do not see since birth. Blindness in the film also carries metaphorical meanings for many of its characters, for Léo is blind to how Gabriel feels about him, Giovanna is blind to what is actually developing in the love relationship between her two best friends, and Léo's parents are blind to the fact that there is more motivation than meets the eye for Léo's desire to study abroad and attain independence and freedom from his sheltered (and heteronormative) home life in Brazil. The exchange of power between the two characters is inverted at the end of the film, where Gabriel is shown holding on to Léo as they ride the bicycle together rather than the customary practice of Gabriel or Giovanna physically helping Léo navigate their world.

THE SEA OF "C"S OF THE TATTOO
THAT MARKS *TATUAGEM*

The tattoo around which the plot of *Tatuagem* is symbolically centered is never concretized or explained during the film. Rather, in a creative display of infinite possibilities, the viewer is left to interpret for themselves the denotations or implications of the "c" that is literally inscribed onto Fininha's (Arlindo) skin. Above all else, it is important to note that the character did not choose this tattoo, much less to be marked by it for life. The first "c," therefore, comes of course from coercion (*coação*) since his military colleagues held down Fininha as they branded him with the tattoo. Branding also brings to mind the possessiveness of *C*lécio, symbolizing that Fininha is permanently marked as the property and propriety of another man. This interpretation co-mingles with the possibility of *C*opyright ©, further objectifying Fininha as belonging uniquely and monogamously to someone else. On a more positive note, the "C"-shaped tattoo could signify *Cu*, utopian alternate universes that transgress reality, created by Clécio's theater troupe *Chão das estrelas*, the very name of which could be inferred by its first capital letter. In a time of military dictatorship-sponsored persecution and torture, the "C" may also come to represent *Censura*, with Fininha's arm bearing the stamp and the stigma of *censurado* or *proibido*. Finally, we cannot overlook the symbolism of the *Cicatriz* (the scar left by the tattoo), as the branding of sexual identity that renders Fininha the permanent possession of another man, literally self-inscribing his own homosexuality. A social manifestation of this possible interpretation emerges at the end of the film, with a tarnished reputation as gay causing the mark of unemployability when it becomes clear that the way in which he has been "marked" and therefore judged by others is the source of his hardship in securing a job in Recife, a goal he is not able to attain by the end of the film. Other "C"s abound, of course, and there are infinite interpretations of what they may come to represent based on the viewer's own values and perceptions. *Consumo* (consumerism), *crise* (crisis), and *capitalismo* (capitalism) all come readily to mind.

TUDO ISSO E NADA DISSO: QUEERING *MALANDRAGEM* AND DISLOCATING IDENTITIES IN *MADAME SATÃ*

Karim Aïnouz opens this remarkable film, based on the life of legendary figure João Francisco dos Santos (Lázaro Ramos), with the headshot and condemnation of a nameless and, almost literally, faceless inmate. Deemed by officials to be a criminal, a misfit, a "threat to society," and a pervert, this figure stares blankly into the camera as his description is read aloud, reduced to a badly beaten prisoner. While this silent and sullen character will take on a dramatic and controversial personality throughout the film, his actions in society and the nature of his relationships with others remain ambiguous. Functioning as a form of both matriarch and patriarch in his household, João looks after Laurita (Marcélia Cartaxo) and Tabu (Flávio Bauraqui) and even has made Laurita's child his own, demonstrating extreme tenderness and care in his moments alone with her. In fact, this is the only character with whom João never exhibits any violence or cruelty, leaving his moments of rage for his close friends and acquaintances. His treatment of Tabu can be particularly cruel and manipulative, and it is those moments in which he is able to exhibit kindness and in which the viewer can perceive his humanity that makes his cruelty even more acute. Hence these two distinct sides of João battle with each other throughout the film, as he appears to struggle with as many demons inside himself as those he encounters in his surroundings.

This film also provides a fascinating historical glimpse into 1930s Rio de Janeiro, in particular the community in which João Francisco dos Santos (*Madame Satã*) inhabited and flourished: *Lapa*. The bohemian vibe from the flourishing artistic community in *Lapa* is one aspect that dates this film; another is arguably the absence of an HIV/AIDS geography among this artistic community and in the lives of characters persistently engaging in unprotected sexual behaviors. In this context, it might be interesting while watching this film to contemplate how new social concerns such as HIV/ AIDS might have affected historical events and even individual histories such as that of João Francisco dos Santos, who despite many significant and some life-threatening challenges, lived to be seventy-six. Other social circumstances and the relationships between different races in Brazilian society that shaped João's life also speak of a past era, even though vestiges of its social and political circumstances do remain present in society today. One of these vestiges of an unjust and discriminatory society is the frustration João experiences in that no matter how hard he works, or how hard he tries, he cannot become someone he is not and, even worse, he is also not accepted by society for who he is.

This social rejection is communicated well by the lighting, music, and scenery, which, together, successfully set the mood of this film. The viewer can literally feel when the characters are crossing over from the dark and often squalid streets of *Lapa* to the ritzy "High Life" Club. Needless to say, this transition cannot be successfully negotiated in a society with extreme social prejudices, and João, Laurita, and Tabu are denied entrance to the "High Life" on suspicion of being bums and prostitutes. Hence this scene confirms exactly what Laurita points out to him after they are rejected from entering the "High Life": that he is different from everybody else, and everybody else is different from him. It appears that João concludes, and perhaps rightfully so, that no amount of money or good deeds would change the way other people perceive him. In a society with very little social fluidity, *Madame Satã* appears trapped between challenging what others have to say about him and making it come true.

Of all the celebrated queer theorists working on queer studies and the divergent opinions as numerous as there are scholars in the field, one point of tension remains consistent: a paradoxical re-membering, dis-membering, and lamenting the impossibility of locating and especially placating a "queer essence," the search for it transitioning a permanent state of movement, of dislocation. In other words, "queer" positions itself precisely as a category of analysis that does not allow itself to be categorized or classified. With our focal point as the historical and mythical "Madame Satã" a queer hero and heroine in a constant state of mutation, Antonio Candido's *Dialética da malandragem* (1970) serves us well, as does Roberto da Matta's seminal study of *malandragem* in *Carnavais, malandros e heróis* (1978). More recently, literary and cultural studies scholars have reinterpreted the idea of *malandragem* in innovative and richly textured theoretical ways. For example, João Cezar de Castro Rocha's work demystifies the legendary *malandro* of Rio de Janeiro's *carnaval* by presenting the thesis that the dialectics of *malandragem*, in modern times, encounters dynamics of marginalization based on a new conception of the *esperteza* (street-smartness, in English) of the *malandro*, as follows: The ability to not only confront but overcome social inequality instead of utilizing his savvy to reconcile or neutralize the conflicts that such injustices generate on a daily basis. Castro Rocha synthesizes his view of the dialectics of *malandragem* as follows: "The dialectic of malandroism suggested that the Brazilian dilemma resided in the oscillation between the world of universal laws and the universe of personal relationships; oscillation which created a special way of negotiating social conflicts." This perspective, endorsed by Antonio Candido and other Brazilian intellectuals, reflects how violence is contained and controlled with the principal objective to reach reconciliation. How is the spectator to reconcile the problematic figure of *Madame Satã*, whether they are reconstructed in historical studies (e.g., James Green) or in the cinematic representation by Aïnouz? How can we take advantage of such a complex character to evaluate the degree of *malandragem* and "queerness" as well as the linkages between the two performative identities? Readers must first address the historical figure described before, João Francisco dos Santos—drag queen, *capoeira* fighter and dancer, cook, prisoner, father, thief—that lived between 1900 and 1976, having spent twenty-seven of those years in jail. Or shall we study the various multi-faceted identities to whom the mythical Madame Satã gave birth and the various heteronyms included in the performative repertoire, such as "Jamacy, the queen of the forest," "*A negra de Bulacoché*" ("The black woman of Bulacoché"), and "*Santa Rita do Coqueiro*" ("Saint Rita of the coconut tree"), among others?

In his article, "Madame Satã (Satan): The Black 'Queen' of Rio's Bohemia," James Green points out how heteronormativity is ruptured when we think of the Brazilian figure of the *malandro*, writing: "Although Madame Satã projected a tough-guy image, his assumed name undercut the traditional association of *malandro* with manliness. Rather, it evoked a mysterious, somewhat androgynous, and sinister figure. And it is precisely this violent and sinister persona that seems to have captured the imagination of the

Pasquim journalists as they interviewed him in 1971. No limp-wristed fairy, no effeminate hairdresser, no artist of 'questionable' sexual proclivities, the Madame Satã of mythic proportions was masculine, virile, and violent, as all *malandros* were supposed to be" (277). I argue that Aïnouz's project goes one big step further than interrogating an explosion of the machista and heterosexist imaginary of *malandragem carioca*. Theoretically, Aïnouz manages to dislodge and put in flux the bohemian neighborhood of *Lapa* in the 1930s—an imaginary where nonconformity was actually the norm, inserting into this new milieu of marginalization, survival, and violence, a new sensibility no less mythical in nature. In aesthetic terms, Aïnouz successfully repaints *malandragem* in the colors of the rainbow, transforming or queering the traditional (hetero)normative imaginary to (dis)occupy that space. As such, the film creates a new mythology of *malandragem*, turning it "queer" not only because of the sexual orientation of our hero(ine) but also in both aesthetic and theoretical senses, particularly as we reflect on Castro Rocha's critique, leading to a new utopian site that parallels just as it contradicts dystopic realities invested with the power to (re)construct itself with irreconcilable paradoxes. In this new imaginary, violence occurs precisely because of the impossibility to resolve culturally constructed dualities exploited as dichotomies to satisfy the rules and conventions of heteropatriarchal institutions. Our *capoeirista* is also a drag queen. Our legendary criminal is also the adoptive father of seven children. Our openly gay man also plays the role of husband to a prostitute with whom he is raising a child. This last case has a special relevance when we recall the whore/mother dichotomy that patriarchal society has imposed. In fact, in the film *Madame Satã*, as we shall see, passion and energy nurture themselves precisely on the practice of resistance against reconciliation.

Nevertheless, it would be worthwhile to consider whether these sites of apparent contradiction may be natural(ized) and even common for an audience of spectators who already sympathize or empathize with certain homocultural sensibilities. For example, a skeptical critic might perceive *Madame Satã* not as innovative but rather just another shameless cliché. In his film review, "Fists and Feathers: Don't Mess with Madame," Gary Morris argues: "Madame Satan . . . was one of those Renaissance Queens who could do it all—one minute in mascara and feathers warbling Piaf-like dirges, the next using Bruce Lee-like kicks to take down a local tough. Madame is in that long-treasured tradition of muscular street queens whose résumés begin with 'doesn't take shit'" (*Bright Lights Film Journal*, Issue 41, August 2003). Frederic Rissover, in his review, "*Madame Satã*: From Rebel to Legend," classifies the protagonist as "an almost stereotypical gay macho man." Celebrated American film critic Roger Ebert positions himself in a similar way, writing: "At home, João rules with the short temper and iron hand of the stereotypical dominant male, and is in many ways the most masculine character I've seen in any recent movie." It is worth noting, however, that even though it is merely one of many heteronymic identities converging in the universe that is Madame Satã, the role of the *machão* remains as a fixed, traditional, patriarchal pattern. In other words and to my mind, Aïnouz manages to demonstrate a multiplicity of roles that the main character performs but does not offer a revision or critical reworking of any of the roles assumed, consequently perpetuating stereotypes of all of them.

In *Madame Satã*, homophobia and transphobia are inextricably entwined with racism and classism. As Green points out, "Gay macho—masculine, stylish, and cool—predicated on middle-class consumption has become a norm. Although most Brazilian gay men are far from having the resources to acquire the sartorial and other accoutrements linked to this sexual lifestyle that reaches far beyond the bed, a new standard of performative masculinity is creeping toward a norm in the country's largest urban centers" (282). Evidently, within Brazil's urban gay male communities, men can out themselves as gay and yet still consider themselves to be "real men." Not really, when we consider Brazil as a misogynistic and homophobic society. Rather, I see this process as a large step backwards in the history of LGBT civil rights. "A real man" spends his life in the gym and/or the beach, regardless of his sexual orientation.

After reading dozens of film reviews in both English and Portuguese, I find it instructive to note a tendency that brings us back to constructions of trans identities. Only the reviews meant for an LGBT audience allude to the character of "Madame Satã" and *also* to João Francisco dos Santos as "she" or *ela*. For instance, I return to Gary Morris's review: "The film opens and closes with stark shots of a pummeled João in a police station, with a rude voiceover declaiming *her* many crimes." After which, the critic writes parenthetically: "(She spent 27 of her 76 years in the hoosegow)."

Another problem rises to the surface when we consider the multifaceted identities of the protagonist as portrayed in the film. Along with the growing complexity of the imaginary of Madame Satã comes a simultaneous dehumanization of the character. Unless, of course, the director's intention was to build a new mythology of Lapa reimagined in the 1930s. The deification or rather the "queenification" of our hero(ine) fits quite well within the paradigms of the legend they represent in addition to the carnivalesque masquerading and parading of versions of Madame Satã to this day. Gary Morris writes, for example, that "Lázaro Ramos' portrayal of João is . . . almost too vigorous, veering into caricature. . . . Literally a drama queen, the character makes hay of every event, and all that screaming and hitting and carry-on may wear down all but the hardiest viewer. . . . [João's] stridency and his abusiveness . . . brings him perilously close to being just another cartoonish Evil Queen."

At the end of the day, or the long Dionysian night, Aïnouz attempts to construct an imaginary of Brazil as a quintessentially queer nation, in both theoretical and aesthetic terms. He is ultimately not successful in this regard, however, because positionality of performative identities, as queer theory claims, maintains itself in permanent flux. Also symptomatic of the *malandro*, to which I now return, da Matta's analysis from decades ago resonates just as loudly today: "In Rio de Janeiro, the symbol of *Carnaval* is the *malandro*. That is to say, the dislocated character. In fact, the *malandro* does not fit in the parameters of order nor outside these parameters: [He] lives in its interstices, between order and disorder, utilizing both and nurturing [him] self as much from those who come from outside as those who are inside the square world of structure." Madame Satã is an interstitial figure inserting and asserting her **self** on multiple axes and sites, thus queering the Brazilian traditional concept of the *malandro*. For this reason, I read the *malandro* as the incarnation of queer spirit, for as renowned queer scholar Annamarie Jagose explains in *Queer Theory*: "Queer . . . is an identity category that has no interest in consolidating or even stabilising itself."

Contemplating whether or not the drag queen can be inscribed as the utopian idealization of *malandragem*, it is not necessary to undress da Matta's affirmation that "In the world of *malandragem*, what counts is voice, feeling, and improvisation, what is defined in our society as belonging to the 'heart' and to 'feeling.' We value, therefore, what is inside emotions and the heart. In the universe of *malandragem*, it is the heart that invents the rules" (217). In other words, the *malandro* as conceived by da Matta, the mythical yet all-too-real figure who proclaims "I am poor, but I have my woman, the moonlight, and my guitar" [*"Sou pobre, mas tenho a cabrocha (mulher), o luar e o violão"*] confronts a new lived experience not altogether different in queer *malandragem*: "I am poor, but I have my *gatinho* (man), my gun, and my dress."

Chapter 8

What's Queer Got to Do with It? Queernormativity and Heterobrasilidade in Brazil's *QueerMuseu*

The August 2018 re-re-inauguration of the "*Queermuseu: Cartografias da diferença na arte brasileira*" (Queermuseum: Cartographies of Difference in Brazilian Art) in Rio de Janeiro, after two highly controversial and successful attempts at censorship, brought to the forefront a multiplicity of intersectional issues that echo, dramatize, and metaphorize (if not metastasize) Brazil's sociopolitical divisions. I am interested in problematizing the victory and, as exhibit curator Gaudêncio Fidelis calls it, the "villainy" of fascist state involvement, religious fundamentalism, and pernicious support for censorship of cultural initiatives that are designed to destigmatize creative production by and/or about Brazilian gender and sexual minorities. To what extent may we argue that these very initiatives to ban, to *invisibilizar* (to make invisible), have the power to restigmatize, that is, if we were to subscribe to queer theory's insistence on "antinormativity as a political goal" (Donald Morton)?

The brief but volatile history of the museum's opening, its subsequent censorship in Porto Alegre, and the use of social media to revive and resituate itself in Rio with "crowdfunding" campaigns reveal larger debates on freedom of speech, citizenship as activism, art as a site of cultural resistance, and the limits of reception and spectatorship on the basis of sexuality, gender, race, and even age of consent. For example, a judge ordered on the eve of its opening that children fourteen and under not be permitted to visit the exhibit. While the order was suspended days later by another judge, these (re)actions stage current debates in Brazil on "ideology of gender" arguments that continue to suppress gender studies and LGBT/queer studies at all levels of the curriculum, from the *kit de anti-homofobia* (Anti-Homophobia Educational Kit) at the secondary level to the repression and commission of aggression against Judith Butler's (physical and scholarly) body of knowledge.

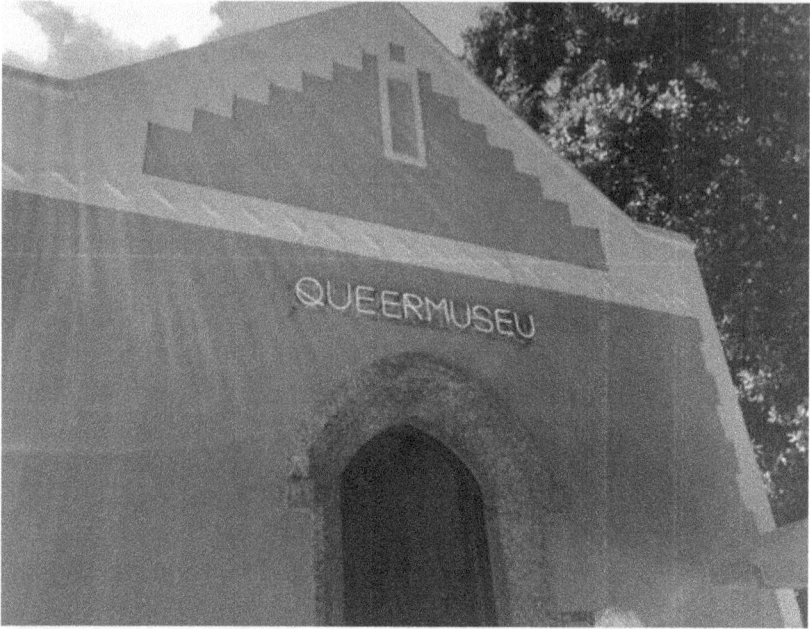

Figure 8.1. Author's Photo of the Outside Entrance of *Queermuseu*.

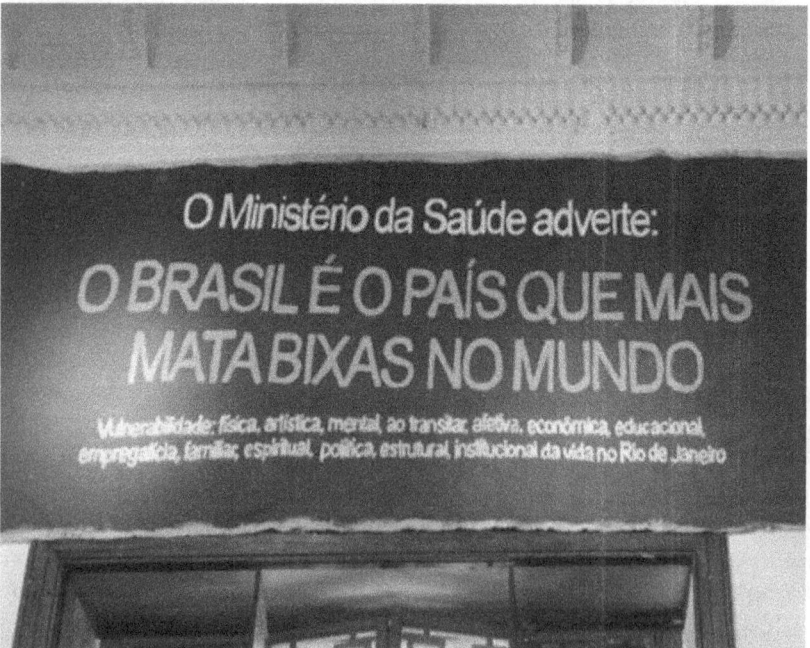

Figure 8.2. Author's Photo of the Inside Entrance of *Queermuseu*.

The photograph in figure 8.2 was the first work of art I noticed upon entrance to the exhibit, prompting the spectator to look up almost to the ceiling to see it and, if heeded, to exercise caution upon proceeding. The giant poster on a black background with three different font sizes and colors imitates and parodies the warnings mandated to be placed on cigarette cartons about the long-term dangers of smoking and tobacco use: "The Ministry of Health warns: 'Brazil kills more faggots than any other country in the world.'" The font size of the content of this warning is enormous, highlighting the magnitude and definitive nature of the problem, comparing the reality and severity of the violent consequences of the addictive "habit"; that is, certain and brutal death that may not come about swiftly but is the inevitable consequence of the world's most violently homophobic society, one where *machismo* is a high-risk vice that causes others to die. The difference, of course, is that this illness is socially constructed rather than chemically formed, and that it does not target the individual who is addicted to the practice but rather the object onto which the consequent hatred is (mis)placed. Written in all capital letters and appearing in a hot pink color, one that universally represents the international LGBT movement, the stern warning, while mimicking governmental intervention in labels and packaging of consumer products, makes no claim that the perpetrator of such crimes will suffer punishment or responsibility, even for murder, as the warning is conceived as an inevitable (even chemical) outcome of a homophobic society. As a spectator viewing an intervening warning before setting foot in the queer journey that is the exposition, it is imperative to ask who is being advised. There is no distinction made here of perpetrator or victim, suggesting that these crimes are conditioned by a society that perpetuates their commission with impunity.

The colloquial use of *bicha*, a pejorative but "reclaimed" slang term we have examined extensively throughout this book, especially in chapter 4, is made even more informal by using the homophonic (and homophobic) "x" in the place of "ch," as if to say "X marks the spot," as the spectator is greeted at ground zero of queer expression and creativity motivated by an egregious social situation that reveals the enormity of Brazil's lethal homophobic legacy and positionality in the present. The use of the present-tense "warns" (*adverte*) indicates that the crime is both present and unavoidable. Despite its naturalization and lack of punishment for its commission, I read the use of capital letters here as an exclamation (which in the age of social media jargon has come to symbolize a shout), a denunciation against this injustice.

The third and final phrase, written in the smallest of the three fonts and in yellow that, for a Brazilian spectatorship, represents the national flag, also signals the eyes to move slowly, pausing so that the words do not go unnoticed or unprocessed. A literal translation of the phrase reads as follows: "Vulnerability: Physical, artistic, mental, in transit, affect(ive), economic, educational, work place, familial, spiritual, political, structural, institutional life in Rio de Janeiro." The inverted syntactic structure of the phrase, while difficult to capture in English translation, requires the reader/spectator to reconstitute the meaning of the words and their grammatical usage. Put another way, each of the adjectives employed to describe vulnerability transcend not only any attempt to define or placate the nature of that vulnerability but also the parts of speech, or better, use of language, to denote it. For example, in Portuguese, the use of the term *institucional* can allude to both "institutional" and "institutionalized." Vulnerability is present in structural factors that include education (even "manners" or etiquette, modes of behavior considered appropriate in the context of the Romance languages) as well as the educational system at large. The multivalent noun *empregância* denotes "the work place" but simultaneously refers to labor rights and conditions. In sum, while the "warning" gives us indicators of possible side effects, much like we would read on a medicine bottle or a prescription label, the list that ensues encompasses every conceivable area of human life, running the gamut from lack of acceptance or rejection from the family unit, to discrimination at the place of employment, to compromising mental and emotional health, to lack of access to educational opportunities, even denying the right to develop a personal spirituality.

After noting the warning and entering the *Queermuseu* at my own risk, I felt at ease, at *quome*, when I noticed the presence of two trans people of color working as docents in the museum, providing clues to help spectators interpret artworks while fielding questions from audience members, a refreshing sign of the exhibit's inclusivity (see figure 8.10).

This chapter problematizes simultaneously conflictual and consensual relationships between aesthetics (artwork), the ethical imperative of the museum as a cultural institution invested in creating space for and representing cultural artifacts of marginalized citizens, the rules of censorship and the roles of freedom of speech in a "democracy" increasingly positioning itself in an ambivalent "queer space and time" (Halberstam) consistently questioning the fragile foundations upon which it is employed—and revoked—in today's Brazil.

To better understand what is at stake in what is one of the most explicit cases of censorship of a cultural artifact since Brazil's military dictatorship, I would like to take a brief step back to highlight a chronological accounting of the key historical events that shaped this trajectory. I will follow this dramatic *novela* with interdisciplinary theoretical insights and international contextualization by dialoguing with the works of scholars of queer curatorship, including, in the United States, art history scholar Jennifer Tyburczy's 2016 *Sex Museums: The Politics and Performance of Display*, notes and observations from Swedish museology scholar Patrik Steorn's methodological reflections while examining Brazilian curator Fidelis's aesthetic apparatus and political goals to consider whether or not queer curatorship as defined in the United States and Northern European circles bears fruit in this specific Brazilian scenario or runs the risk of re-colonizing a linguistic landscape where "queer" is only beginning to be considered part of a countercultural narrative of *brasilidade* in its own (anthropophagic) right. My work is in large part inspired by engaging in conversation with contributions of queer studies scholars like Denilson Lopes, Silviano Santiago, Rafael de la Dehesa, and Ben Sifuentes-Jáuregui, all invested in critiquing Eurocentric and U.S.-centric models and modalities of queer theory and their (in)applicability to Latin American contexts.

Queermuseu: Cartografias da diferença na arte brasileira, containing 264 artworks in various media produced by eighty-five Brazilian artists from the 1950s to the present, opened its doors to the public in Porto Alegre in late 2017. It is worth mentioning that the works featured in the exhibit came from both public and private collections, with thirty-six on loan from Brazilian public museums. As Fidelis argues, approximately 104 of these contributions are part of Brazilian "historical heritage" since they were created at least ten years ago. *Queermuseu* received sponsorship by the Cultural Center of Santander Bank, only to be permanently revoked on September 10, 2017, thirty days before the exhibit's actual closing date. In its initial stage, attendance reports show that the *Queermuseu* received approximately 800 visitors per day. While a group ironically calling itself the *Movimento Brasil Livre* (*MBL*) was the chief instigator in the campaign to defame the exhibit, there are many other voices, including the roles played by Pentecostal religious fundamentalist politicians, of epidemic proportions in Brazilian government and conservative social media campaigns disseminating so-called moral judgments that would accuse a handful of the contributions of inspiring pedophilia, bestiality, pornography, and sacrilegious transgression of religious (read: Christian) symbols. I discuss in the following five of the interrogated and denigrated Brazilian works.

Celebrated *carioca* artist Adriana Varejão, commissioned to produce a seascape mural to encircle the new Aquatics Center built for the 2016 Olympic Games in Rio, contributes to the *Queermuseu* exhibit with an equally "fragmented, reordered and turbulent"—to use the artist's characterization of her own work in a July 13, 2016 interview with *The New York Times*— *Cena de interior II* (1994; see figure 8.3), a sociopolitical denunciation of slavery, racism, sexual exploitation, and violence perpetuated against people of color. Accused by the *MBL* of promoting *zoofilia*, and implying that such work could influence the impressionable to commit acts of bestiality, Varejão resurrects an ancient Japanese art reminiscent of the *Shunga* prints, a type of erotic art in the traditional style of *ukiyo-e* ("Pictures of the Floating

Figure 8.3. *Cena de interior II* (1994). Artist: Adriana Varejão. 120 × 110 cm.

World"), referring to a genre of Japanese woodblock print and painting from the Edo period (1603–1867), in order to critique structural, physical, and sexual violence throughout history and regardless of the location or site in the world. It is worth noting, in a parallel situation to censorship of the *Queermuseu* exhibit, that these artworks, literally translated to English as "spring pictures," were banned in Japan for the majority of the twentieth century. In the *New York Times* article alluded to earlier, Laura van Straaten writes that much of Varejão's work "asks uncomfortable questions about the hidden, bloody stories of racism and subjugation—Portugal's colonization of Brazil in particular, but also England's and Spain's of other parts of the Americas." The piece shown at the *Queermuseu* certainly reinforces this characterization. At first glance, the spectator is prompted to trace this work to another piece that does not exist, an original work perhaps from Japan. The title *Cena de interior II* (Indoor Scene #2) tempts us to find an "authentic" work of art on which this piece is based. Nevertheless, this search would occur in vain because there is no recorded original work (of this artist's authorship or any other) with this title. The implication of a second set implies a series of work or, perhaps metaphorically, a reoccurrence of historical processes, of colonial legacies, that this piece both playfully and repulsively display. Appearances are deceptive in much of Varejão's artistic universe. The object appears to have been produced on rice paper, reminding us of an ancient Japanese scroll kept for centuries, with stains and both horizontal and vertical lines indicating that this document has been preserved for years, folded and wrinkled to connote the old age of the piece, perhaps acquired by an art collector. However, contemporary viewers will recognize that, sadly, this is a tragic (hi)story told over and over again, depicting historical processes that repeat themselves despite time and place There are nine "characters" portrayed, men and women of different racial and ethnic backgrounds, involved in sexual relations with one another. In one case, we witness two white men with an animal. The bottom right corner of the artwork features three men, two white and one black man who is sexually "serving" the other two, both orally and anally, reminding the viewer that even same-sex relations cannot escape from a racist colonial legacies where the animalized bodies of slaves were objects to be "used" for both economic gain and for sexual pleasure. Varejão thus denounces patriarchal exploitation and rape culture in the same brush. Neither the black slaves nor the unidentified animal has a choice about participating in these relations, which are displayed with no judgment (except that which the viewer confers upon them). It is of course no coincidence that the white men in the bottom corner are the only two wearing modern clothes, marking both their racial and gendered privilege while simultaneously reminding the spectator that this painting is as historical in nature as it is contemporary, as if to say "Look what was happening in the past, and look what still happens in the present." This confers a somewhat ahistorical timelessness that may speak more to the universal violence in human nature than to specific cultural contexts. There is also the depiction of an interracial couple (a white woman with a black man), which of course would not have been tolerated in a racist colonial framework. In this complex piece, there are different horizontal levels with separate scenes. However, when the viewer mentally "flips" the painting, all the sexual scenarios are vertically connected with a pillar on the left side, transforming into stair steps. All of the people portrayed are practicing sexual relations in different constellations with the singular similarity that all are having sex. The portrayal of the two women in the top of the drawing appears different than the rest, and only in part because it is upside down. The spectator-voyeur perceives a more intimate exchange of sexual relations, where there is a sense of agency, implying freedom and playfulness in the sexual connection between the two. Of course, tolerance or acceptance of erotic love between lesbian women (and not just sex for the attention and the attainment of pleasure of the male viewer) would turn heteropatriarchal societies on their head.

Bia Leite's *Travesti da lambada e deusa das águas* (also known in international circles as *Queer Child* [2013]; see figure 8.4) features drawings of children covered in words that might equate to (loosely because translation is also problematic here) "faggot" and "tranny." The work denounces bullying and violence against LGBT children but is accused by the *MBL* of promoting pedophilia and censored for partaking in strategies for "recruitment" of otherwise "innocent" Brazilian youth in conjunction with the "ideology of gender" campaign to vilify LGBT populations. Not only do these paintings appear to have been done by a child, but they also offer the queer spectator a glimpse back to our own childhoods to redefine such a formative period of our lives in a way that removes negative judgment or condemnation for not adhering to the heteronormative scripts of childhood. In this "taking back" of shame and bullying, the spectator views children in different phases of psychosocial development. The similarity in the features of the blue-faced boy wearing multi-colored trousers with a younger version of himself in a neighboring panel represents a revisionist rethinking of childhood development in a queer-positive light. The non-binary youngster proudly wears their skirt; the tall child with the yellow sweater is either riding a pony or is himself a centaur, representing the rich fantasies and imaginations of children when creativity is allowed to flourish on its own, uninhibited by heteronormative

Figure 8.4. *Travesti da lambada e deusa das águas* (2013). Artist: Bia Leite. 100 × 100 cm.

impositions. For Bia Leite, queer children clearly represent the freedom of self-expression and to explore identities without censure. This utopian vision of an unfettered childhood contrasts with the damage children regularly suffer because of parental regulation or what they learn is acceptable and "normal" in school classes and on the playground. The return to a happy, spontaneous childhood that Leite's work offers for us is one that nullifies all forms of repression of difference, from left-handedness to conversion therapies to religious "exorcism" to straighten the queer. Social reality, unfortunately, is quite the contrary, and the psychosexual violence perpetuated on children carry permanent lifetime scars when—and sadly in many cases if—we live to become adults.

Fernando Baril's 1996 *Cruzando Jesus Cristo com Deusa Shiva* (*Crossing*, or, alternatively, *Breeding Jesus Christ with the Goddess Shiva*; see figure 8.5) is a piece about transubstantiation and multiplicities of religious icons, represented by the sixteen limbs of the Christ figure, each grasping sporty luxury items or prized artifacts of popular culture. Accused as blasphemous and a moral offense to Christianity, the work fuses the androgynous Hindu divinity

Figure 8.5. *Cruzando Jesus Cristo com Deusa Shiva* (1996). Artist: Fernando Baril. 150 × 125 cm.

Shiva, God of Destruction and the Destroyer of Evil, with Jesus Christ. Also known as the patron god of yoga, meditation, and the arts, the ways in which this deity crosses with Christ are antithetical to the materialistic possessions of Baril's god/dess. In this piece, Shiva is inscribed with female gender and therefore alluded to as *deusa*. The figure depicted on this cross no longer represents forgiveness or pardon, much less martyrdom. The amalgamation of both deities, transexualized and transformed, comes at a priceless cost because of reverence to materialism instead of spirituality, lamenting a contemporary universe driven by hedonism and gross mass consumption on earth rather than subscribing to the promise of an afterlife to come for the sacrifices believers make and the good deeds they perform in their earthly lives.

Antônio Obá's *Et Verbum* (2011; see figures 8.6–8.7), referring to both the word (as a part of speech) and the gospel of a Christian God, features Holy Communion wafers as they have never been packaged before, inscribed with words that carry sexual connotations, if not break silences that repressive "moral" codes of religiosity regularly omit or openly condemn. *Et verbum* is a paraphrased fragment of the Biblical phrase, *Verbum caro factum est*, translating to "The Word made flesh," and marking the beginning of St. John's Gospel, "The Word was made flesh and dwelt among us." Nevertheless, the astute observer will notice that sexually charged words, from actual body parts with both formal (e.g., *vulva* and *pênis*) and informal denotations to erotic sexual behaviors, coalesce and co-exist with words like *poesia*. Within the same open box of verbal communion wafers, these concepts bear equal weight and proportionality, each "dignified" by its presence on the most obvious symbol of Christian communion. With *cu* (asshole) as legitimate as poetry, and a box that remains open, one may interpret that these words and what they (re)present are being given back to us by a divine force and therefore ready to come out to the (Christian) world. The installation also challenges traditional Christian notions of mediation. Since the wafer representing the body of Christ can be distributed only by a priest, it is the institution of the church that makes these rules that congregants are to follow. There is a fair amount of ambiguity, too, about how we perceive this exchange semiotically. In other words, we may argue that when a religious institution dictates words of a sexual or erotic nature, the mediator is literally handling and handing out sacramental manductions to consume that are more along the lines of seductions to quench thirst, inscribed with the subversive power of human language. In fact, the polysemantic *língua* (much like English translating as the "tongue" or "language" itself, or both in the case of this installation) is one of the most repetitive sacraments. If practicing Christians were to receive the "spirit" or even the impure thoughts of the words coating the wafers, whether of poetry (the most common wafer in the box), provocations (such as *Prove meu tato*, "try my touch") or prohibited passions (such

Figures 8.6–8.7. *Et Verbum* (2011). Artist: Antônio Obá. 40 × 54 × 14 cm.

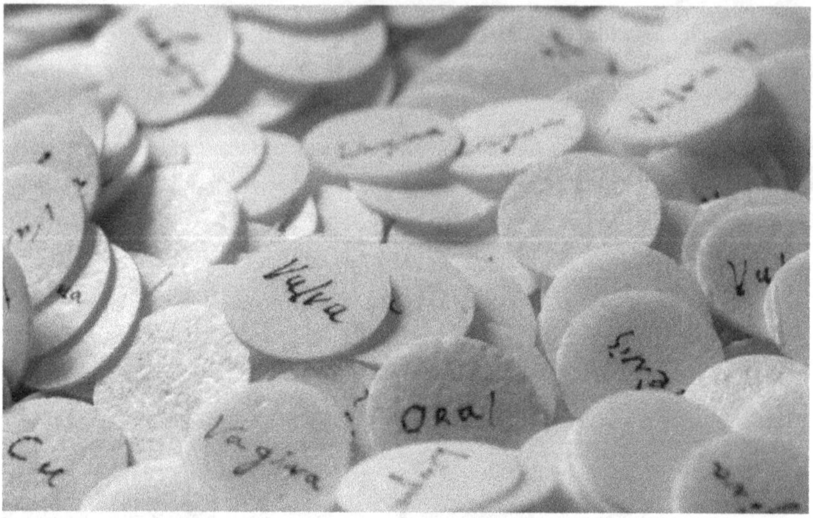

Figures 8.6–8.7.   (Continued)

as anal intercourse), then the believers or followers are held accountable for their commission. Responsibility for hypocritically committing the sin indicated thus confers power to the institution of the church and its leadership to confess or clear those very sins that come from the treasure box of the church, representing an eroticized or sexualized (and thus) irreverent body of Christ. What is clear is that the suggestive wafers come from inside an open box, creating the space for dialogue or interpretation among spectators as they metaphorically consume a language as concrete (and as sinful) as the body of Christ, giving viewers something to chew on regardless of their own religious affiliation or lack thereof.

Flávio Cerqueira's *Amnésia* (2015; see figures 8.8–8.9) boldly speaks for itself, documenting the invisibility and continued marginalization of Afro-Brazilian citizens and culture despite the fact that Afro-Brazilians comprise more than half of Brazil's population and constitute the second largest black population in the world. This sculpture, therefore, is a literal display of *branqueamento* (whitening) internalized by a young black man who wants to *macunaimically* transform his race to white. This attempt to deracialize himself is, of course, doomed to failure. The ephemeral effects of pouring white paint over his skin represent a futile effort to alter his identity and rewrite his origins. The "amnesia" of the title hints at a collective forgetting but also leads the viewer to understand that this boy's decision is not a conscious choice but rather the result of desperate attempt to erase the status of Afro-Brazilians, historically the most vulnerable victims of the disease of white superiority that has caused such deep racial inequality from slavery to the current day.

Tragically, the boy is merely attempting to rectify a historical process over which he has no control, and worse, no say. His action to coat himself with artificial whiteness is instantaneous and occurs in total silence and solitude.

The drama does not end with Santander Bank's decision to close the very exhibit it sponsored. Ruling on the premature closing of the exhibit, the Federal Public Ministry intervened to dismiss all accusations and recommended the immediate reopening of the *Queermuseu*. Santander declined to follow this suggestion. The *Museu de Arte do Rio* (*MAR*) attempted to come to the

Figures 8.8–8.9. *Amnésia* (2015). Artist: Flávio Cerqueira.

Figures 8.8–8.9.   (Continued)

rescue by acting to reopen the event in Rio de Janeiro. I find in this moment a fascinating juncture that geographically mirrors the (physical and political) queer dislocation from a conservative city in Southern Brazil to the "progressive" melting pot of Rio de Janeiro (both stereotypes and generalizations, of course). The exile, or imposed queer diaspora, of the exposition speaks literally to movement from the margins of extreme Southern Brazil to the widely regarded cultural center. Nevertheless, the journey for a home continued, with Rio's fundamentalist mayor, Marcello Crivella, denying (read: repressing) the initiative to move the exhibit to the MAR, remarking pointedly and homotransphobically with a despicable pun that, for this story, is utterly humorless: The exhibit would occupy the space of the museum only *"se fosse para o fundo do mar"* (literally, only if it were at "the bottom of the sea," implying that such an opening would occur at the expense of permanently drowning the museum).

Our story continues on a more positive note now, though no less dramatic. The *Queermuseu* began a crowdfunding campaign, which amassed Brazilian and international donors to raise money to salvage the nomadic exhibit and allow it to find a new (albeit temporary) home. It is worth noting though, as curator Fidelis has importantly contextualized, the exhibit was not meant to be a traveling one. With an overall goal of collecting US$5,000.00, this brilliant strategy to undo a tyrannical act of repression and to redemocratize public space, ended up raising US$327,000. This record pledge, of R$1.081 million in the last quarter of 2017, constituted the most successful crowdfunding campaign

ever conducted in Brazil, according to Fábio Szwarcwald, director and president of the *Escola de Artes Visuais do Parque Lage (EAV)* (School of Visual Arts in Lage Park) in Rio, founded in 1975 in the midst of dictatorship. The generated funding would allow the *EAV* to become the new home for the displaced and embattled *Queermuseu*. I feel compelled to add just a few more notes to this abbreviated story before we move further into how it is illustrative of political and theoretical implications of queer curatorship, which I would like to now contract or collapse into the neologism "cuiratorship" (queeratorship).

One day after the assassination of Marielle Franco, on March 15, 2018, Caetano Veloso performed a benefit concert for the *Queermuseu*, aptly titled "Caetano Veloso against Censorship," with participation of Maria Gadú and Marisa Monte. The mobilization of Brazilians outraged by the forced closure of the exhibit in Porto Alegre would bear fruit in Rio de Janeiro, where eighty-one artists donated works to an auction designed to benefit the *Queermuseu*, also occurring on March 15, 2018. It is worth noting that, according to Fidelis, the majority of the artist donors initially had no connection or professional ties to the exhibit.

Our story has a quasi-Hollywoodesque happy ending, at least quantitatively if not qualitatively: The *Queermuseu*, safely installed at *EAV* from August 18 to September 16, received a total of 8,000 visitors in its first weekend (with a wait time of an hour and a half), 14,000 visitors in its first ten days, and drew a total of 60,000 guests by the end of its brief re-opening.

We begin to wrap up our queer journey that has taken us to a Brazil that has only recently begun to legitimize (Brazilianize) the term "queer," much less perceive itself as a quintessentially queer imaginary as I argue throughout this book. I am especially interested in assessing the movement, disruption, eruption/e-ruption, rupture, location, and dislocation of the *Queermuseu*, whose drastically altered trajectory and ultimately smashing success both paralleled and ironically was guaranteed by similarly successful attempts at censorship. What we are witnessing here is a certain degree of authoritarianism within democratization, a paradoxical process that reflects the critical views of Gaudêncio Fidelis's assumptions about queer curatorship. In the official *Queermuseu* catalog, it is telling that of the several long articles in the catalog, only one is written by someone other than Fidelis—and this one for the most part as a shameless though not undeserving shout-out to the director and president of the *Escola de Artes Visuais*. Is this indicative of an authoritarian nature of the exhibit's curatorship? To be sure, most of these pieces attack or preempt critique by "specialists" or queer theory academics who Fidelis claims do not truly understand the methodology or the aesthetics of the collection. What this reflects, to my mind, a sense of authorship that would come into conflict and contradiction with the expected inclusivity of queer curatorship. However, it also lays bare the continuing "culture wars" with respect to progressive versus conservative politics, to freedom from the constraints of normative gender categories in opposition to the "ideology of gender" arguments to repress and criminalize personal freedoms. But what is also being re-enacted with this display is the drama of how "queer" gets absorbed and, as Fidelis puts it, "cannibalized" in a popular Brazilian context in opposition to academic discourses based on Americentric models of queer theory. As much as Fidelis claims that the installation destabilizes conventional curatorial practice by decolonizing heteronormative, hierarchical, dominant, and essentialist epistemologies that "traditional" art history and historians tend to reinforce, it is useful and, I would argue, necessary to chart the failures of this compelling effort, aesthetically, politically and methodologically speaking.

Without intending to argue or frankly even touch the incessantly clichéd dilemma "Is x or y, in this case, the *Queermuseu*, queer enough?" I contend that the exhibit is crafted with artistic *queeriosidade* but questionable *cuiriosidade* when it comes to what I call *heterobrasilidade* in ironic contrast to *queernormativity*. Gaudêncio's exhaustive and exhausting defensive pleas to concretely define what is queer about the organization and the content of the exhibit defies any ambiguity of the fleeting, floating, and fluid nature of queer that the curator tries so desperately to relocate (read: placate) within and between the confines of the walls of the exposition (and the aesthetically beautiful but utterly conventional catalog to guide the spectator and/or commodify the queer). As Patrik Steorn (2010) points out in his article "Queer in the Museum: Methodological Reflections on Doing Queer in Museum Collections": "Inserting 'queer' as a static label in a museum database would surely be the end of the term itself," contending that identities would become "tagged," reified, fixed, therefore losing their queer meanings. To add to the normative queer cliché discussed before, I would like to queer another: If the book can't be judged by its cover, the cover may be too queer for the template of the patriarchal pages printed within it. One of Fidelis's most compelling essays in the exhibit catalog is his shortest piece with the longest title: "*A energia da forma: elementos de construção morfológica do padrão visual da publicação Queermuseu*" (The Energy of Form: Elements of Morphological Construction in the Visual Pattern of the Queermuseu Catalog). In this article, Fidelis explains the intricate design and, to my mind, the brilliant conception of the cover of the catalog, noting that the graphic elements constitute five possible combinations: XX, XY, XXY, XXX, and XYY. Fidelis attributes this design to Anne Fausto-Sterling's conceptualization of five sexes, published in 1993 but revised in 2000 with further data on intersexuality. The curator's mapping of the cover goes further, and though my translation appears in the following, it is worth quoting in the original Portuguese:[1,2,3,4,5] "The graphical elements used to create the platform on the cover of the *Queermuseum* catalogue originate from combinations of the letters 'X' and 'Y,' representing the respective chromosomes and their five possible combinations: XX, XY, XXY, XXX, and XXY . . . suggesting the five sexes Anne Fausto-Sterling conceived and published in her essay of the same name (*The Five Sexes*, 1993), revised as *The Five Sexes Revisited* in 2000. To graphically represent this, we included a series of other shapes that came into existence in an interchangeable figure/background relation, without being fixed to any of them, continuously undoing the binary relation that constitutes it. . . . We can designate each of them as presenting specific attributions, bearing in mind that this is about transitory shapes which interconnect to the whole at any moment that one wishes to create a distinct combination. . . . The pattern obtained results in an intricate wave-like (undulatory) movement that demands different types of seeing, appearing entangled within a network of movement towards different directions" (Catalog, 132–3).

The "cuirator" continues to assert that even the specific style utilized in the construction of the word *Queermuseu* on the catalog's cover is a unique font never before in existence and designed exclusively for the publication at hand. His contention that the genesis of a brand new font never seen before is a quintessentially queer product of contamination, hybridity, and visibility (133) perhaps goes a bit too far. However, as Steorn (2010) notes, rather cynically, "Temporary exhibitions and collaborations with feminist and queer artists and curators . . . tend to profile themselves as much more radical than they actually are" (120). The critic later does well to remind us of the danger that "an object that is collected in order to represent LGBT community might end up affirming and reproducing normative attitudes and social categories" (135). If representation results in names or labels, then heteronormative finality or completion ensues. This conclusive process, as we know, is the antithesis of queer flux.

I think it is important to keep in mind the strategies and multiplicities of genres and genders in which "the archive" can (and, from a political standpoint, should) be queered, a function I believe the *Queermuseu* fulfills quite successfully. As Jack Halberstam notes, reflecting on the performative function of the archive (or in this case, museum) for queer community, "The archive is not simply a repository; it is also a theory of cultural relevance, a construction of collective memory and complex record of queer activity" (2003), a record that includes video art, pop art, but also ephemeral objects like zines, pamphlets, and music, enriching or challenging the documents and objects that one may expect to find in a conventional museum. What is at the root of this difference is queer affect, as the earlier work of Eve Kosofsky Segwick, Ann Cvetkovich, José Muñóz, and others have articulated, ultimately transforming the *museu* itself into an "alternative archive" that does not constitute its difference from objects per se but rather distinguishes itself as devoting new or renewed energies to differing emotional, political, and aesthetic attachments or detachment (or as the case may be when challenging

Figures 8.10. One of two docents at the *Queermuseu* performatively narrating a series of videos (duration of 33 minutes), "Sudário—Espada de São Jorge I, II, III, IV" (2013), 21 × 65 cm each, an artwork that represents the historic ban to enforce a 12-month "waiting period" for LGBT Brazilians to donate blood, imposed by Brazil's Ministry of Health and lifted on May 9, 2020 after nearly four years in court. The artist, Christus Nóbrega, used his own blood to create the swords of St. George of Cappadocia, a plant of African origin brought by African slaves to Brazil, where it has flourished. It bears spiritual significance in *candomblé*. The format of its leaves is likened to the sword of the *orixá* Ogum, with the capacity to protect, purify, and "cut out" the envy of the evil eye, bringing prosperity to its practitioners and removing negative energies from their homes

hegemonic heteronormativity) from these objects, which may very well be the *same* objects. This project and experiment of *cuiratorship* begs consideration of Tyburczy's bold claim that opens her book, that "All Museums are Sex Museums," provocatively enticing the reader to consider museums as "theatrical spaces of everyday drama, veritable contact zones between bodies and objects" (1).

Epilogue: The (R)evolving Closet Door in LGBT Brazil

In a well-known interview, *gaúcho* novelist, playwright, *cronista* and AIDS activist Caio Fernando Abreu declares: "It's just that homosexuality does not exist and it never existed. What exists is sexuality, connected to any object of desire. [This object] may or may not have identical genitalia, and that is a mere detail. But this, in itself, does not determine a greater or lesser degree of morality or integrity."[1] How does one embrace or even trust an openly gay writer who does not believe in homosexuality? Indeed, at the same time as Abreu attempts to break free from heteronormative hegemonic notions about sexual orientation(s), he also relegates homosexuality (and heterosexuality) to silence by arguing for its erasure in the language of LGBT activism. This perspective may constitute a queer gesture, arguing for liberation from monolithic and overtly oppressive categorizations and classifications of identities. However, is Brazilian Portuguese, so rooted in deeply rigid patriarchal structures, capable of transcending categories of difference without inadvertently erasing them? Or is this wishful thinking of a utopian nature, hoping for the reconstruction of a world that intentionally erases identities to dream of abolishing identitarian politics altogether? This assertion is somewhat reminiscent of another, made by writer Eric Bentley nearly forty years ago, in a compelling 1977 article, "*The Homosexual Question*": "All terms used to describe homosexuality are histories of ideologies [that] assist the dominant social order in promoting and maintaining itself. . . . Homosexual is a descriptive term only in a sexist society; it describes what is *un*heterosexual" (33).

As Denilson Lopes has argued, this game of hide-and-seek, to disappear only to reappear elsewhere, is a beautiful metaphor to suggest the "queerness" of Brazil, even as it continues to resist the designation of this term to define it as recently as the advent of the coronavirus pandemic. But there is much at stake in this "game," including the lives and the loves of countless LGBT citizens who assume great risks in coming out as lesbian, gay, bisexual, or trans in a society still deemed as the most murderous in the world when it comes to homophobic violence. It is by now a rather reprehensible cliché to argue that there is a shadow of truth in every joke, but I assume this risk as I invoke the words of popular Brazilian *cronista*, essayist, and cultural critic Arnaldo Jabor, whose joke in the following is not funny at all given that the number of homophobic assassinations continue well into the thousands and at alarmingly increasing rates: "Homosexuality used to be prohibited in Brazil. Then it became tolerated. Today, it is accepted as something normal. I'm leaving [this country] before it becomes declared obligatory."[2] This "joke," while in poor taste, reminds us of the normalization of the LGBT Pride Parade in São Paulo to such an extent that numerous conservative Brazilian citizens of questionable motives would claim themselves as minorities due to living their heterosexuality amidst a homonormative tradition that has served to empower LGBT Brazilians. This perceived threat to the hegemony of the straights is a discourse not unique to Brazil.

My focus throughout this interdisciplinary study has been on the uses, misuses, and abuses of language. We have analyzed the lexicon of popular mainstream media, reflecting on journalistic discourse as an avenue to interpret and to manipulate knowledge about the São Paulo LGBT Pride Parade, a sociocultural phenomenon enormously significant in both quantitative and qualitative terms. An event that annually brings millions to the street to protest, parade, and party around paradigms of sexual orientation and gender identity is one that deserves careful examination. We have also explored the language of the dictionary, of reference-style manuals and parodic variations thereof and witnessed their ability to redefine, to resignify, and to subvert established and conventional meanings, challenging the privilege and hegemony afforded to them by constraining heteronormative linguistic structures. Our journey has also taken us to the language of illustrations and images, from drawings in our reference book, to the images posted in telephone booths in popular public spaces, to questioning the complex and often contradictory roles photography plays as a medium of communication and influence in public opinion. Notably, we have considered the bodies of LGBT Brazilians, in particular those rendered transgendered, *as* language. Gestures, movements, performance, neologisms all color the lens through which we view meaning in the world. My hope is that the language in this book, though not articulated in the language of Brazil itself, will help promote and inspire additional provocative and productive dialogues to push us further along in our collective human quest to blend two voices that have been deemed incompatible for far too long: the quiet, introspective academic language of the scholar and the angry outbursts and shouts of protest of the activist.

Throughout the pages of this book, I have employed an eclectic and multifaceted theoretical approach to achieve the inattainable *unimultiplicidade*, with the hope of drawing together various cultural vignettes and discourses to frame and construct our examination of LGBT culture and language in today's Brazil. My initial hope was to provide something of a "case study," as it were, to encourage Brazilian and non-Brazilian readers alike to approach the theme from various methodological viewpoints. What I have discovered, however, is that the restrictive language of "case study" itself, while useful, also resists nuanced and textured possibilities of representing itself when analyzing LGBT life or queer politics in a specifically Brazilian context. The slipperiness that such ambivalence inevitably creates can be—and perhaps can only be—unwieldy and unyielding to a construct of sexuality that insists on defining it so as to regulate, moderate, punish, and reward it, as Foucault famously argued. Indeed, and in my final analysis, I believe that the greatest paradox in a country replete of contradictions is the fact that the very fabric of its daily existence is what many North American cultural critics would call "queer" and what attracts many of us to studying its ambivalent landscapes. The flip side of that contradiction is, of course, that the term "queer" itself is all but foreign to that richly ambiguous imaginary.

Appendix

The Queer-stionnaire
(*Queer-Stionário*)

DADOS PESSOAIS:

Nome ou Pseudônimo (sem sobrenome): Name or Pseudonym (no last names):
Local de nascimento: (Place of birth):
Data: (Date):
Estado civil: (Relationship Status):
Instrução: (Level of Education):
Ocupação atual: (Current Occupation):
Renda: (Salary):

PROVINHA DE VOCABULÁRIO:

Procure definir os seguintes 32 vocábulos ou expressões, conforme utilizados na atual gíria da comunidade GLBT.

  1. *África:*
  2. *Aquendar:*
  3. *Ataque epilésbico:*
  4. *Aurélia:*
  5. *Baba-ovo:*
  6. *Bas-fond:*
  7. *Beth Faria:*
  8. *Bi:*
  9. *Bi-curious:*
  10. *Biba:*
  11. *Bicha:*
  12. *Bicha-bofe:*

13. *Bicha carão:*
14. *Bicha-pão-com-ovo:*
15. *Bicha-bofe:*
16. *Bicha-wallpaper:*
17. *Bolacha:*
18. *Bofe:*
19. *Boot:*
20. *Coronel:*
21. *Ebó mal despachado:*
22. *Emma Thompson:*
23. *Helen(inh)a:*
24. *Homossexuellen:*
25. *Irene:*
26. *Jogar o picumã:*
27. *Lesbian chic:*
28. *Meu cu:*
29. *Mona:*
30. *Piti:*
31. *Sapa(tão):*
32. *Viptimização:*

Notes

INTRODUCTION

1. *Brasilidade* translates loosely as "Brazilianness" and is a common trope in Brazilian cultural studies used to assess or determine what constitutes the Brazilian cultural profile, whether in its innate characteristics that create a uniquely Brazilian universe or in its imaginary. The term is problematic, of course, for in attempting to study "culture," whether or not we claim it as our own, scholars often neglect to consider universal truths that characterize the wholeness of human nature and not unique to specific geographical spaces.

2. See Santiago, Silviano. *The Space In-Between: Essays on Latin American Culture*. Trans. Tom Burns, Ana Lúcia Gazzola & Gareth Williams. Durham: Duke U P, 2001.

3. "Order and Progress" are the words inscribed on the Brazilian flag since the Proclamation of the Republic in 1890. Its roots are in positivism, developed by the French philosopher Auguste Comte (1798–1857).

4. There are numerous sources to corroborate that São Paulo is the most ethnically and culturally diverse city in South America and not just in Brazil.

5. The term *transgênero* is the larger umbrella term that is used to refer to transsexuals in Brazil. Many scholars, Benedetti and Kulick among them, have found that transgendered Brazilians tend to self-identify either as *transsexual* or *travesti*.

6. Data on hate crimes does not exist in Brazilian governmental statistics and can be compiled only by referring to newspaper and Internet articles. Moreover, incidence of assassination of LGBT-identified citizens in Brazil has increased 55% in 2008 over 2007: 122 homicides in 2007 as opposed to 190 homicides in 2008, making Brazil the world "champion" in homophobic crimes, followed by Mexico (35 homicides in 2008) and the United States (25 homicides in 2008). Source: *Grupo Gay da Bahia*.

7. For a much more comprehensive analysis of these processes at work, please refer to the sources by Green, MacRae, Míccolis, Mott, and Trevisan listed in the bibliography.

8. For an excellent reference on the influence of radio in Brazil and, in particular, the "Golden Age" of the 1930s and 1940s, see Sterling, Christopher H. Ed. *Encyclopedia of Radio*, Volume 1. London: Taylor & Francis, 2004, especially pp. 311–312.

9. For more information on the gay rights movement in the United States, see D'Emilio, John. *Sexual Politics, Sexual Communities: The Making of a Homosexual Minority in the United States, 1940–1970*. Chicago: The University of Chicago Press, 1983. For further information on the history of gay civil rights activism in France, see Gunther, Scott. "Building a More Stately Closet: French Gay Movements since the Early 1980s." *Journal of the History of Sexuality*. 13, no. 3 (July 2004): 327. Also see Frédéric Martel's *The Pink and the Black: Homosexuals in France since 1968*. Trans. Jane Todd. Palo Alto: Stanford U P, 1999.

10. The title "*Sem lenço, sem documento*" (literally, "Without a handkerchief, without any documents") refers to one of Caetano Veloso's famous protest songs in the heyday of the *Tropicália* movement, expressing frustration with political violence and repression during Brazil's military dictatorship in the 1960s and 1970s. The song's title was used in 1990 to create a "Best of Caetano Veloso" album, which would become a great seller.

11. The award-winning documentary, "Dzi croquettes," was produced in 2009 and directed by Tatiana Issa, the daughter of Américo Issa, choreographer of the band with the same name, "Dzi croquettes." The film is co-directed and produced by Raphael Alvarez. The troupe on which the documentary film is based, "Dzi croquettes," was founded in 1972, during the height of military dictatorship in Brazil. Founded by Brooklyn-born Broadway choreographer and dancer Lennie Dale, who later took up permanent residency in Rio de Janeiro, the group, consisting of only thirteen men, was considered irreverent at the time and remains controversial to this day. The troupe was actively and consciously involved in gender-bending, using high heels, loads of makeup, fake eyelashes, and extravagant dresses covered in glitter.

12. Source: Facchini, Regina. *Sopa de Letrinhas? Movimento homossexual e produção de identidades coletivas nos anos 90*. Rio de Janeiro: Garamond, 2005.

13. See Mascarenhas, João Antônio de Souza. *A Tríplice Conexão: machismo, conservadorismo politico e falso moralismo*. Rio de Janeiro: 2AB Editora, 1997.

14. For an excellent study of both the evolution and the long-ranging effects of the Stonewall riots, see John D'Emilio's work, in particular the study *Sexual Politics, Sexual Communities: The Making of a Homosexual Minority in the United States, 1940–1970*. Chicago: U Chicago P, 1983; revised, 1998. Also notable is David Carter's *Stonewall: The Riots that Sparked the Gay Revolution*. St. Martin's Griffin, 2010 and the DVD *American Experience: Stonewall Uprising*, produced by PBS in 2011.

15. The president singled out the film *Transversais*, which narrates the life stories of five trans Brazilians living in Ceará and the film *Afronte*, about the sociopolitical climate for Afro-Brazilian gay men in Brasília, arguing that these films *não tem cabimento* since *ninguém assiste*, further claiming during a live broadcast that "I admit I didn't understand anything. Nobody has anything to do with someone's personal life, no matter who they are, but I can't understand the reasons for making a film about black homosexuals in the country's capital. One more film that belongs in the

garbage" (*"Não entendi nada, confesso. A vida particular de quem quer que seja, ninguém tem nada a ver com isso, mas fazer um filme sobre negros homossexuais no Distrito Federal, confesso que não dá pra entender. Mais um filme que foi pro saco"*).

16. *"Ninguém pode achar que a homofobia vem de Deus, LGBTfobia é crime. E atenção, padres e pastores que humilham pessoas LGBTs, isso é crime."*

17. *"Paradoxalmente, a mudança sunstancial na forma como parte da população vê o governo Bolsonaro ocorre no momento em que o país vive uma grave crise sanitária e econômica."*

18. *"Já somos vistas como vetor de doenças, e agora também nos olham como responsáveis pela propagação do coronavírus."*

19. *"Como eu falo para elas ficarem a um metro de distância do cliente?"*

20. For the complete lyrics of the song *"Brasil Corrupção,"* and to listen to it in its entirety, the reader may choose to visit the following website: http://letras.mus.br/ana-carolina-seu-jorge/457858/.

21. See Dehesa, Rafael de la. *Queering the Public Sphere in Mexico and Brazil: Sexual Rights Movements in Emerging Democracies*. Durham: Duke U P, 2009.

22. See chapter 3.

CHAPTER 1

1. *"Mesmo para quem tenta desmerecer as Paradas como mero carnaval fora de época, perdura a pergunta: como se chegou a uma consciência coletiva que leva multidões a essa festa celebratória, carregando bandeiras ou vestindo as cores do arco íris? Fica claro que o protagonismo de um novo grupo social aconteceu num processo de aprendizado das ruas. E isso se desdobrou socialmente até contaminar as próprios meios de comunicação, que foram despertados para compreenderem um fenômeno novo."*

2. 2006: *"Homofobia é crime"*; 2007: *"Por um mundo sem homofobia"*; 2008: *"Homofobia mata"*; 2009: *"Mais cidadania sem homofobia"*; 2010: *"Vote contra a homofobia"*; 2011. *"Amai-vos uns aos outros: basta de homofobia."*

3. Though the involvement of labor unions predominate in the most recent incarnations of the Pride Parade, it is important to remember that unions marked their presence from the first parade. For example, the São Paulo Bank workers' union supplied the first sound system, attached to a van, for the 1997 Parade.

4. See Introduction, Note #14.

5. *"Liberdade & igualdade, nada de regras ou leis, nada será imposto a vocês, apenas pensem da seguinte maneira: RESPEITO PARA SER RESPEITADO."*

6. *"Para facilitar a compreensão da sociedade, que até então não se familiarizava com o acrônimo GLBT (utilizado no Brasil até julho de 2008, posteriormente substituído por LGBT), e a disseminação do tema da Parada, decidiu-se por abranger todos os grupos representados pelo movimento na denominação 'Gay.'"*

7. See specific references in the bibliography.

8. I acknowledge the limitations of a study of this nature, which examines ongoing historical and present cultural processes. While I was able to observe the LGBT

Pride Parade in São Paulo in 2012, when the numbers of participants had seemed to dwindle significantly, I was not able to conduct research on this particular edition of the Parade, nor was I able to attend the 2013 edition by the time of publication.

9. *"Orgulho Gay supera expectativa e reúne 400 mil pessoas na cidade."*

10. *"Com roupas coloridas e fantasias, os irreverentes participantes saíram da Paulista e foram até a República."*

11. *"Para organizadores, 700 mil pessoas estiveram na Parada, considerada a maior da América Latina."*

12. *"A Parada do Orgulho Gay passou a ser um programa de família. Além dos grupos de casais homossexuais e simpatizantes, um grande número de pessoas compareceu ao evento na Avenida Paulista simplesmente para conferir a animação e as* **coloridas e exóticas fantasias das 'drag-queens.'"**

13. *"Tomando toda a Paulista, a massa de gays, lésbicas, simpatizantes e curiosos se agitava com a trilha sonora que vinha dos sete carros de som que compunham o desfile."*

14. Paloma Cotes, Fabiane Leite, & Sérgio Duran, *"Orgulho Gay: Parada leva às ruas 400 mil pessoas e bate recorde em SP." Folha de São Paulo* (June 3, 2002).

15. *"Segundo a organização, estiveram presentes grupos estrangeiros vindos dos Estados Unidos e até da África do Sul."*

16. *"O tema deste ano foi o de ampliar o foco nas questões das mulheres homossexuais."*

17. *"Uma comissão de frente com cerca de 10 lésbicas motociclistas abriu o desfile."*

18. *"Uma das principais ações de apoio às lésbicas foi o abaixo-assinado apoiando a concessão da guarda de Chicão, filho da cantora Cássia Eller, para sua companheira, Maria Eugênia."*

19. See Jean Baudrillard's work highlighting the absence of distinction between reality and simulacra in his groundbreaking *Simulacres et Simulation* (1981). In this essay, Baudrillard maintains that contemporary media sources create a tenuous border between fundamentally essential products while manipulating commercial images to arrive at the perception that secondary or non-essential items are also of necessity.

20. *"As lésbicas, homenageadas desta edição, foram o destaque da festa. A cantora Laura Finochiaro convocou as participantes lésbicas a 'mostrarem os peitos' e tirou a camiseta enquanto cantava o hino gay 'Pavão Misterioso,' do compositor Ednardo. Muitas aderiram ao convite."*

21. *"A presença dos dois atores no trio elétrico da revista G Magazine causou tumulto entre as milhares de pessoas que cercavam o carro. A multidão, enlouquecida, ovacionava a dupla e se acotovelava para se aproximar dos atores. Ao descer do carro, a confusão aumentou. Para tentar fotografar Wilker e Muller, os fãs provocaram empurra-empurra na avenida. Os atores retornaram ao carro."*

22. *G Magazine* is arguably the most popular monthly periodical in Brazil, publishing articles, photographs, and art of interest primarily—but not exclusively—to a Brazilian gay male audience.

23. *"Há apenas um carro que é da CUT [Central Única dos Trabalhadores, ligada ao PT]. Ele foi, na verdade, dividido pela central e gays do PT. O abre-alas nunca é do PT, traz apenas os símbolos da associação. Somos suprapartidários."*

24. *"Na primeira parada, todo mundo nos olhava com um jeito **estranho**. Aos poucos, o **respeito** à **diversidade** foi **se impondo**."*
25. *"Uma manifestação como esta só vi nas Diretas-Já."*
26. See http://sfpride.org/heritage/2003.html.
27. *"Parada gay reúne 800 mil e é 3a no mundo." Folha de S. Paulo* (June 23, 2003).
28. *"'O Judiciário já está mais adiantado. Temos jurisprudência em quase tudo. O projeto já está até ultrapassado. O mundo já andou,' disse a prefeita em relação à proposta que já foi uma das suas bandeiras e que a tornou uma porta-voz do público gay."*
29. *"Espero que não tenha sido um melindre dela por nossas cobranças. Não é porque a apoiamos que vamos deixar de criticá-la quando necessário."*
30. *"Outra 'Marta' presente na parada era o travesti Márcia Taylor. Fantasiado com um terno vermelho, peruca loira e coroa, Taylor se autodenominava 'a rainha das taxas.' 'No ano que vem, cobrarei uma taxa para desfilar.'"*
31. *"Com essa manifestação, já está na hora de votar esse projeto. Não depende só do governo, mas vamos defendê-lo."*
32. *"Esse tema é ultrapassado. Temos que trabalhar com uma pauta comum entre todos os segmentos que são minorias políticas."*
33. *"A atual organização já anunciou que, em 2004, haverá um tema direcionado aos idosos e adolescentes."*
34. The disputes between the parade organizers and Suplicy were far more complicated than the media reported. Beto de Jesus, who had been the Parade president and was a close supporter of Marta Suplicy was ousted from his position, and an anti-*PT* faction took over the leadership of the Parade. The movement attempted to keep this conflict out of the press, although it does surface in articles leading up to the Parade.
35. *"A parada gay é o evento de São Paulo que mais reúne pessoas sem precisar fazer rifas ou distribuir prêmios, como carros . . . [Isso] mostra o respeito e o reconhecimento que a população da cidade tem pela diversidade e pela pluralidade. . . . Aqui estão os avós, os filhos e os pais dos homossexuais. [Esse evento] é muito mais que uma religião, é uma **opção**. . . . Nós temos cada vez mais de saber aceitar o diferente e dar cidadania para as pessoas . . . É uma festa linda."*
36. To be fair, though, a second political agenda may have been afoot to help us understand Suplicy's comments. The reference to the Parade as a space where people gather not because they receive prizes or raffle a car may be read as a political critique Suplicy employs to differentiate the Parade and the *PT* from the *Força Sindical*, an anti-*PT/CUT* union confederation that mobilized people to attend its May Day activities by offering shows with car raffles, prizes, and the like. As such, Suplicy's comments may be interpreted as a political compliment to the LGBT march in comparison to her opinion of the populism of the mobilization of other political currents.
37. There are excellent scholarly works that problematize "democracy" and "democratization" in contemporary Brazil. Two such studies include *Corruption and Democracy in Brazil: The Struggle for Accountability*, a collection edited by political scientists Timothy J. Power and Matthew M. Taylor (Notre Dame, Indiana: U Notre Dame P, 2011) and James Holston's award-winning *Insurgent Citizenship: Disjunctions of Democracy*

and Modernity in Brazil (Princeton, NJ: Princeton U P, 2009). Rafael de la Dehesa, a sociologist, whose work is considered in this book, provides an illuminating discussion of the complex discourses revolving around the "secular state" in his *Queering the Public Sphere in Mexico and Brazil: Sexual Rights Movements in Emerging Democracies* (Durham, NC: Duke U P, 2010).

38. This statistic was furnished by Reinaldo Pereira Damião, the president of the Association in an interview for the *Diário de São Paulo* on June 14, 2004 (Viviane Raymundi & Jaqueline Falcão).

39. "*De olho no público da parada, a proprietária da banca de revistas Alfa, na Avenida Paulista, adaptou o esquema de vendas: na vitrine colocou apenas revistas gays.*"

40. "*Parada gay em SP é a maior do mundo: Festa bateu recorde de público ao reunir 1,5 milhão de pessoas na Avenida Paulista.*"

41. "*Os gays e lésbicas, que nos dias normais não costumam ter liberdade nem para andar abraçado ao companheiro do mesmo sexo na rua, vêem na parada o momento ideal para se soltar e trocar carícias.*"

42. Disturbingly, knowledge about the dangers of public displays of affection in Brazil has become so pervasive in popular culture that a reputable travel guidebook for LGBT travelers to Brazil takes special care to warn against exercising such openness, not only in Brazil's rural areas but in the large cities as well: "Outside of the big cities such as São Paulo, Rio de Janeiro, and Salvador, openly gay men or women will certainly draw attention and perhaps be subjected to comments or jokes. Brazil is still a macho culture and any open sign of affection between people of the same sex will meet with disapproval . . . public displays of affection are not common among gays and lesbians even in the cities, and in small towns and communities the level of acceptance is significantly lower—rude remarks and jokes are almost guaranteed." (Source: http://www.frommers.com/destinations/brazil/0813028778.html#ixzz2YbnCqCgJ.)

43. See Da Matta, Roberto. *Carnavais, malandros e heróis: Para uma sociologia do dilemma brasileiro.* Rio de Janeiro: Rocco, 1979. It is important to note that while it is relevant, this reading is somewhat reductive, for it oversimplifies da Matta's *rua*/*casa* dichotomy, which is informed by race, socioeconomic class, gender, and other factors. For further discussion on these dynamics, please refer to da Matta's original text or the numerous essays written on his work.

44. "*Transformistas, drag queens e transgêneros desenham fantasias especiais para a festa, que acaba virando uma vitrine de cor e criatividade. Muita gente chega a pedir para tirar foto junto.*"

45. "*A Paulista foi tomada por uma multidão na marcha que mistura militância e carnaval.*"

46. "*Parada gay reúne 1,5 milhão e bate recorde: São Paulo ultrapassa San Francisco e sedia maior evento homosexual do mundo, afirmam organizadores.*"

47. "*A própria prefeitura armou um camarim em frente ao parque Trianon para que as pessoas pudessem se aprumar para a parada.*"

48. "*Quem é só simpatizante do movimento gay geralmente vai à parada para curtir o clima de descontração, mas ontem havia até gente a procura de outro simpatizante—do sexo oposto. 'Quero ver se acho um,' disse a desempregada Cibele de Almeida, de 18 anos.*"

49. *"Parada Gay lota as duas pistas da Avenida Paulista em SP: O prefeito de São Paulo, José Serra (PSDB), defendeu que a cidade 'tem os braços e a mente abertos às diferenças e às diversidades e não exerce discriminação."*

50. *"São Paulo é o Estado com maior número de assassinatos de homossexuais por ano. A média é de 21 mortos, segundo o relatório 'Assassinatos de Homossexuais no Brasil,' do Grupo Gay da Bahia. 'O número preocupa. A população de São Paulo é grande, mas crimes de homofobia não podem ocorrer em lugar nenhum,' diz Luiz Mott, fundador do grupo."*

51. *"Além de São Paulo, Pernambuco preocupa a entidade. Lá, a media está em 16 crimes por ano, sendo que a população é seis vezes menor que a de São Paulo."*

52. *"O secretário estadual de Justiça e da defesa da Cidadania, Hédio Silva Junior, um dos participantes da marcha, informou que o governo vai anunciar em breve uma série de ações de combate à discriminação homofóbica. Segundo Hédio Silva Junior, uma comissão especial para atender a queixas deste gênero funciona desde 2001 na secretaria, tendo atendido a 32 casos nesse período."*

53. *"Os líderes do movimento pretendem tirar desse evento a força de que necessitam para arrancar da gaveta o projeto de lei que prevê a extensão dos direitos civis entre casais heterossexuais para casais homossexuais."*

54. *"Apesar do caráter festivo da Parada, que contou com milhares de drag queens e participantes fantasiados, a manifestação teve forte teor politico."*

55. *"Eu ainda não sei como o meu projeto não foi aprovado. O assunto é tão sério e forte que já está em jurisprudência no País . . . os principais tribunais do País criaram jurisprudência ao admitir que os casais do mesmo sexo têm os mesmos direitos que os heterossexuais em alguns processos sobre heranças, pensões e custódia de filhos. Os homossexuais e as lésbicas pagam impostos e têm de ter os direitos de qualquer outro cidadão."*

56. *"A presidenta da Amam, a advogada Maria Stella Pires, 62, impede um rapaz de entrar, dizendo: 'O repórter tudo bem, o outro pode ficar aí fora esperando. A Amam nasceu da necessidade de ter uma visibilidade lésbica. Então, se a gente encher de homem aqui, não vai dar. Não sou gay, sou lésbica.'"*

57. *"São Paulo é aberta a diferentes raças e não exercita a palavra discriminação. São Paulo tem mente e braços abertos para a diversidade."*

58. *"Mas ele (Serra) se esquivou de responder quando foi perguntado por repórteres se é favorável à união civil entre homossexuais e se acha importante que a sociedade e a família aceitem os gays. (Ele deu as costas e não respondeu.)"*

59. *"foi assassinado em 2000 por skinheads um dos homossexuais-símbolo da luta antidiscriminação, Edson Neris da Silva."*

60. *"Queremos transformar cada doação e assinatura num voto pelo reconhecimento dos homossexuais como cidadãos e como manifestação ativa contra a violência, desigualdade e qualquer outra forma de racismo neste país."*

61. *"Consideramos a parada um movimento social. Nem o movimento feminista nem o Movimento Sem Terra (MST) levam tantos à manifestação pública. O MST faz uma marcha, mas não tem o apoio que temos. Em quase dez anos mudamos mentalidades. Qualquer gay, jovem ou de terceira idade, pode ir hoje ao evento sem medo de se expor."*

62. *"Parada Gay leva 1,8 mi à Paulista, calcula PM."*

63. *"'Não vou falar disso, vim aqui para outra coisa,'—Marta Suplicy, ex-prefeita de São Paulo, negando que sua presença na parada tivesse interesse eleitoral."*

64. *"Na gíria, 'bolachas' são as lésbicas . . . O evento que reuniu tantas 'bolachas' começou à tarde com uma concentração na avenida Paulista."*

65. *"Motoqueiras com jaquetas de couro, senhoras com perfil de professoras universitárias, jovens estudantes ou darks, como Aline da Silveira Correa, 19, 'bissexual,' segundo a própria definição, piercing no lábio inferior, comissária de bordo. 'A gente veio para mostrar que não temos vergonha do nosso prazer livre e feliz.'"*

66. *"Foi uma enorme brincadeira, regada a litros e mais litros de cerveja, whisky falsificado e vinho barato. Uma diferença e tanto em relação à Marcha para Jesus, acontecida há quatro dias na mesma avenida Paulista, onde o álcool, praticamente proscrito, cedeu lugar ao refrigerante."*

67. See Stam, Robert. *Subversive Pleasures: Bakhtin, Cultural Criticism, and Film.* Baltimore: Johns Hopkins U P, 1989.

68. *"Na 'farra dos invertidos,' como um motorista de táxi irritado pelo trânsito pesado nas imediações da Paulista referiu-se ao evento, cabiam todas as ironias sobre os papéis sexuais. Enquanto os gays homens encharcavam o chão da calçada do parque Trianon, um grupo de meninas na esquina da alameda Casa Branca, fingiu urinar em pé no tronco de uma árvore. Ao lado delas, um amigo, agachado, imitava o jeito feminino."*

69. See Romano de Sant'Anna, Affonso. *O canibalismo amoroso.* Rio de Janeiro: Rocco, 1990.

70. *"O caixa electrônico do Banco Itaú se transformou num 'darkroom'—sala escura, em inglês, típica dos clubes gays. 'Vim aqui sacar R$ 10 e acabei transando com um cara,' contou o produtor Mário (nome fictício), 35. O Itaú patrocinou o 'darkroom' da parada!, brincou."*

71. *"Se tem lésbica no horário nobre da Globo, se pago meus impostos e sou dona do meu nariz, quem vai me proibir de vir com minha namorada?"*

72. *"Gagliasso protaganizou o momento hétero de um grupo de 'bolachas.' De mãos dadas com as namoradas, elas esqueceram suas duplas ao saber que o galã escondia-se em uma van. Com gritinhos de fãs, procuraram papéis onde o rapaz pudesse autografá-los. Conseguida a assinatura, voltavam a segurar as mãos das companheiras."*

73. *"De bonés, calças largas e camisetas de grupos de rap, Edson Dias, 21, e dez amigos metalúrgicos saíram do Jardim Ubirajara (extremo sul) com um único objetivo: caçar mulher. 'Apesar de a maioria aqui ser lésbica e não liberar beijinho nenhum, tem umas minas perdidas por aí. Eu, pelo menos, catei uma,' diz. 'Catei três,' vanglória-se Leandro Guimarães, 19."*

74. *"O personal trainer Rogério Antônio da Silva . . . pediu para não ser associado a 'bichinhas estereotipadas.' Na sua própria definição, Silva é um 'gay com cabeça de hétero': disse que freqüenta reuniões de donos de Tigra, seu carro, gosta de esportes radicais e faz boxe. Ele diz que poucas pessoas sabem que ele é gay. Silva se recusou a posar para fotos ao lado das 'pintosas,' afirmou que não fazia a menor questão de ser associado 'àquelas pessoas.' Só quando subiu à festa regada à champanhe disse: 'Esse é o meu ambiente.'"*

75. "*Parada Gay tenta manter recorde hoje: Nem Copa nem previsão de chuva esfriam expectativa de atrair 2 milhões de pessoas para continuar a maior do mundo.*"

76. "*Parada Gay resiste à Copa e supera recorde de público: Segundo a PM, 2 milhões de pessoas participaram da festa, 200 mil a mais do que no ano passado.*"

77. See Trevisan, João Silvério. *Seis balas num buraco só: A crise do masculino.* Rio de Janeiro: Editora Record, 1998.

78. "*Além dos beijos, muito verde-e-amarelo. Nas camisetas e em vários trios elétricos, as cores da seleção dominaram. O 16⁰ carro passou com bandeiras do Brasil penduradas, arrancando palmas e gritos da multidão.*"

79. "*Não faltou gente nem beijo. Atendendo ao pedido de Pereira, que ao abrir a parada, às 14h10 gritou para a multidão passar a tarde se beijando, os casais não perderam tempo. Paulo Ramos, 21, fazia sua contabilidade ainda no meio da festa: 'Já beijei oito. Tem muito homem bonito por aqui.'*"

80. "*É impossível que uma festa gay não acabe em Carnaval. Somos festivos. Mas não é só oba-oba. O objetivo é que a sociedade nos veja.—Tchaka Drag, 34, que participa desde a primeira parada, em momento-reflexão.*"

81. "*Nossa proposta é mostrar de dia o que o mundo gay é à noite.—Íkaro, 25, performer, que participa todo ano da parada.*"

82. "*Parada se assume como balada: Com o tema Homofobia é Crime, organizadores queriam manter tom politizado, mas 10a edição foi festa eletrônica.*"

83. "'*Isto não é fantasia nem personagem, é o nosso estilo de vida. O Brasil tem de se acostumar cada vez mais com a gente,' disse José Antonio Fonseca, de 45 anos, que trabalha com turismo. Seus amigos, o mascarado Márcio Almeida, de 35, e Eduardo Lima, de 42, endossavam o coro. 'Em outros países, as pessoas andam assim e não são tachadas,' disse Márcio.*"

84. "*Boa parte das pessoas se produz: Minnies, Batmans, Elvis Presleys, anjinhos, capetas, guardas de trânsito, gente levando o parceiro em coleiras, os clássicos marinheiros, marines do Exército americano, travestis de Cinderela, Maria Antonieta e também com seios de fora. Mas o caubói foi uma das fantasias mais populares, inspirada no filme O Segredo de Brokeback Mountain.*"

85. "'*Gay família' é maioria na parada de SP: Maior parte dos participantes em 2005 tinha relacionamentos estáveis, alguns inclusive com filhos, mostra pesquisa. Para coordenador, dados ajudam a combater o senso comum de que relações homossexuais são frágeis e baseadas no desejo sexual.*"

86. "*Esses dados indicam que as relações estáveis são realidade. É por isso que temos que discutir os direitos desta população.*"

87. "*Com turistas, casas noturnas ficam lotadas: Público que vem pela parada quer é se divertir e, para isso, consome e dá lucro à cidade.*"

CHAPTER 2

1. While this is the statistic reported by the official organization of the LGBT Pride Parade in São Paulo, it is important to recall that the Parade organizers are motivated to declare an estimate of the number of participants or the percentage of

foreigners as part of a "numbers game," as it were, to show evidence of momentum, continued growth, to justify financial support from the government for the event, and to show power in numbers.

2. For further information on the current relationship between the Brazilian government and federal banking institutions, with an emphasis on the *Caixa Econômica Federal*, I would refer the reader to Kurt E. von Mettenheim's *Federal Banking in Brazil* (Pickering & Chatto, 2010). A classic and seminal reading on the topic, useful though somewhat outdated, is Werner Baer's most recent (seventh) edition of *The Brazilian Economy: Growth and Development* (Lynne Rienner Publishers, 2013).

3. *"Religião foi o mote central da Parada Gay: Visita do papa no País inspirou figurinos e distribuição de camisinhas; evento reuniu pessoas de todas as idades."*

4. *" 'Eu sou o papa do amor. Não vou morrer por não poder usar preservativos. Usem camisinha, irmãos,' pediu José Ribeiro Fernandes, de 56 anos."*

5. *"Gente de bairros distantes da cidade, a mesma gente que aproveita os outros domingos de sol pra passear no Ibirapuera, pra assistir aos jogos no Morumbi, pra assistir o show do RBD e da Ivete, em suma: é estimulante a real democracia vivenciada num evento como a Parada Gay de São Paulo."*

6. *"A participação dos idosos foi marcante. O escritor Ricardo Moura Aguieiros, de 58 anos, empunhou um cartaz com a simpática mensagem: 'Idosos também são muito gostosos.' 'Quem é idoso e gay sofre o dobro de preconceito. A gente vive nessa ditadura do bonito, do mais novo,' contou."*

7. *"Descer a Consolação num fim de tarde de sol, aos sons dos trios que se misturavam—'drag music' com axé, canções da Xuxa com house progressivo."*

8. *" 'Nunca vi tanta gente feia,' dizem habitués: Freqüentadores reclamam do ecletismo do evento."*

9. *"Esquecido da essência suprapartidária da parada, o fotógrafo carioca Mauro Scur, 32, diz: 'Como vocês dizem aqui em SP, só tem periferia. Lá no Rio, a gente diria suburbano.' Isso diz respeito aos gays também. De acordo com o maquiador Marcos Costa, 32, 'as bonitas são preconceituosas, não vêm mais. Então, a parada tomou outro rumo.' "*

10. *"O stylist Ronaldo Gomes, 30, responde sem rodeios. 'O problema é o baixo poder aquisitivo da maioria. Nem sempre aqui as pessoas são exatamente feias; às vezes são apenas mal tratadas. Presta atenção nos cabelos, nas peles.' "*

11. *"Numa tentativa de explicar matematicamente o fenômeno do 'enfeamento da parada,' o namorado de Edson, o cubano Carlos, arrisca um número: 'No máximo, 10% são bonitos.' "*

12. *"Um monte de 'participantes' caindo pelas tabelas, calçadas, sarjetas. Culpa do vinho barato em garrafa de plástico, imagino."*

13. *"Parada se assume como balada: Com o tema Homofobia é Crime, organizadores queriam manter tom politizado, mas 10a edição foi festa eletrônica."*

14. See http://www.thegailygrind.com/2013/06/04/watch-nearly-4-million-take-part-in-worlds-largest-gay-pride-parade-in-sao-paulo-brazil-this-weekend/.

15. *"Tumultos marcam parada recorde de público. Mais popular das 11 edições da festa gay reúne 3,5 mil: Superlotação na Avenida Paulista provocou empurra-empurra, além de furtos e roubos. Apesar disso, o evento teve empolgação total."*

16. "*Delegacia fica lotada: A reportagem presenciou policiais orientando vítimas a procurarem outras delegacias ou a fazerem um registro pela internet, sob a alegação de que o volume de ocorrências era muito grande.*"

17. "*Neste ano, a Polícia Militar divulgou que não vai fornecer seu cálculo para o público do evento. A assessoria da PM comunicou que seus cálculos se baseiam em número de pessoas por metros quadrados e que, no caso de um evento como a parada, cujos participantes se deslocam, é difícil calcular a população flutuante. A capacidade de público da av. Paulista, isolada . . . é de 1 milhão de pessoas, segundo a PM.*"

18. "*A Parada Gay é para todos, comme il faut. A militância pode não ser tão forte, apesar do lema (no sábado, uma caminhada de lésbicas, mais 'engajada,' na mesma Paulista, reuniu menos da metade do esperado), mas . . . o Brasil não é o país do Carnaval? A Parada, este 'outro Carnaval,' confirma a sina para a mistura e o encontro.*"

19. These statistics are available on the official site of the *APOLGBT*: http://www.paradasp.org.br/home.html.

20. "*Esta é a diversidade que o país quer, a diversidade que nós temos para crescer como um país buscando um nicho turístico entre a comunidade gay.*"

21. "*Especialistas em pesquisas disseram no ano passado que os gays no Brasil têm renda acima da média da população e gastam mais em lazer, mas o Fecomércio diz que 40 por cento dos gays, lésbicas, bissexuais e transgêneros sofrem discriminação como consumidores.*"

22. "*A Associação também apoia os planos da Fecomércio de certificar comerciantes e prestadores de serviços que respeitem diversidade de raça, origem étnica, diferenças físicas e orientação sexual.*"

23. "*40% dos consumidores GLBT são discriminados nos setores de comércio e serviços. Segundo pesquisa da Fecomércio-SP, divulgada ontem, 60% daqueles que se sentem mal atendidos não voltam ao local de compra. Desses, 30% recorrem a órgãos de defesa do consumidor. O órgão quer criar, com a ONG APOGLBT SP, o Selo Diversidade, uma certificação para locais aprovados para atender esse público.*"

24. "*Parada Gay ganha público e economiza brilho: Escassez de drag queens e gente fantasiada deixou festa menos colorida. Público total vai ser divulgado hoje.*"

25. "*Festa tem confusão, furtos e abuso de álcool: Público tentou invadir tenda médica. Pelo menos 500 pessoas foram atendidas. Foram registrados 20 furtos.*"

26. I use the word *machista* in this context to allude to an increasingly aggressive and competitive participation in the "number's game" referred to in this chapter's Note #1. In addition to the motivations already described, the media portrays a heightening of tension in the relationship between the Parade organizers, who insist that the Military Police are underestimating their statistics while the police authorities contend that the *APOLGBT* is exaggerating or inflating the attendance figures. In a sense, then, there is a power struggle between the organizers and authorities who are charged with determining the numbers of attendees at the Parades. For more general definitions of *machismo*, in a Latin American context, I would like to refer the reader to Richard T. Schaefer's *Racial and Ethnic Groups*, twelfth edition. New York: Prentice

Hall, 2011. Variants of *machismo* are succinctly explored in Arciniega, G., Anderson, T.C., Tovar-Blanl, Z.G., and Tracey, T.G.'s collaborative article, "Toward a Fuller Conception of Machismo: Development of a Traditional Machismo and Caballerismo Scale." *Journal of Counseling Psychology* 55, no. 1: 19–33.

27. *"José Maria de Almeida, presidente da Conlutas, nega e diz que o carro de som estava legalizado. 'O que essa Associação faz é utilizar comercialmente dessa manifestação. Fazem convênios com hotéis, empresas e lojas e ganham dinheiro com isso. Sabem que somos contra essa coisa,' disse. Alexandre Santos afirmou, por sua vez, que essa acusação de Almeida não faz sentido."*

28. The exclusion of *CONCLAT* was related to a fight between the *CUT* (pro-*PT*) and *CONCLAT* (pro-*PSTU*) and the fact that the *PSTU* criticized the Lula government and the *PT*; therefore, the organizers did not want its constituents to participate in the Parade.

29. *"Infelizmente, o dia em que mais de 3,1 milhões de pessoas saíram às ruas para pedir respeito às diferenças terminou de forma trágica. . . . O Congresso Nacional ainda não chegou a um consenso sobre o projeto de lei 122/06, que criminaliza a homofobia. A bomba lançada na Rua Vieira de Carvalho, que feriu mais de 20 pessoas, o espancamento de um jovem de 17 anos na Rua Frei Caneca e a morte de Marcelo Barros na Rua Araújo reforçam a necessidade urgente de incluir na legislação brasileira a tipificação desses crimes, cuja premissa é a intolerância."*

30. *"Parada Gay tem tumulto e brigas: Polícia Militar deve sugerir mudanças para o próximo ano."*

31. *"O comerciante Fernando Tabatino, de 30 anos, foi atacado no meio da Avenida Paulista. 'Um grupo de quatro pessoas me cercou, encostou o revolver na minha barriga e pediu a carteira."*

32. *"Na dispersão, alguns participantes continuaram a festa na Avenida Dr. Vieira de Carvalho, em Santa Cecília, por volta das 22h. Incomodado com o barulho, um morador jogou uma bomba caseira sobre o grupo. Segundo a Polícia Militar, 30 pessoas ficaram feridas."*

33. *"Logo após o abre-alas, amigos do professor José Carlos de Siqueira, assassinado há oito dias em Suzano, carregavam faixas para protestar contra a maneira como a polícia tem tratado o crime. 'Deixaram de investigar o caso como deveria quando descobriram que ele era homossexual,' disse a secretária Priscila Lucena, cunhada do professor."*

34. *"Sem trios de boates, política avança na Parada Gay de SP: Sindicatos e entidades de defesa do ambiente e da saúde utilizam evento para divulgar ideias e atrair simpatizantes."*

35. *"Foi a primeira vez em muitos anos que, em meio a reclamações sobre a tarifa de R$10 mil para desfilar, nenhuma casa noturna participou do evento."*

36. *"Já a Comunidade Cristã Nova Esperança chamava a atenção pela militância no chão, com muitos representantes e cartazes. 'Estamos aqui para mostrar que gay não é só boate mas também espiritualidade,' dizia Esdraz Xavier, auxiliar de pastor na igreja."*

37. *"Você sabia que casais do mesmo sexo têm 37 direitos a menos que os demais?"*

38. *"Logo depois que Serra e Kassab foram embora, . . . a ex-prefeita Marta Suplicy surgiu com cabelos curtinhos e blusa estilo tigresa. Tirou algumas fotos com o público e subiu no segundo trio elétrico a entrar na Paulista. Ao som de Age of Aquarius e outros clássicos da década de 70 e 80, não parou de dançar. 'A situação piorou para os homossexuais no Brasil,' disse. 'Os crimes aumentaram e a situação no Congresso não prosperou. Apesar da festa, temos um cenário cada vez mais difícil.'"*

39. *"É de grande valia reiterar que a Parada do Orgulho LGBT de SP é considerada pelos órgãos públicos de segurança o acontecimento de grande porte mais pacífico do Estado."*

40. *"Passou a mensagem de que o esporte é, acima de tudo, um meio de confraternização e que as diversidades de torcedores e esportistas devem ser respeitadas e conviver em harmonia."*

41. While I would like to call the reader's attention to Trevisan's excellent study on machismo and misogyny in Brazilian soccer, there is an abundance of evidence that, in Brazil, soccer is still very much a straight man's sport. As recently as June 22, 2013, a demonstration for women's rights brought 3,000 people to the streets in Brasília. The protesters' two chief complaints were domestic violence and *o machismo no futebol*. The *Estadão* reported on the event with an article entitled *"Machismo no futebol em pauta entre mulheres"*: *"Entre gritos de guerra pela descriminalização do aborto e pelo fim da violência contra a mulher, o futebol também estava em pauta. 'Tem muito machismo dentro e fora de campo. A mulher ainda é vista como incapaz de jogar ou de entender do esporte,' comentou a estudante de serviço social Michelle Pereira. . . . Para Clara, o fato de muitas mulheres serem distantes do futebol é fruto de cultura que vem da infância, quando o menino é presenteado com uma bola e a menina, boneca. 'Infelizmente, o futebol feminino não tem prestígio porque nós somos motivo de piada quando jogamos,' afirma. . . . André citou a questão da homofobia como outro preconceito presente no mundo da bola. 'Chamar um jogador de "viado" só reforça a condição negativa do homossexual no meio do futebol,' argumentou."* ("Among the shouts to decriminalize abortion and to stop violence against women, soccer was also a target. 'There is a lot of machismo inside and outside the soccer field. Women are still seen as incapable of playing or understanding soccer,' commented Michelle Pereira, student of Social Work. . . . For Clara, the fact that many women maintain distance from soccer has cultural origins that come from infancy, when the boy is given a soccer ball and the girl is given a doll to play with. Unfortunately, women's soccer is not seen as prestigious because we are always the butt of the jokes whenever we play,' she affirms. . . . André cited the issue of homophobia as another prejudice present in the world of soccer. 'Calling a player a "faggot" only reinforces the negative condition of homosexuals in soccer.'") Another example is the excessive jokes about Brazil's Marta, nicknamed "Pelé with Skirts." Having received the "World Player of the Year" award on five occasions, Marta was considered one of the greatest female football players in history. Nevertheless, she had to emigrate from Brazil in order to play professionally. According to the latest figures published by FIFA, the world's governing body, 29 million women and girls play football worldwide, representing a significant increase from 1971, when three international teams played just two matches—by 2011 there were 129 teams playing

514 games. But while the women's game has grown in the United States and Europe, progress has been far more difficult to achieve in Brazil. Even the achievements of the national team, which has won two silver medals and finished as runner-up at the last World Cup, has not been enough to get the professional game off the ground. In an August 9, 2013 CNN interview, " 'Female Pele' Marta seeks fair deal for women's soccer," the athlete states: "Football in Brazil is seen as a masculine sport even with a lot of people accepting the female sport. It's that whole macho thing."

42. *"Este é o maior índice de crimes fatais de homofobia no mundo e torna a aprovação do PLC 122/06 a maior reivindicação do movimento brasileiro no momento."*

43. The struggle to criminalize homophobic acts, similar to the hate crimes legislation in the United States, is an ongoing battle in Brazil. There was considerable talk that a reconstituted version of the legislation would have come up for a vote in 2013, but this has still not occurred (as of this writing).

44. *"Finaliza com a posição clara de que, em nenhuma circunstância, apoia a descaracterização da manifestação através da carnavalização de sua identidade ou da criação de espaços privados que elitizam e segregam a participação social."*

45. See Bakhtin, Mikhail. *Rabelais and His World*. Trans. Hèléne Iswolsky. Bloomington: Indiana University Press, 1984.

46. *"O lugar dos LGBT: Senhores e senhoras, o que todos verão marcharem na avenida Paulista, dia 14, são os cidadãos de segunda classe de nossa República."*

47. *"Em vez de comemorar algum avanço legislativo, voltamos às ruas para apelar novamente ao bom senso do Estado brasileiro, para o atraso histórico que o Brasil concorre mais uma vez, depois de ter sido um dos últimos países a abolir a escravidão. Os estrangeiros que acompanham as notícias da maior parada do mundo, devem ficar confusos, sem entender como é possível que um país que permite e financia uma manifestação como esta, seja um dos países onde mais homossexuais são assassinados no mundo e onde não há qualquer legislação que possa coibir crimes de homofobia. Caros amigos, vou tentar explicar. Somos o país da cordialidade. Um país que, por muitos séculos, tratou seus negros como se fossem agregados, apesar de serem escravos, e enquanto não fossem desobedientes. Um país onde, até hoje, se trata a empregada doméstica como alguém da família, até o dia em que ela pede constrangida seus direitos trabalhistas. Com gays, lésbicas, bissexuais,travestis e transexuais, é a mesma coisa. Somos todos muito bem vistos e úteis, enquanto nos colocamos em nossos devidos lugares, sem exigir nossos direitos."*

48. There are a number of excellent studies that critique notions of *cordialidade* and *jeitinho*. Among the most notable include works by philosopher Fernanda Carlos Borges and Lívia Barbosa, a prominent Brazilian sociologist. See bibliography for complete references.

49. See Da Matta, Roberto. *Carnavais, malandros e heróis: Para uma sociologia do dilemma brasileiro*. Rio de Janeiro: Rocco, 1979.

50. *" 'Nós só queremos que as pessoas respeitem o que Jesus Cristo disse há dois mil anos, que todos devem se amar.' Segundo ele, a igreja existe desde 2001 e recebe cerca de 180 pessoas todas as quintas-feiras, dia de culto."*

51. *"Skinhead condenado por bomba na Parada Gay em 2009 volta a cometer crime de ódio."*

52. "*O objetivo é desmistificar a ideia de que todo skinhead é homofóbico. A Parada Gay tem de servir de plataforma para reivindicações e não só para mostrar o orgulho de ser gay.*"

53. "'*A mídia fala que a gente é homofóbico, mas nem todos são. A gente não é,' diz. Ele afirma que também são vímas de intolerância.*"

54. "*Uma semana depois de reunir mais de 3 milhões de gays e simpatizantes, a Avenida Paulista, em São Paulo, voltou a ser palco de uma manifestação de caráter sexual: um grupo de cerca de 50 pessoas realizou no domingo a Primeira Parada de Orgulho Hétero. A manifestação ocorreu em frente ao Museu de Arte de São Paulo.*"

55. "*A Parada do Orgulho Hétero não é uma afronta aos gays. Não queremos ofender ninguém. Rejeitamos qualquer manifestação homofóbica em nossa comunidade no Orkut.*"

56. See Butler, Judith. *Gender Trouble: Feminism and the Subversion of Identity.* London & NY: Routledge, 1990.

57. See chapter 2, Note #45.

58. "*Câmara de SP tenta criar Dia do Orgulho Hetero e trava a pauta do dia: Carlos Apolinário colocou projeto para votação em urgência e tem apoio de bancada evangélica.*"

59. "*A quatro dias da Parada Gay, um dos maiores eventos de São Paulo, a Câmara de Vereadores aprovou nesta quarta-feira, 22, a inclusão do projeto que cria o Dia do Orgulho Heterossexual para ser votado em segunda discussão.*"

60. "*Apolinário . . . promote obstruir qualquer projeto de vereador caso sua proposta não seja colocada para votação. 'Tiraram a Marcha de Jesus da Avenida Paulista e deixaram os gays, isso é um absurdo. Não sou contra os gays, sou contra o lugar do evento,' argumentou o evangélico.*"

61. "*Por trás da parada gay, não há esquemas políticos nem partidários. Na parada evangélica há uma relação que mistura religião com eleições,basta ver o número de políticos no desfile em posição de liderança. Isso para não falar de muitos personagens que, se não têm contas a acertar com Deus, certamente têm com a Justiça dos mortais, acusados de fraudes financeiras. Nada contra—muito pelo contrário—o direito dos evangélicos terem seu direito de se manifestarem. Mas prefiro a alegria dos gays que querem que todos sejam alegres. Inclusive os evangélicos.*"

62. "*Assassinatos de homossexuais batem recorde em 2011, diz entidade.*"

63. According to the *Grupo Gay da Bahia*, 338 LGBT Brazilian citizens were murdered in 2012, representing a 27% increase over the number of homicides reported in 2011 and an increase of 317% since 2005. See http://www.estadao.com.br/noticias/ geral,cresce-o-numero-de-assassinatos-de-homossexuais-em-2012,982836,0.htm.

64. "*A maior visibilidade dos homossexuais—estimulados pelas paradas gays e pela presença de personagens gays e travestis em novelas—provoca maior agressividade dos homófobos.*"

65. "*Se a invisibilidade comumente tem um sentido negativo num primeiro momento de uma política de identidades, talvez agora ela possa significar algo diferente. Ser invisível numa sociedade consumista pode ser uma maneira de fazer uma diferença pela pausa e sutileza. Numa sociedade onde tudo, todos devem ser visíveis a qualquer custo, incluindo mais e mais diversos grupos minoritários; mesmo*

a transgressão e a diferença são apenas estratégias de marketing. Por certo, invisibilidade não significa se esconder, fugir da realidade, mas simplesmente uma forma de enfrentar o poder corrosivo do simulacro, o excesso de imagens e signos, cada vez mais desprovidos de sentido. . . . A desaparição seria, então, uma outra maneira de viver, de se reinventar e de pertencer. A desaparição está sempre em constante tensão com a visibilidade, nos seus vários sentidos, seja político, cultural, comercial ou existencial. Como então desaparecer? Não é só uma questão de saber como lidar com a imagem pública como no caso de pop stars e políticos. É algo mais amplo. A invisibilidade tem menos a ver com o fascínio romântico por outsiders do que por apontar para uma subjetividade formada pelos fluxos do mundo, sem contudo aderir às superteorizações dos sujeitos nômades e pós-humanos. É só uma questão de deixar o mundo exterior ser o interior, a superficialidade ser a profundidade. Desaparecer para reaparecer. Aparecer para desaparecer. Uma brincadeira de pique e esconde."

CHAPTER 3

1. *"A diretoria da APOLGBT SP já se reuniu para pensar a respeito de alguns slogans, mas quer saber também a opinião dos internautas que participam deste nosso movimento LGBTI+. Lembrando que o slogan é uma frase que expressa o nosso sentimento para o mundo, em relação ao tema desenvolvido durante as reuniões com coletivos, ONGs e ativistas/militantes que tem se engajado no Movimento Social LGBTI+."*
2. *"Algumas notícias associando o P a sigla LGBT são tão bem escritas que tem até slogan como 'Amor não tem idade.' "*
3. *"Homofobia tem cura: educação e criminalização."*
4. *"Para o armário, nunca mais. União e conscientização na luta contra a homofobia."*
5. *"País vencedor é país sem homolesbotransfobia: chega de mortes! Criminalização já!"*
6. *"Eu nasci assim, eu cresci assim, vou ser sempre assim: respeitem-me!"*
7. *"Lei de Identidade de Gênero já! Todas as pessoas juntas contra a Transfobia."*
8. *"Independente de nossas crenças nenhuma religião é lei. Todas e todos por um Estado Laico."*
9. *"Dicas para atender bem turistas LGBT."* Available online at the following site: http://www.turismo.gov.br/images/pdf/03_11_2016_Cartilha_LGBT.pdf. The fifty-page pamphlet was awarded the 2017 *Oscar Gay* by the *Grupo Gay da Bahia (GGB)*.
10. *"Poder pra LGBTI+, Nosso Voto, Nossa Voz!"*
11. *"50 Anos de Stonewall: Nossas conquistas, nosso orgulho de ser LGBT+"*
12. World Prides in the past have been held in Rome (2000), Jerusalem (2006), London (2012), Toronto (2014), Madrid (2017), and New York City (2019) for Stonewall 50.
13. *"LGBTIfobia institucionalizada e uma falta de preparo para acolher e lidar com as opressões sofridas por essa população. A pessoa LGBTI+ fica com medo de fazer o registro e de, ao fazer o registro, sofrer alguma nova violência e acaba não fazendo por não ter esse amparo por parte do poder público."*

14. *"Sejamos o pesadelo dos que querem roubar nossa Democracia."*
15. *"Associação da Parada do Orgulho LGBT de SP e Prefeitura cancelam edição deste ano por causa da pandemia. ONG mantém o projeto Parada Solidariedade e informa que em 2021 a data da Parada SP será dia 6 de Junho."*
16. *"Estamos ocupando esse espaço de expressão virtual. Você que está aí, está participando da parada agora, estamos fazendo valer a nossa voz. O nosso tema esse ano é democracia, exatamente por causa de tudo que está acontecendo. Imaginem que vocês estão na avenida Paulista, vamos gritar por democracia, contra a homofobia, contra o racismo!"*
17. *"Na superfície parecemos uma democracia, mas nos falta conteúdo e nos falta a prática da democracia. O que vemos no Brasil é a polícia que mais mata e que mais morre no mundo, manifestações e protestos sendo reprimidos, acusações sem provas e ressurgimento de simaptizantes de regimes ditatoriais."*
18. *"Tem várias pautas que tem tudo a vercom minha história de vida, a caisa da adoção da comunidade LGBT, por exemplo. São pautas importantíssimas que a gente tem que se unir para bater de frente com uma sociedade extremamente preconceituosa. Me identifico com Marielle, a mulher preta da periferia que tem que lutar pra conseguir seu espaço."*

CHAPTER 4

1. My own work, and that of Susana Souto, David William Foster, and Antonio Vicente Seraphim Pietroforte, among others.
2. *"Este dicionário não tem a pretensão de ser politicamente correto. Muitos termos são chulos e pejorativos, podendo ser ofensivos para determinadas pessoas ou grupos. Nesse caso, recomendamos a interrupção imediata da leitura (5)."*
3. *"A obra é fruto de dez anos de pesquisa de Angelo Vip (pseudônimo do jornalista Vitor Angelo) e de Fred Libi, pesquisador que pede para manter só o nome de fantasia."*
4. *"Fred Libi . . . prefere não se identificar e é descrito na obra como um 'gay de nascença que refugiou-se nos estudos para entender o mundo que o hostilizava'* (Inner flap of book cover)."
5. *"(1). Bicha metida e conhecedora profunda do bajubá, jurando que sabe de tudo; (2). Bicha filológica, lexicóloga, eloquente, . . . prolixa e extremamente divertida; (3). Bicha rica, dona de ilha, que não tem medo de comprar os maridos; (4). Meu cu [p. 91]: Expressão usada para designar indignação, negação ou desdém."*
6. *"Tomaria todas as medidas judiciais cabíveis para defender a marca. Quero deixar claro que não é uma prática de homofobia. É proteção a uma marca."* Segundo Caldeira, *"Aurélia"* seria uma *"deturpação do nome."* *"Estão pegando carona em uma instituição muito importante."*
7. *"É interessante que exista no Brasil um dicionário de expressões gays. Só acho que eles pegaram pesado com a brincadeira e erraram na mão. O Aurélio é uma instituição brasileira."*
8. *"No mundo gay, o artigo definido feminino é, em muitos casos, anteposto a substantivos próprios ou comuns do gênero masculino, sendo que, no caso dos*

comuns, o substantivo ele próprio também passa, se possível, para o feminino, criando-se um neologismo." Ex.: A Pedro; A Mário; a prédia; a fota; a relógia; a dicionária.

9. *Para Paulette Pink, a "carão" é uma eterna solitária infeliz. "No fundo, são* **inseguras**, **cheias** *de sentimento de inferioridade. Por isso, criam essa fachada de* **gostosonas**, *que se bastam, mas na verdade são* **ridículas** *e carentes. Bil, desce do salto," provoca. Silvetty Montilla desmascara o falso glamour dessa categoria de gays. "Da carão, não sai nenhum tostão. Passam a noite inteira tomando água ou um único drinque e voltam para casa* **sozinhas**. **Elas** *precisam ser mais humildes." Segundo Divina Núbia: "Nas saunas, são pouco* **pragmáticas**. *Recusam calçar havaianas. Armam barraco se falta uma marca de cerveja no bar. Viram a cara, fazendo biquinho, se o flerte parte de alguém fora dos seus padrões. Preferem dividir um ap de três quartos nos Jardins com* **outras** *oito* **bibas** *a morar no 'centro decadente'"* (emphasis mine).

10. *"São Paulo é a capital brasileira da 'bicha carão,' dizem as drags mais viajadas da cidade. Na gíria, a 'carão' é* **afetada**, *esnobe e blasé. Sente-se* **única**, *superior. Não anda. Desfila . . .* **Despreza pobres**, **negros e nordestinos**. **Humilha garçons**, **porteiros**, **seguranças**, **faxineiro**" (emphasis mine).

11. *"Além disso [da catalogação das expressões gays], o livro pode ser usado para que os pais entendam o que os filhos falam. E também para que bofes (heterossexuais masculinos) compreendam melhor as frases de suas namoradas, já que muitas mulheres falam como os gays."*

12. *"Não teria graça alguma fazer um livro gay politicamente correto. E também, que coisa chata ter que ser chamado de gay. É viado, é bicha. Muitos grupos ficam com essa coisa de chamar de 'homossexualidade,' o que é uma chatice."*

13. *"Espécie be bicha-viada que na Internet quer se passar por bissexual, porque uma vez, quando estava muito louca, se esfregou com a amiga ana cláudia e começou a se sentir meio hétera."*

14. While this analysis is meant to look at Brazilian Portuguese terminology in the context of LGBT language, I take issue with the fact that the term *ana cláudia* finds its English counterparts in objectionable expressions like "fag hag" and "fruit fly," two terms that clearly have misogynist connotations as they are associated with a witch or supposedly an ugly woman whose physical abhorrence assures that she will always remain single and can succeed only in social circles by swarming around her gay friends.

15. *"[pejorativo; SP]: (1). Homossexual pobre culturalmente; (2). Diz-se das bibitas que não têm condições financeiras para comer na rua e levam um pão com ovo para comer na condução, na viagem de volta para casa, depois da balada; (3). Refere-se àquela bicha de moral baixa, sem escrúpulos nem dignidade e com lapsos de caráter."*

16. *"Virar a cabeça, mudando os cabelos de lado, tal como as loiras fazem, só que de um modo um pouco mais inteligente e com a intenção de menosprezar ou ignorar alguém."*

17. *"O bajubá é a língua utilizada nos terreiros de umbanda e candomblé, adotada pelas 'amapoas de canudo,' que a popularizaram, a recriaram e nela enxertaram*

um tanto devivências e línguas que estão presentes na dicionária. Uma combinação de criação e adequação da língua iorubá (nagô) com a velocidade da fala marginal desenvolvida para defesa e ataque. Essas expressões tomaram o universo gay e finalmente desaguaram no mundo como uma catarata criativa e abundante."

18. See chapter 2, Note # 63.

CHAPTER 5

1. *"É importante perceber que, enquanto as autodefinições das travestis se baseiam em critérios e características de gênero ambíguos, fluidos—como, por exemplo, a não-fixidez dos papéis sexuais ativos e passivos em suas sexualidades—as representações construídas pelas transexuais sobre sua condição afirmam um modelo de gênero definido, rígido, em que a separação entre o masculine e o feminino está nitidamente marcada. As transexuais negam qualquer potencial erótico do órgão genital masculino; elas não aceitam utilizar o pênis para o prazer porque, em sua visão, as mulheres não têm pênis. Por isso desejam tanto a cirurgia de transgenitalização. As transexuais parecem negar, em suas explicações e justificativas, a ambigüidade, a principal característica que constrói e define as travestis."*

2. *"É preciso apontar que a categoria travestis sobrepõe-se à categoria **transexuais**, uma vez que esta última é recente e ainda tem pouca presença no universo em pauta, funcionando muito mais por auto-identificação do que por atribuição, talvez pela própria lógica médico-psicológica que a constrói e define."*

3. *"O corpo das travestis é, sobretudo, uma linguagem; é no corpo e por meio dele que os significados do feminino e do masculino se concretizam e conferem à pessoa suas qualidades sociais. É no corpo que as travestis se produzem enquanto sujeitos."*

4. I find it worth noting that, in Portuguese, the noun *modelo* is gender-neutral.

5. *"trata-se de um padrão que não varia muito. Algumas obtêm melhores rendimentos na prostituição. . . . O ideário é, portanto, bastante homogêneo."*

6. *"Exatamente por estarem identificados com uma posição feminina nessa lógica dos valores do gênero, esses clientes 'merecem' ser explorados, segundo às travestis. Freqüentemente são eles as vítimas mais comuns dos pequenos assaltos, furtos e chantagens cometidos por algumas travestis."*

CHAPTER 6

1. A reader may ask, quite rightly, why I am using photographs taken in Rio de Janeiro when the bulk of this book concerns itself with LGBT Brazilians living in São Paulo. It is my conviction that, due to the demographic realities (i.e., the concentration of national population in Southeastern Brazil) as well as massive waves of immigration to both Rio de Janeiro and São Paulo, particularly from within Northeastern Brazil, I view São Paulo and Rio de Janeiro, while maintaining separate and unique geographies, as symbolic of a synthesis of Brazilian culture in general. In no way is

this meant to diminish the presence or importance of other regions in the country. Nevertheless, the cultural manifestations I analyze here are of national if not global proportions. For example, I view the LGBT Pride Parade of São Paulo as a Brazilian event, which absorbs millions of participants from all over the world but primarily from within Brazil itself.

2. "*Ela se chama Bruna Bianchi, é formada em administração de empresas e dona de uma auto-escola. Bruna, aliás, Daniel é um travesti e para não cair na prostituição tem de lutar muito.*"

3. These statistics are certainly not unique to Brazil. One *travesti* organization in Argentina reported in 2005 that 79% of the 302 *travestis* interviewed in Buenos Aires and Mar del Plata work principally as prostitutes. See *La gesta del nombre propio*, edited by Lohana Berkins and Josefina Fernández for ALITT (*Asociación de Lucha por la Identidad Travesti y Transgenero*, "Association for the Fight for Transvestite and Transgender Identity"), published by Ediciones de Plaza de Mayo, Buenos Aires, 2005. To attempt to answer the question as to why the vast majority of *travestis* are sex workers, one need to look only so far as familial and societal rejection. Frequently abandoned by their families, *travestis* often have few if any financial resources, and because of the stigma they suffer, often as both sexual minorities and gender identity minorities, they rarely have opportunities to develop skills to increase their economic mobility. At best, *travestis* can get low-paying jobs as domestic servants or in beauty salons. The majority realize that they can make more money by prostituting themselves. Kulick describes these in-group formations: "She will go to the square in the town where groups of bichas congregate to socialize. She will quickly become part of this group of bichas' she will hang out with them, be called by a female name by them, and learn from them" (61). Through this process of homosocial bonding and identity formation, *travestis* often find themselves accepted into a new social group that boosts their self-esteem in a world that systematically rejects them. Nevertheless, it is important to point out that *travestis* often claim agency, pride, and pleasure in assuming the profession of sex work. As both Kulick and Benedetti relate, *travesti* sex workers, in general, do not regard prostitution as degrading or exploitative, but rather view their work as a job where they can remain virtually autonomous and earn more money than the limited alternative forms of employment that have traditionally been available to them.

4. "*Eles (ou elas) são travestis. Nasceram homens, identificam-se como mulheres e precisam batalhar muito para não cair na prostituição.*"

5. "*O dinheiro acumulado como prostituta serviu de lastro para Cláudia abrir uma empresa—hoje trabalha com softwares na area médica.*"

6. "*Na época a concorrência nas ruas européias era menor, mas não são muitas as que têm planejamento e vontade de deixar essa vida.*"

7. "*No começo vim só porque ela [Bruna] precisava, mas continuava na prostituição. Ganhava lá três vezes mais do que aqui, mas não sinto falta. Faz três anos que só trabalho na auto-escola. Estou menos exposta e vivo com maior segurança.*"

8. The importance of the attainment of "antinormativity as a political goal" (Tim Dean 133) is emphasized in the work of many contemporary queer theorists, including Donald Morton, who argues that one of the most clearly articulated goals of queer

theory is to constantly "test the limits of its [own] radicality" (121). In a similar vein, Lee Edelman writes that queer theory must "refuse itself, resist itself, perceive that it is always somewhere else, operating as a force of displacement, of disappropriation; operating, in short, as a vector of desire" (345). This notion, while perhaps utopian in nature, is entirely antagonistic to the appropriation of any and all heteronormative models, even those that may be adapted by and for the consumption of queer subjectivities.

9. "*Mesmo sendo [uma profissão] legalizada e constando no índice de profissões existentes no Brasil, se autodeclarar profissional do sexo implica em tantos constrangimentos que poucos têm coragem de assumir o estigma. Porém, a informalidade de todo modo é o que existe. Isso implica em ausência de direitos e seguridade, inclusive na aposentadoria de quem passou parte da vida na profissão. Então, pode ser um quadro semelhante aos de muitos trabalhadores informais de vários setores no Brasil.*"

CHAPTER 7

1. "*O exílio coloca você na categoria de migrante. Minha maior dificuldade no exílio é a questão da língua porque eu sou um homem que adora falar português. Eu sei que a língua portuguesa foi dada pelo colonizador. A língua portuguesa é o colonizador em mim. Essa é a minha contradição. Eu amo a língua que o colonizador meu deu porque também é nessa língua que eu atuo contra a colonização. É também por conta dessa língua que eu faço um trabalho de decolonização. O trabalho de decolonização é também um trabalho linguístico.*"

2. It is important to credit Jack Halberstam with the development of notions of queer time and queer space. Please see works cited for the complete reference.

CHAPTER 8

1. See Roberto Da Matta's groundbreaking book, *Carnavais, malandros e heróis: Para uma sociologia do dilemma brasileiro*. Rio de Janeiro: Rocco, 1979.

2. See Jack Halberstam's notions of queer space and time in the visual arts in their groundbreaking study *In a Queer Time and Place*. New York: New York U P, 2005.

3. "*No Rio de Janeiro, o símbolo do Carnaval é o malandro, isto é, o personagem deslocado. De fato, o malandro não cabe nem dentro da ordem nem fora dela: vive nos seus interstícios, entre a ordem e a desordem, utilizando ambas e nutrindo-se tanto dos que estão fora quanto dos que estão dentro do mundo quadrado da estrutura*" (139).

4. "*No mundo da malandragem, o que conta é a voz, o sentimento e a improvisação: aquilo que em nossa sociedade, é definido como pertencendo ao 'coração' e ao 'sentimento.' Vale, assim o que está lá dentro, dentro das emoções e do coração. No universo da malandragem, é o coração que inventa as regras*" (217).

5. "*Para criar esses elementos dentro de uma visão gráfica, adicionou-se uma série de outras formas que passaram a existir em uma intercambiável relação figura/ fundo, sem que em nenhum caso se fixassem em nenhuma delas, desfazendo continuamente a relação binária que a caracteriza . . . podemos designar cada um deles como apresentando uma caraterística que lhe confere atribuições específicas, embora seja importante salientar que se trata de formas em trânsito que se interconectam ao todo a qualquer momento que se deseje promover uma combinação diferenciada. . . . O padrão obtido resultou em um intricado movimento ondulatório que articula diversas demandas do olhar, o qual se vê em uma rede de circulação projetando-se em diversas direções*" (Catalog, 132–133).

EPILOGUE

1. "*Só que homossexualidade não existe, nunca existiu. Existe sexualidade— voltada para um objeto qualquer de desejo. Que pode ou não ter genitália igual, e isso é detalhe. Mas não determina maior ou menor grau de moral ou integridade.*"

2. "*Antigamente o homossexualismo era proibido no Brasil. Depois passou a ser tolerado. Hoje é aceito como coisa normal. Eu vou-me embora antes que passe a ser obrigatório.*"

Filmography of Twenty-First-Century LGBT Brazilian Cinema

FEATURE-LENGTH FILMS

Princesa (Henrique Goldman, 2001)
Amores possíveis (Sandra Werneck, 2001)
Dois perdidos numa noite suja (José Joffily, 2002)
Madame Satã (Karim Aïnouz, 2002)
Carandiru (Hector Babenco, 2003)
Do começo ao fim (Aluizio Abranches, 2009)
Como esquecer (Malu Martino, 2010)
Elvis & Madona (Marcelo Laffitte, 2010)
Tatuagem (Hilton Lacerda, 2013)
Praia do futuro (Karim Aïnouz, 2014)
Do lado de Fora (Alexandre Carvalho & Maitê Romão, 2014)
Hoje eu quero voltar sozinho (Daniel Ribeiro, 2014)
Ausência (Chico Teixeira, 2014)
Mãe só há uma (Anna Muylaert, 2016)
Rodantes (Leandro Leal, 2019)
Aos Nossos Filhos (Maria de Medeiros, 2019)
Carlinhos & Carlão (Pedro Amorim, 2019)
Piedade (Cláudio Assis, 2019)
Cazuza: O tempo não pára (Walter Carvalho & Sandra Werneck, 2004)
Acredite, um Espírito Baixou em Mim (Jorge Moreno, 2006)
Até que a Vida nos Separe (Fabrício Correa, 2010)
Reaching for the Moon (Bruno Barreto, 2013)
A Glória e a Graça (Flávio Ramos Tambellini, 2017)
Copa 181 (Dannon Lacerda, 2017)
Corpo elétrico (Marcelo Caetano, 2017)

Alice Júnior (Gil Baroni, 2019)
Greta (Armando Praça, 2019)
Vil, Má (Gustavo Vinagre, 2020)
Alfabeto sexual (André Medeiros Martins, 2020)

SHORTS (*CURTAS*)

Café com leite (Daniel Ribeiro, 2007)
Hoje eu não quero voltar sozinho (Daniel Ribeiro, 2010)
O Olho e o Zarolho (René Guerra & Juliana Vicente, 2013)
Meu jogador favorito (Adriano Oliveira & Guilherme Luka, 2018)
Depois daquela festa (Caio Scot, 2019)

DOCUMENTARY (*DIDACTIC*)

Dzi croquettes (Raphael Alvarez & Tatiana Issa, 2009)
Meu amigo Claudia (Dácio Pinheiro, 2009)
São Paulo em Hi-Fi (Lufe Steffen, 2013)
Favela Gay (Rodrigo Felha, 2014)
De Gravata e Unha Vermelha (Miriam Chaneiderman, 2015)
Eu, Trans: quero te mostrar quem sou (Empresa Brasil de Comunicação, 2015)
Lampião da Esquina (Lívia Perez, 2016)
Divinas divas (Leandra Leal, 2016)
Bichas, o documentário (Marlon Parente, 2016)
Bicha Preta (Thiago Rocha, 2017)
Meu Corpo é Político (Alice Riff, 2017)
Okama: vozes LGBT nipo-brasileiras (Felipe Massahiro Higa, 2017)
Laerte-se (Eliane Brum, 2017)
A maior parada do mundo (TV Brasil, 2018)
Depois do fervo (Matheus Faisting, 2018)
Abrindo o Armário (Luís Abramo & Dario Menezes, 2018)
Bixa travesty (Claudia Priscila & Kiko Goifman, 2019)
Indianara (Marcelo Barbosa & Aude Chevalier-Beaumel, 2019)
Diga o meu Nome (Juliana Chagas Gouveia, 2020)

DOCUMENTARIES FOR FILMOGRAPHY

Olhe pra mim de novo (Kiko Goifman & Claudia Priscilla, 2012)
Homens Pink (Renato Turnes, 2020)

Bibliography

Acioli, Gustavo. "Verbete cor-de rosa: Dupla de autores brasileiros lança *Aurélia*, o primeiro dicionário de termos gays em língua portuguesa." *Revista Língua*. Especial: Sexo & Linguagem, June 2006. 32–33.

Amin, Kadji. *Disturbing Attachments: Genet, Modern Pederasty, and Queer History*. Durham, NC: Duke U P, 2017.

Andrade, Mário de. *Macunaíma: O herói sem nenhum caráter*. Ed. Crítica de Telê Porto Ancona Lopez. Rio de Janeiro: LTC, 1978.

Anzaldúa, Gloria E. *Borderlands/La Frontera: The New Mestiza*. San Francisco: Aunt Lute Books, 1987.

Arnhold, Jack. "'*Queermuseu*' Opens at Rio's Parque Lage School of Visual Arts this Saturday." *The Rio Times*. August 17, 2018.

Artforum. "Censored 'QueerMuseum' Show in Brazil Reopens to Record-Breaking Crowds." August 21, 2018. https://www.artforum.com/news/censored-queermuseu-show-in-brazil-reopens-to-record-breaking-crowds-76335.

Bakhtin, Mikhail. *Rabelais and His World*. Trans. Hèléne Iswolsky. Bloomington: Indiana University Press, 1984.

Baptista Luz Advogados, Casa Um e ANTRA. *Guia de Retificação de Prenome e Gênero de pessoas não-cisgêneras*. August 2019. https://antrabrasil.files.word press.com/2020/03/guia_retificacao_genero.pdf.

Barbosa, Lívia. *O jeitinho brasileiro: a arte de ser mais igual que os outros*. Rio de Janeiro: Campus, 1992.

Barcellos, José Carlos. "Literatura e homoerotismo masculino: perspectivas teórico-metodológicas e práticas críticas." *Caderno semanal*, Rio de Janeiro 8, no. 8 (2000).

Barifouse, Rafael. "STF aprova a criminalização da homofobia." *BBC News Brasil*. June 13, 2019. https://www.bbc.com/portuguese/brasil-47206924.

Barreto, Leila. *Prostituição: a história recontada: transas sociais e institucionais em Belém*. Belém do Pará, Brasil: Universidade Federal do Pará, 2016.

Barrett, Terry. *Criticizing Photographs: An Introduction to Understanding Images*. 5th Edition. New York: McGraw-Hill, 2011.

Baudrillard, Jean. *Simulacres et Simulation*. Paris: Éditions Galilée, 1981.

BBC News. "Majority in Brazil's Top Court to Make Homophobia and Transphobia Crimes."May 24, 2019. https://www.bbc.com/news/world-latin-america-48391926.

Benedetti, Marcos Renato. *Toda feita: o corpo e o gênero das travestis*. Rio de Janeiro: Garamond, 2005.

Benevides, Bruna G. & Sayonara Naider Bonfim Nogueira, Orgs. Sara Wagner York & Jacob R. Longaker, Trans. "Dossier: Murders & Violence against Travestis & Trans People in Brazil—2018." Brasília: Distrito Drag, 2019. https://www.wash ingtonblade.com/content/files/2019/09/murders-and-violence-against-travestis-and-trans-people-in-brazil-2018.pdf.

Bentley, Eric. "The Homosexual Question." *The American Review* 26 (1977): 288–303.

Bergamo, Monica. "Máscara é 'coisa de viado,' dizia Bolsonaro na frente de visitas." *Folha de S. Paulo*. July 7, 2020. https://www1.folha.uol.com.br/colunas/monicab ergamo/2020/07/mascara-e-coisa-de-v-dizia-bolsonaro-na-frente-de-visitas.shtml.

Bito, Angélica. "*Madame Satã:* Da marginalidade às telas." Cineclick. http://cine click.virgula.terra.com.br/cinebrasil/atual/.

Bollinger, Alex. "Trump Smirks as Brazil's Far Right President Says They Are United against LGBTQ People." *LGBTQ Nation*. March 20, 2019. https://www. lgbtqnation.com/2019/03/trump-smirks-brazils-far-right-president-says-united-lgbtq-people/.

Borges, Fernanda Carlos. *A filosofia do Jeito: um modo brasileiro de pensar com o corpo*. São Paulo: Editora Summus, 2006.

Brasil de Fato. "Engajamento e protestos marcam o carnaval 2020 em todo o país." February 23, 2020. https://www.brasildefato.com.br/2020/02/23/engajamento-e-protestos-marcam-o-carnaval-2020-em-todo-o-pais.

Brito, Ricardo & Marcelo Rochabrun. "Update 1: Brazil Reopens International Flights to Tourists Even as Coronavirus Deaths Spike."July 29, 2020. *Reuters*. https://www.reuters.com/article/health-coronavirus-brazil-travel/update-1-brazil-reopens-international-flights-to-tourists-even-as-coronavirus-deaths-spike-idUSL 2N2F036J.

Brookshaw, David. *Race and Color in Brazilian Literature*. New Jersey: Scarecrow Press, 1986.

Brum, Eliane. "Jair Bolsonaro Has Trashed Brazil's Image But He Hasn't Broken Its Soul: The President Has Fomented Hate, Underplayed Coronavirus and Unleashed a Financial Crash. But There Is Rising Resistance." *The Guardian*. June 3, 2020. https://www.theguardian.com/commentisfree/2020/jun/03/ jair-bolsonaro-brazil-president-coronavirus?CMP=oth_b-aplnews_d-1.

Buarque, Chico. *Ópera do malandro*. São Paulo: Círculo do Livro, 1978.

Butler, Judith. *Bodies That Matter: On the Discursive Limits of "Sex"*. London & NY: Routledge, 1993.

———. *Gender Trouble: Feminism and the Subversion of Identity*. London & NY: Routledge, 1990.

Butterman, Steven F. *(In)visibilidade vigilante: representações midiáticas da maior parada gay do planeta*. São Paulo: nVersos, 2012.

———. *Perversions on Parade: Brazilian Literature of Transgression and Postmodern Anti-Aesthetics in Glauco Mattoso*. San Diego: San Diego State U P/Hyperbole Books, 2005.

Cameron, Deborah & Don Kulick, Eds. *The Language and Sexuality Reader*. New York: Routledge, 2006.

———. "Sexuality as Identity: Gay and Lesbian Language." Chapter 4 in *Language and Sexuality*. Cambridge: Cambridge U P, 2003.

Caminha, Adolfo. *Bom-Crioulo: Texto integral*. Série Bom Livro. São Paulo: Editora Ática, 1983.

Candido, Antonio. "Dialética da malandragem: Caracterização das *Memórias de um sargento de milícias*." *Revista do Instituto de Estudos Brasileiros* 8 (1970): 67–89.

Carneiro, Júlia Dias. "'Queermuseu,' a exposição mais debatida e menos vista dos últimos tempos, reabre no Rio." *BBC News Brasil*. August 16, 2018. https://www.bbc.com/portuguese/brasil-45191250.

Castilhos, Washington. "Travel Resumes as Study Says Brazil Flights Spread Virus." July 31, 2020. *SciDev.Net*. https://www.scidev.net/global/coronavirus/news/travel-resumes-as-study-says-brazil-flights-spread-virus.html.

Chesebro, James W. Ed. *Gayspeak: Gay Male and Lesbian Communication*. NY: Pilgrim Press, 1981. Introduction. ix–xvi.

Ciscati, Márcia Regina. *Malandros da terra do trabalho: Malandragem e boemia na cidade de São Paulo (1930–1950)*. SP: Annablume/Fapesp, 2000.

Collins, Patricia Hill. *Black Feminist Thought: Knowledge, Consciousness, and the Politics of Empowerment*. New York: Routledge, 1999.

Costa, Jurandir F. *A inocência e o vício: estudos sobre o homoerotismo*. Rio de Janeiro: Relume Dumará, 1992.

Costa Netto, Fernando, Isadora Lins França & Regina Facchini. *Parada: 10 Anos do Orgulho GLBT em SP*. São Paulo: Editora Produtiva/Associação da Parada do Orgulho GLBT de São Paulo, 2006.

Couto, Edvaldo Souza. *Transexualidade: o corpo em mutação*. Salvador: Ed. Grupo Gay da Bahia, 1999 (Gaia Ciência).

Crew, Louie. "Lesbian Separation: The Linguistic and Social Sources of Lesbian Politics." *The Gay Academic*. Palm Springs, CA: ETC, 1978.

Cvetkovich, Ann. *An Archive of Feelings: Trauma, Sexuality, and Lesbian Public Cultures (Series Q)*. Durham: Duke U P, 2003.

Dagnese, Napoleão. *Cidadania no armário: uma abordagem sócio-jurídica acerca da homossexualidade*. São Paulo: LTR, 2000.

Damasio, Kevin. "Testes com brasileiros serão decisivos para sucesso das vacinas contra a COVID-19: com altíssimo platô na curva epidemiológica, Brasil chega a 2 milhões de infectados. Enquanto milhares de voluntários recebem a vacina de Oxford, que pode ser registrada ainda esse ano, produto de farmacêutica chinesa será testado em breve no país." *National Geographic Brasil*. July 16, 2020. https://www.nationalgeographicbrasil.com/ciencia/2020/07/vacina-contra-covid-19-brasil-oxford-oms-cura-coronavirus-chadox1-coronavac-sinovac. Accessed July 29, 2020.

Da Matta, Roberto. *Carnavais, malandros e heróis: Para uma sociologia do dilema brasileiro*. Rio de Janeiro: Rocco, 1979.

Bibliography

Dean, Tim. "On the Eve of a Queer Future: A Review of Eve Sedgwick's Tendencies." *Raritan* 15, no. 1 (1995): 116–34.

Declerq, Marie. "'Nós somos invisíveis': trabalhadoras sexuais são afetadas pela pandemia." TAB/ UOL Notícias, March 28, 2020. https://tab.uol.com.br/noticias/redacao/2020/03/28/nos-somos-invisiveis-trabalhadoras-sexuais-afetadas-pelo-coronavirus.htm. Accessed on July 28, 2020.

Dehesa, Rafael de la. *Queering the Public Sphere in Mexico and Brazil: Sexual Rights Movements in Emerging Democracies.* Durham: Duke U P, 2009.

De Hollanda, Sérgio Buarque. *Raízes do Brasil.* Rio de Janeiro: José Olympio, 1984.

D'Emilio, John. *Sexual Politics, Sexual Communities: The Making of a Homosexual Minority in the United States, 1940–1970.* Chicago: The University of Chicago Press, 1983.

Deutsche Welle. "Bolsonaro testa positive para COVID-19 novamente: Terceiro exame realizado pelo presidente desde que contraiu a doença confirma que ele continua infectado pelo coronavírus, segundo o Planalto. Ele segue em isolamento e afirma se tratar com cloroquina." July 22, 2020.

Dixon, Paul B. "Malandro Heaven: Amado's Utopian Vision." In *Jorge Amado: New Critical Essays.* Eds. Keith H. Brower et al. NY/London: Routledge, 2001. 221–30.

Dreger, Alice. *Galileo's Middle Finger: Heretics, Activists, and the Search for Justice in Science.* New York: Penguin, 2015.

Dzidzienyo, Anani & Suzanne Oboler, Orgs. *Neither Enemies Nor Friends: Latinos, Blacks, Afro-Latinos.* New York: Palgrave Macmillan, 2005.

Ebert, Roger. "Madame Satã (Film review). Chicago: *Chicago Sun-Times.* August 22, 2003.

Edelman, Lee. "Queer Theory: Unstating Desire." *GLQ: Journal for Lesbian and Gay Studies.* 2, no. 4 (1995): 343–6.

Eribon, Didier. *Insult and the Making of the Gay Self.* Trans. Michael Lucey. Durham and London: Duke U P, 2004.

Facchini, Regina. *Sopa de letrinhas? Movimento homosexual e produção de identidades coletivas nos anos 90.* Rio de Janeiro: Garamond, 2005.

Fields, Jessica. "The Racialized Erotics of Participatory Research: A Queer Feminist Understanding." In *Imagining Queer Methods.* Eds. Amin Ghaziani and Matt Brim. New York: New York U P, 2019. 63–83.

Figari, Carlos. *@s outr@s cariocas: interpelações, experiências e identidades homoeróticas no Rio de Janeiro séculos XVII ao XX.* Belo Horizonte: Editora da UFMG, 2007.

Foster, David William. *Cultural Diversity in Latin American Literature.* Albuquerque: U New Mexico P, 1994.

Foucault, Michel. *The History of Sexuality, Volume 1: An Introduction.* Trans. Robert Hurley. London: Allen Lane, 1979.

France24. "Brazil's Bolsonaro Dilutes Face Mask Law Again." July 6, 2020. https://www.france24.com/en/20200706-brazil-s-bolsonaro-dilutes-face-mask-law-again?fbclid=IwAR2oByJ1Rx2oh3iqdkETZ9njVoXaEisWUgp5lMJNequCwRdf1ET1UEyel38.

Fry, Peter, & Edward MacRae. *O que é homossexualidade.* São Paulo: Abril Cultural/Brasiliense, 1985 (Primeiros Passos).

Garcia, Wilton. *Homoerotismo e Imagem no Brasil*. São Paulo: FAPESP/UN Nojosa/ Assoc. da Parada do Orgulho GLBT, 2004.

Gatti, Zé. *"Madame Satã*: Filme de Karim Aïnouz retrata o mais famoso dos malandros." February 17, 2003. *MIXBrasil*.

Gay.Blog.BR. "Rio de Janeiro inaugura biblioteca com nome de profesora trans." July 21 2020. https://gay.blog.br/noticias/rio-de-janeiro-inaugura-biblioteca-com-nome-de-professora-trans/.

———. "Padre pede perdão a LGBTs: Ninguém pode achar que a homofobia vem de Deus, LGBTfobia é crime." July 14, 2020. https://gay.blog.br/noticias/padre-pede-perdao -a-lgbts-ninguem-pode-achar-que-a-homofobia-vem-de-deus-lgbtfobia-e-crime/.

Geertz, Clifford. *The Interpretation of Cultures*. New York: Basic Books/Perseus, 1973.

Gonçalves, Robson Pereira. *Macunaíma: Carnaval e Malandragem*. Santa Maria: UFSM Press, 1982.

Goto, Roberto. *Malandragem Revisitada: Uma leitura ideológica de "Dialética da malandragem."* Campinas, SP: Pontes, 1988.

Governo do Estado de São Paulo. "Museu da diversidade sexual inaugura exposição digital Queerentena com 60 obras." May 25, 2020. http://www.cultura.sp.gov.br/ exposicao-digital-queerentena-do-museu-da-diversidade-sexual-sera-inaugurada-dia-25-de-maio-com-60-obras/.

Green, James N. "Madame Satã (Satan): The Black 'Queen' of Rio's Bohemia." *The Human Tradition in Modern Brazil*. Ed. Peter M. Beattie. Wilmington, DE: Scholarly Resources, 2004. 267–285.

———. *Beyond Carnival: Male Homosexuality in Twentieth-Century Brazil*. Chicago: U Chicago P, 2000.

Green, James N. and Ronaldo Trindade, Eds. *Homossexualismo em São Paulo e outros escritos*. São Paulo: Editora UNESP, 2005.

Gunther, Scott. "Building a More Stately Closet: French Gay Movements since the Early 1980s." *Journal of the History of Sexuality* 13, no. 3 (July 2004): 327.

Halberstam, Jack. *In a Queer Time and Place*. New York: New York U P, 2005.

Hall, Stuart. "Cultural Studies and Its Theoretical Legacies." In *Cultural Studies*. Eds. Lawrence Grossberg, Cary Nelson, & Paula A. Treichler. New York: Routledge, 1991. 277–94.

Hayes, Joseph J. "Lesbians, Gay Men, and Their 'Languages.'" *Gayspeak: Gay Male & Lesbian Communication*. Ed. James W. Chesebro. New York: Pilgrim Press, 1981. 28–42.

———. "Gayspeak." *Gayspeak: Gay Male & Lesbian Communication*. Ed. James W. Chesebro. NY: Pilgrim Press, 1981. 45–57.

Jagose, Annamarie. *Queer Theory*. Melbourne: U Melbourne P, 1996.

Jandt, Fred E. and James Darsey. "Coming Out as a Communicative Process." *Gayspeak: Gay Male & Lesbian Communication*. Ed. James W. Chesebro. New York: Pilgrim Press, 1981. 12–27.

Johnson, E. Patrick. "Put a Little Honey in My Sweet Tea: Oral History as Quare Performance." *Imagining Queer Methods*. Eds. Amin Ghaziani & Matt Brim. New York: New York U P, 2019. 45–62.

Karr, Rodney G. "Homosexual Labeling and the Male Role." *Gayspeak: Gay Male & Lesbian Communication*. Ed. James W. Chesebro. New York: Pilgrim Press, 1981. 3–11.

Keegan, Cáel. "Getting Disciplined: What's Trans* about Queer Studies Now?" *Journal of Homosexuality* 67, no. 3. Special Issue: "25 Years On: The State and Continuing Development of LGBTQ Studies Programs." October 22, 2018. 384–97.

Kulick, Don. *Travesti: Sex, Gender, and Culture among Brazilian Transgendered Prostitutes*. Chicago: U Chicago P, 1998.

Lacerda, Hilton. "Amolando a língua no veludo: A história da *Aurélia*, a 'dicionária sem preconceitos.'" *Revista Continuum Itaú Cultural* 20 (December 2007): 42–43.

Lacombe, Andrea. *Para hombre ya estoy yo: Masculinidades y socialización lésbica en un bar del centro de Río de Janeiro*. Buenos Aires: IDES, Centro de Antropología Social, 2006.

Lancet, The. "COVID-19 in Brazil: 'So What?'" 395. May 9, 2020. https://www.thelancet.com/journals/lancet/article/PIIS0140-6736(20)31095-3/fulltext.

Legman, Gershon. "The Language of Homosexuality: An American Glossary." In *Sex Variants: A Study of Homosexual Patterns, Vol. II*. Ed. George W. Henry. New York: Paul B. Hoeber, Inc., 1941.

Lemos, Nina. "Polêmico, 'Aurélia' reúne termos do mundo gay." *Folha de S. Paulo Online: Ilustrada*. 29 de maio de 2006.

Lisboa, Vinícius. "Queermuseu recebe 14 mil pessoas em dez dias e supera expectativas." *Agência Brasil Rio de Janeiro*. August 29, 2018.

Londoño, Ernesto. "In Brazil, 'Queer Museum' Is Censored, Debated, Then Celebrated." *New York Times*. August 26, 2018.

Lopes, Denilson. "Por uma nova invisibilidade." *e-misférica*. November 2007.4.2: Body Matters/Corpografias. http://hemisphericinstitute.org/journal/4.2/por/po42_pg_lopes.html.

———. *O homem que amava rapazes e outros ensaios*. Rio de Janeiro: Aeroplano Editora, 2002.

Lopes, Moacyr Junior. "Judith Butler escreve sobre sua teoria de gênero e o ataque sofrido no Brasil." *Folha de S. Paulo*, September 9, 2015. https://www.folha.uol.com.br/ilustrissima/2017/11/1936103-judith-butler-escreve-sobre-o-fantasma-do-genero-e-o-ataque-sofrido-no-brasil.shtml.

Lorde, Audre. "The Master's Tools Will Never Dismantle the Master's House." *Sister Outsider: Essays and Speeches*. Berkeley, CA: Crossing Press, 1984.

Love, Heather. "How the Other Half Thinks: An Introduction to the Volume." *Imagining Queer Methods*. Eds. Amin Ghaziani & Matt Brim. New York: New York U P, 2019. 28–42.

Lyra, Bernadette, Garcia, Wilton (orgs.). *Corpo e cultura*. São Paulo: Xamã, 2001.

MacRae, Edward. *A Construção da Igualdade: Identidade Sexual e Política no Brasil da "Abertura."* Campinas: UNICAMP, 1990.

Magalhães, Valéria Barbosoa de. "Brasileiros LGBT no Sul da Flórida: Estratégias de documentação em tempos de incerteza." *Alteridades em tempos de (in)certeza: escutas sensíveis*. Eds. Mriam Hermeto, Gabriel Amato, & Carolina Dellamore. SP: Letra e Voz, 2019.

Magalhães, Valéria Barbosoa de, and Steven F. Butterman. "Brasileiros no Sul da Flórida: Novas questões sobre os imigrantes LGBT." *Bagoas—Estudos Gays: gêneros e sexualidades.* Natal, RN. 11, no. 16 (2017): 198–231.

Martel, Frédéric. *The Pink and the Black: Homosexuals in France since 1968.* Trans. Jane Todd. Palo Alto: Stanford U P, 1999.

Mascarenhas, João Antônio de Souza. *A Tríplice Conexão: machismo, conservadorismo politico e falso moralismo.* Rio de Janeiro: 2AB Editora, 1997.

Matos, Claudia. *Acertei no milhar: Malandragem e samba no tempo de Getúlio.* Rio de Janeiro: Paz e Terra, 1982.

Mattoso, Glauco. *Manual do Podólatra Amador: Aventuras & Leituras de um tarado por pés.* São Paulo: Expressão, 1986.

———. *O dicionarinho do palavrão & correlatos: inglês-português, português-inglês.* Rio de Janeiro: Record, 1990.

Mattoso, Glauco & Marcatti. *As aventuras do Glaucomix, o Podólatra.* São Paulo: Quadrinhos Fechou, 1990.

Mendonça, Heloísa. "Queermuseu: O dia em que a intolerância pegou uma exposição para Cristo." *EL PAÍS Brasil* (September 13, 2017).

Mercer, Tim. "Valentina Sampaio Is Sports Illustrated's First Transgender Swimsuit Model." July 12, 2020. *Upworthy.* https://www.upworthy.com/valentina-sampaio-is-sports-illustrateds-first-transgender-swimsuit-model.

Míccolis, Leila. "Literatura Inde(x)pendente." *Vinte Anos de Resistência: Alternativas da Cultura no Regime Militar.* Rio de Janeiro: Espaço e Tempo, 1986. 61–80.

Míccolis, Leila, and Herbert Daniel. *Jacarés e Lobisomens: Dois ensaios sobre a Homossexualidade.* Rio de Janeiro: Achiamé, 1983.

Mills, Robert. "Theorizing the Queer Museum." *Museums and Social Issues* 3, no. 1 (2008): 41–52.

Morris, Gary. "Fists and Feathers: Don't Mess with Madame: *Madame Satã* Reviewed." *Bright Lights Film Journal.* San Francisco International Gay and Lesbian Film Festival. Issue 41. August 2003.

Morton, Donald. "The Politics of Queer Theory in the (Post) Modern Movement." *Genders* 17 (1993): 121–50.

Mott, Luiz. *Homossexualidade: Mitos e Verdades.* Salvador, Ed.GGB, 2003.

———. *O lesbianismo no Brasil.* Porto Alegre: Mercado Aberto, 1987. (Depoimentos, n. 16).

Muñoz, José Esteban. *Disidentifications: Queers of Color and the Performance of Politics.* Minneapolis: U Minnesota P, 1999.

Namaste, Viviane K. *Sex Change, Social Change: Reflections on Identity, Institutions and Imperialism.* Toronto: Women's Press, 2005.

———. *Invisible Lives: The Erasure of Transsexual and Transgendered People.* Chicago: U Chicago P, 2000.

Nogle, Vicki. "Lesbian Feminist Rhetoric as a Social Movement." *Gayspeak: Gay Male and Lesbian Communication.* New York: Pilgrim Press, 260–71.

Parker, Richard G. *Beneath the Equator: Cultures of Desire, Male Homosexuality, and Emerging Gay Communities in Brazil.* New York: Routledge, 1999.

———. *Bodies, Pleasures, and Passions: Sexual Culture in Contemporary Brazil.* 2nd Edition. Nashville: Vanderbilt U P, 2009.

Parker, Richard G., Regina Maria Barbosa, & Peter Aggleton. *Framing the Sexual Subject: The Politics of Gender, Sexuality, and Power*. Berkeley: U California P, 2000.

Peixoto, Mariana. "Estudo mostra que coronavírus sacrifica mais a comunidade LGBT." May 17, 2020. *Estado de Minas Gerais*. https://www.em.com.br/app/noticia/gerais/2020/05/17/interna_gerais,1148046/estudo-mostra-que-coronavirus-sacrifica-mais-a-comunidade-lgbt.shtml.

Penelope, Julia & Wolfe, S.J. "Sexist Slang and the Gay Community: Are You One, Too?" *Michigan Occasional Paper No. XIV*. Ann Arbor, Michigan: U Michigan P, 1979.

Phillips, Tom. "Brazil: Bolsonaro Eeportedly Uses Homophobic Slur to Mock Masks. Top Broadsheet Says President Taunted Staffers Wearing Masks to Protect against COVID-19 by Claiming They Were 'for Fairies.'" *The Guardian*. July 8, 2020. https://www.theguardian.com/world/2020/jul/08/bolsonaro-masks-slur-brazil-coronavirus.

Phillips, Dom & Ian Cheibub. "'If I Don't Have Sex I'll Die of Hunger': COVID-19 Crisis for Rio's Trans Sex Workers." *The Guardian*. May 21, 2020. https://www.theguardian.com/global-development/2020/may/21/if-i-dont-have-sex-ill-die-of-hunger-covid-19-crisis-for-rios-trans-sex-workers.

Pinheiro, Paulo. Resenha do filme *Madame Satã*. www.zerozen.com.br/madame sata.htm.

Preti, Dino. *A linguagem proibida: um estudo sobre a linguagem erótica*. São Paulo: T. A. Queiroz, 1983.

Quinalha, Renan. "Queermuseu, da Diversidade à Intolerância." http://www.justifi cando.com. September 12, 2017. https://www.youtube.com/watch?v=RCGd9KEr 4fs&feature=youtube.

Ribeiro, Irineu Ramos. *A TV no armário: a identidade gay nos programas e telejornais brasileiros*. São Paulo: Edições GLS, 2010.

Ripardo, Sérgio. "São Paulo vira capital do 'gay carão'; leia destaques GLS." *Folha de S. Paulo Online: Ilustrada*. March 7, 2007. https://www.folha.uol.com.br/folha/ilustrada/ult90u69127.shtml.

Rissover, Fredric. "*Madame Satã*: From Rebel to Legend." *The Vital Voice for the St. Louis Gay, Lesbian, Bisexual, and Transgender Community*. May 19, 2004.

Rocha, João Cezar de Castro. *Literatura e cordialidade: O público e o privado na cultura brasileira*. Rio de Janeiro: EdUERJ, 1998.

———. "Do malandro ao antropófago: por uma epistemologia da ausência." *Mester*. Department of Spanish and Portuguese, UCLA. XXIV, no. 1 (1997): 173–84.

Rodrigues, Jorge. "10 Pessoas LGBT Brasileiras para se informar sobre direitos e políticas em tempos de pandemia." *Casa Um*. April 16, 2020. https://www.casaum. org/10-pessoas-lgbt-brasileiras-para-se-informar-sobre-direitos-e-politicas-em-tempos-de-pandemia/.

Romano de Sant'Anna, Affonso. *O canibalismo amoroso*. Rio de Janeiro: Rocco, 1990.

Ruffato, Luiz. Ed. *Entre Nós: Contos sobre Homossexualidade*. Rio de Janeiro: Língua Geral, 2007.

Ruhfus, Juliana. "The Murder of Marielle Franco: What the Death of Brazil's Famous Activist Reveals about the Links between Rio's Militia Groups and Corrupt Politicians." *Al Jazeera*. June 6, 2019. https://www.aljazeera.com/programmes/people andpower/2019/06/murder-marielle-franco-190605100430174.html.

Santiago, Silviano. "O Homossexual Astucioso." *O cosmopolitismo do pobre*. Belo Horizonte: Ed. UFMG, 2004.

———. *The Space In-Between: Essays on Latin American Culture*. Trans. Tom Burns, Ana Lúcia Gazzola & Gareth Williams. Durham: Duke U P, 2001.

———. *Stella Manhattan: Romance*. Rio de Janeiro: Nova Fronteira, 1985.

Santos Junior, Orocil Pedreira. *Bichonário: Um Dicionário Gay*. São Paulo: Sindiquímica, 1996.

Santos, Rick & Gracia, Wilton, Eds. *A Escrita de Adé: Perspectivas teóricas dos estudos gays e lésbic@s no Brasil*. NCC/SUNY P, 2002.

Sedgwick, Eve Kosofsky. *Touching Feeling: Affect, Pedagogy, Performativity (Series Q)*. Durham: Duke U P, 2003.

Shoquist, Lee. Film Review of *Madame Satã*. *The Reel Movie Critic*. 2002. www.reelmoviecritic.com/holiday2002/od1749_m.htm.

Sifuentes-Jáuregui, Ben. *The Avowal of Difference: Queer Latino American Narratives*. New York: SUNY P, 2014.

Silva, Eduardo Cristiano Hass da e Bárbara Virgínia Groff da Silva. "Cena de interior II e Queermuseu: Cartografias das diferenças na arte brasileira silenciadas em Porto Alegre." *Palíndromo* 11, no. 25 (September–December 2019): 254–65.

Simões, Almerindo Júnior. *E havia um lampião na esquina: memórias, identidades e discursos homossexuais no Brasil do fim da ditadura (1978–1980)*. Rio de Janeiro: Multifoco, 2011.

Simões, Júlio Assis & Regina Facchini. *Na trilha do arco-íris: Do movimento homosexual ao LGBT*. São Paulo: Editora Fundação Perseu Abramo, 2009.

Simões, Mariana. "'Eu recebi mais de cem ameaças de morte,' diz curador da exposição Queermuseu." *EL PAÍS Brasil: Cultura*. August 29, 2018.

Skidmore, Thomas. *Black into White: Race and Nationality in Brazilian Thought*. Durham: Duke U P, 1993.

Soboleva, Ksenia M. "The Leslie-Lohman Museum's Choice to Drop 'Gay and Lesbian' from Its Name Is a Great Loss." *Hyperallergic* (November 13, 2019).

Stam, Robert. *Subversive Pleasures: Bakhtin, Cultural Criticism, and Film*. Baltimore: Johns Hopkins U P, 1989.

Steorn, Patrik. "Queer in the Museum: Methodological Reflections on Doing Queer in Museum Collections." *Queer Methodologies* 15, no. 3–4 (2010): 119–43.

Sterling, Christopher H. Ed. *Encyclopedia of Radio*, Volume 1. London: Taylor & Francis, 2004.

Stryker, Susan. *Transgender History*. Berkeley: Seal Press, 2008.

———. "(De) Subjugated Knowledges: An Introduction to Transgender Studies." *The Transgender Studies Reader*. Eds. Susan Stryker & Stephen Whittle. NY: Routledge, 2006.

Teixeira, Fabio. "Brazil's Supreme Court Throws Out Rules that Limit Gay Men Donating Blood." May 9, 2020. *Thomson Reuters Foundation*. https://www.

reuters.com/article/us-brazil-lgbt-blood/brazils-supreme-court-throws-out-rules-that-limit-gay-men-donating-blood-idUSKBN22M05N.

Tesser, Carmen Chaves. "A Postcolonial Reading of a Colonized *Malandro.*" *Jorge Amado: New Critical Essays*. Eds. Keith H. Brower, et al. New York/London: Routledge, 2001. 221–30.

Trevisan, João Silvério. *Devassos no paraíso: a homossexualidade no Brasil, da colônia à atualidade* (Sexta edição revista e ampliada). Rio de Janeiro: Record, 2004.

———. *Seis balas num buraco só: A crise do masculino*. Rio de Janeiro: Editora Record, 1998.

Tyburczy, Jennifer. *Sex Museums: The Politics and Performance of Display*. Chicago: U Chicago P, 2016.

U.S. Network for Democracy in Brazil. "Diálogos pela Democracia." Episódio 1: Jean Wyllys. July 2, 2020. https://www.youtube.com/watch?v=k_jBL3TLNQE.

Vainfas, Ronaldo (org.). *História e sexualidade no Brasil*. Rio de Janeiro: Graal, 1986 (Biblioteca de História).

van Straaten, Laura. "Waves of Dark History Break on an Olympic Pool." *New York Times*. July 13, 2016. https://www.nytimes.com/2016/07/14/arts/design/waves-of-darker-history-break-on-an-artists-seas-in-rio.html.

Venturi, Gustavo & Vilma Bokany, Orgs. *Diversidade sexual e homofobia no Brasil*. São Paulo: Editora Fundação Perseu Abramo, 2011.

Viana, Fabrício. "#Queerentena no Museu da Diversidade Sexual: Artistas LGBTI+, participem até 15/04." *Associação da Parada do Orgulho LGBT de São Paulo*. April 13, 2020. http://paradasp.org.br/queerentena-no-museu-da-diversidade-sexual-artistas-lgbti-participem-ate-15–04/.

———. "Colabore com o primeiro Centro de Convivência e Referência para a população LGBT+ idosa ou em processo de envelhecimento." *Associação da Parada do Orgulho LGBT de São Paulo*. December 13, 2019. http://paradasp.org.br/colabore-com-o-primeiro-centro-de-convivencia-e-referencia-para-a-populacao-lgbt-idosa-ou-em-processo-de-envelhecimento/.

———. "Justiça Federal determina que Ancine retome edital censurado por conteúdo LGBT." *Associação da Parada do Orgulho LGBT de São Paulo*. October 8, 2019. http://paradasp.org.br/justica-federal-determina-que-ancine-retome-edital-censurado-por-conteudo-lgbts/.

———. "STF proíbe que uniões homoafetivas sejam excluídas de políticas públicas." *Associação da Parada do Orgulho LGBT de São Paulo*. September 16, 2019. http://paradasp.org.br/stf-proibe-que-unioes-homoafetivas-sejam-excluidas-de-politicas-publicas/.

———. "Nota pública da APOGLBT SP para a Secretaria de Cultura e Economia Criativa SP sobre o Museu da Diversidade Sexual." *Associação da Parada do Orgulho LGBT de São Paulo*. September 2, 2019. http://paradasp.org.br/nota-publica-da-apoglbt-sp-para-a-secretaria-de-cultura-e-economia-criativa-sp-sobre-o-museu-da-diversidade-sexual/.

———. "Baptista Luz Advogados, Casa 1 e ANTRA lançam Guia de Reificação de Prenome e Gênero de pessoas não-cisgêneras. Compartilhem!" *Associação da Parada do Orgulho LGBT de São Paulo*. August 22, 2019. http://paradasp.org.br/

baptista-luz-advogados-casa-1-e-antra-lancam-guia-de-retificacao-de-prenome-e-genero-de-pessoas-nao-cisgeneras-compartilhem/.

———. "Jair Bolsonaro proíbe Ancine de liberar verbas para filmes com temática LGBT." *Associação da Parada do Orgulho LGBT de São Paulo*. August 20, 2019. http://paradasp.org.br/jair-bolsonaro-proibe-ancine-de-liberar-verbas-para-filmes-com-tematica-lgbt/.

———. "Centro de Referência da Diversidade em SP não será fechado." *Associação da Parada do Orgulho LGBT de São Paulo*. July 1, 2019. http://paradasp.org.br/centro-de-referencia-da-diversidade-em-sp-nao-sera-fechado/.

———. "STF concede liminar e 'cura gay' volta a ser proibida no Brasil." *Associação da Parada do Orgulho LGBT de São Paulo*. April 24, 2019. http://paradasp.org.br/stf-concede-liminar-e-cura-gay-volta-a-ser-proibida-no-brasil/.

———. "Curso de inglês gratuito para travestis e pessoas trans no RJ." *Associação da Parada do Orgulho LGBT de São Paulo*. April 2, 2019. http://paradasp.org.br/curso-de-ingles-gratuito-para-travestis-e-pessoas-trans-no-rj/.

———. "Ministério da Saúde retira do ar cartilha para população trans." *Associação da Parada do Orgulho LGBT de São Paulo*. January 7, 2019. http://paradasp.org.br/ministerio-da-saude-retira-do-ar-cartilha-para-populacao-trans/.

———. "Bolsonaro retira população LGBT das diretrizes dos Direitos Humanos." *Associação da Parada do Orgulho LGBT de São Paulo*. January 3, 2019. http://paradasp.org.br/bolsonaro-retira-populacao-lgbt-das-diretrizes-dos-direitos-humanos/.

———. "Enem 2018 tem questão sobre Pajubá, 'dialeto' usado pela comunidade LGBT." *Associação da Parada do Orgulho LGBT de São Paulo*. November 5, 2018. http://paradasp.org.br/enem-2018-tem-questao-sobre-pajuba-dialeto-usado-pela-comunidade-lgbt/.

———. "O prazo para a inclusão social acabada nessa quarta-feira." *Associação da Parada do Orgulho LGBT de São Paulo*. May 7, 2018. http://paradasp.org.br/o-prazo-para-a-inclusao-do-nome-social-acabada-nessa-quarta-feira/.

Villarreal, Daniel. "Here's Why Some Gay Brazilians Support Their Country's Rabidly Anti LGBTQ President: He Said He'd Rather Have a Dead Son that a Gay One, But Here's How He Won over Some Gay Voters." *LGBTQ Nation*. January 13, 2019. https://www.lgbtqnation.com/2019/01/heres-gay-brazilians-support-countrys-rabidly-anti-lgbtq-president/.

Vip, Ângelo and Fred Libi. *Aurélia: A Dicionária da Língua Afiada*. São Paulo: Editora da Bispa, 2006.

Walcott, Rinaldo. *Queer Returns: Essays on Multiculturalism, Diaspora, and Black Studies*. London, Ontario: Insomniac Press, 2016.

Walsh, Nick Paton, Jo Shelley, Eduardo Duwe, & William Bonnett. "The World's Hope for a Coronavirus Vaccine May Run in These Health Care Workers' Veins." *CNN*. July 27, 2020. https://www.cnn.com/2020/07/27/americas/brazil-covid-19-sinovac-vaccine-intl/index.html.

Webb, Simon. "Masculinities at the Margins: Representations of the *Malandro* and the *Pachuco*." In *Imagination beyond Nation: Latin American Popular Culture*. Eds. Eva P. Bueno & Terry Caesar. Pittsburgh: U Pittsburgh P, 1998. 227–64.

Wellspring. "Official Website of the Film *Madame Satã*." www.wellspring.com/movies/text.html?page=synopsis&movie_id=7.

Wilmington, Michael. "Film Review of *Madame Satã.*" *The Chicago Tribune.* August 21, 2003.

Winter, Brian. "Messiah Complex: How Brazil Made Bolsonaro." *Foreign Affairs.* The Council on Foreign Relations, September/October 2020. https://www.foreign affairs.com/articles/brazil/2020-08-11/jair-bolsonaro-messiah-complex.

Wolfe, Barry Michael. "Transsexuals of Brazil." Ethnographic essay on Travestis in *glbtq.com*. 2006.

Zé, Tom & Ana Carolina. "Brasil Corrrupção (Unimultiplicidade)." *Ana Carolina e Seu Jorge Ao Vivo*. São Paulo: HSBC Brasil, 2005.

NEWSPAPER ARTICLES AND PERIODICALS
CITED IN CHAPTERS 1–3

AGÊNCIA Brasil. "Parada GLBT paulista ganha importância econômica e social." *Rede Brasil Atual*, June 26, 2011. <http://www.redebrasilatual.com.br/temas/ cidadania/2011/06/parada-glbt-paulista-ganha-importancia-economica-e-social>.

ALBUQUERQUE, C. "Brasil tem maior parada gay, mas lidera em violência contra homossexuais." *Deutsche Welle*, August 23, 2011. <http://www.dw.de/dw/ article/0,,15336560,00.html>.

ALONSO, Antonio. "Memória: Parada LGBT de São Paulo começou em 1997 e está no Guiness." *Memorial da Democracia*. Museu Virtual da Fundação Perseu Abramo e do Instituto Lula, June 23, 2019. <https://fpabramo.org.br/2019/06/23/ parada-do-orgulho-lgbt-de-sao-paulo-comecou-em-1997-e-esta-no-guiness/>.

"APÓS 'Dia do Orgulho Hétero,' vereador de SP quer banheiro gay." *Terra Notícias*, February 8, 2012. <http://noticias.terra.com.br/brasil/noticias/0,,OI5600965-EI7896,00-Apos+Dia+do+Orgulho+Hetero+vereador+de+SP+quer+banheiro+ gay.html>.

ARRAIS, D.; KAWAGUTI, L. "Direção da Parada Gay barra carro de central sindical." *Athos GLS*, May 26, 2008. <http://www.athosgls.com.br/noticias_visualiza. php?contcod=23548>.

BBC.com. "São Paulo Gay Pride Draws Huge Crowd and Call to Protect Rights." June 19, 2017. < https://www.bbc.com/news/world-latin-america-40325944>.

"'BEIJAÇO' gay reúne 2.000 em shopping center de SP." *Folha de S. Paulo*, São Paulo, August 3, 2003. <http://www1.folha.uol.com.br/folha/cotidiano/ult95u 79567.shtml>.

BERGAMASCO, D. "Sem trios de boates, política avança na Parada Gay de SP." *Folha de S. Paulo*, São Paulo, June 15, 2009. <http://www1.folha.uol.com.br/ folha/cotidiano/ult95u581051.shtml>.

BERGAMASCO, D.; TÓFOLI, D. "Parada Gay cresce; diversão e problemas, também." *Folha de S. Paulo*, São Paulo, June 11, 2007. <http://www.ccr.org.br/ noticias-detalhe. asp?cod=853>.

BERGAMIN JR, G.; IZUMI C. "Camelôs vendem vinho e whisky na Parada Gay de São Paulo." *Folha de S. Paulo*, São Paulo, June 26, 2009. <http://www1.folha.uol.

com.br/ cotidiano/935089-camelos-vendem-vinho-e-whisky-na-paradagay-de-sao-paulo.shtml>.

"BOMBA caseira explode e deixa três feridos no centro de São Paulo." *Folha de S. Paulo*, São Paulo, June 14, 2009. <http://www1.folha.uol.com.br/folha/cotidiano/ult95u580948.shtml>.

"CÂMARA de SP discute aprovação do Dia do Orgulho Heterossexual." August 2, 2011. <http://g1.globo. com/sao-paulo/noticia/2011/08/camara-de-sp-aprova-diadoorgulho-hetero.html>.

CAPIGLIONE, L.; MENA, F. "Parada Gay tem ampla presença feminina." *Folha de S. Paulo*. <www.folha.uol.com.br/fsp/cotidian/ inde30052005.htm>.

CARDOSO, M. "Até Obama virou fantasia." *O Estado de S. Paulo*, São Paulo, June 15, 2009. <http://www.estadao.com. br/noticias/impresso,ate-obama-virou-fantasia,387283,0.htm>.

CARDOSO, M.; BRANDALISE, V. H.; BRANCATELLI, R.; ODA, F.; ALCALDE, L.; OSCAR, N. "Parada Gay tem tumulto e brigas." *O Estado de S. Paulo*, São Paulo, June 15, 2009. <http://www.estadao.com.br/noticias/impresso,parada-gay tem-tumulto-e-brigas,387282,0.htm>.

CATOIRA, E. "Ecce homo." *CartaCapital*, São Paulo, March 27, 2012. <http://www.cartacapital.com.br/sociedade/eccehomo/>.

COGUMELO LOUCO. "Dia do Orgulho Hetero é aprovado por vereadores de São Paulo." August 3, 2011. <http:// www.cogumelolouco.com/dia-do-orgulho-hetero-e-aprovado-por-vereadores-de-sao-paulo/>.

"COLETA de lixo na Parada Gay de SP aumenta 90%." *Folha de S. Paulo*, São Paulo, June 28, 2011. <http://www1. folha.uol.com.br/cotidiano/935906-coleta-de-lixo-na-paradagay-de-sp-aumenta-90.shtml>.

CONTIER, J. "Religião foi o mote central da Parada Gay." *O Estado de São Paulo*, São Paulo, June 11, 2007. <http:// www.ccr.org.br/noticias-detalhe.asp?cod=833>.

COSTA, D. *Diário de S. Paulo*, São Paulo, June 15, 2009.

COTES, P.; LEITE, F.; DURAN, S. "Orgulho Gay: Parada leva às ruas 400 mil pessoas e bate recorde em SP." *Folha de S. Paulo*, São Paulo, June 3, 2002. <http:// www1.folha.uol. com.br/fsp/indices/inde03062002.htm>.

DIMENSTEIN, G. "São Paulo é mais gay ou evangélica?" *Folha de S. Paulo*, São Paulo, June 24, 2011. <http://www1. folha.uol.com.br/colunas/gilbertodimenstein/934389-sao-paulo-e-mais-gay-ou-evangelica.shtml>.

DOMINGOS, R. "Câmara de SP discute aprovação do Dia do Orgulho Heterossexual." *G1*, São Paulo, June 22, 2011. <http://g1.globo.com/sao-paulo/noticia/2011/06/camara-desp-discute-aprovacao-do-dia-do-orgulho-heterossexual.html>.

———. "Câmara de SP aprova Dia do Orgulho Hétero." *G1*, São Paulo, August 2, 2011. <http://g1.globo.com/saopaulo/noticia/2011/08/camara-de-sp-aprova-dia-do-orgulhohetero.html>.

DRUMOND, D. "Evento em São Paulo discute lei anti-homofobia." March 12, 2012. <http://douglasdrumond.virgula. uol.com.br/2012/03/evento-em-sao-paulo-discute-lei-antihomofobia/#.T3-E89WRSJA>.

DUQUE, T. "Disparatada: 2012, o ano do orgulho hétero!" *A Capa*, January 5, 2012. <http://acapa.virgula.uol.com.br/colunas/disparatada-2012-o-ano-do-orgulhohetero!/10/104/15485>.

"EXPLOSÃO de bomba caseira fere 22 e surpreende pessoas que dispersavam da Parada Gay." *Folha de S. Paulo*, São Paulo, June 15, 2009. <http://www1.folha.uol.com.br/folha/cotidiano/ult95u581105.shtml>.

"EXTRA: Notícias Bizarras." *O Globo*, Rio de Janeiro, June 17, 2007.

"FECOMERCIO-SP quer criar Selo Diversidade."*O Estado de S. Paulo*, São Paulo, 26 May 2008. <http://www. estadao.com.br/noticias/impresso,fecomercio-sp-quer-criar-selodiversidade,177929,0.htm>.

FERRAZ, A.; NUNES, J.; FOLHA de S. Paulo. "Festa da Parada Gay tem tumulto e violência."*Folha de S. Paulo*, São Paulo, June 15, 2009. <http://www.agora.uol.com.br/saopaulo/ ult10103u580943.shtml>.

FONTOURA, C. "Parada gay leva milhões a pedir por mudanças no Brasil." *O Globo*, Rio de Janeiro, May 26, 2008. <http://oglobo.globo.com/cultura/parada-gay-leva-milhoespedir-por-mudancas-no-brasil-3616536>.

FRANCISCO, A. "Grupo gay faz exposição em que sugere 'intimidade' entre santo e o menino Jesus." *Agência Folha*, Salvador, June 24, 2006. < http://www.jornal ismogospel. com.br/modules.php?name=News&file=print&sid=106>.

G1. "Parada LGBT de 2019 movimentou R\$493 milhões em SP, diz prefeitura." 29 June 2019. <https://headtopics.com/br/parada-lgbt-de-2019-movimentou-r-403-milh-es-em-sp-diz-prefeitura-6611278>.

———. "Homem atropelado por trio elétrico na Parada Gay passará por cirurgia." *G1*, São Paulo, May 25, 2008. <http://g1.globo.com/Sites/Especiais/Noticias/0,,MUL535506–15561,00.html>.

GALLO, R. "Casamento coletivo com 10 gays reúne 300 pessoas em SP." *Folha de S. Paulo*, São Paulo, June 23, 2011. <http://www1.folha.uol.com.br/cotidiano/934970-casamentocoletivo-com-10-gays-reune-300-pessoas-em-sp.shtml>.

GLAUBER, W. "As diferentes maneiras de contabilizar a multidão gay." *O Estado de S. Paulo*, São Paulo, May 26, 2008. <http://www.estadao.com.br/noticias/impresso,as-diferentesmaneiras-de-contabilizar-a-multidao-gay,177927,0.htm>.

GOIS, A.; TÓFOLI, D. " 'Gay família' é maioria na parada de SP, diz pesquisa." *Folha de S. Paulo*, São Paulo, June 16, 2006. <http://www1.folha.uol.com.br/folha/ilustrada/ult90u61475.shtml>.

HALLOWELL, B. "Are You Ready for Sao Paulo's "Heterosexual Pride Day?" *The Blaze*, August 4, 2011. <http://www.theblaze.com/stories/are-you-ready-for-sao-paulos-heterosexualpride-day/>.

HARTMAN, K. I. " 'Heterosexual Pride Day' Awaits Mayor's Signature in Sao Paulo." *Digital Journal*, August 5, 2011. <http://www.digitaljournal.com/article/309975>.

IZIDORO, A.; LEITE, P. D.; LAGE, A. "Parada Gay dobra e leva 800 mil à Paulista." *Folha de S. Paulo*, São Paulo, June 23, 2003. <http://www.aids.gov.br/noticia/paradagay-dobra-e-leva-800-mil-paulista>.

"LEIS anti-homofobia: O Brasil não precisa disso." <http://www.marciopacheco.com.br/?p=1194>.

LEITE, F. "Parada defenderá a união civil entre gays." *Folha de S. Paulo*, São Paulo, May 23, 2005. <http://www1.folha.uol.com.br/fsp/cotidian/inde 23052005.htm>.

LEITE, P. D.; MENA, F.; LAGE, A. "Parada Gay reúne 1,5 milhão e bate recorde." *Folha de S. Paulo*, São Paulo, June 14, 2004. <http://www.aids.gov.br/noticia/parada-gay-reune15-milhao-e-bate-recorde>.

LOPES, D. "Por uma nova invisibilidade." *e-misferica*, New York, v. 4, n. 2, November 2007. <http://www.hemi.nyu.edu/ journal/4.2/por/po42_pg_lopes.html>.

MANSO, B. P.; RAMPAZZO, F. "Parada se assume como balada." *Ministério da Saúde*, June 18, 2006. <http://www.aids.gov.br/noticia/parada-se-assume-como-balada>.

MANSO, B. P.; ZANCHETTA, D.; OSCAR, N.; FRANÇA, V. "Parada vira palanque eleitoral." *O Estado de S. Paulo*, São Paulo, May 26, 2008. <http://www.estadao.com.br/noticias/impresso,parada-vira-palanque-eleitoral,177926,0.htm>.

MARQUES, C. "SP tem maior parada gay do mundo pelo 2° ano consecutivo." *Folha de S. Paulo*, São Paulo, May 29, 2005. <http://www1.folha.uol.com.br/folha/ilustrada/ult90u51010.shtml>.

MARSON, D. "Orgulho Gay supera expectativa e reúne 400 mil pessoas na cidade." *Diário de S. Paulo*, São Paulo, June 3, 2002.

"MARTA diz que seu projeto de união civil do mesmo sexo está 'ultrapassado.'" *Folha de S. Paulo*, São Paulo, June 23, 2003. <http://www1.folha.uol.com.br/folha/cotidiano/ult95u77232.shtml>.

MASUTTI, V. "Festa tem confusão, furtos e abuso de álcool." *Agora São Paulo*, São Paulo, May 26, 2008.

MEISSNER, G. M. "Deus pune países com leis anti-homofobia?" *EntreMundos*, January 1, 2012. <http://www.midiaindependente.org/pt/blue/2012/01/501698.shtml>.

MINISTRO de Estado do Turismo. "Dicas para atender bem turistas LGBT." *Ministro de Estado do Turismo*. November 3, 2016. <http://www.turismo.gov.br/images/pdf/03_11_2016_Cartiliha_LGBT.pdf>.

MOREIRA, M. "Parada Gay lota as duas pistas da Avenida Paulista." *O Estado de S. Paulo*, São Paulo, 25 May 2005.

MOREIRA, M. E GABRIEL, J. "SP adia Carnaval de 2021 para blocos de rua e escolas de samba e cancela parada LGBTQUI+: Festa pode acontecer entre maio e junho; Data foi definida em reunião com Liga das Escolas." *Folha de S. Paulo*. São Paulo, July 24, 2020. <https://www1.folha.uol.com.br/cotidiano/2020/07/coronavirus-leva-sp-a-adiar-desfile-e-blocos-no-carnaval-de-2021-e-a-cancelar-parada-lgbtqui.shtml>.

MORENO DE CASTRO, C. "Skinheads também participam de Parada Gay." *Folha de S. Paulo*, São Paulo, June 26, 2011. <http://www1.folha.uol.com.br/cotidiano/935117-skinheadstambem participam-de-parada-gay.shtml>.

MOTT, L. "SP tem maior número de mortes de homossexuais." *Folha de S. Paulo*, São Paulo, June 17, 2006. <http:// www1.folha.uol.com.br/fsp/cotidian/ff1706200616.htm>.

NBC News Out & Proud. "Brazil's Largest City Draws Hundreds of Thousands for Pride March." *NBC News Out & Proud*. Associated Press, June 24, 2019. <https://www.nbcnews.com/feature/nbc-out/brazil-s-largest-city-draws-hundreds-thousands-pride-march-n1020971>.

OLIVEIRA, N. "Turismo feito com diversidade: Parada LGBT de São Paulo é o maior evento do segmento no mundo e acontecerá neste domingo (3), movimentando o turismo na cidade." *Ministério do Turismo*, Brasília, May 30, 2018. <http://www.turismo.gov.br/%C3%BAltimas-not%C3%ADcias/11457-turismo-feito-com-diversidade.html>.

———. "Parada LGBT movimenta turismo em São Paulo: Em sua 21ª edição, evento reforça sua importância para o turismo local. Ministério do Tursimo produziu guia com dicas para atedner bem o turista LGBT." *Ministério do Turismo*, Brasília, June 21, 2017. <http://www.turismo.gov.br/%C3%BAltimas-not%C3%ADcias/7899-parada-lgbt-movimenta-turismo-em-s%C3%A3o-paulo.html>.

PADILHA, T. "União entre dois homens consumada em cartório surpreende moradores de Manhaçu." *Estado de Minas*, Belo Horizonte, March 23, 2012. <http://www.em.com.br/app/noticia/gerais/2012/03/23/interna_gerais,285008/uniao-entre-dois-homens-consumada-em-cartorio-surpreendemoradores-de-manhuacu.shtml>.

PAGNAN, R. "Organizadores do evento pedem apoio ao projeto que criminaliza a homofobia." *Folha de S. Paulo*, São Paulo, June 11, 2007. <http://www.ccr.org.br/noticias-detalhe.asp?cod=852>.

"PARADA Gay bate recorde, dizem organizadores." *Folha de S. Paulo*, São Paulo, June 10, 2006. <http://www1.folha.uol.com.br/folha/ilustrada/ult90u303251.shtml>.

"PARADA Gay divulga público de 5 milhões sem comprovação científica." *Folha de S. Paulo*, São Paulo, May 25, 2008. <http://www1.folha.uol.com.br/folha/ilustrada/ult90u405292.shtml>.

"PARADA Gay perde em glitter e ganha em diversidade." *Folha de S. Paulo*, São Paulo, 26 May 2008. <http://vesetomavergonha.blogspot.com/2008/05/parada-gay-perde-emglitter-e-ganha-em.html>.

"PARADA Gay registra cerca de 2,5 milhões de participantes." *Jornal @Hora Online*, 30 May 2005.

"PARADA LGBT de 2019 movimentou R$403 milhões em SP, diz prefeitura." *G1*, June 29, 2019. <https://headtopics.com/br/parada-lgbt-de-2019-movimentou-r-403-milh-es-em-sp-diz-prefeitura-6611278>.

"PARADA LGBT de SP na web tem manifesto pela democracia e Daniela Mercury: Canais no YouTube exibem a Parada LGBT de São Paulo: evento começou às 14h deste domingo (14)." *UOL Online/Universa*. June 16, 2020. <https://www.uol.com.br/universa/noticias/redacao/2020/06/14/parada-lgbt-online.htm>.

PETROV, A. "Even Under Bolsonaro's Criticism, LGBT Parade in São Paulo Should Attract 12 Percent More Tourists." *The Rio Times*. Rio de Janeiro, June 22, 2019. <https://riotimesonline.com/brazil-news/sao-paulo/even-under-bolsonaros-criticism-lgbt-parade-in-sao-paulo-should-attract-12-percent-more-tourists/>.

RAYMUNDI, V.; FALCÃO, J. "Parada gay em SP é a maior do mundo: Festa bateu recorde de público ao reunir 1,5 milhão de pessoas na Avenida Paulista." *Diário de S. Paulo*, São Paulo, June 14, 2004.

"RECORDE vai para o 'Guinness,' dizem organizadores." *Folha de S. Paulo*, São Paulo, June 10, 2007. <http://www1.folha.uol.com.br/folha/ilustrada/ult90u303293.shtml>.

"RELIGIÃO foi o mote central da Parada Gay que reuniu cerca de 4 milhões na Avenida Paulista." *Instituto Humanitas Unisinos*, São Leopoldo, June 11, 2007. <http://www.ihu.unisinos.br/noticias/noticias-anteriores/7732-religiao-foi-omote-central-da-parada-gay-que-reuniu-cerca-de-4-milhoes-naavenida-paulista>.

RICARDO, S. "SP terá 2ª Parada Hétero no MASP, no dia 1." *Folha de São Paulo*, São Paulo, May 21, 2008. <http://www1.folha.uol.com.br/folha/colunas/destaques gls/ult10009u404340.shtml>.

RIGOBELO, F. "Comentário: Em festa, verdadeiros 'donos' da cidade celebram Parada Gay." *Folha de S. Paulo*, São Paulo, June 11, 2007. <http://www1.folha. uol.com.br/folha/ilustrada/ult90u303297.shtml>.

ROSSI, A. "Pesquisador canadense lança livro sobre desafios do Parada LGBT de SP." *SpressoSP*, June 8, 2012. http://spressosp.com.br/2012/06/08/pesquisador-canadense-lanca-livro-sobre-representacoes-e-desafios-do-parada-lgbt-de-sao-paulo/.

SAMPAIO, P. "Siameses usam roupas iguais em parada."*Folha de S. Paulo*, São Paulo, May 23, 2005. <http://www1.folha.uol.com.br/fsp/cotidian/inde30052005.htm>.

———. "'Nunca vi tanta gente feia,' dizem habitués." *Folha de S. Paulo*, São Paulo, June 11, 2007. <http://www.aids.gov.br/noticia/nbspnunca-vi-tanta-gente-feia-diz-o-estudante-bombado-descamisado-e-depilado-victor-prado-19>.

———. "Gay 'separatista' prefere festa a desfilar na parada." *Folha de S. Paulo*, São Paulo, June 11, 2007. <http://www1.folha.uol.com.br/fsp/cotidian/inde3005 2005.htm>.

"SÃO PAULO Gay Pride Draws Huge Crowd and Call to Protect Rights." *BBC News*. June 19, 2017. <https://www.bbc.com/news/world-latin-america-40325944>.

SCHMIDT, Axel. "Fact Check: The LGBTQ Community Is Not Adding 'P' to Their Acronym." *Reuters*. May 29, 2020. <https://www.reuters.com/article/uk-fact check-lgbtq-community-p-acronym/factcheck-thelgbtq-community-isnotadding-p-to-their-acronym-idUSKBN2352J8>.

SILVEIRA, C. "Parada Gay ganha público e economiza brilho." *Agora São Paulo*, São Paulo, May 26, 2008.

TALENTO, A. "Assassinatos de homossexuais batem recorde em 2011, diz enti-dade." *Folha de S. Paulo*, São Paulo, April 3 2012. <http://www1.folha.uol.com. br/cotidiano/1071307-assassinatosde-homossexuais-batem-recorde-em-2011-diz-entidade.shtml>.

TÓFOLI, D. "Parada Gay tenta manter recorde hoje." *Folha de S. Paulo*, São Paulo, June 17, 2006. <http://www1.folha.uol.com.br/fsp/cotidian/ff1706200615.htm>.

———. "Parada Gay resiste à Copa e supera recorde de público." *Ministério da Saúde*, June 18, 2006. <http://www.aids.gov.br/noticia/parada-gay-resiste-copa-e-supera-recorde-de-publico>.

TRINDADE, P. "Kassab oficializa veto ao Dia do Orgulho Hétero." *Jornal da Tarde*, São Paulo, August 31, 2011. <http://blogs.estadao.com.br/jt-cidades/ kassab-veta-dia-do-orgulhohetero-em-sp/>.

"TUMULTOS marcam parada recorde de público." *Agora São Paulo*, São Paulo, June 11, 2007.

VIANA, F. "Associação da Parada do Orgulho LGBT de SP e Prefeitura cancelam edição deste ano por causa da pandemia." *Associação da Parada do Orgulho LGBT de São Paulo*. July 24, 2020. <http://paradasp.org.br/associacao-da-parada-do-orgulho-lgbt-de-sp-e-prefeitura-cancelam-edicao-deste-ano-por-causa-da-pandemia/>.

————. "Agradecimentos: 1ª Parada Virtual do Orgulho LGBT de São Paulo." *Associação da Parada do Orgulho LGBT de São Paulo*. June 16, 2020. <http://paradasp.org. br/apoglbt-sp-agradecimentos-1a-parada-virtual-do-orgulho-lgbt-de-sao-paulo/>.

————. "Vídeo: Chamada da Primeira Parada Virtual do Orgulho LGBT de São Paulo." *Associação da Parada do Orgulho LGBT de São Paulo*. June 5, 2020. <http://para dasp.org.br/video-chamada-da-primeira-parada-virtual-do-orgulho-lgbt-de-sp/>.

————. "Comunicado: Mês do Orgulho LGBT+ é alterado de Junho para Novembro por conta do Coronavirus!" *Associação da Parada do Orgulho LGBT de São Paulo*. March 19, 2020. <http://paradasp.org.br/apoglbt-sp-mes-do-orgulho-lgbt-e-alterado-de-junho-para-novembro-por-conta-do-coronavirus/>.

————. "Tema da Parada do Orgulho LGBT de SP em 2020: 'Democracia.' Slogan: 'Sejamos o pesadelo dos que querem roubar nossa Democracia. Leia o manifesto/justificativa!' " March 9, 2020. <http://paradasp.org.br/tema-da-parada-do-orgulho-lgbt-de-sp-em-2020-democracia-slogan-sejamos-o-pesadelo-dos-que-querem-roubar-nossa-democracia-leia-o-manifesto-justificativa/>.

————. "Relatório informa que maioria das vítimas de LGBTIfobia não fazem boletim de ocorrência." *Associação da Parada do Orgulho LGBT de São Paulo*. May 30, 2019. <http://paradasp.org.br/relatorio-informa-que-maioria-das-vitimas-de-lgbtifobia-nao-fazem-boletim-de-ocorrencia/>.

————. " '50 anos de Stonewall," leia a jsutificativa/manifesto sobre o tema da Parada do Orgulho LGBT de 2019." *Associação da Parada do Orgulho LGBT de São Paulo*. March 22, 2019. <http://paradasp.org.br/50-anos-de-stonewall-leia-a-justificativa-manifesto-sobre-o-tema-da-parada-do-orgulho-lgbt-de-2019/>.

————. "Parada do orgulho LGBT de São Paulo agora faz parte da rede Interpride." *Associação da Parada do Orgulho LGBT de São Paulo*. February 25, 2019. <http:// paradasp.org.br/parada-do-orgulho-lgbt-de-sao-paulo-agora-faz-parte-da-rede-interpride/>.

————. "Ajude a escolher o Slogan da Parada do Orgulho LGBT de SP de 2019!" *Associação da Parada do Orgulho LGBT de São Paulo*. February 14, 2019. <http:// paradasp.org.br/ajude-a-escolher-o-slogan-da-parada-do-orgulho-lgbt-de-sp-de-2019/>.

————. "Datafolha: 74% dos brasileiros acham que a homossexualidade deve ser aceita por toda a sociedade." *Associação da Parada do Orgulho LGBT de São Paulo*. October 29, 2018. <http://paradasp.org.br/datafolha-74-dos-brasileiros-acham-que-a-homossexualidade-deve-ser-aceita-por-toda-a-sociedade/>.

————. "ALERTA: A inclusão do P, de pedófilos, na sigla LGBT é fake news." *Associação da Parada do Orgulho LGBT de São Paulo*. July 19, 2018. <http://paradasp .org.br/alerta-a-inclusao-do-p-de-pedofilos-na-sigla-lgbt-e-fake-news/>.

————. "TV Brasil lança documentário *A Maior Parada do Mundo* nesta quinta (28/6), Dia Internacional do Orgulho LGBTI+." *Associação da Parada do Orgulho LGBT de São Paulo*. June 27, 2018. <http://paradasp.org.br/tv-brasil-lanca-documentario-a-maior-parada-do-mundo-nesta-quinta-28–6-dia-internacional-do-orgulho-lgbti/>.

————. "Comunicado importante: Vai ter Parada do Orgulho LGBT em São Paulo sim! Repassem!" *Associação da Parada do Orgulho LGBT de São Paulo*. May 27,

2018. <http://paradasp.org.br/comunicado-importante-vai-ter-parada-do-orgulho-lgbt-em-sao-paulo-sim-repassem/>.

———. "Antes de criticar a Parada, leia este texto!" *Associação da Parada do Orgulho LGBT de São Paulo*. April 28, 2016. <http://paradasp.org.br/antes-de-criticar-a-parada-leia-este-texto/>.

ZANCHETTA, D. "Câmara de SP tenta criar Dia do Orgulho Hetero e trava a pauta do dia." *O Estado de S. Paulo*, São Paulo, June 22, 2011. <http://www.estadao.com.br/noticias/cidades,camara-de-sp-tenta-criar-dia-do-orgulho-hetero-e-travaa-pauta-do-dia,735736,0.htm>.

Index

Note: Page references for figures are *italicized*.

285

About the Author

Associate professor of Portuguese and director of the Portuguese language program since 2000, **Steven F. Butterman** teaches Portuguese language courses and Brazilian literature and cultural studies in the Department of Modern Languages and Literatures at the University of Miami (UM), where he also directed the Gender & Sexuality Studies (GSS) Program and launched

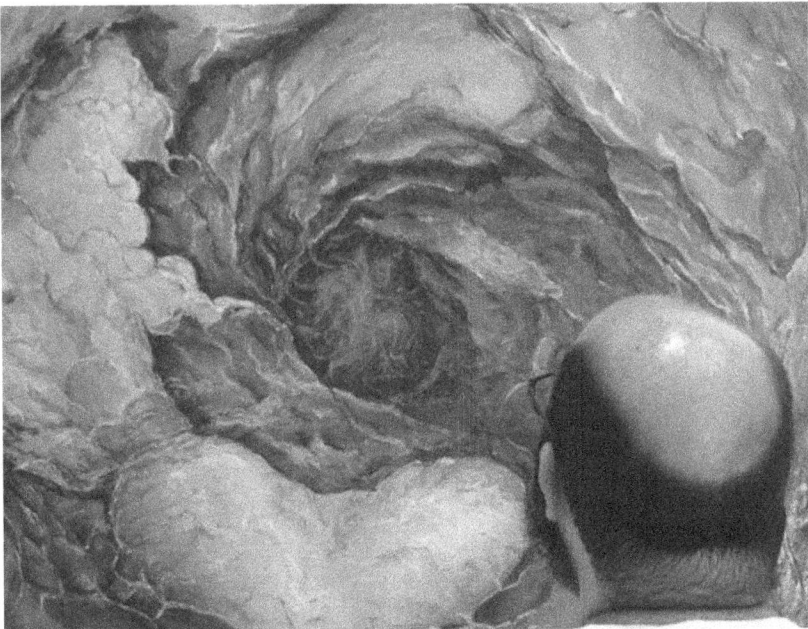

Figure E.1.   Author Gazing into *O Buraco* (2004) by Telmo Lanes. 130 × 130 cm. Photo by Laura Guerim.

the minor in LGBTQ studies. While at UM, Butterman has also held visiting professor/scholar posts at Middlebury College, Tulane University, the University of São Paulo (USP), and Unilasalle in Canoas, Rio Grande do Sul, Brazil. He has delivered over forty invited talks and keynote addresses at universities throughout Brazil, Canada, Denmark, France, Germany, the United Kingdom, and the United States and dozens of academic conference presentations throughout the world. Butterman earned a PhD from the University of Wisconsin–Madison in 2000. A recipient of a National Endowment for the Humanities Summer Institute in 2002 and Summer Seminar in 2010 and a winner of the Brazilian International Press Award, Provost's Excellence in Teaching Award, and the 2004 University of Miami Scholarly and Creative Activity Award, Butterman has published books and articles on a wide range of topics, focusing on transnational LGBTQ+ studies and gender and feminist studies in the cultural contexts of Portuguese-speaking countries. Butterman is the author of *Perversions on Parade: Brazilian Literature of Transgression and Postmodern Anti-Aesthetics in Glauco Mattoso* (2005) and *(In)Visibilidade Vigilante: representações midiáticas da maior parada gay do planeta* (2012). In addition to his academic work, Butterman has served as an expert witness on asylum petition cases involving homophobia, lesbophobia, transphobia, and domestic violence in Brazil and other countries.